The Massacre That Never Was

The Myth of Deir Yassin
and the Creation of the Palestinian Refugee Problem

ASMEA
ASSOCIATION FOR THE STUDY
OF THE MIDDLE EAST AND AFRICA

Toby

Eliezer Tauber

The Massacre That Never Was

The Myth of Deir Yassin
and the Creation of the Palestinian Refugee Problem

ASMEA
The Toby Press

The Massacre That Never Was
The Myth of Deir Yassin
and the Creation of the Palestinian Refugee Problem

First English Edition, 2021

The Toby Press LLC
POB 8531, New Milford, CT 06776–8531, USA
& POB 2455, London W1A 5WY, England
www.tobypress.com

ISBN 978-1-59264-543-5, *hardcover*

Printed and bound in the United States

Contents

Abbreviations

ACICR	Archives du Comité International de la Croix-Rouge
AIR	Air Ministry
BUPA	Birzeit University Palestine Archive
CID	Criminal Investigation Department
CO	Colonial Office
CZA	Central Zionist Archives
FBIS	Foreign Broadcast Information Service
FO	Foreign Office
HA	Haganah Archives
HQ	Headquarters
IDFA	Israel Defense Forces Archives
ISA	Israel State Archives
IWM	Imperial War Museum
JA	Jabotinsky Archives
LC	Larry Collins Papers
MEC	Middle East Centre
NARA	National Archives and Records Administration
PACE	Palestinian Association for Cultural Exchange
RAF	Royal Air Force
RG	Record Group
RH	Rhodes House
UNISPAL	United Nations Information System on the Question of Palestine
WO	War Office
YTA	Yad Tabenkin Archives

Introduction

On 9 April 1948, forces of the Etzel and Lehi Jewish underground military organizations attacked the Arab village of Deir Yassin west of Jerusalem. The nature of this attack became one of the most controversial issues in the history of the Arab-Israeli conflict. Most of accounts of what transpired that day were biased, representing, variously, the attackers' viewpoint, the Jewish mainstream Haganah viewpoint or the Arab viewpoint. There was virtually no agreement about anything relating to the affair, with the different narratives presenting, not only differing perspectives, but also entirely different stories. The focus of the debate was whether the assailants committed a massacre in the village, as claimed by the Arabs, the Haganah and some foreign writers, or whether it was a legitimate battle, as claimed by Etzel and Lehi, albeit one that resulted in the unfortunate but inevitable death of many civilians.

The Deir Yassin affair deserved serious and in depth research, not only because this incident and its ramifications were unique enough to merit it, but also because the story is too complicated to be discussed in just a few pages of a book on the 1948 Israeli War of Independence. The purpose of this book is to discover what really happened in Deir Yassin. The primary methodology I have adopted in this book is to integrate the testimonies of both Etzel and Lehi's combatants, on the one hand, and the Arab survivors, on the other hand, into one combined narrative of the events, in order to yield the true and complete story. Where relevant, I have supplemented these accounts with those of others who witnessed, or claimed to have witnessed the events. Some previous attempts to describe events that day have ignored or disqualified the testimonies of one or more of the sides involved, either Jews or Arabs, and in doing so made it impossible to develop an accurate account. Yet, when the testimonies of all parties were heeded, the accounts of the Jewish attackers and the Arab survivors proved to be surprisingly similar, at times almost identical. Although this might defy expectations, it actually should not be so surprising, since both parties were there when it happened.

The Palestinians faced a fundamental dilemma when forming their narrative of the 1948 war. On the one hand, when a people narrates its historical past it may wish to underline heroics and determination. On the other hand, the results of the 1948 war compelled the Palestinians to rely on external sympathy, making it necessary for them to emphasize their tragedies in order to arouse compassion. In the particular case of Deir Yassin, it created a conflict of interests. The villagers wanted to emphasize their determined resistance and that, rather than going like lambs to the slaughter, they fought "to the last bullet." This, however, was contrary to the general Palestinian interest in presenting the village as an innocent and defenseless victim of inhumanity. These political considerations, however, are of no concern of the historian, whose task is to write history "*wie es eigentlich gewesen*" – "as it really happened" to cite Ranke's words, without trying to force the facts to accommodate any of the parties involved.

In order to produce a complete and reliable narrative of the affair it was necessary to answer scores of formerly unasked questions; some seemed trivial, but actually proved to be crucial. There were no shortcuts, and in this particular case, seeing the forest was dependent on first discerning all the trees. It became clear that in order to decipher what had happened in Deir Yassin and avoid empty phrases regarding the "plausibility" or "impossibility" of a massacre, the only option was to ascertain the exact circumstances of death of each of the individuals killed. "I do not think the investigator will be able to reach his research goals," declared a skeptical reader on behalf of the Israel Science Foundation who examined the research proposal of this book. However, the wealth of survivor testimonies available made it possible.

Many details relating to the Deir Yassin story remain controversial. In several places in this book, especially when quantitative issues were concerned, I put forward all the views available, but always end with a clear-cut decision as to which of them is the correct one, with an explanation why that is the one that should be accepted. Each of the text paragraphs relies on a large number of sources, accumulated in the reference at the end of each paragraph. Actually, each of the sentences usually relied on many sources. The order of the sources within the notes is usually in accordance with the order of the sentences they refer to within the paragraph. At times, Jewish sources were put first and then the Arab ones, or the other way around, as relevant to the text. The sources of this book mainly encompass archival records, typescripts of interviews, many memoirs, the contemporaneous press, secondary literature, and internet sources including video clips (in the latter type, I indicated the exact second when the relevant segment begins).

Quite a few books written by people directly involved in the affair were published recently. Mordechai Gichon (Gicherman) was a Haganah intelligence officer in Jerusalem in 1948. In 2010, as a retired archeology professor of Tel Aviv University, he published his memoirs in a private edition (a copy he donated to his former place of employment was used for this book). Da'ud Ahmad As'ad Radwan, a survivor of Deir Yassin living in the United States, published his memoirs in 2010 in English, and two years later, in Arabic. Shimon Moneta, a Haganah spy inside Lehi, published his memoirs in 2011. Yehoshua Matza, former Knesset member and minister, and in 1948 a Lehi combatant in Deir Yassin, published his memoirs in 2014. The family of Col. (res.) Meir Pa'il (Pilavsky), whose controversial role will be discussed in detail, also published his memoirs in 2014, based on his personal records. Finally, 65 years after he had written them, in 2014 the family of Husayn Fakhri al-Khalidi, the secretary of the

Arab Higher Committee, published his memoirs in Amman. All of these memoirs were used in the present research.

Many Etzel and Haganah members changed their surname later in life. Etzel men usually adopted their code name in the underground as their new surname. For example, Mordechai Kaufman changed his surname to Raanan, his code name in Etzel. Haganah men usually used a phonetically similar Hebrew name to replace their former non-Hebrew surname. For example, Meir Pilavsky changed his surname to Pa'il while Mordechai Gicherman changed his surname to Gichon. For the text, I used the surnames they were called by during the events of 1948. However, if, when interviewed many years later, they already used their new surnames, these ones were used for the notes when indicating the interviews and later testimonies.

For Arabic and Hebrew I used the ordinary professional transliterations used by academics, but without diacritics or indications of long vowels, except for a single open quotation mark for *ayn* and a single close quotation mark for *hamza*. Widely known place names, however, were spelled as they have come to be accepted and not in accordance with their exact transliteration (for example, Deir Yassin, not Dayr Yasin). Authors' names were spelled (where available) the way they themselves rendered them in English, but titles of publications were always spelled in exact transliteration.

Professor Benny Morris provided me with copies of the documents on Deir Yassin available in the IDF archives, which he had photocopied when the documents were open (see "The Historiography" in chapter 11), thus enabling me to "legally" see and use these "forbidden" documents. Professor Yehuda Lapidot, formerly deputy commander of Etzel's force in Deir Yassin, was always ready to help and answer my many bothersome questions. Many others helped me on various occasions, answering questions or providing sources, and they were noted in the respective notes. The Association for the Study of the Middle East and Africa (ASMEA) awarded me three research grants and significantly contributed toward the publication of this book. It was in its seventh annual conference in

October 2014 in Washington, DC, that I first presented the results of my research. My sincere thanks are extended to them all. I also wish to thank my literary agent Andrew Stuart of the Stuart Agency, my publisher Matthew Miller and his team at The Toby Press, as well as the book's editor, David Olesker, who did excellent work. Special thanks go to my wife, Rachel, whose art has always been a source of inspiration for me.

Eliezer Tauber

Chapter 1

Why Deir Yassin?

THE VILLAGE

Deir Yassin was an Arab village west of Jerusalem. It stood about 700 meters south-west of the Jewish suburb Givat Shaul, and about one kilometer west and north-west of the Jewish suburbs of Montefiore (nowadays Kiryat Moshe), Beit ha-Kerem and Yefe Nof. Further south was the Jewish suburb of Bayit ve-Gan. Located on the eastern slopes a of hill that rose 800 meters above sea level, it was separated from the Jewish suburbs by a valley planted with fig, almond and olive trees. A narrow road at the north of the valley led from Deir Yassin to Givat Shaul and it was the only direct link between the village and Jerusalem. The closest Arab village to Deir Yassin was 'Ayn Karm, about two kilometers south-west of it. There were other Arab villages in the vicinity, Lifta, northeast of it and Qalunya and Qastal to the north-west, but they were farther away and lacked a direct connection. From its position, the village overlooked the main Jerusalem-Tel Aviv road, laying less than two kilometers north of the village.

Officially, Deir Yassin extended over a large area of 2,857 *dunam*s (decares), yet about one third of it was cultivated lands and

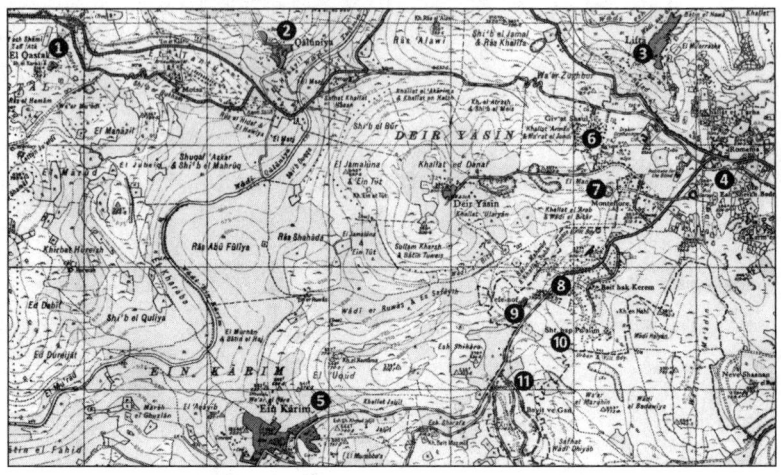

Fig. 1 Arab villages and Jewish neighborhoods around Deir Yassin: 1. Qastal, 2. Qalunya, 3. Lifta, 4. Sheikh Badr, 5. 'Ayn Karm, 6. Givat Shaul, 7. Montefiore, 8. Beit ha-Kerem, 9. Yefe Nof, 10. Ha-Poalim, 11. Bayit ve-Gan

only 12 *dunam*s were built up. There were 144 houses in Deir Yassin in 1948, most of them made of stone, with some of the newer houses constructed from concrete. Most of the houses were located in blocks with narrow alleys between them. The blocks and the individual houses were scattered over a large area, with stretches of empty space between them. According to official figures of the British authorities, 2,701 *dunam*s out of the 2,857 belonged to Muslim Arabs. The surprising figure, however, is, that 153 *dunam*s belonged to Jews, most of them cultivated lands. It seems that, while these lands were formally part of Deir Yassin, in practice they belonged to the neighboring suburb of Givat Shaul.[1]

How many people lived there? The number is controversial. The number of 400 is quoted by a number of sources including the commander of the Etzel force that attacked Deir Yassin, the representative of the Red Cross who visited the village two days after the attack, and an Arab survivor who was 9 years old in 1948.[2] Others, both Jews (the Haganah) and Arabs (the secretary of the Arab Higher Committee), put it at 500 or 600. Other Arab survivors, some of them babies at the time, raised the estimate to 650, 670 or even 700. A spokesman on behalf of Etzel also stated this last number in a press

2

Fig. 2 Deir Yassin – general view from the east (picture taken in 1949)

conference after the attack.³ The Palestinian researcher, Salman Abu-Sitta, calculated the number to be exactly 708. He based his number on a 1944 British census, according to which the number of inhabitants in Deir Yassin was 610. Applying the 3.8 percent Muslim annual natural growth rate for the years 1944 to 1948 yielded that figure.⁴ Most sources, be they Arab (including adult survivors), Jewish or Western, put the number at 750, or 800 at most.⁵ There are a few researchers that increased it to 1,000, while two Jewish researchers further raised it to 1,200, contending that number to include refugees from other Arab villages and neighborhoods. There is no solid evidence that such refugees arrived in Deir Yassin in early 1948.⁶

It seems, however, that the higher estimates are the correct ones. On 20 April 1948, the social affairs committee of the Jerusalem National Committee (*al-Lajna al-Qawmiyya*) requested the Arab Higher Committee to provide it with financial resources to support 730 survivors from Deir Yassin. Taking into account that the number of dead was about one hundred (see below), than the overall population of Deir Yassin certainly exceeded 800. Furthermore, in a booklet about Deir Yassin, the two Palestinian researchers, Sharif Kana'na and Nihad Zaytawi, cited genealogical trees of all the families of

Deir Yassin. Altogether, these trees included 498 names and in most cases covered five to six generations of the respective families. While it is clear that not all of these people lived in the village at the same time, there is evidence that the last three to four generations lived in April 1948 (people from these generations appear amongst those killed during the attack). Deducting the names of the first two generations yielded 469 names. On the other hand, the trees included only males, and in most cases did not include the small children of 1948. In other words, in order to compensate for the missing women and children in these trees one must double the number, if not more, to achieve the correct figure of inhabitants in Deir Yassin in early 1948. It seems, therefore that the number of inhabitants in Deir Yassin prior to the attack was about 1,000.[7]

The Deir Yassin population was divided into three main *hamulas* (clans, enlarged families) and several additional families. The *hamulas* were Shahada (comprising the families Sammur, Zaydan, Hamdan and Khalil), 'Aql (comprising the families Radwan, Zahran, 'Atiyya and 'Ata Allah-Farhan) and Hamida (comprising mainly the families 'Alya, Salah, Salih and Qasim). Additional families were Jabir, 'Id, Muslih and Jundi.[8]

Until the early 1920s, Deir Yassin's villagers depended on agriculture, growing grains, grapes, olives, plums, almonds, dates and figs. Some of the produce was sold to the inhabitants of the Jewish neighborhoods. The economic basis of the village started to change in the wake of increased Jewish immigration and the need for stones for extensive construction projects in Jerusalem. Many of the villagers shifted to working in the stone industry as the village lands were rich in high quality limestone (*hajar yasini*). In 1927, the first quarry was dug and a stone crusher was brought in to expedite the work. By the second half of the 1940s, there were already seven quarries, three north of the road to Givat Shaul and four south of it, with four crushers belonging to the Radwan, Sammur and Jundi families. At that point, most of villagers worked in the stone industry, either as stonecutters and processors or as truck drivers transporting the product. Only fifteen percent of the villagers remained in agriculture. Other villagers worked in the British army and police facilities, some were self-employed, and a few dozen worked in the Jewish neighborhoods.[9]

The stone industry made Deir Yassin a prosperous village. It had two mosques, one called the Sheikh Yassin mosque, after whom the village was named, and the other one was named after Mahmud Salah, a wealthy notable who had died several years before. There were two primary schools in the village, one for boys established in 1940 and one for girls established in 1943. The village boasted three shops and a bakery. The latter was owned by the mukhtar, the village headman, but operated by a baker from Hebron and his son. There were five wells in the village, but no regular water supply from Jerusalem or electricity. There were, however, two phones in the village, one in the house of Muhammad Zaydan, near the village center, and the other near the crusher of the Radwan family, very close to Givat Shaul. A bus belonging to a company from Lifta would arrive at the village from Jerusalem three times a day. There was no physician in Deir Yassin.[10]

DEIR YASSIN AND ITS JEWISH NEIGHBORS

Relations between Deir Yassin and its Jewish neighbors dated back to 1906, when villagers from Deir Yassin and Lifta sold the lands of the future Givat Shaul to a group of Jewish settlers. In the years that followed, villagers from Deir Yassin worked in construction works in the new neighborhood but were also involved in thefts and burglaries. Although protection money paid to the mukhtar brought some tranquility, the economic depression on the eve of World War I, saw the thefts resume. In March 1914, some of the villagers planned a raid on Givat Shaul. Villagers armed with guns and cold steel attacked the neighborhood, robbing and injuring. One of the first homes attacked belonged to Yosef Tzvi Goldschmidt, who would father Yehoshua, who would grow to be the Etzel's operations officer in 1948. Yosef Tzvi was lightly injured but managed to halt the attackers until his neighbors came to his help. Turkish forces were summoned and they opened fire on the attackers. The Arabs ran back to Deir Yassin, but one of them was caught. A note from the leader of the attack was found on him with instructions. Consequently, the soldiers arrested many villagers and searched Deir Yassin, finding weapons and goods stolen from the army. The Turkish commanding officer warned the villagers that, unless they handed over their leader, he would destroy the village. The leader was surrendered, court-martialed and executed by firing squad. During World War I, the villagers collected arms left by the Turkish army and the Germans and hid them underground. When the war was over they sold some of them to 'Ayn Karm and Lifta.[11]

On the Jewish festival of Simchat Torah 1927, Arabs from Deir Yassin again attacked Givat Shaul, resulting in six Jews "officially" injured and others who refused medical treatment due to the sanctity of the day. A committee representing the Jews of Givat Shaul asked their municipal representatives to demand that the government punish the rioters and station police between Givat Shaul and the village. A compensation for those injured was later arranged, paid by the village in order to avoid trial. Less than two years later, on 23 August 1929, in the framework of countrywide attacks against the Jews, villagers from Lifta, Deir Yassin and 'Ayn Karm attacked the nearby Jewish neighborhoods of Romema, Givat Shaul, Montefiore, Beit ha-Kerem, Yefe Nof and Bayit ve-Gan. The Arabs of Deir Yassin played a key role in this violence, attacking the central suburbs of Givat Shaul, Montefiore and Beit ha-Kerem. An attempt was also made to block the Jerusalem-Tel Aviv road. The Jewish self-defense organization, the Haganah, repulsed the attackers. Two defenders and one Jewish policeman were killed. The attack on Givat Shaul renewed at dawn and this time a police armored car arrived and machine-gunned Deir Yassin. The fire from the village stopped, but not before a British officer had been killed.[12]

Relations improved during the economic boom of the early 1930s, to the point that the Sammurs took a Jewish partner for their quarry. The partnership lasted three years, during which the Jewish partner brought machinery from Britain and hired a Jewish engineer. However, when the Arab revolt of 1936–1939 broke out all the economic ties were cut. Most of the villagers supported the Grand Mufti of Jerusalem, Amin al-Husayni, and his Palestinian Arab Party. Tension escalated into skirmishes and the British authorities arrested

Fig. 3 The Jewish western suburbs: 1. Givat Shaul, 2. Montefiore,
3. Beit ha-Kerem, 4. Yefe Nof, 5. Ha-Poalim, 6. Bayit ve-Gan

several villagers. Rebels from the village would attack the Jewish neighborhoods and kill Jews, leading to British raids and searches, the confiscation of arms and the imprisonment of villagers. Finally, the British set up a temporary checkpoint in the village, staffed by 10 to 15 soldiers, and would intermittently declare a curfew. They issued a list of people ordered to report daily to prove their presence in the village, anyone failing to do so would be punished. The villagers were undeterred and continued to use the nearby hills for attacks on British patrols and vehicles. Rebels from Deir Yassin also

7

derailed a supply train arriving from the coastal plain to Jerusalem. British planes appeared and the rebels took refuge among the trees. Some villagers joined the band of irregulars commanded by Ahmad Mahmud Abu Sha'ban from Lifta.[13]

The Jews, for their part, would retaliate by ravaging Arab plantations close to the Jewish neighborhoods. Combatants on behalf of the Haganah and the smaller Jewish underground organization, Etzel, defended the Jewish neighborhoods from Arab raids, including Givat Shaul. Members of the Jewish underground organizations who would drive on the Jerusalem-Tel Aviv road encountered ambushes laid by villagers from Deir Yassin. In August 1937, an attempt for a *sulha* (reconciliation) was made between Givat Shaul and Deir Yassin. Exchanges of fire nevertheless continued until the outbreak of World War II. During the war, the hostilities died out, and following it, the economic ties with the Jews resumed, especially with regard to the quarries. Calm reigned until late 1947.[14]

The adoption of the Palestine partition resolution by the United Nations General Assembly, on 29 November 1947, escalated the situation in the whole of Palestine, particularly in Jerusalem. Jews and Arabs were locked in a civil war. The road from Jerusalem to Deir Yassin via Givat Shaul became unsafe. Villagers who wanted to reach Jerusalem had to take a long walk through 'Ayn Karm and Maliha further south. An emergency committee (*lajnat tawari*) was formed, composed of seven elders representing the village families, to organize the defense of Deir Yassin. They resolved to set up patrols, to fortify the village and to purchase arms. An important additional decision was made: not to take any aggressive steps against the neighboring Jewish suburbs because of the delicate position of the village. Notwithstanding this policy, some of the younger villagers joined the Palestinian military organization, the Army of Sacred Jihad (*Jaysh al-Jihad al-Muqaddas*), led by 'Abd al-Qadir al-Husayni. In late December and early January, on several occasions, there was fire from Deir Yassin aimed at Givat Shaul, which only stopped when the police arrived. The Jews classified Deir Yassin one of the hostile villages endangering the road from Jerusalem to Tel Aviv.[15]

Fig. 4 Trenches dug by the Turks during World War I on the hill north of Deir Yassin, overlooking the Jerusalem–Tel Aviv road

Haganah started to distribute leaflets near the village calling on the villagers to remain on friendly terms with the Jews and to forbid foreign elements from entering the village. The villagers were promised protection if they complied with this. A Haganah messenger infiltrated into the village with such leaflets, was brought to the mukhtar, and then returned safely to Givat Shaul by the mukhtar's son. When the mukhtar, Muhammad Isma'il Sammur, visited Jerusalem, he was offered the opportunity to sign a non-belligerency agreement with the Jews. Although he hesitated to sign a formal peace agreement with Givat Shaul, by late December, he had promised his interlocutors to notify Givat Shaul when foreigners visited the village. From that point the Haganah considered him an "informer," though evidently he was not, divulging to the Jews only what he felt suited the interests of his village. On 11 January 1948, a small band of irregulars tried to enter Deir Yassin and settle in the bakery, with the intention to use it as a base for attacking the Jewish neighborhoods. The

9

villagers denied them entry, and in the ensuing exchange of fire one of the villagers was killed (not the mukhtar's son, as some claimed). Givat Shaul was asked to call the police. The irregulars were ousted and at that point, the notables of Deir Yassin were ready to sign an agreement with their Jewish neighbors.[16]

On 20 January 1948, the two sides signed a "good neighborly relations" agreement. The mukhtar and some of the village notables represented the Arabs, while the Jews were represented by Peri Friedman, the "mukhtar" of Givat Shaul, Nahum Bushmi, a police officer on behalf of the Jewish Agency, and Akiva Azulay, the Haganah regional second-in-command. Yitzhak Navon, head of the Arab department of the Haganah's intelligence in Jerusalem, as well as the district command, sanctioned the agreement. The accord comprised five articles. In the first article, the villagers pledged to inform the Jews about the presence of any irregulars whom they would not be able to drive away by themselves. During daylight, they would hang certain articles of laundry at a certain place to announce that they had such information. Flashlight signals would be used during the nights. Then the two sides would convene, after an exchange of passwords. The second article dealt with passwords for people from Givat Shaul patrolling near Deir Yassin. The third article discussed traffic from Deir Yassin through Givat Shaul. Such traffic was only allowed from 7:00 to 9:00 a.m. and from 3:00 to 5:00 p.m. The number of vehicles was limited and their registration numbers had to be delivered to Givat Shaul in advance. Although the Jews had the right to search the cars, they were responsible for their safety while in Givat Shaul. The fourth article prohibited Arabs from entering Givat Shaul on their own. Finally, the fifth article established the need to negotiate the fate of several of the quarries close to Givat Shaul. The Arabs had to set a price for handing them over to the Jews until the end of the hostilities. The agreement did not include mutual defense from attacks, as some have claimed.[17]

Besides the signatories, the people of Deir Yassin, Givat Shaul and the Haganah, who knew about this agreement? "The entire city knew," said Yitzhak Levy, the commander of the Haganah's intelligence in Jerusalem. "It must have been that Etzel also knew about it." Etzel member Yoel Kimhi insisted in an interview that he knew nothing about it and doubted whether his commander knew. Lehi definitely knew. Yehoshua Zettler, the commander of Lehi in Jerusalem, reported on the agreement in March, indicating that "so far" it had been maintained. His report was almost verbatim cited in *Ha-Ma'as*, Lehi's organ. News about the agreement also reached the Arab Higher Committee, the supreme political authority of the Palestinian Arabs, and Muhammad Isma'il Sammur was summoned to Jerusalem to supply explanations. He told the Committee that the villagers were living in peace with the Jews. He later informed his Haganah liaison that the Committee was satisfied by his words, but the Haganah learned from other sources that the agreement had, in fact, been subject to sharp criticism by the Committee. The Committee's secretary, Husayn Fakhri al-Khalidi, would recall this after the attack, when he was to indicate that Deir Yassin was the only Arab village that had not sought the protection of the Arab Higher Committee.[18]

A brother of the mukhtar was also dissatisfied with the agreement and at times would shoot at Givat Shaul, following which the mukhtar would apologize, while Akiva Azulay would "run from house to house" to prevent reciprocation and the collapse of the agreement. It became evident that the villagers did not have much faith in the pact. Parallel to the continuation of the negotiations with Givat Shaul, whether through a Jewish liaison or by phone (which the Haganah tapped), the villagers continued to promote defensive measures. Already by late December 1947, Arabs had been seen training north of the quarries. Again, during the first months of 1948, Arabs were repeatedly spotted training in shooting, first aid and field exercises in various locations in and around the village. On several occasions Haganah observers noted the instructor was wearing the uniform of the Arab Legion (actually he served in the Transjordan Frontier Force – see below). The vicinity of the village cemetery became a training ground for the use of hand grenades.[19]

In late January, a large group of the Army of Sacred Jihad, some say 400 men, headed by 'Abd al-Qadir al-Husayni himself, arrived in Deir Yassin. They were looking for volunteers to join them, but found none. When asked about the relationship between the village and the Jews, the mukhtar answered that they were living in peace. Husayni, nevertheless, promised to help the village when needed (he would die the day before the attack on the village). Husayni was given to understand that the presence of his men in the village was undesirable and they left. A fortnight later, another band of irregulars arrived in Deir Yassin with the intention of attacking Givat Shaul. The villagers objected and the band retaliated by slaughtering the village sheep. An attempt by Husayni to use Deir Yassin as a base for attacking Givat Shaul and Yefe Nof was rebuffed by the village notables between late February and early March. In the third week of March, a delegation from the Arab Higher Committee arrived in the village, asking it to host Iraqi and Syrian volunteers of the Rescue Army (*Jaysh al-Inqadh*), who in turn would defend the village. The delegation left empty-handed.[20]

Fig. 5 Standing in the middle, with two bandoliers crossed on his chest, 'Abd al-Qadir al-Husayni, commander of the Army of Sacred Jihad; to his right his second-in-command, Kamil 'Arikat (photo taken by a Jewish spy)

On 22 March, two Haganah men disguised as supernumerary police approached the village to investigate the presence of foreign combatants there. An old man, apparently an informer, came out of one of the houses on the edge of the village and talked with them. When they began driving back to Givat Shaul, an exchange of fire started. After some twenty minutes of shooting, a group of Haganah men started to advance on Deir Yassin and tried to gain control over the Radwan family's stone crusher, the closest to Givat Shaul. The watchman of the Radwan stone plant opened fire on them, injuring two. Reinforcements from both sides started to join in, the emergency committee of Deir Yassin trying to calm the situation down. After two and a half hours of shooting a British police armored car intervened and the Jewish fighters retreated. Following the incident, the emergency committee reached an understanding with representatives of the Haganah that no villager would pass Radwan's crusher in the direction of Givat Shaul and vice versa. Any transgressor would be shot. The Jews, in any case, closed the road from the village to Jerusalem.[21]

In late March, the Haganah received information from an Arab source that about 150 Iraqi and Syrian irregulars had entered Deir Yassin. Observations by the Haganah of a large group of people approaching Deir Yassin from 'Ayn Karm, seemed to corroborate this information. Mordechai Gicherman (later Gichon), the regional intelligence officer of the Haganah's Etzioni brigade , hurried to the observation post to see for himself, and managed to observe the last of them entering the village. According to him, they numbered more than several dozens. The regional command was updated about the development. The information proved to be incorrect. The notables of Deir Yassin denied that foreign forces had taken control of the village or that any foreigners were even present. Although the denial was corroborated by a Jewish source and reported to the district commander, nevertheless, on 9 April, the day of the attack on Deir Yassin, the original information about the 150 foreigners was circulated by the Haganah's intelligence. Rumors about a foreign presence persisted, and when Etzel and Lehi attacked Deir Yassin, they would be utterly convinced that the village was packed with foreigners.[22]

As if to confirm the information about the foreign combatants, on Friday night, 2 April, Deir Yassin and 'Ayn Karm opened fire on Beit ha-Kerem, Yefe Nof and Bayit ve-Gan (but not on Givat Shaul!). The shooting continued throughout the night and was intense enough for some of Sunday's morning newspapers to report on it. On Sunday, shots were fired at vehicles on the Jerusalem-Tel Aviv road below Deir Yassin. At 6:00 a.m., a Lehi armored car under the command of David Gottlieb was attacked from above, just before the turn near Motza. Another car coming from Motza was also attacked in the same place by rifle fire. Motza also came under fire. Early that morning the Haganah seized the Sharafa ridge facing 'Ayn Karm (today's Mount Herzl). Arabs from all around – including combatants from Maliha and Deir Yassin – returned fire throughout that day and the next.[23]

On that Sunday, amidst the crucial and bloody battle over Qastal (captured by the Haganah the day before), Kamil 'Arikat, 'Abd al-Qadir al-Husayni's second-in-command, arrived in 'Ayn Karm and met with its notables as well as notables from Deir Yassin. He offered both villages foreign combatants to secure their villages. 'Ayn Karm's notables agreed while those of Deir Yassin refused, claiming that the entry of foreigners into their village would endanger their relationship with the Jews. Nevertheless, when the next day a runner came from Qastal to Deir Yassin asking for assistance, twelve fighters were sent from the village, with one of the mukhtar's sons, Musa Muhammad Isma'il, among them. They first stopped at 'Ayn Karm for a brief exercise in military tactics, and on 7 and 8 April, they participated in the Arab counter attack on Qastal. Some of them were injured. Etzel and Lehi believed that Deir Yassin was serving as a rear supply base for the Arab fighters in Qastal.[24]

On 8 April, the Arabs managed to regain Qastal from the Haganah for several hours, but at the cost of 'Abd al-Qadir al-Husayni's life. Most of the Arab combatants left for Jerusalem after the battle to participate in Husayni's funeral the next day. The Haganah exploited their absence to recapture Qastal. Some of the fighters from Deir Yassin, too, remained for the funeral, while others returned to the village in the evening. The villagers clearly understood the severity of the situation following the fall of Qastal. Already by January and

February, other Arab villages in the vicinity, like Lifta and Sheikh Badr, were evacuated under Jewish pressure, as well as the Arabs who lived in the mixed neighborhood Romema. There was a substantial fear that Deir Yassin was going to be the next and at 4:30 p.m., the emergency committee declared a state of emergency. All villagers under arms were called to be on the alert.[25]

FIGHTERS, ARMS AND FORTIFICATIONS IN DEIR YASSIN

Controversy surrounds the number of armed fighters in Deir Yassin on the eve of the attack. Forty was the lowest estimate, related a few days after the attack by a hospitalized young girl to a reporter.[26] Older witnesses, who participated themselves in the defense of the village, estimated the number to be between 60 and 70. This also was the opinion of the commander of the Etzel force that attacked Deir Yassin.[27] Most Arab writers, however, supported by one of the adult survivors, give a higher estimate of 80 to 85.[28] Others, including one of Etzel's seconds-in-command and a native of Deir Yassin who was not in the village during the attack, give an even higher number of 100.[29] Finally, one of the adult survivors established the number of combatants to be 200, a figure also stated by Etzel in a press conference after the attack.[30] It seems likely that, if the much smaller number of Jews who attacked Deir Yassin had faced 200 armed fighters, the result of the battle would have been different. It seems more likely that the number of defenders in Deir Yassin corresponded with the testimonies of the Arab survivors who participated in the battle and was about 70, perhaps 80 at most.

All the youths able to carry arms were regularly trained in their use and in patrolling. One of their instructors, 'Ali Qasim, a veteran of the 1936–39 revolt, would later lead the Arab resistance against the Jewish attackers. Another instructor served in the Transjordan Frontier Force. A night watch was also set up, composed of 40 fighters, who took turns standing guard in assigned positions with particular attention focused on the entrances to the village. One watch would stand guard from 6:00 p.m. to midnight, when they would be relieved by the other group who would be on duty from midnight until 6:00 a.m. Husayn Zaydan of the emergency committee was appointed inspector of the guards.[31]

"Maybe some people had rifles," Anwar Nusayba, secretary of the Jerusalem National Committee in 1948, said to a reporter. Some of the Deir Yassin survivors claimed that the villagers only had their own private rifles, with a few bullets each, possibly also a few pistols. The rifles were old, said others, Turkish rifles from World War I. "Wrecked rifles," another survivor (a baby in 1948) added. Twenty to 25 rifles at most, averred the commander of the Haganah's intelligence in Jerusalem at the time.[32]

This was not the case. Although some of the villagers had their own shotguns, understanding the gravity of the situation, the emergency committee had decided to send a delegation to Egypt to buy weaponry left from World War II. A large sum of money was raised, the women of Deir Yassin donating some of their jewelry, and a four-man delegation set out. Failing to buy enough weapons from official sources, they decided to seek more on the black market. One of the delegates, Husayn Muhammad 'Atiyya, was caught red-handed by Egyptian intelligence, jailed, the weapons he had bought, confiscated. It was only after a month in prison that his friends managed to convince the Egyptian military to release him whereupon the Egyptian army brought the weapons to Rafah. Altogether, the delegation had managed to buy two Bren guns and some 25 rifles (40, according to another version) and a considerable amount of ammunition. They hid the weapons in a truck carrying vegetables to Jerusalem, and via 'Ayn Karm, brought it by means of pack-animals to Deir Yassin, reaching there on 4 April.[33]

By late March, the British authorities delivered ten semiautomatic rifles with 10-round magazines to Deir Yassin in a framework of a plan to establish a rural police parallel to the municipal police. British soldiers delivered some rifles to the villagers on their own initiative, probably for money. It seems that the British also supplied the village with appropriate ammunition, since during the battle the attackers discovered several cases of ammunition sealed with the inscription "Palestine Police." During the battle, the Jewish attackers would find at least two armories in the village. In one, they found 18 rifles, 20 pistols and ammunition, and in the second position they found several Tommy guns (Sten guns, according to Arab sources) and two bags full of bullets. An Etzel fighter found an additional 20 Bren magazines in one of the houses. In addition, explosives and some steel helmets were discovered. Finally, there is much evidence, from both sides, that the Arab defenders used hand grenades during the battle.[34]

According to most Arab sources, on the eve of the attack the villagers possessed two Bren guns, four Sten guns, some 60 rifles (mainly British, but also Italian, French, German and even one American), some of them semi-automatic, appropriate ammunition and a considerable number of hand grenades. According to Jewish sources, they also had some pistols and explosives.[35] Etzel and Lehi had no advance knowledge of the presence of such a large store of weaponry available to the villagers. "They did not realize the intensity of the fire they were going to face," a Haganah man was to say many years later. The regional second-in-command on behalf of the Haganah tried to warn them, but was not taken seriously.[36]

As early as late December 1947, the inhabitants of Deir Yassin started to build firing positions, mainly on the roofs of their houses. Some were constructed from concrete, while others were built from sandbags. In early February 1948, Mordechai Gicherman, the Haganah regional intelligence officer, submitted a report indicating twelve such positions. The first, a hut on a roof with firing ports was directed at Beit ha-Kerem. The second, made of sand bags, was directed at Yefe Nof and Beit ha-Kerem. The third, made of stones and barrels, was also directed at Yefe Nof and Beit ha-Kerem. The fourth, of reinforced concrete, overlooked Beit ha-Kerem and Montefiore. The fifth, a concrete post manned only at nightof, overlooked Beit ha-Kerem and the quarries south of the road. The sixth, made of stones and cans, also manned only at night, was directed at Beit ha-Kerem and Montefiore. The seventh, of sand bags, also faced in that direction. He was not sure about a possible eighth position. The ninth was made of concrete and directed at Montefiore and Givat Shaul. The tenth, also made of concrete, overlooked the road. The eleventh, of sand bags, faced westward, while the twelfth, of concrete, was directed to the northwest. Other positions were identified later. A forward position dominated the entrance to the village, near the crusher of the Sammurs.[37]

This last position was part of the most important decision taken by the emergency committee, one that would have significant consequences. The committee decided to secure the road from Givat Shaul by digging trenches across it, in order to prevent the passage of

Figs. 6 and 7 Firing positions on the roofs of Deir Yassin's houses

18

hostile vehicles. The most significant trench was dug several meters away from the crusher of the Sammurs, a few meters east of the first houses of the village. At that part of the road, there were two quarries, one to the north and the other to the south. With no way to bypass it the trench effectively blocked all passage along the road. The excavation was five meters long, two meters deep and at least two meters wide, impassable not only for armored cars but even for tanks. It was disguised with a covering of branches and dirt.[38]

HAGANAH, ETZEL AND LEHI IN EARLY 1948 JERUSALEM

The Haganah (the name literally means, "Defense") was the main and largest military organization of the Jewish community in Palestine from the early days of the British mandate until the establishment of the state of Israel. It was founded in 1920 to cope with the increasing Arab hostilities against Jews. Etzel (the acronym of *Irgun Tzva'i Le'umi*, National Military Organization) was established in 1931 when a group of Haganah members seceded from it. The new faction opposed the relatively defensive character of the Haganah and wanted to be more pro-active. Lehi (the acronym of *Lohamey Herut Yisra'el*, Fighters for Israel's Freedom) seceded from Etzel in 1940, following Etzel's decision to cease its struggle against the British in order not to impede their war with Germany. Lehi believed in the necessity of continuing the struggle against British rule. The latter two organizations were considered "dissidents" (*porshim*) by the Haganah since they differed from the mainstream position of the Jewish community. In 1947, after Britain had referred the Palestine question to the United Nations, the Haganah began the process of consolidating into a countrywide army able to overcome the Arabs. With the outbreak of hostilities following the adoption of the Palestine partition resolution, Etzel and Lehi also realized that the struggle had to shift from fighting the British to Arabs.[39]

The Palestine partition resolution adopted by the United Nation established that Jerusalem be placed under UN control. Both Etzel and Lehi openly and vehemently opposed both the partition of Palestine and the internationalization of Jerusalem. The Jewish Agency and the Haganah likewise did not intend to abandon Jewish Jerusalem, but they hesitated

about the proper way to handle the situation, and Etzel and Lehi interpreted this hesitation as a betrayal of Jerusalem. In early February 1948, David Shaltiel was appointed the Haganah's district commander of Jerusalem (and commander of the Etzioni brigade). Etzel's commander in Jerusalem, Mordechai Kaufman, apparently detested him, while his relations with the local Lehi's commander, Yehoshua Zettler, were likewise cold. Nonetheless, Shaltiel repeatedly attempted to achieve cooperation with the

Fig. 8 David Shaltiel, the Haganah's district commander of Jerusalem

other two organizations for the sake of Jerusalem's defense, efforts that exasperated his superior, Yisrael Galili, the Haganah's chief of staff. Because of Jerusalem's delicate status and the possible implications, upon his appointment his superior instructed Shaltiel to seek instructions before taking any initiative against the Arabs. However, Shaltiel would report directly to Ben-Gurion and bypass Galili.[40]

In the early months of 1948 Etzel's Jerusalem branch comprised some 350 to 400 members, of whom about 100 were active combatants. Its main base was located near the entrance to Jerusalem, in the Etz Haim neighborhood. The base's commander was Ben-Zion Cohen, who had served with the British naval commandos. The Lehi Jerusalem branch was much smaller, comprising some 80 members, about half of them combatants. Due to the circumstances, Lehi's supreme command decided that the Jerusalem branch would operate autonomously of headquarters in most fields, nonetheless requiring permission for operations. Its commander, Yehoshua Zettler, had been persuaded to move to Jerusalem in late 1947 due to tense relations between him and one of Lehi's supreme commanders, Nathan Fried-man-Yellin. Zettler introduced a new spirit into the branch, attacking Arabs in the mixed neighborhood of Romema, as well as the Arab villages Sheikh Badr and Lifta, soon to be evacuated by their inhabitants. A Lehi base was set up in the abandoned village of Sheikh Badr.[41]

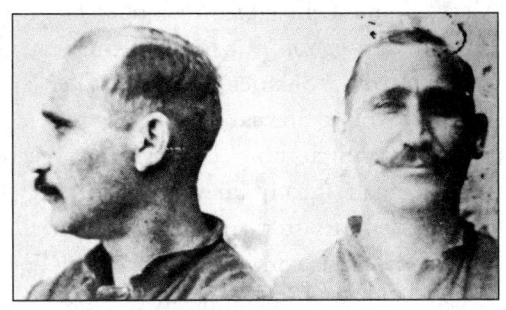

Fig. 9 Yehoshua Zettler, Lehi's commander in Jerusalem (prison photograph; he escaped from the British prison in May 1947)

A short while after his arrival, Shaltiel appointed Eliyahu Arbel, an operations officer in the Etzioni brigade, as liaison between the Haganah and the other two organizations. He instructed him to negotiate with the underground organizations to set up a coordinated operation against an Arab target. Various villages were proposed, Biddu, Nabi Samwil and Qalunya, and eventually they decided to attack Maliha, a base for the Arab irregulars that assaulted southern Jerusalem. He, along with a representative of the two underground organizations studied the village and discussed the details of the operation. The representative asked the Haganah to supply them with one or two machine guns and ammunition. The Haganah agreed to put two machine guns on a ridge overlooking the village, but the underground organizations insisted that they operate the machine guns for use in the village itself. Fearing that would lead to the loss of the weapons, the Haganah refused, and Etzel and Lehi canceled the operation. Before he left, the representative asked Arbel for his opinion about Deir Yassin as a target. Arbel answered that since the village was not belligerent, it would be a waste of resources.[42]

Another liaison was Zalman Mart, the commander of the Moriah battalion of the Etzioni brigade. His connections were mainly with Lehi members, and via them to Etzel (according to him, Etzel was only interested in financial subvention and nothing came of it).

Mart first met Mordechai Ben-Uziyahu, the operations officer of the Lehi branch, and afterwards with Zettler, offering them coordination between the organizations. The meetings turned out well. Mart informed Shaltiel about them, who next met Zettler himself in Mart's home. Lehi agreed to cooperate with the Haganah in the war, though Zettler too put forward financial demands, which seemed exaggerated to Shaltiel and Mart. Zettler met several times with Shaltiel, who expressed willingness to supply Lehi's men with salaries, food and clothing, even without receiving their names (which the Haganah already knew). In return, Lehi had to pledge not to operate contrary to the instructions of the Haganah. Zettler refused. The negotiations continued, and Shaltiel offered him various targets. Zettler suggested operating in the Qatamon, which Lehi did on 13 March, destroying an Arab house and damaging another under covering fire of the Haganah. Zettler further offered Sheikh Jarrah, but Shaltiel doubted the wisdom of this since it would mean opening a front against the British who were still in that neighborhood. Shaltiel in turn suggested that Lehi should mine the road from Jericho, and this time Zettler was reluctant. He formed the impression that the Haganah wanted to keep them far from the Old City and busy in marginal tasks.[43]

Fig. 10 Zalman Mart, commander of the Moriah battalion

On the other hand, Zettler responded positively to a request from Ben-Uziyahu to supply the Haganah with several barrels of explosives in exchange for bullets. Lehi had a warehouse full of explosives, sent to them regularly from Tel Aviv, while the Haganah was manufacturing bullets. The bullets that Lehi would use in Deir Yassin would come from this transaction. Zettler and Ben-Uziyahu were not the only Lehi men to communicate with the Haganah.

Moshe Edelstein, from Lehi's intelligence department, discussed an operation in Qalunya with his acquaintance Yaakov Weg, a company commander in the Palmach, the elite force of the Haganah (Edelstein himself was a past member of the Palmach). Other Arab targets he examined with Haganah men included Sheikh Jarrah and a possible attack in the direction of Ramallah. Shaltiel's negotiations with Lehi soon reached the ears of Yisrael Galili (Ben-Gurion told him about it). "Note, with the utmost seriousness, that you are not allowed to reach a settlement with the dissidents without getting prior authorization, so that we will not have to annul your commitments, as has been done before," Galili wrote to him.[44]

Since the adoption of the Palestine partition resolution Jewish Jerusalem had been under siege. The Jewish failure to cope effectively with the Arab challenge in Palestine generally, and in Jerusalem in particular, posed the danger of the United Nations retracting its partition resolution. In early April 1948, the Haganah crossed the Rubicon and launched Operation Nahshon, aimed at opening the road to Jerusalem and removing the Arab siege. An unprecedented 1,500 men was allocated to the operation, with the intention of conquering all the Arab villages endangering the road. The Etzioni brigade was responsible for the portion of the road from Kiryat Anavim to Jerusalem. The operation progressed relatively smoothly, with one complication: the battle for Qastal. It was the peak of the military effort of the Palestinian Arabs against the Jews as far as coordination and cooperation between their various forces were concerned. The price the Arabs paid was high, their preeminent military leader, 'Abd al-Qadir al-Husayni, was killed in the fighting. Initial Arab success in regaining the village from the Haganah was squandered when the Arab fighters abandoned their positions in order to participate in Husayni's funeral. In the early hours of 9 April, when the forces of Etzel and Lehi were operating in Deir Yassin, the Haganah recaptured Qastal for good.[45]

Yeshurun Schiff, commander of the Michmash battalion of the Etzioni brigade, also was one of Shaltiel's liaisons with Etzel and Lehi. Lacking manpower, during the battle for Qastal he sought the participation of the other two underground organizations. He suggested that they should lie in wait in the Suba quarry at the rear of Qastal and block Arab reinforcements. They responded with several preconditions, that they should get an authorization from their headquarters in Tel Aviv, that they would command their forces by themselves and that the Haganah would supply them with arms. Schiff was willing to supply them with firearms (and according to him, did supply them, along with some hand grenades, which they used in Deir Yassin instead). Yet they also wanted Shaltiel himself to officially ask them to help. Therefore, Schiff went to Shaltiel trying to convince him that their assistance was necessary. Shaltiel seemed "very upset" to hear all this, and instructed Schiff to discontinue the negotiations.[46]

At the time that Shaltiel pushed Schiff aside, he himself was trying to reach a settlement with both Etzel and Lehi. At the beginning of April, he met with Mordechai Kaufman in the house of Chief Rabbi Isaac Herzog. During the previous month, Etzel was involved in the "expropriation" of various goods and food for its bases from

Fig. 11 Left to right, in uniform: David Shaltiel; Yeshurun Schiff, commander of the Michmash battalion; and Zion Eldad, Shaltiel's operations officer

both the British and Jewish merchants, which at times ended in violent engagements with the Haganah. Shaltiel demanded that Etzel should halt all such actions. Kaufman answered that so long as the municipal food supply committee did not apportion food rations to them, they had no choice but to continue with the seizures. Shaltiel threatened to open fire, to which Kaufman retorted that fire would be met with fire. Shaltiel then took a different approach and suggested that the Haganah would take upon itself to supply Etzel with all the necessities, including arms, if Etzel pledged not to operate independently. Etzel would be allowed to preserve its organizational independence and only be subordinate to the Haganah operationally. Shaltiel further noted that Lehi had already agreed to a similar arrangement. Kaufman refused, arguing that the Haganah in Jerusalem was getting its instructions from Tel Aviv, and Tel Aviv was willing to deliver Jerusalem to international rule. If the Haganah pledged to conquer the Old City and annex Jerusalem to the Jewish state, then they would agree to the proposal.

Fig. 12 Mordechai Kaufman (left), Etzel's commander in Jerusalem, with Etzel's leader, Menachem Begin

Two days later Kaufman returned with a counter proposal. He suggested that Shaltiel take measures focused on the local needs of Jerusalem: to widen the bottleneck west to Jerusalem, and to conquer Sheikh Jarrah and strengthen the Jewish presence in Mount Scopus in order to dominate the approaches to the city from Jericho and Nablus. All the Arab villages besieging Jerusalem had to be conquered and Etzel would assist in this. Shaltiel retorted that he was not looking for advice or suggestions from anyone and refused to commit himself. He reiterated that Zettler had already signed such an agreement and urged Kaufman not to remain alone. Kaufman left.[47]

On 4 April, the Haganah and Lehi exchanged letters regarding the arrangements to integrate Lehi's combatants in the campaign for Jerusalem. In order to achieve full coordination, Lehi agreed to deliver to the Haganah all necessary details before any operation. These were to include the size and makeup of the participating unit, the number of weapons available to it, the code names of the commanders and the means of communication with them. The Haganah, for its part, undertook to provide the unit with food, clothing and salary and after the action, replace any weapons that had been lost. The next day Shaltiel and Zettler met to conclude the agreement. Zettler made two demands; firstly, the need to conquer the Old City, which Shaltiel refused to commit himself to, and secondly, that the commanders of Lehi join the city's high command, which was refused by the Haganah commander. Still trying to convince Zettler to agree, Shaltiel told him that Kaufman had already agreed to that arrangement and Lehi was therefore on the verge of being isolated. "Go and hang yourself," Zettler replied and left. Lehi issued a statement explaining to the public why unity had not been achieved.[48]

Two hours after the meeting between Kaufman and Shaltiel reached no results, Kaufman heard that Zettler was calling him "the greatest bastard of all the Etzel people so far" because he had reached an agreement with Shaltiel. Kaufman immediately met with Zettler and they realized that Shaltiel was playing one against the other by telling each that the other had already reached an agreement, and therefore his organization was about to be isolated. Evidently, Shaltiel was trying to gain their cooperation this way, or, as they believed, sow discord between their organizations. At this point, they reached the decision that it was up to their two underground organizations to initiate their own joint operations to deliver Jerusalem from the Arabs.[49]

THE DECISION IS TAKEN

The next step was to decide on the first Arab target to operate against, taking into account the limited manpower and facilities at the disposal of the two underground organuzations. Both operations officers, Etzel's Yehoshua Goldschmidt and Lehi's Mordechai Ben-Uziyahu, were called to join the discussion. Zettler suggested conquering the village of Shuʻafat north of Jerusalem. In doing so, they would be able to cut Arab Jerusalem off from the north and paralyze Sheikh Jarrah. The occupation of Shuʻafat would create Jewish continuity in the north of Jerusalem by connecting Atarot, Neve Yaakov and Mount Scopus with Jewish Jerusalem. It would also be an appropriate punishment of the Arabs for the attack, near Shuʻafat, on the convoy to Atarot some ten days earlier, which had cost the lives of 14 Jews. Goldschmidt opposed the proposal since Shuʻafat lay on the evacuation route of the British forces northward. British forces would therefore interfere and prevent its conquest. Kaufman, too, opposed the proposal, pointing out that Shuʻafat was too far away from the closest Jewish neighborhood, Sanhedria, and that, even if it could be taken, they would not be able to hold it. He mentioned that several months earlier his men had operated there, blowing up several houses, but they returned exhausted because of the distance. The Shuʻafat proposal was rejected.[50]

Kaufman suggested advancing through Silwan to take the Mount of Olives, but they realized they did not have the necessary manpower for such an operation. Another location considered was the village of Sur Bahir in southern Jerusalem, near the kibbutz of Ramat Rachel. Its conquest would remove the threat from Jewish Talpiot, Arnona and Ramat Rachel, but they feared the members of the kibbutz would obstruct the operation on the grounds that it was a quiet village. Other options considered were Bayt Hanina, which

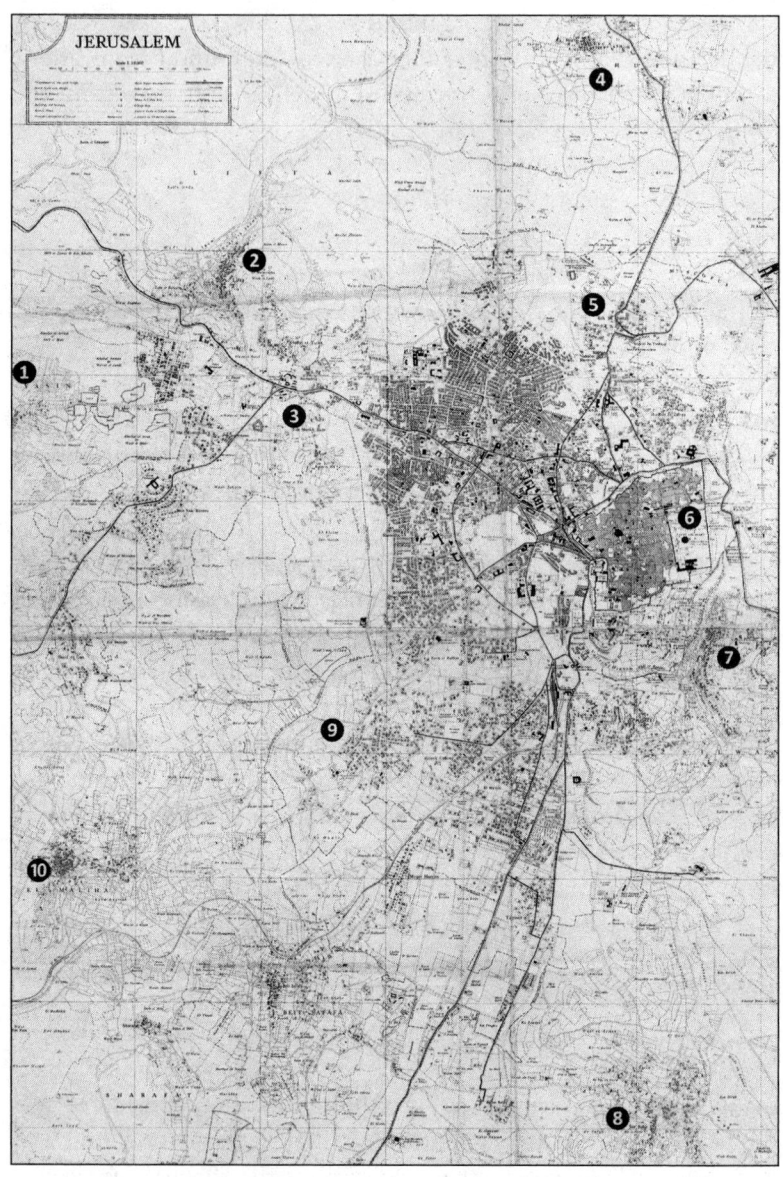

Fig. 13 Arab villages and neighborhoods around Jerusalem: 1. Deir Yassin, 2. Lifta, 3. Sheikh Badr, 4. Shu'afat, 5. Sheikh Jarrah, 6. The Old City, 7. Silwan, 8. Sur Bahir, 9. Qatamon, 10. Maliha

was too far in the north, and Lifta. Lehi sent patrols to both locations. Lehi had received intelligence that a band of Arab irregulars had settled in Lifta and was endangering the road to Jerusalem, but the scouts found the village empty.[51]

It was Etzel's operations officer, Yehoshua Goldschmidt, who suggested Deir Yassin. It was rumored that he proposed it because his father had urged him to settle the account with the village. Whatever his private motives might have been, Goldschmidt had some substantial arguments to support his proposal. Deir Yassin was remote from the British lines of evacuation, so they would not interfere. No obstructions were expected from Jews either, since the residents of Beit ha-Kerem feared Deir Yassin and sympathizers with the underground organizations in Givat Shaul supported an operation against the village. Goldschmidt argued that Deir Yassin was an important link between Arab Mount Hebron and Qastal, via Bethlehem, Bayt Jala, Maliha and 'Ayn Karm, and that its strategic location provided a base for the Arab siege of Jerusalem. Not only that, the village commanded kilometers 4 to 6 of the road from Jerusalem to Tel Aviv, enabling it to block Jewish reinforcements to Motza and Qastal. Conquering it would therefore be an important addition to the campaign to break up the siege and would ease the pressure on Qastal. He, like the others, was entirely convinced that foreign combatants, mainly Iraqis, inhabited the village. The frequent sniping from it at the Jewish suburbs as well as the traffic between them, had to be stopped. Zettler agreed to the proposal. After the Arabs had abandoned Romema, Sheikh Badr and Lifta, the conquest of Deir Yassin would complete the Jewish continuity in western Jerusalem.[52]

Fig. 14 Yehoshua Goldschmidt, Etzel's operations officer

A further reason for the attack was the need to raise the morale of Jewish Jerusalem by the permanent taking of an Arab area, which, at the same time would damage Arab morale. A Jewish woman who offered the assailants coffee before the attack remembered how enthusiastic they had been about the larger object of scaring the Arabs beyond the village into fleeing. According to Yehuda Lapidot, one of Etzel's seconds-in-command, the attackers had two options of dealing with the villagers, either to let them stay in their homes under Jewish control had they surrendered, or to transfer them to Arab Jerusalem. The underground organiztions prepared themselves for taking prisoners. Kalman Bergman, head of Etzel's intelligence in Jerusalem, later related that the instruction was to take all the Arab men prisoners in order to exchange them for Jewish captives. In contrast, Lehi's fighters understood that the intention was to evacuate all the inhabitants from the village to Arab Jerusalem.[53]

A secondary reason for the attack was the need for provisions. The underground organizations' bases needed supplies and Deir Yassin was a prosperous village. Looting in Deir Yassin was not a casual consequence of the attack but a significant motive for undertaking it in the first place. The fighters expected to find flour, cooking oil, petrol and other essential commodities and intended to appropriate them, not just for themselves, but also for distribution in the needy neighborhoods of Jerusalem. It was two weeks before Passover and Jerusalem under siege was starving. Since they believed Deir Yassin was packed with foreign volunteers, they also hoped to find considerable amounts of weaponry there.[54]

Finally, there was another reason why Deir Yassin was chosen: it was close to the Jewish neighborhoods and the underground organizations, especially Etzel, were convinced it was going to be an easy victory. Goldschmidt believed the village would be conquered easily, and prior patrols conducted by Etzel (discussed below) seemed to them to verify this assumption.[55] They were wrong.

Dov Yosef, the civil governor of Jerusalem on behalf of the Jewish Agency in 1948, would argue in his memoirs that the "dissidents" had attacked the village for political reasons. To a certain extent, he was right, but probably not just for the "political reasons" he inferred. Like many others, Yosef interpreted the attack as a public relations exercise. He speculated that, since the two organizations had just come out of the underground, they wanted to prove that they were not just guerrillas. They therefore needed an achievement that would publicize their presence and justify the continuation of their separate existence. It was as if they had to compete with Operation Nahshon being carried out by the Haganah, an operation on a scale that was beyond their resources to carry out. Therefore, according to this interpretation, attacking a village independently seemed to them more attractive than just being an auxiliary in a Haganah operation, such as assisting the Haganah in Qastal.[56]

However, there were other "political reasons." Operation Nahshon was interpreted by the underground organzations as part of the implementation of the partition plan they wanted to frustrate. Fearing that Ben-Gurion would agree to the internationalization of Jerusalem, or to a deal with King 'Abdallah, they wanted to widen the war to the utmost, in order to prevent partition. The Jewish Agency was operating a strategy of minimizing friction with the Arabs in the hope of preventing an Arab invasion. The organizations wanted to sabotage this approach and push the Jewish community into an overall confrontation with the Arabs that would be decided by force of arms alone. They wanted to prove that the Jews could and should take Arab controlled areas, rather than being continually on the defensive. The taking of an Arab village would be the means to achieve this goal.[57]

Chapter 2

Preparing for the Attack

INFORMING THE HAGANAH

The Haganah learned of the decision to attack Deir Yasin immediately after it had been reached, via a Haganah agent inside Lehi, Shimon Moneta. Schiff brought the information to Shaltiel, who later heard about it directly from Zettler and Kaufman. Shaltiel disapproved of the plan. He told them both that, in his opinion, the proposed attack was pointless. He considered Deir Yasin a quiet village constituting no security threat, and there were other, more important targets. He furthermore intimated to them that the Haganah was planning to build an airstrip between Givat Shaul and Deir Yassin, which their attack might hinder. It would therefore be much more useful if they assisted in the battle over Qastal. Shaltiel had two specific suggestions to offer: 'Ayn Karm, serving as a base for Arab reinforcements sent to Qastal, or Qalunya, from where fire was being directed at Jewish convoys and at Motza. They could blow up the houses there and expel the inhabitants. He was even willing to supply them with arms. However, Etzel and Lehi refused on the grounds that the suggested operations were beyond their capabilities. They did not have enough manpower in Jerusalem to divide their forces, so they had decided to concentrate their efforts in the city, leaving the battle over the road to the Haganah. Furthermore, they argued, an operation in Deir Yassin would draw Arab combatants away from Qastal. When Shaltiel realized that the organizations were adamant about Deir Yassin, he agreed, but urged them to remain in the village after its capture, to prevent foreign forces from recapturing it.[1]

On 7 April, Shaltiel sent an identical, seemingly official, letter summing up his position regarding the issue to Zettler and Kaufman. Once again, he acted without seeking instructions or permission from his superiors in Tel Aviv. Zion Eldad, the operations officer of the Etzioni brigade, assisted Shaltiel in wording the letter:

> It has come to my attention that you intend to carry out an operation in Deir Yassin. I would like to draw to your attention that the capture and holding of Deir Yassin forms one phase of our general plan. I have no objection to you carrying out the operation, on condition that you have the ability to hold the objective. If you are unable to do so, I warn you against blowing up the village, which would cause its abandonment by its residents and the capture of the deserted houses and ruins by foreign forces. Such a situation would impede rather than aid the general campaign, and a re-occupation of the location would cost our men heavy losses. A further point you should consider is, that if foreign forces are attracted to the site, it may hinder our plan to build an airdrome.[2]

The last sentence of Shaltiel's letter might lead one to conclude that, because of its plan to build the airstrip, the Haganah would eventually have to conquer Deir Yasin anyway. Under siege conditions, such a landing strip could constitute an important link between Jerusalem and the coastal plain. By early April work on the proposed facility was under way, and an area 300 meters by 40 meters had been cleared of rocks. This was still not big enough to land planes on. On 9 April, the day of the attack, Meir Batz, the engineering officer of the Etzioni brigade and a member of Shaltiel's staff, wrote that if the runway were to be extended to a length of 700 meters Deir Yassin had to be distanced from the worksite. Because the site of the air-strip was within firing range of the village, he feared that the Arabs could obstruct construction by sniping and attacking the workers. Therefore, "It is imperative to do everything to cleanse Deir Yassin of its inhabitants," he wrote.[3]

One who did not like the so-called authorization given by Shaltiel was Meir Pilavsky (better known as Meir Pa'il). Since late 1947, he had headed a Haganah unit that operated against the "dissidents" in Jerusalem. The unit was disbanded in mid-March, but Pilavsky remained in Jerusalem for the time being. When he heard about the forthcoming attack and Shaltiel's green light (he was later to claim that Moshe Edelstein of Lehi had told him, an assertion fiercely denied by Edelstein), he hurried to Shaltiel to make him change his mind. He reminded Shaltiel of the agreement the village had with the Haganah and, according to one version, even offered to fire on Etzel and Lehi. Shaltiel admitted that he had authorized the operation. He explained that the organizations would probably attack in any case and he was unable and unwilling to stop them by force. "I have enough trouble as it is. I couldn't shoot them in the back – they are Jews, you know." He preferred, therefore, authorizing the operation on condition that they remained in the village after its seizure and defended it against counter-attacks.[4]

Fig. 15 Meir Pilavsky (left) as Palmach soldier in 1948

Yitzhak Levy, the commander of the Haganah's intelligence in Jerusalem, also protested to Shaltiel and reminded him about the agreement with the village. Shaltiel explained to him that since the organizations would attack anyhow, it was better that it appeared as if the attack was carried out with his agreement than against his will.

This way, he was able to maintain some measure of authority over them. Furthermore, a few hours earlier, Qastal had fallen into the hands of the Arabs, and Shaltiel feared that as a result Deir Yassin might turn hostile. He refused a proposal by Levy at least to warn the villagers to evacuate the village. He said he was unwilling to endanger an operation carried out by Jews, which had been sanctioned by him, by hinting to the Arabs that something was going to happen.[5]

When the underground organizations sent out patrols before the attack to reconnoiter the terrain, this was coordinated with the Haganah. An Etzel patrol visited the Haganah positions facing Deir Yassin and was accompanied by a Haganah man to the vicinity of the village. A Lehi patrol, too, visited a Haganah position near Givat Shaul facing Deir Yassin, and even established a password with its men ("We shall hit the enemy"). On the other hand, Shaltiel did not bother to supply the organizations with any of the ample intelligence on Deir Yassin he had (such as the location of the firing positions there that Gicherman had reported on in February), which they so badly needed.[6]

On the evening of 8 April, Zalman Mart met with Mordechai Ben-Uziyahu, Lehi's operations officer, and Moshe Barzilai, Lehi's intelligence officer, and asked them, in Shaltiel's name, to start their attack the next day at dawn. They forwarded his request to Zettler. A similar request was submitted from Shaltiel to Kaufman. The Haganah was preparing a counter-attack on Qastal early the next day, and a coordinated attack on Deir Yassin could assist in Qastal's recapture. The Palmach was to bear the main brunt of the attack on Qastal, and past member Moshe Edelstein was also asked by one of its officers to coordinate the attacks, a request he, too, forwarded to Zettler. Zettler hesitated. It was Thursday evening. There were many Orthodox Jews in Lehi, and he would prefer not to start an operation on Friday morning lest it would continue into the Jewish Sabbath. But since Shaltiel was asking it, Zettler and Kaufman decided to comply and start the attack at dawn. Ben-Uziyahu and Petahya Selivansky, who was slated to command Lehi forces in the attack, informed Mart of the decision. "Do it and be successful," were Mart's parting words to them.[7]

Ben-Uziyahu also updated Mart as to when zero hour would be and coordinated the communication arrangements with him. Following this, instructions were given to the Haganah positions in western Jerusalem regarding allowing passage of the attackers through their lines. The Haganah guards in Givat Shaul were informed about the upcoming attack, and were asked to keep the district headquarters informed about events. Apparently, Akiva Azulay, Givat Shaul's second-in-command, had not been updated. On Thursday, he noticed a group of young men concentrating near the brewery in Givat Shaul. When asked, they told him that the Haganah had sent them. He did not believe them and demanded that they disperse. One of them, identifying himself as a liaison between Lehi and the Haganah, asked him amazed: "Didn't you get a message from Shaltiel?" Soon Azulay had a phone call from Yosef Ben-Nun, the commander of the entire area, instructing him not only to give Lehi a position to operate from, but also to assist them with covering fire in case they had to retreat. Astounded Azulay asked the instructions in writing, which he got. A similar dialogue occurred between Selivansky and the Haganah regional commander, Yonah Ben-Sasson, who, failing to find a senior commander to consult with, decided not to interfere. The Lehi men settled into a Haganah position in the cellar of the brewery, at which stage Azulay decided to share the information he had about the village with Selivansky. He informed him about the abundance of weaponry in Deir Yassin and about the trenches, but was not taken seriously.[8]

The commanders of the Haganah guards in Beit ha-Kerem and the nearby ha-Poalim neighborhood also updated them about the forthcoming attack. Even civilian residents of the areas there learned of it. The Haganah allowed the Etzel force, which set out from Beit ha-Kerem, to commandeer rooms in private houses to serve as first aid posts. On their way to Deir Yassin, the Etzel fighters passed through Haganah guard posts, whose personnel wished them success. Haganah efforts to assist went beyond good wishes, the Haganah's posts facing Deir Yassin received instructions to extend medical aid to the attackers and to assist them in case of retreat. Furthermore, following a request by Lehi, and after consultation with Mart, Shaltiel agreed to secure the routes leading to the village in order to prevent the arrival of Arab reinforcements, especially from the direction of 'Ayn Karm. Mordechai Gicherman and a colleague from the Moriah battalion spent the night in Givat Shaul, to be ready to place a Spandau machine gun the next morning on the Sharafa ridge dominating the route between Deir Yassin and 'Ayn Karm.[9]

PLANS, DISCUSSIONS AND RECONNAISSANCE PATROLS
After Kaufman and Zettler had jointly taken the decision to attack Deir Yassin, the task of working out the details was entrusted to the two operations officers of the underground organizations, Goldschmidt and Ben-Uziyahu. Ben-Zion Cohen was also called in to assist in the formulation of the plan, accompanied by Yehuda Lapidot, Michael Harif and Yehuda Treibisch of Etzel, and Petahya Selivansky, David Schneeweiss and Amos Kenan of Lehi. They decided to attack the village in a pincer movement. An Etzel force would set out from Beit ha-Kerem and attack the village from the southeast, while a Lehi force would start from Givat Shaul and attack it from the north. An additional blocking force would head to a hill south of the village to obstruct possible reinforcements from 'Ayn Karm. Although it would be a coordinated attack, the two organizations would operate independently and meet inside the village. "Fighting unity" (*ahdut lohemet*) would be their password. It was Zettler's view that Lehi should operate separately, as he considered his men better trained and operating with different methods than Etzel. Yet the two operations officers ruled that at least 110 combatants were needed for the attack, making the cooperation between the organizations essential. Cohen was appointed commander of the Etzel force, with Lapidot and Harif his deputies and Treibisch commanding the blocking force, while Selivansky was appointed commander of the Lehi force.[10]

There were, however, differences of opinion in the preparatory meeting regarding the fate of Deir Yassin's inhabitants. According to Lapidot and Cohen, some of the representatives of Lehi suggested killing them, or at least all the men and anyone else who would resist the attackers. It emanated out of a desire for revenge (this was shortly after several deadly Arab attacks on Jewish convoys) as well as a desire to break the Arab morale, and turn the engagement into a turning point in the battle for Palestine. The Etzel representatives disliked the idea and insisted on referring it to their superiors. Kaufman consulted with his intelligence officer and finally referred the matter to his superiors in Tel Aviv. Etzel's leader, Menachem Begin, ordered them to avoid unnecessary bloodshed and to follow the Geneva Convention. Kaufman delivered the instruction to his representatives, with the interpretation to take all Arab men prisoners and avoid harming women and children. Zettler, too, opposed unnecessary killing of the civilian population. Kaufman further suggested using a car with a loudspeaker before the attack to warn the Arabs to evacuate, leaving the south-west exit of the village open for them. It would mean losing the element of surprise, and Lehi's men did not like the idea at all. Actually, some of Etzel future commanders of the attack, including Lapidot, also opposed the idea, for the same reason. Etzel however, made their participation in the operation conditional on the use of the loudspeaker car, and Lehi, being the minority, reluctantly had to accept it.[11]

Although Cohen opposed indiscriminate killing, he was of the opinion that the attackers should not enter houses before throwing a hand grenade inside or using explosives. When Etzel's combatants exercised in built-up area warfare on the day before the attack, they were instructed to throw hand grenades into every house and shoot bursts into every room before entering. One of the decisions taken in the preparatory meeting was that Etzel should supply the attackers with rifles, Sten guns and Bren guns, while Lehi would bring pistols and explosives. As early as 7 April, the underground organizations started bringing the arms and ammunition (along with scores of steel helmets) to their positions and began checking that they were serviceable.

Fig. 16 A Sten manufactured by Etzel.
They gave the combatants a hard time during the battle.

A large shipment of new home made Sten guns reached Etzel from Tel Aviv. Excited, Lapidot tried one of them, only to learn that the weapons were defective, capable of only semi-automatic fire. These Sten guns would give the fighters much trouble during the attack. Kalman Bergman, Etzel's head of intelligence, used the time leading up to the attack to prepare a place to hold prisoners – a two-story building with a spacious yard surrounded by a two and a half meter high wall. Until the attack, the yard was used for parking the trucks Etzel had robbed from the British forces.[12]

On the two nights before the operation, Etzel sent patrols to survey the terrain. Cohen led a patrol of everyone who would command the attack. They started with a daylight reconnaissance near Beit ha-Kerem, Cohen explaining the plan of attack and each of the commanders' assignments. This was followed by a night patrol simulating the route of the assault during which they were able to advance within 150 meters of the village without any of the Arabs noticing them. It was only when the village dogs started to bark that they halted and returned to base. The fact that the village lookouts had not spotted them made them confident of the operation's success. When they returned, Kaufman explained to them that, although the village looked quiet, it actually defended a new route opened by the Arabs between 'Ayn Karm and Suba. Taking the village was therefore an essential part of the campaign to break the siege of Jerusalem. Yehuda Treibisch led another patrol whose mission was to pinpoint barricades and defensive positions. Only some of these were successfully identified, they also failed to discover the trench blocking the entrance to the village. Lehi conducted a patrol of its own two days before the attack, setting out from Givat Shaul. It reported the topography of the region and possible paths for attack and retreat. Like their Etzel counterparts, they did not notice the trench either.[13]

Despite the patrols, Etzel and Lehi had very little intelligence about Deir Yassin prior to the attack, having received none from Shaltiel. They were completely in the dark about the number of combatants they faced or their weaponry. Goldschmidt drew a map of the village, indicating the assault routes, and Etzel's intelligence department prepared enlarged copies for distribution among the attacking forces. However, the map was inaccurate and very general.[14]

The day before the attack, Lehi's commanders met in an apartment in Yefe Nof to observe the village and receive their battle orders (this was an unwise choice of vantage point, since the Yefe Nof neighborhood was located southeast of Deir Yassin, and they were supposed to operate on the northern side of the village). Ben-Uziyahu informed them that they were going to operate together with Etzel and explained to them the route of the attack as well as the plan to use a car with a loudspeaker to warn the Arabs. They were instructed to transport all the Arab prisoners by trucks to eastern Jerusalem and to take every precaution to not harm women and children. They were also ordered to confiscate all the essential supplies in the village for distribution in Jewish Jerusalem. No instruction was given to them regarding the disposal of the Arabs dead, either because they did not think the battle would be very intense or because they simply did not think about it in advance.[15]

The information delivered to Lehi's junior commanders was unavailable to Lehi's high command, which knew nothing about the operation. This was due not only to the difficulties in communicating with Tel Aviv, but also due to Zettler tense relations with Nathan Friedman-Yellin, Lehi's acting supreme commander. Zettler did not deem it necessary to seek his authorization or even to consult him, since he considered Lehi's branch in Jerusalem to be autonomous. While Friedman-Yellin acknowledged that circumstances dictated the need for independent operations in Jerusalem, he was nonetheless furious when he heard of the operation, in part due to the precedent of a joint operation with Etzel without prior authorization from Lehi's central command.[16]

In fact, even Etzel's leader, Menachem Begin, knew nothing concrete about the operation because, due to the difficulties in communications between Jerusalem and Tel Aviv, Etzel's Jerusalem branch was also authorized to operate autonomously without getting prior permission from Tel Aviv. The radio connection between the branch and Tel Aviv was both unreliable and insecure and Kaufman feared that the enemy was listening to his messages. He therefore declined to divulge any logistic details in his transmissions to Tel Aviv. Begin was only informed of the general intention to operate against the Arabs in the suburbs of Jerusalem, which he applauded, but not even the name of the village. Begin only learned the details of the attack after the fact, at which point Kaufman also radioed to him Shaltiel's letter of 7 April verbatim.[17]

ZERO HOUR

On the evening of 8 April, at 8:00 p.m., Etzel's combatants convened in their base in the Etz Haim neighborhood. Such was the secrecy of the underground organization that some were surprised to discover friends and acquaintances amongst their fellow members of Etzel. Kaufman explained to them the objectives of the operation: to free the western suburbs of Jerusalem from Deir Yassin's threat and to transform the Jews from mere responders to Arab attacks into those who took the fight to the enemy. This would obviously produce a positive impact on Jewish morale. A fundamental change in concept was afoot; Jews would no longer be limited to defensive actions, but would capture, and permanently hold, an Arab village. However, he warned his men not to harm the elderly, women or children. Any Arab who wished to surrender, even a combatant, would be taken prisoner and had to be treated according to the Geneva Convention. Goldschmidt explained the plan of the attack and informed the combatants of the password ("fighting unity"). He told the combatants: "Today, for the first time in the history of Etzel, we are going to an open war, an offensive war, a war to conquer and occupy territory." Goldschmidt, reiterated the warning not to shoot unarmed men, the elderly, women or children.[18]

At about midnight, the Etzel force traveled from Etz Haim to Beit ha-Kerem in three trucks with doused lights, to a location near Yefe Nof. From there, at 2:00 a.m., they continued on foot through a wadi to approach Deir Yassin from the southeast. At this instant, Treibisch's blocking squad separated from them, heading to its destination south of the village. At about 3:00 a.m. the main force, under Cohen's command, reached the low ground below Deir Yassin and started climbing the terraces in the direction of the village. Then they crawled silently to a distance of about thirty meters from the village, reaching there at 4:10 a.m., twenty minutes before the zero hour, at which time the assailants expected the villagers to be in deep sleep, unable to resist. The sign to start the attack was supposed to be the shooting of tracer bullets, at which time Lapidot's platoon was to attack the area extending from the Givat Shaul road to the village center, while Harif's platoon was to attack the area from the village center southward.[19]

Lehi's fighters convened on 8 April at noon in a school near Mea Shearim for a briefing. Ben-Uziyahu, elated, explained their mission, pointing out that the attack was coordinated with the Haganah and integrated into its general strategy. They were about to free the western suburbs of Jerusalem and raise Jewish morale. They would

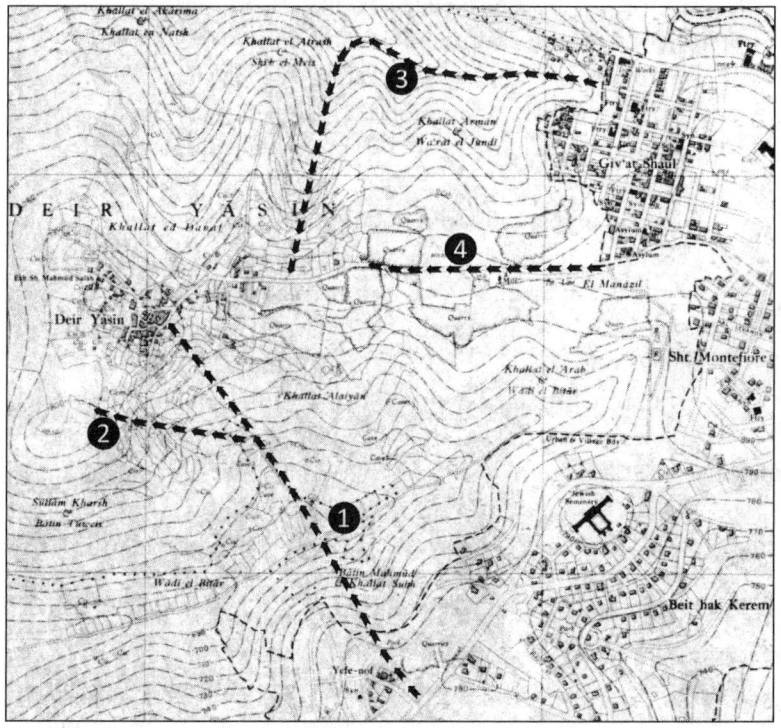

Fig. 17 The attack on Deir Yassin: 1. Etzel's force, 2. The blocking squad, 3. Lehi's force, 4. The loudspeaker car

shift the war into the enemy's territory. For the first time, they would conquer Arab territory and hold it permanently. Since they did not have enough manpower to carry out the task alone and Iraqi combatants were expected in the village, they would be cooperating with Etzel. He noted that Etzel was opposed to harming women and children during the operation and Zettler too, warned against unnecessary killing. When asked how they could evade harming women and children when the latter were intermixed with the combatants, Ben-Uziyahu informed them that a loudspeaker would be used to warn the elderly, women and children to evacuate the village.[20]

Close to midnight, Lehi's combatants were transported from their base in Sheikh Badr to the brewery in Givat Shaul for final orders and the distribution of arms. They were supposed to set out from there at 2:00 a.m., but they were not ready till 4:00 a.m. They walked to the northwestern edge of Givat Shaul, near a leather factory, from where they continued in a column through a wadi westward and then southward in the direction of the village. They passed through a plantation, and approached the village from the north. Meanwhile, a Lehi armored car carrying a loudspeaker approached from the east.[21]

All these preparations did not escape the eyes of the Arabs. The village guards noticed that there was too much traffic in the Jewish neighborhoods facing them and became suspicious. In accordance with the January agreement one of the villagers started to signal with a flashlight to apprise Givat Shaul that a meeting with its liaison was sought. Yonah Ben-Sasson, the Haganah's regional commander, refused to allow this, fearing that the villagers might take the liaison hostage, and the signals went unanswered.[22]

On the day after the attack, the Arab daily *Filastin* reported that the number of the attackers was 300. Foreign observers, British and American (and Shaltiel in one of his reports) put the number at 200.[23] These estimates doubled and even tripled the actual number of attackers. Many sources claimed that the overall number of the attackers was 130 (or 132), divided into 70 (or 72) Etzel fighters and 60 Lehi fighters.[24] This was a gross overestimation of Lehi's abilities, as in early 1948 its Jerusalem branch could not mobilize 60 combat personnel. Others, mainly Haganah sources, quoted the figure 120, made up of 80 Etzel fighters and 40 Lehi fighters.[25]

The only accurate way to assess the true number is to use each of the underground organizations' own figures. Even testimonies given by Etzel members regarding Lehi and vice versa would not be accurate, since each of the organizations operated independently. With regard to Etzel, Kaufman, Cohen and Lapidot stated on several occasions that the overall number of Etzel fighters was between 70 and 80. According to Etzel sources, their force was composed of two platoons, comprising three squads each, while each squad was made up of ten combatants and their commander. Adding the platoon commanders and their deputies (four), yields 70 for the two platoons. To this, one has to add the force commander (Cohen) and Treibisch's blocking squad composed of 12 combatants, giving a total of 83 men.[26]

Lehi's force was composed of Selivansky's platoon and the squad that accompanied the car with the loudspeaker. Ezra Yakhin, a Lehi member who participated in the battle, recalled that their number was 40. In his memoirs, Shimon Moneta, a Haganah agent within Lehi, wrote that their number was about 50. However, in an earlier interview he put it at 30 to 40, figures he also reported to his superiors in the Haganah at the time (under the code name Esther; his code name in Lehi was Gad). In one of his reports, he actually delivered his operators an incomplete list of 38 names (subsequently censored by the IDF archives, who only left their code names in the document). In another report he indicated that Lehi's force would be composed of five infantry squads of six men each (that is, 30 altogether), and one mobile unit, totaling 40. Friedman-Yellin, of Lehi's supreme command, also wrote in his memoirs that the number of Lehi's fighters was one third of 120 (he was, however, in Tel Aviv at the time of the operation).[27]

Thus, the total number of the attackers was a little more than 120, two-thirds of them belonging to Etzel and one third to Lehi. This corresponds with the estimates of the Haganah, which is not surprising, taking into account that the Haganah operated a spy in Lehi. Actually, Lehi committed all its forces in Jerusalem (including women) to the Deir Yassin operation and Etzel used most of its fighting manpower for the task. Both used new, inexperience recruits side by side with the veterans, of whom only a few aged above twenty. (Cohen was 21 years old at the time of the operation, while Selivansky was 24). Even though both organizations deployed almost every weapon they possessed in Jerusalem, there was still not enough to arm all the fighters they sent.[28]

Yosef Danoch, an Etzel quartermaster and one of Cohen's squad commanders, brought the weapons and ammunition from every Etzel depot in Jerusalem. However, they were still not enough. Some of the fighters went into battle without appropriate arms, with the intention to find weapons in the village, either from dead Arabs or from their fallen comrades. Lapidot was to relate that he – like the rest of the commanders – was only issued a pistol, an unsuitable weapon for this kind of battle due to its short range. When he complained to Goldschmidt about this, the latter responded that he was counting on him to find his weapon in Deir Yassin, which is exactly what Lapidot did, taking a rifle from a dead Arab.[29]

Altogether, the attackers had three Bren guns (Etzel two and Lehi one), about 40 sub-machine guns (mainly Stens, many of them defective, and some Tommy guns), 36 rifles (mostly British, but some Canadian, Czech and Turkish) and about 30 pistols. Each Etzel squad carried four Sten guns, four rifles, and pistols for the commander and the stretcher-bearer. Each Lehi squad got two Sten guns, two rifles and two pistols. Forty bullets were allocated for each rifle and 100 for every Sten gun. Each combatant had two hand grenades, for a total of more than 240 odd (300, according to Cohen). In addition to this, the attackers brought a substantial amount of explosives with them: 28 charges of 10–15 kilos each with detonators, light enough for the combatants to carry them in rucksacks, as well as sticks of gelignite for breaching doors. The attackers did not bring with them any wireless devices for communicating, and had to rely on runners for delivering information during the battle.[30]

The following table presents a summary of the manpower and weaponry of the two sides at the beginning of the battle:

	Jews	Arabs
Combatants	approx. 120	70–80
Machine guns	3	2
Sub-machine guns	approx. 40	4
Rifles	36	approx. 60
Pistols	approx. 30	at least 20
Hand grenades	approx. 240	a significant number
Ammunition	approx. 4,000 for sub-machine guns, 1,440 for rifles	a significant amount
Explosives	28 charges as well as gelignite sticks	a certain amount

The combatants were accompanied by two physicians, a certified nurse and ten female paramedics. An advance first aid post was set up in an apartment in Givat Shaul, less than a kilometer from the battlefield. Also in Beit ha-Kerem, young women were waiting to extend first aid. An Etzel underground hospital was located inside Jerusalem, in an apartment in the Rehavia neighborhood.[31]

Chapter 3

The Attack

ETZEL ATTACKS

Isma'il Muhammad 'Atiyya was guarding the village at the early hours of Friday, 9 April, from a position on the roof of his home. He had returned only a few hours earlier from the battle of Qastal. Together with him was his younger brother Mahmud. Their uncle, Rubhi Isma'il 'Atiyya, was standing guard in another position on the roof, and they were later joined by their father, Muhammad Isma'il. At 4:25 a.m., Mahmud fired a round from his rifle. Isma'il turned to him in surprise and asked for an explanation. "I shot a Jew," Mahmud shouted. "Jews are attacking us!"[1]

A quarter of an hour earlier, Cohen's force had crawled to a distance of some thirty meters from the southeastern edge of the village, facing the houses of the 'Atiyya family. The Arab guards in front of them were talking. Five minutes before the zero hour, one of Etzel's combatants, crawling ahead, rolled a stone down the hilly slope. One of the Arab guards said: "Mahmud..." Squad commander Danoch mistook the name "Mahmud" for the first part of the Hebrew password – *ahdut* ("unity"). It must be other Etzel fighters, he thought,

49

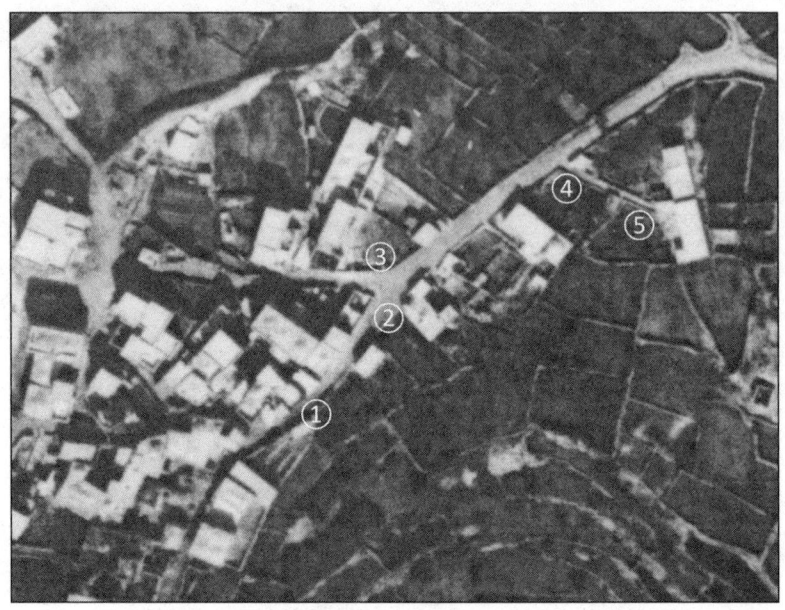

Fig. 18 Eastern Deir Yassin: 1. The 'Atiyya family complex, 2. Mustafa 'Ali Zaydan's house, 3. The village center, 4. The bakery, 5. The mukhtar house

and answered with the second half of the password, *lohemet* ("fighting"). Mahmud heard it, and having no doubt that he was hearing Hebrew, shot in Danoch's direction, hitting one of Etzel's combatants in the hip. The Arab guards noticed them and started shouting, and a hail of bullets quickly followed the single shot. With no other choice, Cohen immediately instructed squad commander Yehuda Segal, carrying the force's Bren gun, to shoot tracer bullets, the signal to start the attack.[2]

Heavy Sten fire was directed at the Arab position, followed by a hand grenade, resulting in the position's destruction. Muhammad Isma'il was injured (and later killed), Rubhi escaped (and was later caught and killed), Mahmud was injured and fled to 'Ayn Karm (he later returned and was killed). Soon thereafter, the attackers broke into the house. Aged Isma'il 'Atiyya, father of Muhammad and Rubhi, confronted them shouting that they had betrayed their agreement with the village. The attackers probably did not understand what he was talking about and when he slapped one of them on the face, they shot him. Within ten minutes, the entire village was awakened by the noise of the shooting and the first explosions.[3]

At 4:45 a.m., as the sun rose, the attackers found themselves in the open and exposed to gunfire. Arabs snipers began shooting at them from their positions and from inside the houses. Many of the attackers, untrained in this kind of combat (some, in any kind of combat), were hit. An Etzel fighter who had removed his helmet was shot in the head and died on the spot. At 5:00 a.m., Michael Harif, one of Cohen's two deputies, and his platoon had passed the first row of houses. He saw a man in khaki fleeing and gave chase. The running man abruptly turned around and fired at him, wounding Harif in the leg. Harif hopped back to an already occupied yard and sat there. Etzel's advance slowed down and now involved house-to-house fighting. At 6:00 a.m., while fighting over the third row of houses, Cohen himself was wounded in the knee. Having no bandages, his subordinates tore the sleeves off

Fig. 19 Ben-Zion Cohen, the commander of Etzel's force

his shirt to dress the wound (despite losing a lot of blood, he remained on the battlefield until 11:30). Lapidot, age nineteen, remained the only senior Etzel commander in the field unharmed. According to him, at this point, about half of Etzel's men were neutralized, either wounded or attending the wounded. A Haganah armored car evacuated some of the injured.[4] Some of Etzel's combatants started thinking about retreat.

At 7:00 a.m. a messenger from Etzel reached Lehi's sector in the northeastern part of the village and told Ben-Uziyahu, who had arrived with the loudspeaker car, that Etzel were considering a retreat due to lack of ammunition. Ben-Uziyahu told him to hold their ground as Lehi was already inside the village. As early as 6:00 a.m. Lehi's forces had arrived at the center of the village. Etzel arrived there much later, close to 9:00 a.m. Even then, many of Etzel's combatants lagged behind in the outer houses of the village. To reach the village center, Etzel's force had to attack eight houses belonging to the 'Atiyya and 'Id families. During this assault their machine-gunner, Yehuda Segal, was severely wounded in his stomach by a burst of enemy fire. Eventually Etzel's combatants met with Lehi's at the center of the village. At this point, most of the eastern part of the village was in the hands of the attackers. However, there was no reason to rejoice. Jewish fighters had reached the open field in the center of the village, only to find themselves pinned down there by Bren and rifle fire from a two-story house at the northwestern edge of the village, which dominated the space. This house had belonged to the late Mahmud Salah (deceased already for some years) and was now occupied by his brother Muhammad. Fire from the roof of the building impeded the movements of the attackers and prevented them from advancing into the western part of the village, which still remained in Arab hands.[5]

At this stage, the attackers faced two urgent problems: they were running out of ammunition and they had to evacuate their wounded. Luckily, they had discovered at least two depots of weaponry in the village during the battle. In one armory, they found rifles, pistols and cases of ammunition, and in the second, they found several sub-machine guns and bags full of bullets. Additional Bren magazines were found in one of the houses. In addition, they received some ammunition from Yonah Ben-Sasson, the Haganah's regional commander (subsequently dismissed by Shaltiel for distributing materiel without permission, even though Shaltiel himself was later to supply them with ammunition). His deputy, Akiva Azulay, also gave them ammunition and then added several rifles and Sten guns. They also took a Lewis gun that belonged to the Haganah and was posted in Givat Shaul without obtaining consent.[6]

Most of the injured combatants belonged to Etzel. The lightly wounded made their own way to Givat Shaul on foot. The more seriously wounded were scattered across the battlefield and fire from Mahmud Salah's house made it difficult to reach, much less, evacuate them. Finally, they were transferred to the yard of one house where they received initial first aid. Lapidot began organizing them for evacuation. An ambulance, summoned for them by Zalman Mart, awaited between Givat Shaul and Deir Yassin, but the problem was how to reach it under heavy fire. They put the wounded on beds or doors they took from the houses, to carry them out of the village. However, an attempt to evacuate Segal this way failed, the two combatants carrying him being hit themselves by Arab snipers. Cohen therefore ordered that Arab prisoners be used to carry the wounded, in the hope that the Arab snipers would cease fire in order not to harm them. The snipers, however, continued to shoot, hitting two of the Arab prisoners. Segal was nevertheless evacuated (he would later die of his wounds). At about the same time, Lehi's commander Selivansky, with the same idea in mind, issued instructions to use Arab women to carry the wounded. Here, too, the Arab snipers shot some of these women. Some of them later related their experience in carrying the wounded and the bodies of dead Jews.[7]

Fig. 20 Yehuda Segal, Etzel's Bren-gunner. He was seriously wounded and died two weeks later.

Yehuda Treibisch's blocking squad fared even less well. After splitting off from the Etzel force, it sought to capture the hill south of the village in order to block access to any possible Arab reinforcements from 'Ayn Karm. Conquest of this hill would confer the additional advantage of a secure route for the Jewish combatants to bring in supplies and evacuate casualties. After climbing the hill, they were attacked by Arab fighters who misinterpreted their appearance as an attempt to deny the villagers the chance to flee to 'Ayn Karm. One of the squad members was killed and two others were injured, one of them seriously. In addition to these setbacks, they were rapidly running out of ammunition. Treibisch therefore decided to retreat. His squad initially descended back to the wadi and from there to Beit ha-Kerem, Treibisch himself later joined the main Etzel force in Deir Yassin. The Arabs succeeded in reoccupying the hill, allowing them to keep the route to 'Ayn Karm open. They had also secured a vantage point to shoot at Etzel's forces inside the village, a move that would later hinder the evacuation of the Jewish wounded to Beit ha-Kerem.[8]

As these events were taking place, Kaufman and Zettler were observing the fighting from an abandoned, British built pillbox

located on the western edge of Givat Shaul. Alongside the Jerusalem commanders of Etzel and Lehi, photographer Ben Oyserman was present, documenting the battle with a movie camera. At 9:30 a.m., a runner from the village arrived and reported that three of the Jewish combatants had been killed and some twenty injured, Cohen and Harif among them. He added that Cohen was seeking instructions. Kaufman and Goldschmidt immediately entered the village and went to the first aid post where the wounded were

Fig. 21 Mordechai Kaufman (in jacket) walking in Deir Yassin

being tended. Cohen told Kaufman that in his opinion they had to retreat. Lapidot, too, was of the opinion that the price of the action was becoming too high. The weapons in the hands of the attackers could not penetrate the stone houses of the villagers or their iron doors and shutters. Goldschmidt suggested an alternative: to blast their way into the houses with explosives, a tactic they had used in the underground struggle against the British. Under covering fire, two attackers would crawl to the door of a house, one would use a gelignite stick to blow a hole in the door, and the other would throw a primed satchel charge through the breach. With Kaufman's acceptance of this proposal, a new phase in the battle was about to begin, to be discussed below.[9]

LEHI ATTACKS

Lehi's force, under Petahya Selivansky's command, set out from Givat Shaul at 4:00 a.m. with the intention of attacking the village from the northeast. It was an easier walk than the Etzel fighters had faced, and the force approached the village rapidly. Although some of the village guards on the road near the Sammur family's crusher heard steps approaching from the northeast, they seemed to be far away and they could not see anything. A thin rain started to fall.[10]

Shimon Moneta and another fighter were leading the column of Lehi's combatants. As they neared the village, they encountered residents on their way to work. The Jewish attackers opened fire, some of the villagers were hit, and the group of Arabs fled. This encounter clearly attracted attention, because, when the Jewish combatants reached an olive grove near the village, they came under light fire. One of the attackers was hit. Moneta and the other fighter leading the column returned fire. They succeeded in entering the village just as dawn broke. To their right were the houses of the Zahran family and then some of those of the 'Id family. In front of them were a few houses of the Radwan family and the boys' elementary school. The guards in the forward position near the Sammur family's crusher spotted them as they approached the school. After a brief firefight, Lehi's men captured the school. The Lehi force then exchanged fire with the Zahran family houses, supplementing their attack with hand grenades, resulting in the capture of the buildings. From there, at about 5:30 a.m., part of the Lehi force continued along the road toward the center of the village, under fire all the way.[11]

Fig. 22 Petahya Selivansky, the commander of Lehi's force

The remaining Lehi combatants were still engaged in the capture of the Arab houses in this part of the village. Unlike Etzel, Lehi's force had started to use explosives from the very beginning.

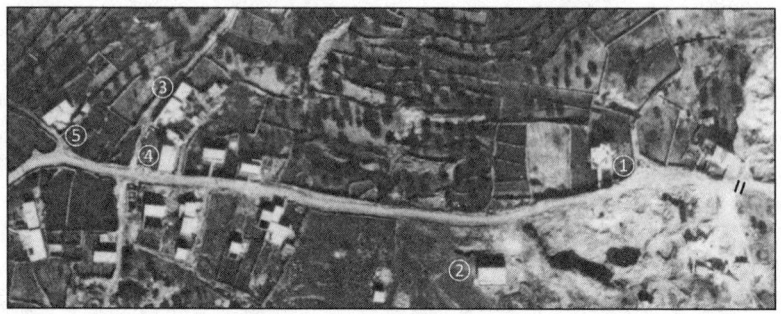

Fig. 23 Northern Deir Yassin: 1. Ahmad As'ad Radwan's house, 2. The boys' school, 3. The Zahran family complex, 4. The house of Mustafa 'Id, where the prisoners were later confined, 5. The 'Alyas' house

A hand grenade thrown into a house was not enough to neutralize it since the defenders took shelter behind the furniture and continued firing. An initial attempt to break down an iron door with a hand grenade proved unsuccessful (the fighter had forgotten to pull out the pin – an example of some of the fighters' lack of training). Subsequently, they started to breach doors with explosives. Fighters would crawl under covering fire to the doors and blow them open with gelignite sticks. Another tactic was to lay a several-kilos charge near a house, and encircling it with stones to direct the blast into the house. Even these methods did not always break the spirit of the defenders, some of whom continued to fire at the Jewish attackers even after they had entered the houses. Lehi combatants were also encountering serious problems with their Etzel-manufactured Sten guns. Some proved undependable while others would not fire at all. Working behind cover, squad commander David Schneeweiss began repairing some of them. However, this was a time-consuming task, and while he worked, Lehi's fighters were continuing to take casualties.[12]

The Lehi force that had set off for the center of the village arrived there at 6:00 a.m. Its members too, took fire from houses in the western part of the village, including that of Mahmud Salah. By the time they had reached their objective, they had suffered casualties, although less than the Etzel contingent. One of the first to be injured had been squad commander Amos Kenan, accidentally shot in the heel by one of his fellow combatants. Moneta's partner in leading Lehi's column suffered a bullet wound in the neck and three more in the leg. Two more fighters were injured when they failed to withdraw far enough from their own explosives. The wounded were taken back to the shelter where Schneeweiss was repairing the Sten guns, where they were attended by female paramedics who had by now arrived.[13]

THE LOUDSPEAKER CAR

Because of Etzel's insistence on avoiding unnecessary bloodshed, and in accordance with Kaufman's proposal, it was decided to use a car with a loudspeaker to warn the Arab residents to evacuate the village before the attack. Lehi was entrusted with the task of bringing the car and the loudspeaker. They expropriated a small, lightly armored car from a Jewish taxi company in Jerusalem (the car was occasionally used by the Haganah, which caused Shaltiel later to accuse them of stealing the car from the Haganah). The loudspeaker was taken from a Jewish appliances dealer, a Haganah member. He at first declined their request but eventually agreed to rent it to them, demanding a record deposit of 57 Palestine pounds.[14]

The unit accompanying the armored car was the last to arrive at Deir Yassin, when the battle had already started. It left Givat Shaul at about 4:15 a.m. and comprised ten Lehi men, some of them inside the car and the rest walking after it. Ben-Uziyahu commanded the force, which included a Jew of Iraqi origin who was to announce the warning in Arabic via the loudspeaker. They encountered a trench and managed to fill it with stones and sand. Some sixty meters later, they encountered a second trench and managed to pass it too after a delay. Shortly after dawn, they reached a third trench, a few meters east of the first houses of the village. This was the deep trench dug by the villagers to prevent hostile vehicles from entering the village. Since the trench was covered with branches and dirt, they did not notice it and the car rolled down into the trench and was stuck there. An attempt to extricate the car from the trench by laying stones and steel helmets under it failed, the car crushing the helmets. Fire was directed at them from the roof of one of the houses of the Radwan family facing them, and one of Lehi's combatants was killed while others were injured. The car's tires were punctured.[15]

With no other option, the Arabic-speaker started to broadcast the announcement from where they were. The villagers were warned that superior forces of Etzel and Lehi were about to attack and they were advised to either run to 'Ayn Karm through the western exit of the village, or to seek shelter in the hillsides. The villagers were told to stop fighting, lay down their weapons and run for their lives. It was more than twenty minutes after the beginning of the battle, and due to the noise of the shooting and the distance from the bulk of the village, it was difficult to hear the loudspeaker. Furthermore, after the announcement had been made several times, the loudspeaker malfunctioned, apparently having been hit by a bullet. The message was mainly heard in the houses close to the car. Shimon Moneta, leading Selivansky's force, said that he heard it only faintly, although they were operating close by. Similarly, an Arab survivor living in this area also said that it was barely audible. Although two Arab fighters testified that they heard the loudspeaker clearly in the western part of the village, this may have been due to the greater elevation they enjoyed. The message was not heard in the center of the village, even though it was closer.[16]

The Arab guards on the roof of the house dominating the entrance to the village continued to shoot at the car until their ammunition was exhausted. At a certain point, the Lehi combatants decided to leave the car. They first attacked the house closest to them, belonging to the Muslih family, and then the house they had been fired upon from. In both cases they threw hand grenades through the windows. At this point, a few Etzel fighters, apparently belonging to the right wing of Lapidot's platoon, joined them. At this stage, a first aid unit arrived from Givat Shaul to attend to the wounded at the car and one of

Fig. 24 Mordechai Ben-Uziyahu, Lehi's operations officer

its female paramedics was injured. When Ben-Uziyahu noticed that the combatants were taking shelter behind fences and terraces, he told them, "We haven't come here to defend ourselves behind stone fences, we've come to conquer the village." Ben-Uziyahu advanced and four other fighters (two from Lehi and two from Etzel) accompanied him, while another Lehi combatant laid down covering fire from a Bren gun. Climbing on a roof, Ben-Uziyahu succeeded in hitting several snipers, enabling the group to move forward toward the center of the village. Due to their limited number, they did not enter the houses, hoping that other combatants would do so later. They left the two Etzel fighters in one of the houses to secure their rear. At this point, at about 7:00 a.m., they met with the first members of Cohen's force.[17]

THE ATTACKERS TACTICS

Etzel and Lehi's members were trained in guerrilla warfare. They were used to operating as part of an underground group that blew up buildings and carried out assassinations. Most of them had undergone no training in field operations and had no notion in fighting in either open or built-up areas. They had no experience in house-to-house fighting. Except for a few veterans of World War II, like Cohen, they had never participated in a full-scale battle, or even in a skirmish with other forces. They definitely had no experience whatsoever in the taking of populated areas. "No one in the country, the Palmach included, had then any real notion how to conquer a village," Lapidot was to say many years later. Furthermore, many of the combatants were newly enrolled members in the organizations, teenagers with no prior operational experience.[18]

They did what they knew, which Lapidot was to characterize as, "toss grenades and spray gunfire." It turned out that some did not even know how to do that properly. Moneta related that some of Lehi's men did not know how to operate their weapons, since they had never practiced on a rifle range. Although they had learned to shoot pistols, their rifle training was carried out without bullets in order to save ammunition: "We would lie on the ground with an English rifle. The instructor would sit in front of you holding a target with a pinhole in the bullseye. When you, the shooter, would aim the rifle, lining up both the foresight and the back-sight, directly at the bullseye. The instructor was able to see through the pinhole if you were aiming properly." They learned to dismantle Sten guns and Tommy guns. They also were trained to use hand grenades, but, again, without throwing live grenades. Consequently, on at least on one occasion during the battle a fighter forgot to pull out the pin before he threw the grenade.[19]

Fig. 25 Yehoshua Goldschmidt (left) in training

The underground fighters were used to operating in ad hoc units of variable size, depending on what operations they were tasked with. They therefore lacked experience in fighting in coordinated units such as squads and platoons. The result was that the attack progressed in a disorderly manner, with each small unit fighting on its own, resulting in diminished firepower. There was no systematic coordination, nor even communication, between the units (let alone radio contact). The fighters lacked discipline, did not know how to make use of dead spots in the terrain, and did not supply each other with covering fire while advancing. When day dawned, the attackers were caught in the open, exposed to Arab fire, and many of them, advancing recklessly, were hit. After the battle, Etzel's commanders met several times to analyze their faults and learn lessons. Goldschmidt's conclusion was that all units needed to undergo comprehensive field training, a policy later implemented.[20]

As mentioned above, when it became clear that the weapons in the possession of the attackers made no impact on the stone houses of the villagers, Goldschmidt had suggested blasting their way into the houses. Under covering fire, two combatants would crawl to the door of a house, one would lay a gelignite stick to make a hole in the door, and the other would throw a satchel charge through the hole into the house. Etzel started using this method at about 11:00 a.m. According to Kaufman, they blew up eleven houses that way, one every fifteen minutes, burying the occupants under the debris. Finally, the occupants of the twelfth house surrendered. At a press conference held by Etzel after the battle, its spokesman mentioned ten houses blown up, although an early announcement by the organization only spoke about five demolished homes in the eastern part of the village. Lapidot further reduced the number to "several" ("a few," he said in a later interview).[21]

Etzel's men claimed that they warned the occupants of each house in Arabic to surrender before blowing up the building and the villagers were told to leave the houses with their hands up. Some of the Arab survivors confirmed this. Kaufman later gave evidence that they brought a battery-powered loudspeaker from Jerusalem for this purpose. Akiva Azulay, the Haganah's second-in-command in Givat Shaul, related that they heard this loudspeaker throughout the day. Also one of the Palmach's combatants who arrived in Deir Yassin later (at about noon), testified that he heard a loudspeaker calling the populace to surrender. However, the Arabs did not surrender even after Etzel had begun blowing up the houses. Kaufman was to surmise that the villagers, locked in their houses, heard the explosions but did not understand their meaning, and this was the reason they did not surrender after the first warnings. Lehi's fighters, too, used the method of blowing up houses after they had encountered heavy fire from them, but without issuing warnings.[22]

Matthew Hogan, one of the main adherents of the deliberate massacre narrative, claimed, in an article, that there was no substantial destruction of houses in Deir Yassin. The question whether houses were blown up in Deir Yassin, burying their occupants beneath them, is important. Etzel and Lehi claimed that this occurred many times, partially explaining the high number of civilian deaths. The other view was that the underground fighters had intentionally shot the villagers to death individually. Hogan based his claim on an interview with Meir Pa'il (formerly Pilavsky), who had told his interviewer, Daniel

McGowan, that no house was blown up in Deir Yassin. (McGowan and Hogan were both members of an organization memorializing the affair.) In a testimony deposited in the Jabotinsky archives, Pa'il insisted that no Arab was killed in Deir Yassin due to the demolition of a house. Pa'il's testimonies and interviews will be discussed in more detail later. Hogan also based his argument on the words of Yehoshua Arieli, who commanded the Haganah burial party assigned to inter the Arabs, who told him that he saw no systematic destruction of houses. Hogan further mentioned Eliyahu Arbel, a Haganah officer who visited Deir Yassin on Saturday and reported that he saw people killed by gunfire but not by the demolition of houses.[23]

The day after the battle, the newspaper *Filastin* reported that five houses had been demolished in Deir Yassin. Although this report could be dismissed as merely echoing the announcement issued by Etzel the day before, there are also many independent testimonies of Arab survivors that houses were blown up in Deir Yassin. According to these accounts, houses collapsed over their occupants, killing them. One survivor attested that the number of demolished houses amounted to four or five and that women were killed under the debris. Another survivor said that not too many houses were destroyed, but some were. The mukhtar, Muhammad Isma'il Sammur, who had left the village before the attack, had asked the British military to assist in rescuing the villagers trapped under the debris (a request refused by the British). The British also reported that explosives destroyed five houses, but it could be that they, too, were relying on Etzel's initial announcement. Yet there are also testimonies by Haganah members who visited the site that houses had been destroyed. Gicherman saw houses partly destroyed by explosives. Moshe Vachman, one of the Palmach's men who later came to assist the attackers (see below), related that he saw houses systematically broken into by explosives, the blast killing the occupants. Inhabitants of Beit ha-Kerem also reported hearing the explosions.[24]

In contrast to these accounts of demolitions of buildings stands the fact that Deir Yassin was one of the few Arab villages whose buildings and facilities remained mainly intact after the 1948 war. When in late 1948 officials of the Jewish Agency visited the village to examine its potential as accommodation for new immigrants, they reported that the houses were in good condition and needed only minor renovations. There also exist two aerial photos of Deir Yassin, one from early 1946, before the attack, and the other from late 1951, after the attack, which clearly show that almost all of the houses that existed in 1946 remained in 1951. Three of the houses of the Jawda (Hamdan) family, northeast of the village center and adjacent to the house of the mukhtar, did not exist in 1951. Also the house of 'Ali Mustafa Zaydan, near the eastern crossroad of the village center, seemed to be partly destroyed in the 1951 photo, but the story of this family was completely different and will be discussed below. Two houses of the Jabir family were also missing in 1951, one southeast of the mukhtar house and the second in the center of the village. However, three houses of the Jundi, Jabir, and Qasim families, in the southwestern corner of the village, could not have been demolished in the attack, despite being missing in the 1951 photo, because this region was the last to remain in Arab hands. They were probably demolished later.[25]

How to resolve these conflicting testimonies and narratives regarding demolition? How can one reconcile the fact that the destruction in Deir Yassin was relatively small with the later testimony of Kaufman who described a house that "went up in flames, exploded and collapsed, really crumbling down"? The solution is that, although houses were blown up in Deir Yassin, the number completely destroyed (the kind of event described by Kaufman), was low. In other instances, although the blasts caused massive internal damage, they did not destroy the houses' structural integrity and they continued to stand in their place, as attested to by several sources. In many other instances, the charges were used just to break down the doors. Lehi's Amos Kenan and Etzel's Kalman Bergman related that the attackers broke down doors with petards (breaching charges). The blast and shrapnel would kill the people inside. Arab sources corroborate the use of this method.[26]

Etzel's commander in the field, Cohen, ordered the attackers not to take unnecessary risks and enter any houses without first throwing in hand grenades. Attempts to enter houses without doing so invariably ended in a firefight with those inside the house and casualties among the attackers. "I gave the order that our fighters should not enter a single house without using explosives or throwing a grenade or two inside. That I guess caused the enemy many losses." After throwing the grenades, the fighters would pour automatic weapons fire into the house before entering, causing further casualties among the occupants. Many women and children died this way. Lehi's fighters, too, faced fire from within the houses and they reacted similarly, throwing hand grenades and shooting automatic fire inside, inflicting casualties among the occupants. Many of the Arab survivors also mentioned the throwing of hand grenades into the houses, killing and injuring those inside. The results were especially severe for the Zahran family, living in a four-house complex in the northeastern part of the village. They were attacked by Lehi's force coming from the north. After an exchange of fire, Lehi's combatants threw hand grenades into the complex and burst in firing on full automatic. More than twenty members of the family were killed, making it the incident with the highest casualty count of the day.[27]

Selivansky, Lehi's commander in the field, related that his force blew in doors with gelignite sticks, threw hand grenades into the houses, and sprayed them with fire.[28] This description summarizes both Lehi's and Etzel's tactics in facing the fire from the local inhabitants and seizing their houses. The residents did not stand much of a chance to survive this three-phased method of consecutively using explosives, hand grenades, and automatic fire when breaking into the buildings.

Chapter 4
The Arabs Fight Back

LOCAL COMBATANTS RESIST THE ATTACK

A complex of houses in the southeastern corner of the village, inhabited by the 'Atiyya family, was the first to be attacked by Etzel's force. On the roof of the complex there was an Arab observation position guarded by three members of the 'Atiyya family, Isma'il, who had just returned from the battle over Qastal, his younger brother Mahmud and their uncle Rubhi. As related earlier, at 4:25 a.m. Mahmud heard one of Etzel's combatants and fired in his direction, hitting another Jewish combatant. Mahmud shouted to his brother that the Jews were attacking them. Etzel's fighters started to advance, but were forced back by Muhammad, father of Isma'il and Mahmud, who fired bursts from his Sten at them. The firing position was situated on the roof of the third floor with a ladder leading to it from inside the house. Muhammad hurried to climb to the roof, asking a younger brother of his, 'Azmi, and other members of the family, to pass up to them all Sten and rifle ammunition in the house. After a heavy exchange of fire, the Etzel men threw a hand grenade into the position, Muhammad was seriously injured in the explosion. Mahmud, too, was injured, but managed to escape together with Isma'il and Rubhi. Immediately after this clash, Etzel took the complex.[1]

Mahmud's shot was heard by the guards in the advance post near the crusher of the Sammur family, dominating the entrance to the village. The position contained more than the usual number of personnel because some villagers, who had finished their guard duty by midnight, had preferred to rejoin the guards of this position instead of going to sleep. Husayn Zaydan, the inspector of the guards, was also there and he asked one of them to return to the village and tell whoever had

Figs. 26 and 27 Some of Deir Yassin's complexes of houses

opened fire to stop it. Before long, they heard the noise of the battle coming from the southeastern side of the village. A short while later, they observed Lehi's force approaching the boys elementary school behind them. Although they exchanged fire with the Lehi fighters, they could not prevent them from capturing the school. At this point, the seven guards decided to retreat to the house of Ahmad As'ad Radwan, half way to the school and facing the main trench dug by the villagers at the village entrance. Minutes later Lehi's loudspeaker car arrived and was trapped in the trench. The guards, standing on the roof of Radwan's house, started shooting at it from behind a parapet. A veteran of the Transjordan Frontier Force who was posted nearby also opened fire with a Bren gun. The car's occupants tried to heave it free while the guards sought to stop them, killing one of Lehi's combatants and injuring others. The guards continued shooting until they ran out of ammunition. Then, they escaped through the olive trees to the western, upper region of the village. Only Radwan As'ad Radwan, Ahmad's brother, failed to escape. He had been injured during the exchange of fire and descended from the roof into the house and continued to shoot through a window. The attackers threw in a hand grenade and broke in. Radwan intended to pretend to be sleeping, hiding his rifle beneath the bed, but was identified as the sniper and shot dead.[2]

After the capture of the school, Lehi's force turned to the houses of the Zahran family. Among the buildings' defenders were Jum'a Zahran, his father, brother and nephew. Jum'a's father was hit whilst Jum'a fired at one of the attackers, but missed. His target grappled with him, trying to seize his rifle. Having failed, the Lehi man turned his back, and Jum'a shot him. Jum'a was, in turn, shot from several directions. He escaped to the western, upper region of the village and joined other Arab combatants who had regrouped there. Khalil Sammur, son of the mukhtar, was fighting side by side with the Zahrans. At one point, he left for the house of Yusuf 'Alya, some fifty meters to the west, adjacent to the village main well (the Jawza well) to fetch more ammunition. At the same time, the Lehi force started to move toward the center of the village. As they passed by 'Alya's house, Sammur, 'Alya and 'Alya's three sons opened fire on them and the Lehi combatants shot back. However, it was not just Jewish bullets that were directed at the Arab fighters, the Arab combatants on the high ground in the west also opened fire on the area of the Jawza well in order to thwart Lehi's advance, and Sammur and the 'Alyas were caught in the cross fire. Sammur managed to slip away through the trees. Heading first to rescue some of his family, he then continued west to the house of 'Arif Sammur, which dominated the main road of the village. From the roof, he and others fired on the Jewish combatants, hindering their advance.[3]

Fig. 28 Deir Yassin's main road, near the Jawza well (picture taken in 1949)

One of the most prominent Arab fighters in the western sector of the village was 'Ali Qasim, a veteran of the 1936–39 revolt. It fell to him to repulse the Etzel squad which was trying to conquer the hill south of the village. Although the unit's intention was to block possible Arab reinforcements from 'Ayn Karm, the villagers interpreted their arrival as an attempt to block their way out of the village. The hill was already in Jewish hands, when Qasim with several other Arab combatants counter-attacked, firing and throwing hand grenades. They killed one of the Etzel combatants and injured two more. The Etzel squad retreated, descending back to the wadi, and the Arab combatants reoccupied the site. Despite the death of one of the Arab combatants the route to 'Ayn Karm remained open, and Qasim and his men urged the villagers to flee. The Arab combatants also took advantage of their position to snipe from the hill at the Jewish fighters inside the village, hitting some of them. Qasim tried to exploit his success by attempting to expel the Jews from the southeastern corner of the village, where Etzel's main force was operating. He threw a hand grenade at a group of Jewish fighters taking shelter in a nearby porch. Some were injured, but one fired back, hitting Qasim in the stomach. Qasim's men carried him back to the western part of the village, from where he was later evacuated to 'Ayn Karm.[4]

Mahmud Salah's house, located in the northwestern edge of the village, occupied the highest point in Deir Yassin. The second Bren gun of the village was brought there, put on the roof, and Muhammad Salah, brother of the late Mahmud, fired it throughout the battle, delaying the Jewish advance for hours. Downhill from this house was a two-building complex belonging to the Radwan family. When the battle broke out, Hasan As'ad Radwan left his home to take up a position behind a stone fence affording a view of the entire village, and fired from there. He had one of the rifles brought from Egypt and about thirty magazines, holding five rounds each. At dawn, he could see the attackers clearly. He chose his targets well in order to save ammunition, and shot about twenty bullets per hour until the early afternoon. At 7:00 a.m., he had been joined by Jum'a Zahran and later by Khalil Sammur and other members of the Sammur family. In the early afternoon, Khalil Sammur and Muhammad Salah launched an attack and succeeded in getting back to the house of 'Arif Sammur, about one hundred meters to the east, a lower position, but still well above the level of the village center. However, they could not hold the location for long, as they were running out of ammunition.[5]

The snipers' fire was persistent, effective and lasted for hours. In addition to the specific clashes listed already, throughout the village, Arab defenders were fighting the attackers "from house to house and from street to street," as one Arab combatant put it. They returned fire, threw hand grenades and sometimes fought hand-to-hand. The occupants of many of the houses would shoot at the attackers from behind stone fences, from roofs and through windows, and sometimes would continue fighting even after the attackers had broken into their buildings. Selivansky related an encounter with an Arab whose right arm had been blown off by a hand grenade, who continued to try to fire with his left arm. The Arab fighters gradually started to retreat as their ammunition ran out, the survivors fleeing to ʿAyn Karm. Fighting only ended at about 2:00 p.m., after almost ten hours, when the defenders completely ran out of ammunition.[6]

Fig. 29 A narrow alley in Deir Yassin

There are three additional questions to be answered with regard to the Arab military effort in Deir Yassin. Did foreign warriors assist the local combatants? Did women participate in active combat? Did some of the combatants disguise themselves as women?

Since late March, there had been rumors that some 150 Iraqi and Syrian irregulars were in Deir Yassin. Although the notables of Deir Yassin had denied the rumors, they continued to circulate. Etzel and Lehi were convinced that foreign soldiers, mainly Iraqi but also Syrian, were reinforcing the village, and the attacking forces were told to expect to encounter such forces.[7] Thus primed, the attackers interpreted what they saw as proof of the presence of Arab soldiers. The most common evidence cited was the presence of Arabs in military uniforms. There were many testimonies of Arabs dressed in khaki. Some Arabs were seen to be wearing red-and-white checkered *keffiyeh*s. One Arab was observed to be wearing a British steel helmet, a blue coat, and a pair of khaki pants.[8] While there is no reason to doubt these testimonies, they definitely do not prove the presence of foreign soldiers in Deir Yassin. Arabs, especially youngsters but also adults, commonly wore khaki clothing. A red-and-white checkered *keffiyeh* did not necessarily mean a Transjordanian or Iraqi soldier; Palestinians too wore such *keffiyeh*s (some of the survivors were wearing them in later filmed interviews). Helmets and other articles of military clothing also did not necessarily denote soldiers. The same applies to swastikas and Iraqi military insignia found in Deir Yassin, which might just as well have been interpreted as some sort of souvenirs and not as a proof for the presence of foreigners, Nazi soldiers among them, as some claimed.[9]

One or two Iraqi soldiers were identified by their papers (some of the attackers could read Arabic), but these were exceptions. Selivansky claimed that Lehi killed a deserter from the Arab Legion and a Muslim Yugoslavian officer. On one occasion, an identity card identified a dead Arab as a leader of one of the bands of irregulars (his name was not indicated by the source). If true, he was most likely to have been a local villager since some of the villagers had fought with the irregulars in the 1936–39 revolt and later. A veteran of the Transjordan Frontier Force was present in the village, but he was not amongst the fatalities. The Haganah men who later buried the corpses found no bodies in foreign uniforms. According to the available evidence, there is no solid proof for a significant presence of either the Rescue Army or the Army of Sacred Jihad in Deir Yassin. A significant number of Iraqi volunteer soldiers, belonging to the Rescue Army, had encamped in 'Ayn Karm (see below), but not in Deir Yassin. The Arab combatants in Deir Yassin were locals.[10]

There is considerable testimony, both Arab and Jewish, that Arab women took an active part in the combat, some of them firing weapons. One of the more famous stories is that of Hilwa Zaydan

Khalil, whose son was killed in battle, followed by her husband before she herself fell in battle. Another woman let a Jew enter the house but then drew a pistol and aimed at him (he subdued her). When Etzel eventually captured Mahmud Salah's house, a dead woman holding a rifle was found on its roof. Several Arab women participated in the fighting by distributing ammunition, some paying with their lives. Others would leave their houses under fire to retrieve weapons from combatants killed. Women would also dress the wounded, at times under fire. The most famous story from that respect is that of Hayat al-Balabsa, the teacher of the girls' school. She was not a resident of the village but could not return to Jerusalem because the road was cut. Since she was trained in first aid, instead of fleeing the village at the start of the attack she went to attend the wounded, was hit by a bullet and died. One of the accounts of the events of Deir Yassin by an Arab historian lists the names of eighteen women who, according to him, died in combat.[11]

There is also testimony, from both Arab and Jewish sources, that Arab combatants disguised themselves as women. Arab sources mostly report fighters trying to escape from the village disguised as women, while most Jewish sources claimed that those disguising themselves did it so in order to attack the Jewish forces more easily. Arab eyewitnesses mentioned several names of combatants killed when trying to escape disguised as women, among them Rubhi 'Atiyya, who fought in the first position attacked by Etzel's force. Etzel and Lehi's sources describe Arab fighters disguised as women who hid their firearms beneath their clothes, approached the Jewish combatants and shot them. A group of veiled Arab "women" were unmasked as men by a female Lehi fighter, who proved faster than one of the Arabs who drew his weapon. Several dead combatants disguised as women were found in Mahmud Salah's house. Jewish sources claimed that altogether thirty such cases were discovered in the village. Even if this number is an exaggeration, the phenomenon existed, and according to their own evidence, it caused Jewish combatants to shoot women when they found their behavior suspect.[12]

Nonetheless, the majority of the village women did not take part in the battle, and the survivors were to relate how they coped with the events. Zaynab 'Atiyya lived in the center of the village. A group of attackers demanded that she open her door. She refused and they blasted it in, injuring her and her two daughters. They shot her brother to death and took the female survivors to a house where the children and female prisoners were kept under guard by female Jewish combatants. 'Aziza 'Atiyya, Zaynab's aunt, was at the bakery when the attack began. The attackers broke into the bakery shooting the baker and his son, while she and some other thirty women fled. 'Aziza found shelter of the nearby house of Muhammad Jawda, whose relative, Muhammad Mahmud Sammur, soon turned up armed with a rifle. There were a total of five people in the house at that point, including Muhammad Jawda's wife and son. The attackers arrived and demanded the door be opened. 'Aziza opened the door and came out. When the Jewish fighters saw the rifle, they threw in a hand grenade, killing all the men inside. 'Aziza then ran to the mukhtar's house where she was caught by three Jewish fighters, who were, themselves, soon wounded by gunfire. She ran again and was caught and brought to the house where the women and children were being held. Shafiqa Sammur, the mukhtar's daughter, gave shelter to ten women who had run from the bakery. At 11:00 a.m., they were ordered to open the door and refused. At 2:00 p.m. they were warned that the house be blown up unless they opened the door, whereupon they did open up and were taken to the compound for children and female prisoners[13]

The children's fate was similar. A typical story is that of Naziha Radwan, daughter of Ahmad As'ad. After the guards of the advance post retreated and the Jewish combatants broke into the house (and killed her uncle Radwan As'ad, see above), she, her brother and grandmother were instructed to stay in a hencoop. Her grandmother decided to try to reach a house of their relatives through the trees, but they were shot at on the way and her grandmother and brother were killed. She reached the house of her aunt Basma, wife of Jum'a Zahran, only to find everybody there dead. Suddenly, she heard someone crying in the house. It was her cousin Fatima who had been seriously injured (she was evacuated two days later by a representative of the Red Cross, but died a couple of days later). At this point, a Jew arrived telling her to follow him. She asked to be taken to her mother, who was supposed to be in the nearby house of her uncle Ibrahim 'Atiyya. When she arrived there his wife, Safiyya, opened the door holding a white flag. They were then all taken to the house where the women and children were being held. Many of the women and children were not taken prisoner by the attackers, and after hiding – at times for days in cellars, stables and the like – they managed to flee to 'Ayn Karm.[14]

THE FLIGHT TO 'AYN KARM

Many of the villagers heeded the warnings to run for their lives that had been broadcast by the loudspeaker car at the beginning of the battle. They were advised either to seek shelter in the hillsides or to flee to 'Ayn Karm through the western exit of the village. Even those who did not hear the loudspeaker quickly understood the situation and followed their neighbors fleeing to 'Ayn Karm, the closest Arab village to Deir Yassin, about two kilometers to the southwest. An eyewitness from Beit ha-Kerem related that within minutes of the start of the battle, a stream of villagers could be seen running over the hills. The number of those escaping at the beginning of the battle was estimated at two hundred.[15]

Except for the fighters and those taken prisoner during the fighting, everyone capable of leaving had left – children, youngsters, men and women. Whole families left. Sakina, daughter of 'Aziza 'Atiyya (mentioned above), was living in the northwestern edge of the village. Her mother was at the bakery. When she, her sisters and her elder brother heard the noise of the shooting and explosions they ran toward the center of the village, saw all the women and children fleeing, and followed them in the direction of 'Ayn Karm. Another youngster described how he was running to 'Ayn Karm carrying his sister on his back. Mothers were carrying their babies. Many ran out of the back doors of their houses. Some left injured. Others crawled on hands and knees to escape. Still others did not flee at once, but hid in their houses until nightfall and then seized the opportunity to leave for 'Ayn Karm. Since there were more houses in Deir Yassin than attackers, it was a time consuming task to gain control of the entire village, and people continued to slip out of the village long after the battle was over. It is clear that most of the inhabitants of Deir Yassin managed to escape throughout the day. The total number of escapees was estimated at seven hundred, corresponding to the total number of villagers, less those killed and taken prisoner.[16]

Some of the young men capable of fighting panicked and fled too. Of these, some later returned and joined the fighting. Mahmud 'Atiyya, the first to notice the Etzel force (see above), suffered a wound to the face from the hand grenade thrown at his position and fled to 'Ayn Karm. When he learned that his brother and family were still trapped in their house in the village, he returned to Deir Yassin and shot at the attackers to keep them away from the house. They returned fire and killed him. Nonetheless, his brother and family managed to escape and reached 'Ayn Karm. Others who fled the attackers took up positions on the hills surrounding the village and shot at the Jewish forces for hours. Eventually, when they ran out of ammunition, all the Arab combatants remained alive withdrew to 'Ayn Karm, taking their weapons with them.[17]

It was not only the Arabs who used the surrounding hills to fire into the village, Mordechai Gicherman was operating a Spandau machine gun from the Sharafa ridge, which dominated the route from Deir Yassin to 'Ayn Karm and had been taken some days before by the Haganah. At about 7:00 a.m., the Haganah in Givat Shaul received information that Arab reinforcements were advancing from 'Ayn Karm and Maliha to Deir Yassin. Although Gicherman only saw Arabs fleeing from Deir Yassin, it seemed to him that some force was gathering south of the village (he possibly saw 'Ali Qasim and his fellow combatants), so he opened fire. Other Haganah positions in the western suburbs joined in. The Spandau's bursts not only hit Arabs fleeing from the village, but may have also struck Etzel fighters who were within range. Lapidot was later to relate his surprise at being shot at from the ridge. Etzel's early announcement about the battle interpreted these shots as being fired by a large group of Arab reinforcements arriving from 'Ayn Karm.[18]

APPROACHING ARAB NEIGHBORS FOR HELP

In fact, no Arab reinforcement came from 'Ayn Karm or from anywhere else. A company of more than one hundred Iraqi and Syrian soldiers was camped in 'Ayn Karm, belonging to Fawzi al-Qawuqji's Rescue Army. Some of the fugitives arriving at 'Ayn Karm, approached their officers to ask for help, only to be told that they could not intervene without instructions from their commanders, all of whom were in Jerusalem attending the funeral of 'Abd al-Qadir al-Husayni. They were not even prepared to provide them with arms and ammunition. Amina Zaydan, who had lost both her husband and a son in the battle, approached some of the soldiers urging them: "Please, in Allah's name, our women are massacred, our children are dead, and you are sitting here? Go and fight them!" Their response was, "Shut up, old woman." In a statement to the Arab daily *Filastin*, a spokesman of the Rescue Army's information office blamed the inhabitants of Deir Yassin for what had happened to them, saying that, instead of defending the village, they had left for Husayni's funeral, and that they should not have given the Jews the opportunity. The Rescue Army,

Fig. 30 'Abd al-Qadir al-Husayni's funeral

on the other hand, he said, had sent a relief force there to defend the region until further notice.[19]

Local fighters from 'Ayn Karm's likewise failed to assist their brethren in Deir Yassin, except for two who had relatives there. Other villages in the vicinity still in a position to extend help, such as Maliha and Suba, also stood aloof. Some attributed the failure to offer aid to the shock of 'Abd al-Qadir al-Husayni's death and the fall of Qastal, or that they simply were afraid. The Arab daily *al-Difa'* would report that Arabs from the neighboring villages had been eager to save their brethren in Deir Yassin, but the Jews were too many and were using artillery against them.[20]

Muhammad Qasim, 'Ali's brother, was one of the refugees ignored by the officers of the Rescue Army in 'Ayn Karm. He immediately continued on to Jerusalem, where he turned to Yasin al-Bakri, one the Arab military commanders in the Old City. Al-Bakri phoned the British police, but the officer who answered him said he could not act without orders. Two other refugees who reached Jerusalem turned to a senior Arab officer serving in the Kishle police station. He, too, turned down their appeal to intervene, claiming that to do so would exceed his authority. They next went to the National Committee in Jerusalem, which, in turn, contacted the British army asking for its intervention, all to no avail. The National Committee took no further steps at this stage. Deir Yassin's mukhtar, Muhammad Isma'il Sammur, had left the village before the attack and also was in Jerusalem at the time, where he learned that none of the many combatants of the Army of Sacred Jihad, present there for Husayni's funeral, showed any interest in the fate of his village. No help would reach the Arabs of Deir Yassin that day from the Arabs of Jerusalem, who were completely absorbed in the funeral.[21]

Only when it was already too late, did the National Committee decide to actively intervene. It planned to mobilize three hundred fighters and send them to 'Ayn Karm in order to reoccupy Deir Yassin. This plan was never carried out due to trivial difficulties, such as lack of fuel to transport the combatants. In any case, the inhabitants of 'Ayn Karm themselves were by then more concerned for their own safety. A senior Arab officer in the Palestine Police would later tell the secretary of the Arab Higher Committee that, had the British authorities allowed him to do so, he could have captured Deir Yassin with three hundred Arab policemen, however, they refused to permit it. During the following few days, sporadic, ineffective fire was directed from 'Ayn Karm and the area toward the southern slopes of the village, harming no one.[22]

APPEALING TO THE BRITISH FOR HELP

It was not until the afternoon, after Husayni's funeral, when Husayn Fakhri al-Khalidi, secretary of the Arab Higher Committee, learned of events in Deir Yassin. He immediately contacted the British police. An assistant to the Inspector-General denied the village had been attacked but promised to look into the matter. An hour later, he called Khalidi back to inform him that a Jewish police officer and a British policeman had been sent to the village and reported back that everything was quiet, except for one building that had been partially demolished. He went on to assure Khalidi that reports of fighting were no more than rumors. In fact, no policeman, Jewish or otherwise, had visited Deir Yassin. Nevertheless, that night the police issued an official announcement reiterating these words. Richard Graves, mayor of Jerusalem, wrote in his diary that according to the Jewish police officer one Arab had been killed.[23]

Khalidi also approached the British Chief Secretariat, who gave him the impression that he was the first to tell them of events in the village. In reality, Chief Secretary Henry Gurney had apprised High Commissioner Alan Cunningham of the news already by 9:30 a.m. "We must bust the hell out of these people," was Cunningham's first reaction. He wanted to send the army. "At last, you have got those bastards there," he told the General Officer Commanding, General MacMillan. "For God's sake, go and get them." MacMillan refused. Although the army had learned what was going on as early as 9:00 a.m., when the National Committee had approached it, MacMillan was of the opinion that the war between Jews and Arabs was none of their business. His priority was to safeguard British lives and not Arab ones. British forces were there to secure their lines of communication and not to get involved in the civil war in Palestine. The conquest of Arab villages by Jews was an internal matter between Jews and Arabs, so long as it did not compromise the British plans of evacuation. He therefore instructed General Murray, the regional commander, "There has been an engagement with D[eir Yassin], you will not intervene in any circumstances." "If you get an order that's as straightforward as that one was, you don't lightly disregard it," Murray was later to say. It was a military matter, so Cunningham had to accept MacMillan's position.[24]

Muhammad Isma'il Sammur, the mukhtar, also approached the headquarters of the Rural Division of the Jerusalem police at about 9:00 a.m., asking that British troops should be sent to the village. His request was passed on to the army, which answered that "the military authorities were not prepared to send troops to Deir Yassin because they might become involved in Arab/Jewish fighting." At 4:00 p.m., the first women and children who had been taken prisoner by the attackers were released on the border of Arab Jerusalem. At this point, the National Committee again approached the army, begging it to intervene. At this point Khalidi, too, contacted the army, which denied what had happened and in any case refused to intervene. Khalidi asked to send some tanks or armored cars, but the army was unwilling to go near the village. The next day the army also refused a request made by the representative of the Red Cross in Jerusalem to escort him to the village. It was too dangerous and they did not intend to intervene.[25]

The British officials were well aware of the bed impression generated by their inactivity, made public by Khalidi, who threatened to lodge a complaint about it to the British government and the United Nations. The National Committee, too, issued a statement denouncing the British indifference with regard to Deir Yassin. It was "the general Arab view," the British themselves noted, "that had the military rendered assistance when the mukhtar requested it" they could have prevented the entire event. The British were informed of events in real time and the village was within walking distance of their centers of government. Nonetheless, they did nothing. The British inactivity was interpreted by both British and foreign reporters as proof of the British inability to impose their authority. Indeed, when Cunningham wanted to publish some details of the affair, MacMillan expressed his doubts as to the wisdom of such a move, "as he was afraid that explanations of our inability to assist the Arabs might show up our military weakness." Cunningham was to write to his minister, "I should make it clear that the military authorities are not, repeat not, in a position to take action in the matter owing to their falling strength and increasing commitments." Many years later he would explain, "Our powers got less and less as the situation got worse and worse."[26]

Chapter 5

The Haganah Intervenes

THE HAGANAH FOLLOWS THE BATTLE

Haganah commanders followed the battle throughout the day, with several of them, junior and senior, being involved in one way or another. Yosef Ben-Nun, who was the Haganah commander for the whole area, instructed Akiva Azulay, Givat Shaul's second-in-command, not only to give Lehi a base for their attack, but also to assist them with covering fire in case they retreated. When Etzel and Lehi were running out of ammunition, they received additional supplies from Yonah Ben-Sasson, Givat Shaul's regional commander (subsequently dismissed by Shaltiel for doing so without permission). Azulay also gave them 1,500 bullets, eleven rifles, and some Sten guns (he faced charges for acting without authorization). When Azulay learned of the difficulties of the attackers and the many casualties in their ranks, he called Ben-Nun and Shaltiel and asked for their help.[1]

Aid of a different kind came from Mordechai Gicherman, the regional intelligence officer, who early in the morning reached the Sharafa ridge and posted a Spandau machine gun there. At about 7:00 a.m. he and a partner from the Moriah battalion opened fire on Arabs fleeing from Deir Yassin, hitting some. Haganah positions in the western suburbs joined in. The Spandau's bursts not only hit Arab escapees, but possibly also Etzel fighters who were in the line

of fire. They further shot at Arab fighters gathered in the western part of the village, and according to Gicherman, inflicted substantial losses upon them, forcing them either to expose themselves to their fire or that of the attackers. At 8:30 a.m., when they ran out of ammunition, they returned to Givat Shaul.[2]

The Haganah's senior commanders set up a command post in Givat Shaul to follow the battle. Zalman Mart, the commander of the Moriah battalion, spent most of the day there. Other senior officers, Shaltiel himself, his operations

Fig. 31 Mordechai Gicherman, the Haganah's regional intelligence officer

officer, Zion Eldad, and the commander of the Michmash battalion, Yeshurun Schiff, came there several times during the battle. Shaltiel arrived before noon and met with Zettler, who asked for help in the evacuation of the wounded. Shaltiel reproved him for attacking Deir Yassin in the first place, but agreed to help. As early as 8:00 a.m., Mart phoned a Magen David Adom station (the Jewish emergency medical service) asking for an ambulance. When it arrived it was only able to evacuate some of the wounded, the rest would have to wait. Following a request by Shaltiel, Yosef Tabenkin, commander of the fourth battalion of the Palmach, sent an armored car from Kiryat Anavim, which arrived at Deir Yassin at about 11:30 a.m. and evacuated the seriously wounded. In addition, Shaltiel supplied the attackers with four thousand rounds of ammunition for the Stens as well as some for the rifles.[3]

In the early afternoon, Kaufman received a summons from Shaltiel to meet with him. He returned from Deir Yassin to Givat Shaul and updated Shaltiel about the situation. Shaltiel instructed Gicherman to accompany Kaufman back to Deir Yassin to tour the village. According to his own testimony Gicherman did so only after the battle was over, and when he returned he reported to Shaltiel that bodies of people were scattered throughout the village. When, later on, Kaufman would meet Shaltiel again and ask him that the Haganah would take over the village, Shaltiel would only agree on condition that the bodies be buried first.[4]

THE PALMACH ARRIVES

During the first hours of the attack, when the Jewish troops were running out of ammunition and suffering significant casualties, Zettler instructed Moshe Edelstein to go to Schneller Camp near Romema, where a Palmach company was stationed, and bring ammunition. Edelstein was part of Lehi's intelligence department and a former Palmach member who served as a liaison between Lehi and the Palmach and occasionally would exchange ammunition of various calibers with the Haganah. Edelstein took a case of German bullets found in the village, which did not fit Lehi's weaponry, and rode a motorcycle to Schneller. He was later followed by two other Lehi representatives seeking help, his direct commander, Lehi's intelligence officer Moshe Barzilai, and Lehi's senior member David Gottlieb.[5]

Fig. 32 Lehi's member Moshe Edelstein

While most of the Palmach's sixth battalion was far away in the coastal plain, its fourth company was based at Schneller, tasked with escorting convoys and securing the road between Jerusalem and Bab al-Wad. Throughout 8 April, the company commander, Yaakov Weg, and some of his men had been patrolling the portion of the road from Qalunya to Jerusalem, a task they completed at 1:00 a.m. and returned to base. In the early hours of the morning Weg's second-in-command, Moshe Vachman, was awakened by Edelstein, asking him for weapons and ammunition in exchange for bullets. Weg was away and Vachman refused to grant the request without permission from his superiors. At 6:30 a.m., Weg returned and learned about the situation in Deir Yassin and the difficulties in evacuating the wounded. He refused to deliver weapons but agreed to supply Lehi with three thousand rounds suitable for their arms in exchange for the rounds brought by Edelstein. He further approached Shaltiel to seek permission to go to Deir Yassin and assist the attackers. After several hours, Shaltiel, with Yosef Tabenkin's approval but without consulting Ben-Gurion, authorized Weg to go to Deir Yassin and assist the attackers in evacuating the wounded and to lay down covering fire for the evacuation.[6]

The day before, the Palmach company had received new weaponry from Czechoslovakia, which included a German MG 34 machine gun. The guns were unpacked and cleaned from grease. Weg instructed some of his men to go to the Jewish Agency's building, where they had an arms depot, and bring an additional mortar with ammunition. Finally, Weg and twelve of his men set out to Deir Yassin in two armored cars, equipped with two 2-inch mortars with six shells each, the MG 34 and seven rifles.[7]

Weg and his men arrived at the pillbox that served as the Etzel and Lehi command post on the western edge of Givat Shaul shortly

Fig. 33 Yaakov Weg (standing in the middle) and his men in Schneller camp with the MG 34

before noon. Akiva Azulay, the Haganah's second-in-command in Givat Shaul, gave them an overview of the situation, and then Weg went on to meet with Zettler and Kaufman. Zettler did not like

Figs. 34 and 35 The Haganah in Deir Yassin: The Palmach (above) and the military police (below). Those wearing helmets are Etzel's men. The one with the jacket and tie is Mordechai Kaufman.

85

their presence. "Take them away," he told Edelstein. Kaufman was more accommodating and offered the Palmach officer the opportunity to fire several mortar bombs at what he called "the mukhtar's house" (Mahmud Salah's house), in order to stop the shooting from there and enable the evacuation of the wounded. Weg demanded a large-scale map of the village (which he did not receive) and an exact description of the situation, the locations of the wounded and the disposition of the enemy. Not finding the answers he received satisfactory, he decided to explore the village by himself. He went to the center of the village, met with some of the attackers, assessed the situation and returned to his men. He and Vachman reached the conclusion that it was necessary to enter the village and silence the enemy fire if the wounded were to be evacuated. Although contrary to Shaltiel's instructions not to take an active part in the battle, they interpreted their initiative as merely assisting in the evacuation of the wounded.[8]

One of the Palmach combatants, Avraham Zeidenberg, climbed to the roof of the pillbox with the MG 34 and started to shoot at Mahmud Salah's house. Since the MG 34's range was two kilometers, the fire was effective until, after several bursts, the weapon malfunctioned. It was a different story with the mortars. Since the effective range of a 2-inch mortar was less than half a kilometer, they had to move them closer to the village, near the quarries. They were apparently still out of range when Shimon Moneta came to them out of the village with a note from his squad commander "Shell the mukhtar's house." They hesitated about the effectiveness of the mortars at that range, but Weg ordered them to fire three shells at Mahmud Salah's house. The effects of the explosions were primarily psychological, scaring some of the defenders into fleeing. The fire from the building stopped for a while but later resumed. While one of the Arab survivors testified that the mortar fire had caused "almost no harm," others, non-residents, claimed that some inhabitants had been killed.[9]

Weg divided the rest of his men into two squads, sending one of them, under Vachman's command, on the main road into the village to evacuate the wounded. According to his own testimony, Vachman's squad was more engaged in combat than in evacuation.

The Palmach troops cooperated with a group of the attackers in the center of the village and responded, with heavy fire, to some Arab snipers. They were moving forward, hopping from house to house, throwing a hand grenade or two into every house before entering it. The squad advanced rapidly toward the upper, western region of the village, still occupied by Arab fighters, seizing a row of houses belonging to the Khalil and Zaydan families. However, before it managed to reach the western region, they received an order from Shaltiel to leave the village immediately. Vachman took some of the wounded and returned to the pillbox.[10]

Figs. 36 and 37 Moshe Vachman (in Schneller) and Yaakov Weg

The second squad, under Weg's own command, circled around the village from the north, with the intention of reaching the western part of the village from that direction, primarily to reach Mahmud Salah's house. However, Weg, too, did not reach that building. Within less than an hour, he returned with his men to the eastern edge of the village. The Bren gun on Mahmud Salah's house continued to fire and Weg explained that it was not worth destroying the house because of it. Weg returned to Givat Shaul and updated Shaltiel about the developments. Shaltiel did not like the situation at all. He ordered the Palmach to exit the village at once, warning Weg not to intervene in any combat activity but did permit him to supply the attackers with professional advice, if they requested it. Weg remained in the village until 2:30 p.m., advising Lapidot how to prepare for its defense from a counter-attack. Then he returned to Schneller.[11]

THE BATTLE IS OVER

Mahmud Salah's house and the nearby two-house complex of the Radwan family remained the last Arab stronghold in Deir Yassin. Located in the northwestern corner of the village, Salah's house was built on the highest spot in Deir Yassin. It dominated both the center of the village and the main road and hindered the efforts of the attackers to advance into the western part of the village for hours. Muhammad Salah, brother of the late Mahmud, was operating a Bren gun from the roof of the house, supported by some other fighters using rifles. Many of the attackers suffered hits by this fire. According to the original plan, it was up to Lehi's force to seize that house, but because the building was surrounded by open space, the attackers could not approach it, leaving them pinned down about 150 meters to the southeast. The Bren-gunner from Ben-Uziyahu's force returned fire, according to him hitting two snipers, but seemingly with little effect. The house, made of thick solid stone, withstood the Bren shots and later the Palmach's mortar bombs.[12]

When the Palmach's troops left, the Arab defenders were still holding their position, despite suffering from a serious shortage of ammunition. At this stage, Kaufman instructed a final assault on Mahmud Salah's house. The available Etzel combatants divided into three groups. Squad commander Yosef Danoch moved northwest with some men on the road leading to the house. Squad commander Yehoshua Gorodenchik took some men to circle around from the east through the trees, while squad commander Yehuda Treibisch and a few combatants laid down covering fire for them. Treibisch was firing a Bren gun. A charge placed next to the building did little damage. One of the Jewish combatants then placed gelignite sticks on the door, and after it was breached, Danoch entered the house spraying Bren fire. Danoch was injured by counter fire, but the house was finally taken. Three dead Arab males were found in the house, along with a dead woman holding a rifle. It seems that the rest of the defenders

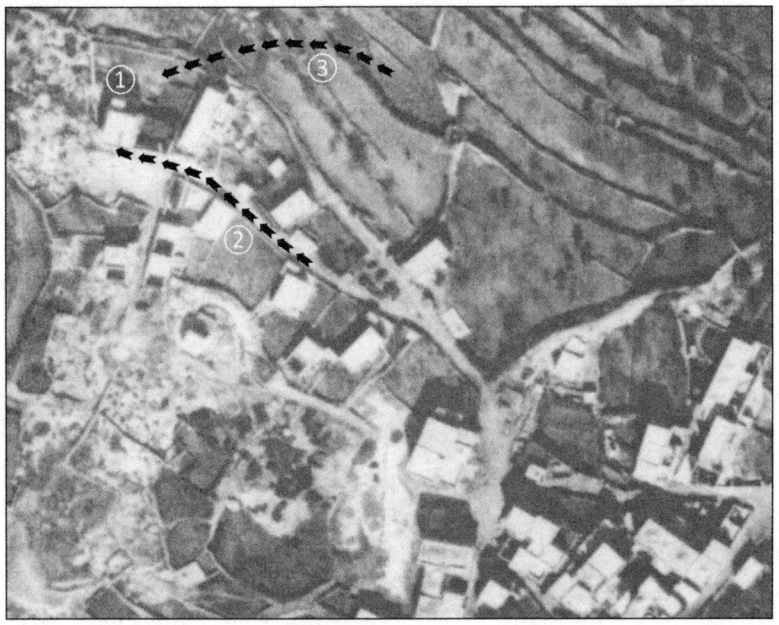

Fig. 38 Western Deir Yassin: 1. Mahmud Salah's house, 2. Danoch's force, 3. Gorodenchik's force

had managed to escape. By 2:00 p.m., Lapidot and Selivansky waved a flag from the roof of the building.[13]

In the early afternoon, the Arab fighters began to retreat from the village as their ammunition ran low. Finally, only nine of them remained, mostly from the Salah and 'Alya families. They, too, soon ran out of ammunition and the fighting stopped. According to most Arab sources, the Arab resistance terminated between 2:00 and 2:30 p.m., after about ten consecutive hours of fighting. Sporadic sniping continued in the hours that followed, mainly from the surrounding hills, dying down only at dusk. Lapidot related that after the battle he was standing on the roof of one of the houses when a bullet suddenly whistled past his ear making him jump down to the yard. For the next two days, Jewish combatants continued to comb the village for hiding Arab fighters.[14]

Altogether, four Etzel combatants were killed during the battle or as a result of it. Gershon Manoah took off his helmet at the beginning of the battle and was shot in the head.[15] Efraim Yaacobi, a member of Treibisch's blocking squad, was killed by 'Ali Qasim and his fellow fighters on the hill south of the village.[16] Squad commander Yehuda Segal, in charge of Etzel's Bren gun, was severely wounded in the stomach by a machine gun burst. He was operated on successfully and on 13 April was supposed to be transferred to Hadassah hospital for further treatment. The convoy he was travelling in was part of the ill-fated Mount Scopus convoy that was attacked by Arabs in Sheikh Jarrah. Although his ambulance managed to escape the attack, the jolting he endured as the vehicle made its escape caused the stiches in his abdomen to open and he died several days later.[17] Amos Baranes was seriously wounded and was not found by his comrades until next day. Suffering from severe blood loss, he was transferred to hospital and died of his wounds several days later.[18] Lehi lost one combatant in the battle, Yosef Yagen who was struck by a bullet in the neck while trying to extricate the loudspeaker car from the trench.[19]

There are differences of opinion regarding the number of Jewish casualties from the battle. In a 1971 letter to Menachem Begin, Yitzhak Levy, the Haganah's intelligence chief in Jerusalem in 1948, claimed that only ten Jewish fighters were wounded in the battle. There are no sources, reliable or otherwise, which corroborate this figure. On the other hand, in a speech he gave in November 1948 in New York, Kaufman claimed that 57 were injured (and eight killed), which was definitely an exaggeration.[20] Most Jewish sources indicated the number of combatants injured to be slightly more than 30, almost certainly 32. Those supporting this figure include Levy himself (in a report he circulated on 12 April), Kaufman (in a testimony he gave in 1952), a broadcast of *Kol Zion ha-Lohemet*, Etzel's broadcasting station (on 11 April), a poster issued by Etzel following the attack, some of the newspapers published on the Sunday morning, the Jewish Agency's *Digest*, and Lapidot (in an interview to the author).[21] There were some sources, however, which raised the number of Jewish combatants injured to almost, about, or exactly 40. These included Begin, Cohen, Lapidot (in a testimony he gave the authors of *O Jerusalem!* in the late 1960s), Etzel member Yehoshua Ofir, Meir Avizohar, an officer in the Moriah battalion, and the *New York Times*.[22] When one considers of all the available evidence, one may safely conclude that the number of combatants injured was between 30 and 40, more probably closer to the lower number. Given that the total number of attackers was about 120, then the attacking forces took about 30 percent casualties. Of these, Etzel suffered the majority, not necessarily because Lehi's combatants were better trained in this kind of fighting (they were not), but probably because the Etzel combatants fought in a more densely popu-lated area. Most of Etzel's

Fig. 39 Etzel's physician Leon Farhi dressing Dvorah Simhon, an Etzel female paramedic injured while evacuating the wounded

commanders were injured in the early stage of the attack, including the force's overall commander, Cohen, and Michael Harif, one of his deputies. In addition, some of their squad commanders were also injured during the battle. In the end, the only senior Etzel commander in the field who was left unscathed was Lapidot.

In the final hours of the attack, the Etzel and Lehi forces began to loot the village, a task they continued with greater vigor after the battle ended. As explained earlier, looting was not a random con-sequence of the attack, but explicitly one of the motives for it. The underground's bases needed supplies and Deir Yassin was a prosper-ous village. It was also their intention to distribute some of the booty in the poor neighborhoods of Jerusalem, which were suffering from hunger due to the Arab siege. The fighters were looking primarily for flour, sugar, pulses, cooking oil, petrol and other essentials, of which they found large quantities. They also collected all the available cattle, some sheep, a herd of goats, and hens. The houses were stripped of housewares and the village shops were emptied of their products. In some of the houses, large sums of money were found (hundreds of gold pounds, according to one version). Some of the women prison-ers offered their captors money as ransom for the lives of their sons. The attackers took all jewelry from the women captives. When the prisoners were taken to Arab Jerusalem (see below), the trucks carrying them stopped at Givat Shaul, where a blanket was unfolded on the ground and two women combatants ordered the women to throw all their valuables onto it. Body searches were also carried out.

Figs. 40 and 41 A pocket watch looted by Yehoshua Goldschmidt and given as a gift to his father. The inscription says: "A souvenir for a dear father from a loving son, Yehoshua, Passover Tashah [1948]."

The plundering of the village continued on Saturday.[23]

Goldschmidt and a representative of Lehi distributed the spoils equally between the two organizations who transferred it to their respective bases in Jerusalem. Some of the booty was divided among their supporters in the poor neighborhoods of Jerusalem. It seems that some of the fighters took money and small items for themselves. The Palmach combatants also took their share of the spoil, bringing with them chickens and other articles when they returned to their base. Three days later, when the Haganah took over the village, Solel Boneh (the construction company of the major Jewish labor union, Histadrut, with which the Haganah was connected), arrived and took the crushers and construction materials.[24]

During Friday, in response to rumors, local and foreign journalists arrived at Givat Shaul to investigate. Their efforts to enter the village to seek information prompted the decision of Kalman Bergman, head of Etzel's intelligence in Jerusalem, to hold a press conference. Kaufman agreed, but told Bergman that he was too tired to attend it in person and asked him to substitute for him. Only American and Jewish correspondents were invited to the conference, British journalist being excluded by the organizers, who considered them "untrustworthy." Etzel telephoned selected reporters to invite them to the conference, and that evening they were taken by car to the house of Yehoshua Goldschmidt in Givat Shaul. Armed combatants surrounded the house and the journalists were led inside to meet with Bergman and a Lehi representative. Attending were Dana Adams Schmidt of the *New York Times*, Fitzhugh Turner of the *New York Herald Tribune*, the correspondent of the Associated Press and several others. Over tea and cookies, they listened to Bergman's statement.[25]

Bergman explained that Etzel and Lehi had launched the operation because of the repeated provocations of the residents of Deir Yassin against their Jewish neighbors. It was more than just an attempt to teach the Arabs a lesson or a move to forestall a possible attack by local Arabs, assisted by Syrians and Iraqis, on western Jerusalem; it was also the first step of a new policy. "We intend to attack, conquer, and keep until we have the whole of Palestine and Transjordan in a Greater Jewish State." One hundred combatants had taken part in the attack, which had been carried out with the knowledge of the Haganah. Although the attackers had been ordered not to harm women and children, the fact that the village was well fortified and offered resistance (by two hundred armed men), meant that they had had no choice but to demolish houses with explosives, blast down doors, and throw hand grenades into the houses. This had resulted in "a good many civilian casualties," which was unfortunate but inevitable under the circumstances. Two hundred Arabs had been killed, half of them women and children, two hundred were wounded and 140 were transferred to Arab Jerusalem. The rest escaped. "We hope to improve our methods in future and to make it possible to spare women and children." Bergman also mentioned the Jewish casualties and concluded that, while it was their intention to deliver the village to the Haganah, "if the British come, we shall fight them." After a few questions, the conference ended, with the journalists taken back to where they came from, without being permitted to tour the village. Years later, Schmidt would observe that at the time, none of the journalists present realized the significance of the story.[26]

Chapter 6

The Toll

HOW MANY ARABS WERE KILLED?

In the press conference held by Etzel and Lehi following the attack, Bergman reported that the number of Arabs killed was 200. This figure was an invention, not of Bergman but Kaufman, who had asked Bergman to stand in for him at the event. In fact, Kaufman did not know how many Arabs had been killed, as nobody had bothered to count them. He had estimated the number to be between 100 and 150, but decided to report a higher number in order to intimidate the Palestinian Arabs psychologically. Bergman's words soon reached the ears of the High Commissioner and his staff, and were made public that night by the BBC, and the next day by the *Times* and the *New York Times*.[1] Kaufman further inflated the number to 240 in a 7:00 p.m. report by radio to Etzel's headquarters in Tel Aviv. The report and the figure were soon to be cited by *Kol Zion ha-Lohemet*, Etzel's broadcasting station, and by some of the Sunday morning newspapers. One of them, *ha-Mashqif*, aligned with the Revisionist Party (and consequently with Etzel), added that according to "Etzel and Lehi circles," 245 Arabs were killed.[2]

When the first escapees from Deir Yassin to 'Ayn Karm arrived in Arab Jerusalem, they told Husayn al-Khalidi, secretary of the Arab Higher Committee, that 400 villagers were killed. Because of the chaos that existed, they believed all unaccounted for persons that had been killed, including those taken prisoner. The estimate was quickly reduced, especially after the arrival of the prisoners (see below), but on Saturday Khalidi still believed that 250 people had been killed. On Sunday, 11 April, Khalidi met with Jacques de Reynier, the representative of the Red Cross in Jerusalem, who had just returned from a visit to Deir Yassin. De Reynier told him that 150 bodies had been thrown into an excavation, though he admitted that he had not witnessed it with his own eyes. He had seen 40 to 50 bodies, and had been told that a further 50 bodies were scattered around the village. In the evening Khalidi convened his own press conference and announced that 250 Arabs had been killed. His claim was circulated throughout Palestine by Arab broadcasts and the Arab press, and was cited the next day by the *New York Times*. Khalidi was also quoted the next morning by the *Palestine Post*, as if having said that 254 Arabs were killed, following which the *New York Times* revised its number for the third time, publishing the next day the 254 figure.[3] The 254 number became the most cited figure in the literature about Deir Yassin for the next four decades,[4] with the 240, 245 and 250 figures sharing second place.[5]

When the Palestinian researchers Sharif Kana'na and Nihad Zaytawi established in 1986 that 107 people – less than half of the accepted figure – had been killed, it came as a surprise to the scholarly community and, perhaps, to the rest of the world, but not to the survivors. They had always known that the real number of villagers killed was much lower than the accepted estimates. After the first few days of confusion, Deir Yassin's surviving notables had counted the number of those killed as approximately 100. Some of them told the Palestinian historian 'Arif al-'Arif that 110 were killed, while Bahjat Abu Gharbiyya, a commander in the Army of Sacred Jihad who had met with the first fugitives, determined the number to be around 90. Over the years, many of the survivors gave evidence about the number of those killed. Muhammad Mahmud As'ad

Radwan stated he possessed a list of 93 names, checked "with the utmost scrutiny," yet when the list was published by his cousin Da'ud Ahmad As'ad Radwan in the latter's memoirs, it actually included 96 names. Muhammad 'Arif Sammur spoke of 94 people killed. In a later interview, he related that several days after the attack the heads of the clans met in Jerusalem and made a list of 116 people missing. Khalil Sammur had a list of 94 names. Khumays Zaydan testified that 96 had been killed. Mahfuz Sammur mentioned 99 names in a booklet he wrote. 'Abd al-Qadir Zaydan related that he and other survivors counted 105 people killed. 'Ayish Muhammad 'Ayish Zaydan gave the same number, although he later rounded it to 110, while his father said 106.[6]

The Haganah, too, knew immediately after the fighting ended that the number of Arabs killed was just over 100. Gicherman, who had toured the village after the battle, related that there were four concentrations of bodies, with 20 bodies each, and additional few dozen bodies in a quarry. A Haganah's intelligence officer who visited the village the next morning reported 80 bodies. The very same day the Haganah received information from an Arab source that the number of the Arabs killed was about 100. Yehoshua Arieli, who later handled the burial operation for the Haganah, also related that they had buried some 70 bodies in a mass grave and the blowing up of houses over two concentrations of 20 bodies each, altogether about 110 bodies. In another interview, Arieli talked about 120 bodies buried, possibly more, up to 140, but he was not sure about the exact number.[7]

It seems that the only way to ascertain the exact number of people killed in Deir Yassin is to prepare a complete list of all the people who died there. Several attempts to prepare such lists have been made in the past. The present list is based on fourteen such lists. It comprises people that answered at least one of the three following criteria:

1. The exact circumstances of death were known – this is definitely the most reliable criterion.
2. The person's name appeared in a considerable number of former lists. (One must bear in mind, though, that some of

these lists were based on previous one, as detailed below, in which case a name appearing in two such lists is only counted once.)

3. The person appeared in the lists and in the genealogical trees of Deir Yassin's families brought by Kana'na and Zaytawi, which at least implied that the person really existed (this criterion could only apply to adult males; see above).

People were not entered into the list, even if they answered one of these criteria, where there was clear evidence that they had survived (for example, they were hospitalized and recovered). The lists used were as follows:

1. The list published by *al-Difa'*, one of the two Palestinian 1948 dailies, three days after the attack, comprising 106 names. There was still much confusion, and according to Kana'na some of the people mentioned there were still alive many years later.[8]

2. A list prepared by Khalil Muhammad Sammur, son of the mukhtar, comprising 94 names. Some of the people whose names appear at the end of the list died later, rather than at Deir Yassin.[9]

3. Names of 87 people from Deir Yassin collected from 'Arif al-'Arif's general list of Arabs killed in the 1948 war, (although 'Arif had mistakenly stated that he had 91 names from Deir Yassin).[10]

4. A list of 59 names prepared by the Palestinian historian and journalist 'Arafat Hijazi, defined by him as "killed during the resistance fighting against the deceitful forces." He claims an additional 250 non-combatants killed without providing names.[11]

5. A list compiled by the Palestinian journal *Sawt al-Bilad* on the 37th anniversary of the event, comprising 75 people, not all of them identified by name.[12]

6. A handwritten list posted on the Internet site of Birzeit University Palestine Archive, comprising 107 names. Some of

the materials which served as basis for Kana'na and Zaytawi's project (see next item) were posted there.[13]

7. The list prepared by Kana'na and Zaytawi ("the most accurate list of its kind hitherto"), comprising 107 names. In 1984 Kana'na was appointed director of the Research and Documentation Center in Birzeit University and embarked on a project to anthropologically document the Palestinian villages destroyed in 1948. Deir Yassin was the fourth village investigated. His list was based on four sources: the *al-Difa'* list, 'Arif's list, a list prepared by Sa'id Sammur, and information collected in interviews with survivors.[14]

8. Kana'na's project served as one of the sources for Walid Khalidi's 1992 *All That Remains*, which documented the Palestinian villages depopulated in 1948. The Arabic version of that book, *Kay la Nansa* (So We Would Not Forget), published in 1997, included an appendix listing all the Palestinians killed in the 1948 war, divided into villages. The list for Deir Yassin comprised the names of 107 Arabs killed, identical to Kana'na's list, though sorted according to surnames, with the addition of two Arabs who had been injured.[15]

9. In 1999, Khalidi published a major work about Deir Yassin, which included partial genealogical trees of its families, underscoring the names of 100 Arabs killed. He based his findings on many testimonies of survivors and materials supplied to him by Yusuf Ahmad As'ad Radwan.[16]

10. A list in a booklet on Deir Yassin written by the Palestinian historian 'Abbas Nimr and published by the Islamic heritage department in the Ministry of Awqaf of the Palestinian Authority, comprising 106 names.[17]

11. A list delivered by Mustafa Hamida, chairman of *Jam'iyyat Dayr Yasin al-Khayriyya* (Deir Yassin's charitable organization), to the Palestinian journalist Wadi' 'Awawda, comprising 93 names.[18]

12. A list included in an online booklet on Deir Yassin, published by an association commemorating the 1948 *Nakba*, comprising 102 names.[19]

13. A list prepared by the Palestinian researcher Fadi Salayima ("the most accurate written") for a book he wrote about Deir Yassin, comprising 115 names. The list was identical to that of Kana'na and Zaytawi, with the addition of eight other people at the end.[20]

14. A list prepared by the survivor Muhammad Mahmud As'ad Radwan ("with the utmost scrutiny") and published by another survivor, his cousin Da'ud Ahmad As'ad Radwan, in his memoirs, comprising 96 names.[21]

Cross-referencing data from all fourteen lists, and applying the above-mentioned criteria for inclusion, yielded the following list (all the married women were entered according to the surname of their husbands):

Name	1	2	3	4	5	6	7	8	9	10	11	12	13	14
1. 'Alya, 'Isa Ahmad Yusuf	+	+	+	+	+	+	+	+	+	+	+	+	+	+
2. 'Alya, Muhammad 'Isa Ahmad					+	+			+	+	+	+		+
3. 'Alya, Yusuf Ahmad Yusuf	+	+	+	+	+	+	+	+	+	+	+	+	+	+
4. 'Atiyya, Amina Husayn al-Kawbariyya	+	+	+	+		+	+	+	+	+	+	+	+	+
5. 'Atiyya, 'Ayisha Radwan	+	+	+	+	+	+		+	+	+	+	+	+	
6. 'Atiyya, Isma'il	+	+	+	+	+	+	+	+	+	+	+	+	+	
7. 'Atiyya, Mahmud Muhammad Isma'il	+	+		+	+		+	+	+	+	+	+	+	
8. 'Atiyya, Muhammad Isma'il	+	+	+	+	+	+	+	+	+	+		+	+	+
9. 'Atiyya, Musa Muhammad Isma'il	+	+	+	+	+	+	+	+		+	+	+	+	
10. 'Atiyya, Rubhi Isma'il	+	+	+	+			+	+	+	+	+	+	+	+

Name	1	2	3	4	5	6	7	8	9	10	11	12	13	14
11. 'Atiyya, Sara al-Kawbariyya	+	+	+	+	+		+	+	+	+	+	+	+	+
12. Balabsa, Hayat	+	+	+	+	+	+	+	+	+	+	+	+	+	+
13. Farhan, Hasan Ya'qub Muhammad 'Ali				+		+	+	+				+		
14. Hamdan, Mahmud Muhammad Jawda	+	+	+	+	+	+	+	+	+	+	+	+	+	+
15. Hamdan, Muhammad Jawda	+	+	+	+		+	+	+	+	+	+	+	+	+
16. Hamida, 'Abd al-Rahman Husayn	+		+			+	+	+	+	+	+	+	+	
17. Hamida, 'Ali 'Abd al-Rahim	+					+	+	+				+		
18. Hamida, 'Ali Husayn 'Ali	+					+	+	+	+	+		+		
19. Hamida, Hamid 'Abdallah	+					+			+	+				+
20. Hamida, Fatima Salih	+					+			+					+
21. 'Id, 'Ali Khalil	+	+	+	+	+	+	+	+	+	+			+	+
22. 'Id, 'Isa Muhammad 'Isa	+	+	+	+	+	+	+	+	+	+	+	+	+	+
23. 'Id, Isma'il Muhammad Khalil	+	+	+	+	+	+	+	+	+	+	+	+	+	+
24. 'Id, Isma'il Shakir Mustafa	+					+	+	+	+	+	+	+	+	+
25. 'Id, Jamil 'Isa Muhammad	+	+	+	+	+	+	+	+	+	+	+	+	+	+
26. 'Id, Salihiyya Muhammad 'Isa	+	+	+	+	+	+	+	+	+	+	+	+	+	+
27. Jabir, Ahmad Hasan	+	+	+	+	+	+	+	+	+	+	+	+	+	+
28. Jabir, Fu'ad Khalil	+	+	+	+		+	+	+	+	+	+	+	+	+

Name	1	2	3	4	5	6	7	8	9	10	11	12	13	14
29. Jabir, Jabir Mustafa	+	+	+	+	+	+	+	+	+	+	+	+	+	+
30. Jabir, Jabr Tawfiq Jabr	+	+	+	+	+		+	+	+	+	+	+	+	+
31. Jabir, Khalil Mustafa	+	+	+	+	+	+	+	+	+	+	+	+	+	+
32. Jabir, Mahmud Mustafa	+	+	+	+	+	+	+	+	+		+	+	+	+
33. Jabir, Muhammad Khalil Mustafa	+		+			+	+	+	+	+			+	+
34. Jabir, Sa'id Muhammad Sa'id	+	+	+			+	+	+		+	+	+	+	+
35. Jabir, Salim Muhammad Isma'il	+	+	+	+	+	+	+	+	+	+	+	+	+	+
36. Jabir, Tawfiq Jabr	+	+	+		+	+	+	+	+	+		+	+	+
37. Khalil, 'Ayish	+	+	+	+	+	+	+	+	+	+	+	+	+	+
38. Khalil, Hilwa Zaydan	+	+	+		+	+	+	+	+	+	+	+	+	+
39. Khalil, Muhammad 'Ali	+	+	+	+	+	+	+	+	+	+	+	+	+	
40. Khalil, Muhammad 'Ayish	+	+	+	+	+	+	+	+	+	+	+	+	+	+
41. Khalil, Zarifa Muhammad 'Ali	+						+	+					+	+
42. Muslih, 'Ali Husayn		+	+	+		+	+	+		+	+	+	+	
43. Muslih, 'Aziza	+	+	+	+		+	+	+	+	+	+	+	+	+
44. Muslih, Muhammad 'Ali Hasan	+	+	+	+	+	+	+	+	+	+	+	+	+	+
45. Muslih, Watfa Muhammad 'Ali Hasan		+	+			+	+	+		+	+	+	+	
46. Radwan, As'ad	+	+	+	+	+	+	+	+	+	+	+	+	+	+
47. Radwan, Muhammad As'ad			+	+		+				+	+	+		

Name	1	2	3	4	5	6	7	8	9	10	11	12	13	14
48. Radwan, Radwan As'ad	+	+	+	+		+	+	+	+	+	+	+	+	+
49. Radwan, Sabha	+	+	+	+	+	+	+	+	+		+	+	+	+
50. Radwan, 'Umar Ahmad As'ad	+	+	+			+			+	+	+	+		+
51. Sammur, 'Abdallah 'Abd al-Majid	+	+	+	+	+	+	+	+	+	+	+	+	+	+
52. Sammur, Fiddiyya Isma'il al-Qaryutiyya		+	+	+		+	+	+	+	+	+	+	+	+
53. Sammur, Husayn Isma'il Muhammad	+	+	+	+		+	+	+	+	+	+	+	+	+
54. Sammur, Mansur 'Abd al-'Aziz		+	+	+	+	+	+		+			+		
55. Sammur, Muhammad Mahmud Isma'il	+	+	+	+	+	+	+	+	+	+	+	+	+	+
56. Sammur, Musa Isma'il	+	+	+	+	+	+	+	+	+	+	+	+	+	+
57. Sammur, Najma Isma'il	+	+	+	+		+	+	+	+		+	+	+	+
58. Sammur, Sammur Khalil Muhammad	+	+	+	+			+	+	+	+	+	+	+	+
59. Sharif, 'Abd al-Ra'uf Husayn		+				+			+	+	+	+		+
60. Sharif, Husayn		+	+			+	+	+	+	+	+	+	+	+
61. Zahran, 'Ali Muhammad	+	+	+	+	+	+	+	+	+	+	+	+	+	+
62. Zahran, Basma As'ad Radwan	+	+	+	+		+	+	+	+	+	+	+	+	+
63. Zahran, Fathi Jum'a	+	+	+		+	+	+	+	+	+	+	+	+	+
64. Zahran, Fathiyya Jum'a			+			+	+	+		+	+	+	+	

Name	1	2	3	4	5	6	7	8	9	10	11	12	13	14
65. Zahran, Fatima Isma'il 'Atiyya	+	+	+			+	+	+	+	+	+	+	+	+
66. Zahran, Fatima Jum'a	+	+	+	+		+	+	+	+	+	+	+	+	+
67. Zahran, Fatima Muhammad 'Id	+	+	+	+		+	+	+	+	+	+	+	+	+
68. Zahran, Hamda						+		+	+					+
69. Zahran, Muhammad	+	+	+		+	+	+	+	+	+	+	+	+	+
70. Zahran, Muhammad 'Ali	+	+	+			+	+	+	+			+	+	+
71. Zahran, Muhammad Mahmud	+	+	+			+	+	+	+	+	+	+	+	+
72. Zahran, Muhammad Musa	+	+	+	+	+	+	+	+	+	+	+	+	+	+
73. Zahran, Nazmi Ahmad	+	+				+	+	+	+	+	+	+	+	+
74. Zahran, Nazmiyya Ahmad	+	+	+			+		+	+	+	+			+
75. Zahran, Rasmiyya Jum'a		+				+		+		+	+			+
76. Zahran, Rasmiyya Musa	+	+				+	+	+	+	+	+	+	+	+
77. Zahran, Ruqya 'Ilyan al-Subaniyya	+	+	+	+	+	+	+	+	+	+	+	+	+	+
78. Zahran, Safiyya Jum'a		+	+			+			+	+	+			+
79. Zahran, Sa'id Musa		+	+			+	+	+	+	+	+	+	+	+
80. Zahran, Samiha Ahmad	+	+	+			+	+	+	+	+	+	+	+	+
81. Zahran, Yusra Jum'a						+				+	+			

Name	1	2	3	4	5	6	7	8	9	10	11	12	13	14
82. Zahran, Zaynab Jum'a	+					+	+		+			+		
83. Zahran, Zaynab Muhammad Husayn al-Malihiyya			+	+		+	+	+	+	+	+	+	+	+
84. Zahran, Zaynab Musa Muhammad			+			+				+	+	+		
85. Zaydan, 'Ali Hasan 'Ali	+	+	+	+	+	+	+	+	+	+	+	+	+	
86. Zaydan, Amina 'Ali Mustafa			+			+	+		+			+		
87. Zaydan, Amina al-Baytuniyya					?	+			+	+				
88. Zaydan, 'Ayida al-'Umuriyya	+	+	+	+	+	+	+	+	+	+	+	+	+	+
89. Zaydan, 'Aziza 'Ali Mustafa	+					+	+	+	+	+			+	+
90. Zaydan, Fatima Sammur	+	+	+	+	+	+	+	+	+	+	+	+	+	+
91. Zaydan, Hasan 'Ali	+	+	+	+	+	+	+	+	+	+	+	+	+	+
92. Zaydan, Khudra al-Baytuniyya	+	+	+	+	?		+	+				+	+	
93. Zaydan, Mahmud 'Ali Mustafa	+	+	+			+	+	+	+	+		+	+	+
94. Zaydan, Mustafa 'Ali	+	+	+	+	+	+	+	+	+	+	+	+	+	+
95. Zaydan, Muyassar Musa Mustafa	+	+				+	+	+			+	+	+	
96. Zaydan, Ni'ma 'Ali Mustafa		+			+				+		+			+
97. Zaydan, Samiyya Musa Mustafa											+	+	+	

Name	1	2	3	4	5	6	7	8	9	10	11	12	13	14
98. Zaydan, Shafiq Musa Mustafa	+	+				+	+	+	+	+	+	+	+	+
99. Zaydan, Shafiqa Musa Mustafa		+	+			+	+	+	+	+	+	+	+	+
100. Zaydan, Tamam Muhammad ʿAli Hasan Muslih	+	+	+	+		+	+	+	+	+	+	+	+	+
101. Zaydan, Yusra Musa Mustafa	+	+	+			+	+	+	+		+	+	+	+

While it is possible to establish the approximate number of those killed in Deir Yassin, it is more difficult to determine the number of those injured. This question, of how many were injured in Deir Yassin is of crucial importance. Matthew Hogan and Daniel McGowan, leading advocates of the massacre narrative, claimed that the low number of Arabs injured, in comparison with those killed, was evidence of a massacre. Based on a list of twelve Arabs hospitalized for injuries, published by Kanaʿna and Zaytawi in addition to their list of 107 Arabs killed, Hogan and McGowan claimed that such a proportion (1:9, or 2 percent of the entire population, according to their calculation), attested to a massacre. They asserted that, in a battle, the number of those injured would have been significantly higher. In the chaos of a real battle, the injured would be scattered everywhere, but, they claimed, Etzel and Lehi had intended to kill and not leave the wounded alive. When one intends to commit a massacre, one continues to shoot until death is verified.[22]

However, Hogan and McGowan's figure of twelve people injured (based on Kanaʿna and Zaytawi's list), only includes those seriously wounded by bullets and shrapnel and hospitalized in the government hospital in the Russian Compound. Although the figure of 200 Arabs wounded, stated in the press conference held by the underground organizations after the battle, and later cited by Arthur Creech-Jones, the British Secretary of State for the Colonies, was inflated, the total number of the injured was much higher than

Hogan and McGowan's estimate. Apparently, in addition to these twelve seriously wounded, there were dozens of others. Furthermore, casualties were treated in other locations as well. A nurse, working at the time in the government hospital, recounted that tens of injured people were brought to her hospital. Other Arabs casualties were admitted to the local hospital in the village of Bayt Safafa, which only had limited facilities. Still others were treated for their wounds in 'Ayn Karm. [23]

The Red Cross representative reported to Geneva that more than 50 out of the 150 Arabs prisoner had been wounded. In his personal diary, however, he wrote that the number of wounded was between 60 and 70. Senior Lehi member, David Gottlieb, related that some of the prisoners' wounds had been dressed by the Jewish combatants before they were evacuated to Arab Jerusalem. This figure of 50 to 70 was came to be cited by some as the total number of injured in Deir Yassin, although it actually related only to the number of injured prisoners. There were other Arabs injured, both fighters injured in battle (like 'Ali Qasim), including women who took part in the fighting, and non-combatants. The latter, mainly women and children, were mainly hurt by the hand grenades thrown into the houses. Some of the injured non-combatants who had fled to 'Ayn Karm were later transferred to the hospital in Bayt Safafa. Ten days after the fighting, the social affairs committee of the Jerusalem National Committee wrote to the Arab Higher Committee informing it that they had quite a few injured survivors to provide for. Considering all these factors, one may suggest that the number of those injured in Deir Yassin was similar to that of those killed.[24]

The following table compares the casualty figures of the villagers and the attackers:

	Total	Dead	Percentage of total	Injured	Percentage of total
Villagers	c 1,000	101	10	c 100	10
Attackers	120+	5	4	30+	c 25

HOW DID THEY MEET THEIR DEATHS?

Due to Etzel's insistence on avoiding unnecessary bloodshed, it was decided to use a loudspeaker car to warn the Arabs to evacuate the village before the attack, a fact that, alone, rules out the possibility of a premeditated massacre. Despite their efforts, many non-combatant villagers were killed during the attack, including children, women, and old people, mostly indoors. As explained earlier, the villagers inside the houses had little chance to survive the three-phased method of the attackers of consecutively using explosives, hand grenades and automatic fire when breaking into the houses. The following is an interview held many years later with one of the survivors, Muhammad 'Ayish Zaydan:

> Q: It is said that they killed women, men, and small children.
>
> A: It is all lies. They only killed men. The women were killed under the debris. The houses crumbled over them.
>
> Q: They demolished houses over people?
>
> A: Yes, they demolished four or five houses.
>
> Q: It is said that they killed children in the arms of their mothers and pregnant women.
>
> A: It's a lie.
>
> Q: You mean that it did not happen?
>
> A: They did not kill women. They did not kill small children. Only men above the age of 15 or 16.[25]

The Arab combatants were fighting the Jewish fighters "from house to house and from street to street," as one of them put it. In contrast to battles as that at Qastal, the battle for Deir Yassin took place in the presence of a non-combatant population. Combatants and non-combatants lived in the same houses. In many instances, the heads of the families, with their sons or other relatives, would shoot at the attackers from within the houses, in the presence of the rest of their families. The Jewish combatants would return fire, not always correctly identifying the sources of enemy shots. "I believe that most of those who were killed were among the fighters and the women and children who helped the fighters," another survivor recounted. Other Arabs were killed by crossfire when trying to escape. Cohen was to

Fig. 42 Yehoshua Zettler addressing Lehi members. Behind him is a photo of Lehi's founder, Avraham Stern, killed by the British in 1942, and a map of Jerusalem.

explain that at the first phase of the battle they shot everyone standing before them in order to avoid being attacked from the rear once they had passed. Zettler later explained that although the original intention was to avoid the killing of women and children, circumstances made it inevitable. It became a matter of life and death for the attackers ("If he lives, I will die"). "The moment the inhabitants of Deir Yassin resolved to fight, they determined their fate," he added.[26]

The Zahran family, living in a four-house complex in the northeastern edge of the village, was to suffer most from this course of events. Some Arab and foreign sources claimed that 35 members of the family were lined up against a wall and shot. The reality was quite different. In an early stage of the battle, Lehi's force, advancing from the north, approached the complex. Aged Muhammad Zahran, two of his sons and a grandson, defended the houses. After a heavy exchange of fire, Lehi's combatants threw hand grenades into the complex and burst in firing automatic weapons. Twenty-four members of the family were killed in the assault, the grandfather and his grandson included. The two brothers managed to escape.[27]

The story of Mustafa 'Ali Zaydan and his family was completely different, and formed the basis for the stories about people being lined up against walls and shot. Mustafa had two married sons, 'Ali and Musa, each with large families. They all lived in a three-house complex near the eastern crossroad of the village center. They were about to flee the village when Etzel combatants approached the complex. 'Ali threw a hand grenade at them. They shot back and wounded him in his shoulder. He shouted to his family to leave the house and then ran away. His elder son, Mahmud, went out to assess the situation, but returned immediately telling the others that there was nowhere to run to as the Jews had surrounded them. They hid in the house and were soon joined by Musa and his family, who told them that their grandfather was already dead. After a while, Etzel combatants ordered them to open the door or else they would blow up the building. When they refused to open, the Etzel men blew the door down and ordered them out. Not far from the house, Etzel's machine-gunner, Yehuda Segal, was lying severely wounded. A young Etzel combatant holding a Bren gun was standing near him. When the family came out with their hands up, the Etzel man squeezed the trigger shouting, "This is for Yiftah" (Segal's code name in Etzel). The Arabs were hit, some being killed and others wounded. Kaufman, who attended the scene, shouted at him: "What have you done..." "One of them held a rifle and was about to shoot," he answered. Other Etzel combatants present confirmed his words.[28]

One may doubt the combatant's excuse and wonder why he should exclaim, "This is for Yiftah," if he was acting in self-defense, and not for revenge. In any case, the immediate result of the incident was that other families refused to surrender fearing for their lives. The incident, however, had more far-reaching consequences. Many had seen it. Zaynab 'Atiyya, living in the center of the village, heard the shots and shouts and could see the entire episode from her second floor window. Twenty-seven people they killed there, she was to say. In fact, 11 people were killed in this incident (and 17 from the entire Zaydan family). However, the story soon spread not just in Palestine, but also in the Arab world and beyond. Fahima, a daughter of 'Ali, survived the shooting and was being treated for a chest wound in the government hospital when an Associated Press correspondent interviewed her and heard her version of the story. The story of the Zaydan family would serve as a major proof for allegations of shooting villagers against the walls and the massacre narrative.[29]

Several years later squad commander Yehoshua Gorodenchik gave testimony that a group of 80 Arab prisoners was killed, after they had opened fire and killed one of the Jewish combatants who approached them to deliver first aid. The proponents of the massacre narrative used his testimony as a proof that even one of Etzel's commanders admitted to there having been a massacre.[30] None of them ever bothered to question the feasibility of 80 people being killed in a single incident in Deir Yassin, even when it became clear, following Kana'na and Zaytawi's research, that the total number of villagers killed was just over 100. Furthermore, no Jewish combatant was killed in the circumstances described in Gorodenchik's testimony and the most severe multi-casualty incident of the day was the death of the 24 members of the Zahran family.[31]

Nevertheless, it seems that a few, a very few, prisoners were killed during the battle. In his testimony, for what it was worth, Gorodenchik also said that when that Etzel was contemplating retreat, some wounded prisoners were killed. A Lehi member, not actually present during the battle, claimed that one guard, fearing that he was going to be surrounded by Arabs, killed two to three prisoners. An unnamed witness reported two wounded Arab combatants found in Mahmud Salah's house, "whom we assisted in getting rid of the pains." One Arab combatant attempted to leave the village with the female prisoners, trying to board a truck disguised as a woman. He was identified by Etzel combatants as a sniper and was shot dead. Another combatant disguised as a woman was more successful in boarding one of the trucks, but when the trucks arrived in Givat Shaul, the women were searched for valuables. He was identified by Lehi men as "a notorious gang member" and shot. There also were stories of children or youngsters killed in the arms of their mothers. One seems to have been true, that of the teenager Fu'ad Khalil Jabir, whose mother lost her mind due to suffering the ordeal. Other stories were clearly imaginary, like Gicherman's account of the mukhtar's son being killed after the battle in front of his mother. This could not be true for at least two reasons: none of the mukhtar's sons was killed, while their mother, on the other hand, was killed during the fighting.[32]

One of the more controversial issues related to the massacre narrative is the allegation that the Jewish combatants executed Arabs in the quarries. The gist of the story is that a group of male prisoners, apparently captured fighters, was taken by truck on a victory parade in Jerusalem and then returned to the village and executed. The number of those allegedly executed ranged between seven through fourteen, twenty-one and twenty-five to forty. The problem with this accusation is that none of the Arabs reporting the shooting saw it with his own eyes. Muhammad Mahmud Radwan, who in one interview claimed to have seen it himself, admitted on other occasions that he did not, because at the time of the alleged event he was fighting in the western side of the village. Jamil Ahmad 'Alya, who lived near the quarries, also claimed to see it, but could recall only two names of the victims, one of whom really died on the other side of the village, while being attended to by Hayat al-Balabsa before she was killed. Gicherman, too, reported the episode, but he arrived at the village after the battle. Kaufman, on the other hand, denied any such execution, as did Yonah Ben-Sasson, the Haganah's regional commander, while Lapidot insisted that no truck with prisoners ever returned to the village. Actually, the Arabs themselves were not sure about the returning truck element of the story. The only one to claim to be personally present at the executions was Meir Pa'il, whose testimonies will be discussed later on. In fact, some of the Arabs based their testimonies on his.[33]

A problem for the historian of these events is the prevalence of hearsay evidence among the survivors of Deir Yassin. In an interview on the 50th anniversary of the incident, Muhammad Mahmud Radwan admitted that he did not see cold-blooded killing, just bodies riddled with bullets. "I did not see them actually slaughtering women or children in front of me." When the interviewer asked another interviewee on the same occasion if anybody saw the Jews spraying people with bullets in the quarries, the answer was "Whoever was busy in a battle could not see." A third interviewee, describing the death of the Zahrans, was asked if he had actually witnessed it, to which he answered: "I was in the western side of the village but we heard the heavy firing from the other edge." These kind of answers was not limited to Arabs. Gideon Sarig had come with the Palmach force, but remained with its armored cars near the pillbox at a distance of 500 to 600 meters from the first houses of the village. In an interview, he was to relate, "I saw with my own eyes that Arabs had been shot after they had surrendered." Then, just a few sentences later, he added, "I did not really see them shooting Arabs, but it is inconceivable that they shot for nothing, since ammunition was scarce."[34]

Unlike Sarig, Moshe Vachman actually entered the village. "I saw the killing, not just the dead," he said, "and not just in circumstances necessitated by the fighting." He asked one of the commanders for explanations. "We have men injured and killed, and we are not going to finish it otherwise," he answered. "I do not know what the definition of massacre is," Vachman was to say many years later, "but we saw them killing Arabs and using them as a human shield around the stretchers with the wounded." Nonetheless, another Palmach man was to point out that when the Palmach personnel returned to their base, "nothing was said about a massacre in the village." Muhammad Mahmud Radwan had his own definition for massacre. "When we say massacre, we mean that the Jews shot indiscriminately at anyone who was running away."[35]

It seems that, if one wants to establish what happened in Deir Yassin on that day, there is no choice but to try to find out the precise circumstances of the death of each of the people killed there. The information in the following list was gathered from the various sources used for this book. (In the age column, an age range was often listed, since there were almost no instances in which two sources agreed on the age of a particular individual.)

Name	Age	Circumstances of Death
1. 'Alya, 'Isa Ahmad Yusuf	50–55	Combatant. Injured by shrapnel. Died while being treated by Hayat al-Balabsa.[36]
2. 'Alya, Muhammad 'Isa Ahmad	20	
3. 'Alya, Yusuf Ahmad Yusuf	58–62	His house served as an arms depot. His sons fired at Lehi's force. Captured and killed.[37]
4. 'Atiyya, Amina Husayn al-Kawbariyya	80	Shot while running from a house to a house through the olive groves.[38]
5. 'Atiyya, 'Ayisha Radwan	50–60	Shot.[39]
6. 'Atiyya, Isma'il	90–96	His house served as a defense position. Shot after slapped the face of one of Etzel's force who broke in.[40]
7. 'Atiyya, Mahmud Muhammad Isma'il	15–20	Combatant. Discovered Etzel's force and hit one of them. Injured by a hand grenade. Fled to 'Ayn Karm, returned and killed in exchange of fire.[41]
8. 'Atiyya, Muhammad Isma'il	45–50	Combatant. Fired at Etzel's force. Injured by a hand grenade and later killed.[42]
9. 'Atiyya, Musa Muhammad Isma'il	13–16	Shot after attackers had broken into his sister's house. Looked older than he was.[43]
10. 'Atiyya, Rubhi Isma'il	16–22	Combatant. Fired at Etzel's force. Tried to escape disguised as a woman, was identified in Givat Shaul and shot.[44]

Name	Age	Circumstances of Death
11. ʿAtiyya, Sara al-Kawbariyya	35–45	Her house served as a defense position. Killed by a hand grenade when Etzel's force broke in.[45]
12. Balabsa, Hayat	18–23	Shot when treating the injuries of ʿIsa Ahmad ʿAlya.[46]
13. Farhan, Hasan Yaʿqub Muhammad ʿAli		
14. Hamdan, Mahmud Muhammad Jawda	24–25	Killed by a hand grenade at the side of a relative holding a rifle.[47]
15. Hamdan, Muhammad Jawda	52–66	Killed by a hand grenade at the side of a relative holding a rifle.[48]
16. Hamida, ʿAbd al-Rahman Husayn	52–54	Blind.[49]
17. Hamida, ʿAli ʿAbd al-Rahim	10	
18. Hamida, ʿAli Husayn ʿAli	35–40	
19. Hamida, Hamid ʿAbdallah	70	
20. Hamida, Fatima Salih	50	
21. ʿId, ʿAli Khalil	20–30	Combatant. Injured in battle and later taken by the attackers. One source says that he was killed in the quarries.[50]
22. ʿId, ʿIsa Muhammad ʿIsa	15–20	Combatant. Captured by the attackers. One source says that he was killed in the quarries.[51]

Name	Age	Circumstances of Death
23. 'Id, Isma'il Muhammad Khalil	31–40	Combatant. Shot while firing from a foxhole he had prepared.[52]
24. 'Id, Isma'il Shakir Mustafa	1–6	Killed with his mother in their home.[53]
25. 'Id, Jamil 'Isa Muhammad	27–35	Combatant. Captured by the attackers and allegedly shot in the quarries. According to another version, he was killed in fighting.[54]
26. 'Id, Salihiyya Muhammad 'Isa	20–24	Shot in her home.[55]
27. Jabir, Ahmad Hasan	40–45	
28. Jabir, Fu'ad Khalil	12–16	Killed in the arms of his mother.[56]
29. Jabir, Jabir Mustafa	75–85	Paralyzed. Killed in his home.[57]
30. Jabir, Jabr Tawfiq Jabr	23–27	Combatant. Captured by the attackers. One source says that he was shot in the quarries.[58]
31. Jabir, Khalil Mustafa	35–38	Killed while searching for his children; according to another version, was shot in the quarries.[59]
32. Jabir, Mahmud Mustafa	50–60	Blind.[60]
33. Jabir, Muhammad Khalil Mustafa	5	
34. Jabir, Sa'id Muhammad Sa'id	15–20	

Name	Age	Circumstances of Death
35. Jabir, Salim Muhammad Isma'il	25	Combatant. Killed in fighting; according to another version, was captured by the attackers and killed.[61]
36. Jabir, Tawfiq Jabr	44–55	Killed while searching for his children; according to another version, he was shot in the quarries.[62]
37. Khalil, 'Ayish	55–58	Combatant. Killed while fighting near his home.[63]
38. Khalil, Hilwa Zaydan	48–50	Killed while fighting near her home.[64]
39. Khalil, Muhammad 'Ali	25–26	
40. Khalil, Muhammad 'Ayish	23–25	Combatant. Killed while fighting near his home.[65]
41. Khalil, Zarifa Muhammad 'Ali	16	Shot.[66]
42. Muslih, 'Ali Husayn	38	Combatant. It was said that he was captured by the attackers.[67]
43. Muslih, 'Aziza	52	Killed in her home after her armed husband was killed.[68]
44. Muslih, Muhammad 'Ali Hasan	45–55	Combatant. Killed when trying to reach a firearm.[69]
45. Muslih, Watfa Muhammad 'Ali Hasan	15	Killed in her parents' home after her armed father was killed.[70]
46. Radwan, As'ad	75–85	Shot when assailing an attacker with his walking stick.[71]
47. Radwan, Muhammad As'ad		Combatant. Killed in fighting.[72]

Name	Age	Circumstances of Death
48. Radwan, Radwan As'ad	18	Combatant. Fired at Lehi's loud-speaker car. Injured and then shot.[73]
49. Radwan, Sabha	75–80	
50. Radwan, 'Umar Ahmad As'ad	2	Killed when he fell from his grandmother's shoulders.[74]
51. Sammur, 'Abdallah 'Abd al-Majid	22–24	Combatant. Tried to escape disguised as a woman, was identified and shot.[75]
52. Sammur, Fiddiyya Isma'il al-Qaryutiyya	52–60	Killed in her home when the attackers broke in.[76]
53. Sammur, Husayn Isma'il Muhammad	14–18	Killed in his grandfather's home.[77]
54. Sammur, Mansur 'Abd al-'Aziz	24–27	Combatant. Fought to keep the route to 'Ayn Karm open.[78]
55. Sammur, Muhammad Mahmud Isma'il	30–35	Combatant. Killed by a hand grenade holding a rifle.[79]
56. Sammur, Musa Isma'il	40–50	Found near his home with amputated arms.[80]
57. Sammur, Najma Isma'il	65	
58. Sammur, Sammur Khalil Muhammad	11–12	Killed in his grandfather's home.[81]
59. Sharif, 'Abd al-Ra'uf Husayn	18	Shot in the bakery when the attackers broke in.[82]
60. Sharif, Husayn	50–65	Shot in the bakery when the attackers broke in.[83]
61. Zahran, 'Ali Muhammad	25–30	Combatant.[84] Killed during Lehi's attack on the Zahran houses.

Name	Age	Circumstances of Death
62. Zahran, Basma As'ad Radwan	23–25	Shot by a sub-machine gun when Lehi broke into her house.[85]
63. Zahran, Fathi Jum'a	2–3	Killed during Lehi's attack on the Zahran houses.
64. Zahran, Fathiyya Jum'a	girl	Killed during Lehi's attack on the Zahran houses.
65. Zahran, Fatima Isma'il 'Atiyya	37–45	Killed during Lehi's attack on the Zahran houses.
66. Zahran, Fatima Jum'a	6–8	Wounded during Lehi's attack on the Zahran houses. Evacuated by de Reynier to a hospital and died two days later.[86]
67. Zahran, Fatima Muhammad 'Id	40–52	Shot by a sub-machine gun when Lehi broke into her daughter's house.[87]
68. Zahran, Hamda	50	Killed during Lehi's attack on the Zahran houses.
69. Zahran, Muhammad	65–75	Was firing at Lehi's forces when hit.[88]
70. Zahran, Muhammad 'Ali	2–8	Killed during Lehi's attack on the Zahran houses.
71. Zahran, Muhammad Mahmud	14–18	Killed during Lehi's attack on the Zahran houses.
72. Zahran, Muhammad Musa	17–22	Combatant. Fought Lehi's force coming from the north.[89]
73. Zahran, Nazmi Ahmad	2	Killed during Lehi's attack on the Zahran houses.
74. Zahran, Nazmiyya Ahmad	5–8	Killed during Lehi's attack on the Zahran houses.
75. Zahran, Rasmiyya Jum'a	8 months	Burned to death during Lehi's attack on the Zahran houses.[90]

Name	Age	Circumstances of Death
76. Zahran, Rasmiyya Musa	16–19	Killed during Lehi's attack on the Zahran houses.
77. Zahran, Ruqya 'Ilyan al-Subaniyya	30–35	Killed during Lehi's attack on the Zahran houses.
78. Zahran, Safiyya Jum'a	3–6	Killed during Lehi's attack on the Zahran houses.
79. Zahran, Sa'id Musa	7–11	Killed during Lehi's attack on the Zahran houses.
80. Zahran, Samiha Ahmad	7–10	Killed during Lehi's attack on the Zahran houses.
81. Zahran, Yusra Jum'a		Killed during Lehi's attack on the Zahran houses.
82. Zahran, Zaynab Jum'a	4	Killed during Lehi's attack on the Zahran houses.
83. Zahran, Zaynab Muhammad Husayn al-Malihiyya	18	Killed during Lehi's attack on the Zahran houses.
84. Zahran, Zaynab Musa Muhammad	22	Killed during Lehi's attack on the Zahran houses.
85. Zaydan, 'Ali Hasan 'Ali	25–30	Combatant. Killed in fighting holding a rifle.[91]
86. Zaydan, Amina 'Ali Mustafa	girl	Machine-gunned by Etzel fighter.
87. Zaydan, Amina al-Baytuniyya	65 ?	
88. Zaydan, 'Ayida al-'Umuriyya	38–40	Machine-gunned by Etzel fighter.[92]
89. Zaydan, 'Aziza 'Ali Mustafa	12–17	Machine-gunned by Etzel fighter.[93]
90. Zaydan, Fatima Sammur	45	Shot when running to help her husband.[94]

Name	Age	Circumstances of Death
91. Zaydan, Hasan 'Ali	48–50	Combatant. Continued firing from his position until shot to death.[95]
92. Zaydan, Khudra al-Baytuniyya	52–60	Shot.[96]
93. Zaydan, Mahmud 'Ali Mustafa	17–22	Combatant. Machine-gunned by Etzel fighter.[97]
94. Zaydan, Mustafa 'Ali	70–72	Former bandsman. Shot.[98]
95. Zaydan, Muyassar Musa Mustafa	2	Machine-gunned by Etzel fighter.
96. Zaydan, Ni'ma 'Ali Mustafa	5 months	Machine-gunned by Etzel fighter.[99]
97. Zaydan, Samiyya Musa Mustafa		Machine-gunned by Etzel fighter.
98. Zaydan, Shafiq Musa Mustafa	3	Machine-gunned by Etzel fighter.
99. Zaydan, Shafiqa Musa Mustafa	5	Machine-gunned by Etzel fighter.
100. Zaydan, Tamam Muhammad 'Ali Hasan Muslih	23–24	Machine-gunned by Etzel fighter.[100]
101. Zaydan, Yusra Musa Mustafa	8	Machine-gunned by Etzel fighter.

The list of fatalities comprises 60 males and 41 females. The following table lists the percentages of males and females in accordance with their ages, in order to establish the percentages of children, adults and elderly killed. (When only the range of ages was known for a person, he or she was calculated according to the major bulk of years of that range that fell within one of the ranges of years in the table.)

Age	Percentage of Males	Percentage of Females	Percentage of Both Males and Females
0–5	10	20	14
6–13	5	10	7
14–18	15	15	15
19–40	34	20	28
41–60	22	23	22
61–70	5	4	5
71 and above	5	4	5
Unknown	4	4	4
Total	100	100	100

Kana'na claimed that 75 percent of the people killed were children, women and the aged (which denoted higher probability that a massacre had occurred).[101] However, according to this table, males between the ages of 14 and 60 formed 42 percent of the total of both sexes killed (the third row of the table). In other words, 58 percent of those killed were children up to the age of secondary education, women, and elderly. However, neither age nor sex necessarily denote the ability or inability to fight. For example, Muhammad Zahran, who was over sixty, continued to fire his rifle until hit, and Hilwa Zaydan Khalil took part in the fighting despite being a woman.

'Arif al-'Arif claimed that only seven of the Arabs killed were armed combatants, while 103 were non-combatants, mainly elderly, women and children.[102] The above list tells quite a different story. There were between seventy to eighty Arab combatants in the village, and according to this list, 24 of the Arabs killed were amongst that number. The question however is not, what was the ratio of combatants to noncombatants killed, but the circumstances in which they died. The exact circumstances of death of 17 people out of the 101 remains unknown. According to the above list, of the remaining 84 people, 61 were killed under battle conditions. Of the remaining 23, eleven were machine-gunned by the Etzel Bren gunner in the after-math of the surrender of the Zaydan family, as described earlier. As to the alleged executions in the quarries, if they ever happened, they totaled, at most, six people, significantly fewer than most claims.[103] These numbers completely refute the assertion by many of two phases to events in Deir Yasin; that after the battle had ended and the Palmach had left, Etzel and Lehi perpetrated a full-scale massacre. It is clear that most of the people killed were killed under battle conditions and not in a subsequent deliberate massacre. Generally speaking, when the battle ended, the killing stopped.

WERE THERE RAPES?
In their book *O Jerusalem!*, the authors Larry Collins and Dominique Lapierre provide a vivid description of the rape of an Arab woman from Deir Yassin called Safiyya 'Atiyya. Allegedly, she reported the assault to Richard Catling, Assistant Inspector-General of the CID, further asserting that she witnessed the rape of other women. Collins and Lapierre drew this information from a series of reports about Deir Yassin sent by Catling to Chief Secretary Gurney, starting from 13 April. On 15 April, he reported a visit to the village of Silwan, where a large number of villagers from Deir Yassin found refuge. He wanted to interview women about sexual assaults, but, according to him, they were embarrassed, hysterical, and did not want to talk. He therefore concluded that many sexual offences had undoubtedly been committed, adding that many schoolgirls had been raped and then murdered. Yitzhak Levy, the Haganah intelligence chief in Jerusalem, also issued a report (on 13 April) stating a claim that "Etzel members raped and then murdered a number of Arab young women (we do not know if this is true)."[104]

Safiyya 'Atiyya was not raped. As described in chapter 4, when discussing the fate of the children of Deir Yassin during the battle, a Jewish fighter agreed to escort Naziha Radwan to her mother, supposed to be in the nearby house of her uncle Ibrahim 'Atiyya. When they arrived there, Ibrahim's wife, Safiyya, opened the door holding a white flag, and she, Naziha and Naziha's mother were taken to a neighboring house in which the Arab women and children prisoners were being held under the guard of Jewish women.[105] If it was just a matter of Safiyya 'Atiyya, then one might still believe that somehow, somewhere, she had been raped, despite Naziha Radwan's testimony refuted this possibility. However, according to Catling, she told him that other women were raped in her presence. There were no testimonies of other women, or anyone else, which corroborated this claim.

So what was the source for all the stories of rape? One of the first to meet with the fugitives of Deir Yassin when they arrived in Arab Jerusalem was Hazim Nusayba, the Arabic news editor of the Palestine Broadcasting Service. He asked Husayn al-Khalidi, the senior Arab authority in Jerusalem at the time, how to cover the story. "We must make the most of this," Khalidi answered. "I think we should give this the utmost propaganda possible because the Arab countries apparently are not interested in assisting us and we are facing a catastrophe." "So," Khalidi said, "we are forced to give a picture – not what is actually happening – but we had to exaggerate a little bit so that maybe the Arab countries would become enthusiastic to come and assist us." Khalidi also hoped that such stories would strengthen Palestinian *sumud* (determination to resist). He issued Nusayba a strongly worded communiqué containing stories of rapes and all kinds of other atrocities, which was quickly broadcast and published all over the country. Some of the fugitives were summoned to Khalidi's headquarters. "We want you to say that the Jews slaughtered people, committed atrocities, raped, and stole gold," he said to them. When the fugitives protested against the false accounts of rape, Khalidi insisted that they had to say so in order to pressure the Arab armies to free Palestine from the Jews. Sa'd al-Din 'Arif, a prominent Arab activist and a member of the Jerusalem National Committee, was also of the opinion that they had to attribute brutal crimes to the attackers.[106]

As Nusayba was to describe it, the accusations of rape touched "a raw nerve in the Palestinian psyche," achieving the opposite result intended. The moment the Palestinians heard about the rapes they started to leave. Local leaders told Nusayba that "we are not afraid of death, but when it comes to honour it is another topic completely, we cannot bear with it. We cannot bear that our women should be raped." The impact was overwhelming, as attested to by many Palestinian refugees. Everyone believed that women and girls were raped, to the extent that when a woman from Deir Yassin told an Arab woman in Jerusalem that it was not true, the latter retorted: "Away with you, you liar!" She had heard that 200 girls had been raped. According to a Palestinian doctor, the Palestinians heard that "most of the women of Deir Yassin from the ages of six to seventy were raped." Some added other horrific descriptions of atrocities, such as the ripping open of the bellies of pregnant women. As one Palestinian woman stated with certainty to an interviewer "It is all recorded in history." Following the rule of *al-'ird qabla al-ard* (women's honor [comes] before land), whole families decided to leave.[107]

Nusayba himself was convinced that there were no rapes in Deir Yassin: "It was a battle that took place in the night till the morning, and under such circumstances there would be no time for rape." The first to protest against the rape allegations were the people of Deir Yassin themselves. A member of the Jabir family told Sa'd al-Din 'Arif that if he wanted to incriminate the Jews, he should not do it at the expense of Deir Yassin and its women. "I would like to stress on the fact that no rape incidents took place. That was part of a big lie that some of the Arabs and some of our leaders invented," he was to tell an interviewer. "We cannot say they amputated women's breasts, slashed their bellies or raped them." Muhammad Mahmud Radwan also insisted, "There were no rapes. It's all lies. There were no pregnant women who were slit open. It was propaganda...so Arab armies would invade." Other survivors delivered similar testimonies. Bahjat Abu Gharbiyya, a commander in the Army of Sacred Jihad who met with the first fugitives from Deir Yassin, was also to testify: "Frankly speaking, I never heard from them anything about any incident of sexual assault." Anwar Nusayba, secretary of the Jerusalem National Committee (and Hazim's brother), also confirmed that he heard nothing of rapes, which he considered inconceivable in the circumstances of the event.[108]

A Jewish doctor, who accompanied the representative of the Red Cross to Deir Yassin, searched the houses and was to testify that he saw no evidence of rape. Two Jewish doctors, who came the day after, also confirmed that all the bodies they saw were fully clad.[109] This was not enough for Hogan and McGowan, staunch believers in the massacre narrative, who insisted that women and girls were raped in Deir Yassin. The matter was of importance for them, "because questioning of sexual assault allegations at Deir Yassin has been used to suggest that the entire massacre is subject to doubt" (as put by Hogan). They dismissed the testimonies of the Jewish doctors on the ground that the bodies of the women raped might have been taken away, or that the women raped remained alive. Furthermore, Hogan was to say about the statements of the villagers that no rape had occurred, "these denials carry minimal, if any, weight." Why? Because the subject of war crimes against women was very sensitive for Muslims. In other words, all the Arab witnesses denying rapes lied, as they wanted to defend the honor of Deir Yassin's women.[110] While this argument might have some merit if Arab witnesses would defend the honor of their own wives or daughters, it has none at all when dealing with an amorphous defense of the good name of an entire village. One cannot conduct historical research from the starting point that everyone is lying.

Chapter 7

The Prisoners

Prior to the attack, Kaufman consulted with his superiors in Tel Aviv regarding the fate of the villagers. Begin ordered him to avoid unnecessary bloodshed and to follow the Geneva Convention. Lehi, too, accepted this policy, albeit somewhat reluctantly. Before they set out, Kaufman and Goldschmidt warned their fighters not to shoot unarmed men, women, children or the elderly, nor any Arab who wanted to surrender, even a combatant, and to treat prisoners according to the Geneva Convention. Zettler and Ben-Uziyahu, too, warned their combatants against unnecessary killing during the operation, especially of women and children, explaining that Etzel had made this a condition for the joint operation.[1]

At about 9:30 a.m., after they had occupied the center of the village, Etzel and Lehi forces started to gather up the prisoners. The first stage consisted of confining those who had fallen into their hands during the fighting. Lehi placed their prisoners in the house of Mustafa 'Id, close to the entrance to village, while Etzel theirs in Mustafa Zaydan's house, near the eastern crossroad of the village center. At about 2:00 p.m., after the fighting had ceased, Goldschmidt and Lapidot, assisted by other Etzel and Lehi combatants, rounded up the survivors from all the houses, assembling them in the eastern crossroad of the village center, from where they marched them to Mustafa 'Id's house. Close to 4:00 p.m. four open trucks, two of them heavy, 15-ton Leylands, and two smaller, 5-ton trucks, arrived from Etzel's transport base in order to transfer the prisoners to Arab Jerusalem. They parked on the border between Givat Shaul and Deir Yassin, not far from the pillbox, and the prisoners, mainly women, children, and the elderly, but also some adult males, boarded. Many of the prisoners boarding the trucks were suffering from various injuries. The trucks traveled a short distance to Givat Shaul and then stopped to allow a search of the prisoners for valuables. After being stripped of their valuables, the prisoners resumed their journey to Arab Jerusalem.[2]

On its way to Arab Jerusalem, the convoy's drivers, on their own initiative, drove through some of Jewish Jerusalem's main streets, in order to raise the population's morale with the sight of Arab prisoners. The guards accompanying the prisoners were singing, "Deir Yassin is ours," and were greeted by some of the spectators with cheers and applause. For some of the audience along Jaffa Road, especially near Mahane Yehuda, this was not enough and they started cursing the prisoners, spitting at them and throwing stones and empty cans. On the other hand, allegations that women prisoners were stripped of their clothes during the journey were baseless. Although they were driven through Jerusalem bareheaded and without a veil, as some of the women would testify, no one was naked, as other sources would later claim.[3]

Gicherman was very troubled by the way in which the "enthusiasm" aroused among the Jewish audience made the "dissidents" more popular. He advised his superiors to counteract this by undermining perceptions of both their morality and their military prowess. Soon, the Haganah accused Etzel and Lehi of holding a "victory parade" and humiliating the prisoners for publicity purposes. Many years later Zettler would argue that they never thought of a victory parade, as they were too tired for that. In order to correctly assess the intention of the trek, one must ascertain its exact route to Arab Jerusalem, which is possible as there is abundant testimony from people who saw the convoy at various points along the route. The trucks left Givat Shaul in the direction of Romema and then continued along

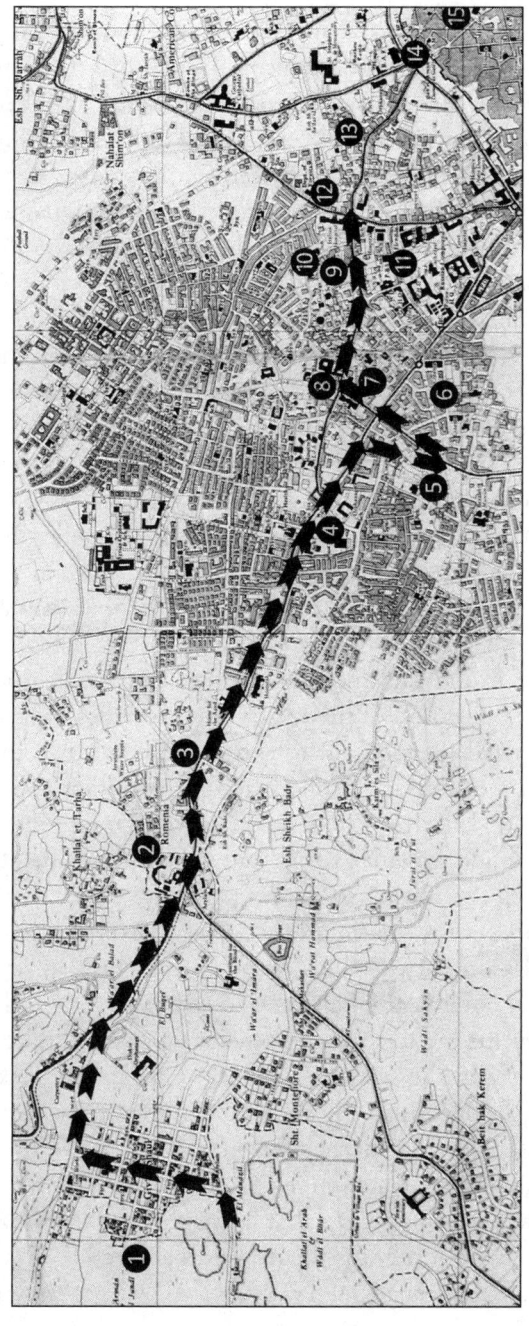

Fig. 43 The trek from Deir Yassin to Arab Jerusalem: 1. Givat Shaul, 2. Romema, 3. Jaffa Road, 4. Mahane Yehuda, 5. King George Avenue, 6. Ben-Yehuda Street, 7. Chancellor Avenue, 8. Bikkur Cholim Hospital, 9. Prophets Street, 10. Mea Shearim, 11. Security Zone C, 12. Italian Hospital, 13. Musrara, 14. Damascus Gate, 15. Muslim Quarter (Old City)

Jaffa Road, passing north of the Mahane Yehuda neighborhood, up to King George Avenue in central Jerusalem. They drove up King George Avenue to Ben-Yehuda Street, reversed direction, continued to Chancellor Avenue (now Straus Street), passed Bikkur Cholim hospital and turned right onto Prophets Street. On Prophets Street, they continued east, south of the Mea Shearim neighborhood, passed the Haganah positions, and stopped near the Italian hospital, on the border of Arab Musrara. To their right was British security zone C and to their left headquarters of the RAF (both apparently unaware of what was going on) where the prisoners were disembarked from the trucks. Except for the deviation on King George Avenue, it was one of the shortest routes possible from Deir Yassin to Arab Jerusalem.[4]

"Go to King 'Abdallah!" the guards told the prisoners as they released them and pointed them in the direction to Damascus Gate and the Muslim quarter. "Go to your people, and they'll look after you," they told the children. It was shortly after 4:00 p.m. when the released prisoners arrived in Musrara. Bahjat Abu Gharbiyya was at the headquarters of the Army of Sacred Jihad in Musrara when he got a phone call from an Arab advance post saying that many people were coming from the direction of the Jewish zone but they looked like Arabs. He instructed his men not to shoot and hurried to the post. There he found the released prisoners, according to him about 200, and took them to a nearby school in order to segregate them from the local population in order to prevent demoralization. He later delivered them to the National Committee in the Old City. A group of girls was brought to the house of Anwar Nusayba, secretary of the National Committee. The Committee put most of the released prisoners in a hotel near Jaffa Gate and soon the entire Old City learned of the events in Deir Yassin. Some of the small children were roaming aimlessly in the streets of the Old City for the next few days, until Hind al-Husayni, a cousin of 'Abd al-Qadir, gathered them together and started an orphanage for them.[5]

In what appeared to be an attempt to distance himself from the affair, Shaltiel reported to his superiors that it was the Haganah that had freed the prisoners from the "dissidents" and delivered them to the British authorities. This strange claim was repeated by a spokesman of the Jewish Agency and cited in the local and foreign press. (Etzel and Lehi protested against it in a later poster.) The Arabs, for their part, announced that it was the National Guard (*al-Haras al-Watani,* a local military force established by the National Committee), which released some of the prisoners from "the enemies of humanity."[6]

These prisoners were not the only villagers who fell into the hands of the Jewish forces. As early as Friday morning, Lehi had transferred two truckloads of old people, women and children (some forty prisoners in all) to its base in Sheikh Badr. There they were locked in a warehouse under armed guards until the evening, when most of them were transferred to Arab Jerusalem (some women and children still remained under detention in Sheikh Badr on Saturday morning). Lehi, responsible for guarding Deir Yassin on Friday night and Saturday morning, continued to search the village for Arabs in hiding, and, according to Shimon Moneta, on Saturday morning they found 30 women and children hiding in one room. Lehi found additional Arabs, mainly children, during the following hours, and transferred them all via trucks to Arab Jerusalem. A Lehi driver was to relate that altogether he drove the route from Deir Yassin to Arab Jerusalem four times; he did not notice curses or the like, he said. The British detected at least one of these trips on Saturday, but did nothing about it.[7]

There were variant reports of the number of the Arab prisoners released. The *New York Times* announced 70 Arabs turned over to the British army, but this was an inaccurate early report.[8] Most sources, including individual members of the underground organizations (and an official announcement circulated by Etzel and Lehi), Arabs (Husayn al-Khalidi among them), and British (Gurney), spoke of about 150 prisoners.[9] Kaufman, however, claimed, that 40 to 50 Arabs boarded each of the four trucks on Friday afternoon, and altogether 200 prisoners were released. Abu Gharbiyya also claimed, both in his memoirs and in a later interview, that the number of released prisoners he admitted to Musrara was about 200 (and his description of events was generally reliable).[10] Lapidot, on the other hand, was of the opinion that since only two of the trucks were big, it was more likely that the number of the prisoners was lower, about 120.[11]

It seems that the solution to this difference of opinion is that while the number of prisoners in the main round of Friday afternoon was between 120 and 150, one has to add Lehi's prisoners, those first taken to Sheikh Badr and those found on Saturday, to bring the total to about 200.

Chapter 8

The Aftermath

THE RED CROSS ARRIVES

At 2:00 a.m. on Saturday morning, Jacques de Reynier, the representative of the Red Cross in Palestine who was in Jerusalem, received a phone call from a British nurse, urging him to set out to Deir Yassin to save lives. He ignored her. At 4:00 a.m., she called again. This time, it sounded more serious, yet he still took no concrete action until 5:00 p.m., when he was contacted by Husayn al-Khalidi, secretary of the Arab Higher Committee. After failing to obtain the help of the British authorities, Khalidi had decided to approach the Red Cross. Although new to Palestine, de Reynier reached the decision to intervene without consulting with Geneva. He phoned the Jewish Agency, only to be told that the attackers belonged to Etzel, over whom the Agency had no control. They warned him that it was unsafe to go to Deir Yassin, so he approached the British, who confirmed the identity of the attackers but refused to intervene. Consequently, de Reynier contacted Etzel itself, through Leon Farhi, a French-speaking physician who was a member of the underground organization, and obtained Bergman's permission to visit the village. A Jewish police officer approached Moshe Barzilai, Lehi's intelligence officer, on de Reynier's behalf and secured his permission as well. Finally, de Reynier secured the assistance of two Jewish doctors, Alfred Engel of Magen David Adom (the Jewish equivalent of the Red Cross) and the district physician of the Haganah, and together with several nurses, an ambulance, and a truck, they started off the next morning for Deir Yassin.[1]

It was 9:00 a.m. on Sunday, 11 April, when the convoy rendezvoused with an armed Etzel officer assigned to escort them to the village. He joined de Reynier's car and they continued on to Deir Yassin. On the border between Givat Shaul and the village, they were stopped at an Etzel checkpoint. A lengthy argument ensued, which only ended when Barzilai appeared on the scene and accompanied them into the village. Several journalists found hiding in the ambulance were sent away. De Reynier next met with Selivansky and explained to him the mission of the Red Cross, to evacuate the wounded and the dead. Selivansky responded that there were no wounded Arabs in the village, only about 200 dead. From his interlocutor, de Reynier understood that 150 bodies had been thrown into some sort of an excavation (which he could not see for himself due to Arab sniping), twenty bodies lay in a "no-man's-land" between the Jews and the Arabs, and fifty more were scattered within the village. De Reynier insisted on touring the village to see things for himself. Selivansky agreed and de Reynier began entering the houses, accompanied by Barzilai, Bergman, the physician from Etzel, and some other combatants. The physicians from Magen David Adom and from the Haganah also entered houses and observed the dead (about 100, Engel later related).[2]

After visiting several houses, de Reynier entered the house of Jum'a Zahran. He found many bodies of people who had died due to blast, hand grenades, and automatic weapons fire (he added in his memoirs that someone had been stabbed). When he was about to leave he heard a noise and saw a leg moving. It was a girl, Fatima Jum'a Zahran, seriously injured in her head by blast, unconscious, but still alive. He carried her out of the house and delivered her to the Haganah physician, instructing him use the ambulance to rush her to British security zone B (she would die two days later). When he asked Selivansky about his earlier assertion that there were no wounded Arabs in the village, the latter answered that they had not yet finished searching the village. Later, another old woman, injured in her arm, was found hiding, and was transferred in the afternoon to security zone B.³

In the early afternoon, after searching only a small portion of the village near its entrance, de Reynier left Deir Yassin, instructing the Haganah physician to bring another truck for the evacuation of the dead. Actually, the original request of Khalidi from de Reynier was to assist in bringing the bodies to Arab Jerusalem and this, in addition to the evacuation of the wounded, was de Reynier's main objective. Therefore, immediately on his arrival he had requested the commanders of the attacking forces to allot personnel to load the dead onto the truck that he had brought with him for transfer to Arab Jerusalem. They agreed, and saw to it that their men started loading the bodies onto the truck. When de Reynier and the Haganah physician left, Engel, the Magen David Adom doctor, was to supervise the loading of the deceased. However, when the Haganah physician returned to the village with a second truck, he found that only a small number of bodies had been loaded on the first truck. Engel informed him that the combatants had refused to continue the loading.⁴

Meanwhile, de Reynier returned to Jerusalem and met with Leo Kohn, secretary of the Jewish Agency's Political Department, to protest officially against what he viewed as a clear violation of the Geneva Convention, which the Agency had pledged to respect. Kohn regretted the incident, but noted that the Agency was unable to curb the Jewish "extremists" and that they too were suffering from Etzel and Lehi. De Reynier retorted that it did not release the Agency from responsibility, since it represented the entire Jewish community in Palestine. De Reynier next went to meet with Khalidi, to ascertain the position of the Arab Higher Committee regarding the burial of the dead. Khalidi was furious and it took time to calm him. It appeared that the Arabs had now changed their minds. They no longer wanted the bodies brought to Arab Jerusalem, for both health reasons (fearing the spread of epidemics), and political considerations (to prevent panic and demoralization). Therefore, Khalidi now asked de Reynier

Fig. 44 Jacques de Reynier, the Red Cross representative (standing left),
in front of the Arab hospital in Bayt Safafa

to have the bodies buried in Deir Yassin itself. Since he understood from de Reynier that some 150 bodies had been thrown into some sort of a well, while the rest were scattered throughout the village, he suggested moving the rest of the bodies to the same place and sealing it. De Reynier therefore had to return to the Jews with new requests.[5]

De Reynier's new instructions were to bury the dead in a decent manner in Deir Yassin, to supply him with a list of names of all the dead, to bring him their identity cards, and to transfer any wounded found to the barrier of security zone B. He delivered the instructions in writing and later in person to Etzel and Lehi's commanders in the village, who promised to comply with them. Subsequently, the Lehi members who were guarding the village, started to unload the bodies from the truck. De Reynier demanded the burial of all the dead. The Haganah physician suggested covering the bodies with lime, in order to prevent disease. It turned out to be impossible to fulfill de Reynier's instruction to identify the dead, since none carried identification papers. At 5:00 p.m., de Reynier returned to his headquarters, which swarmed with journalists, but he refused to respond to their questions. The next day he traveled to Amman.[6]

On Monday morning, 12 April, two additional physicians arrived at Deir Yassin. One was Zalman Avigdori, the chairman of the Jerusalem branch of the "Hebrew Medical Association in the Land of Israel." He was familiar with Deir Yassin, having previously treated patients there. He was accompanied by the vice-chairman. They had come at the request of the Jewish Agency to examine the dead. At this point, the Haganah was about to take over the village, and relations with Etzel and Lehi were so tense as to be on the brink of a clash (see below). The two doctors later related that they had to intervene to calm the situation down and prevent bloodshed. Avigdori told Lapidot and Selivansky that if they were given permission to freely inspect the village, they would only report the truth. Permission was granted and the two toured the village for several hours. At this point, the bodies were still unburied. They inspected some of them and saw additional bodies without inspecting them individually, altogether 46 bodies. Their impression, reported to the head of the Haganah's medical service of the Jerusalem district, was that the cause of death of all the people examined was shooting or explosions. All the deceased were in their clothes and there were no signs of mutilation. When Avigdori informed Lapidot and Selivansky of his findings, Selivansky asked for it in writing. Avigdori promised to supply it shortly.[7]

On Tuesday, de Reynier returned to Jerusalem and the next morning he revisited Deir Yassin, which was now in the hands of the Haganah, who had already buried most of the bodies. He toured the village with Yeshurun Schiff, commander of the Haganah's Michmash battalion, asking him to prepare a map indicating all the mass graves and the number of people buried in them. Since the Haganah was talking about 100 bodies buried, and according to what he had heard in his former visit there should have been more than 200 bodies, he was looking for the rest. They only existed in Etzel's imagination, the Haganah's answer was. He nevertheless followed the smell and found a pile of burned bodies in the bottom of a quarry north of the road, following which they too were buried. Schiff prepared the requested map, indicating seven graves, on the very same day, delivered to the Red Cross two days later through Shaltiel.[8]

When de Reynier returned to his office, two Etzel officers were waiting for him with a document to sign, that Etzel rendered all possible assistance to him to complete his mission. When he refused to sign, they threatened his life (according to him), he still refused, telling them that he had already sent his report of the affair to Geneva, and they left. Selivansky met with a similar failure when he tried to get a written statement from Avigdori about the findings of his visit to Deir Yassin. A week later, he came to Avigdori's office but the latter put him off telling him to come back in two days. When he returned the office was closed. Attempts to reach him by phone also failed; he was always not at home. One day Selivansky met him in the street and asked for the statement. Avigdori refused, telling him that he was under pressure although he declined to say from who. Zettler told Selivansky to leave him alone, since he suffered from heart problems.[9]

Etzel was not the only group to request a written statement from de Reynier, both the Jewish Agency and the Arabs sought the same thing. Unsure of how to respond, de Reynier sought the advice of Geneva regarding the possibility of issuing identical reports to all parties concerned, which he had so far tried to avoid. On the one hand, issuing such a report would improve public perceptions of the role of the Red Cross. On the other hand, it might involve him with differences of opinion regarding details and legal controversies. Geneva was of the opinion that he should not issue a report to any of the parties. The Jewish Agency claimed to have no control over the perpetrators and could not assume responsibility for their actions. Etzel could not expect a report before it had followed the lead of the Jewish Agency and the Arabs in recognizing the Red Cross and committing itself to the Geneva Convention. As to the Arab request, his role in Deir Yassin had been to help the wounded and assure the burial of the dead, not to determine the facts.[10]

ATTEMPTS TO BURY THE DEAD

When Gicherman visited the village after the battle, he saw people dragging bodies to a quarry east of the village. He told Kaufman that they had to clear the village of bodies, but by burying them and not by burning them or by throwing the corpses into wells, the first place liable to be checked by foreign observers. Kaufman answered that his men were too tired to do so and Gicherman threatened to use force to coerce them to do so and reported the situation to Shaltiel. When Kaufman later asked Shaltiel to have the Haganah take over the village, Shaltiel made the burial of the bodies a precondition for this. He made it clear that the Haganah did not intend to clean up the mess and bury the dead for them, and he, too, threatened that unless they cleaned the village there would be "ta-ta-ta." Yeshurun Schiff, the commander of the Michmash battalion, urged Kaufman to make an effort and Kaufman eventually agreed. Zettler also acquiesced, after Schiff had threatened to hold a gun on them if necessary. Kaufman instructed Lapidot to start collecting the bodies. In many cases, they had to move heavy chunks of concrete and stone to extract the dead. The combatants were exhausted and although they collected some remains, they then stopped. They lacked both the tools and the expertise to tackle the task. Lapidot told Kaufman that they could not continue and he concurred. Lehi continued to gather bodies on Saturday morning, but no burial operation was carried out.[11]

On Sunday, de Reynier arrived and found bodies still scattered throughout the village. His changing instructions contributed to the delay in interning the bodies. At first, he asked to assign personnel to load the bodies on the truck that came with him, in order to transfer them to Arab Jerusalem. Lehi's combatants started loading the bodies on the truck, but after about a couple of dozen, refused to continue. In the meanwhile, in Arab Jerusalem, Khalidi asked de Reynier to bury the bodies in Deir Yassin. He told him to remind the Jews that they could find themselves in similar situations and therefore they should assist in the burial operation. Khalidi wanted to send some Arab physicians and laborers to Deir Yassin to handle the burial, and an *imam* (prayer leader) to conduct the burial ceremony, but there was no chance that Lehi would agree to it. A suggestion to send some Arab boy scouts for that purpose, accompanied by several survivors from the village who could identify the dead, was also refused. Subsequently, de Reynier asked the commanders in Deir Yassin to bury the bodies on site, and Lehi's combatants reluctantly started unloading the bodies from the truck, piling them up in the main street.[12]

An attempt to dig a mass grave in the rocky ground failed and Lehi's combatants tried to dispose of the bodies by burning them. They poured three jerry cans of kerosene over the pile of bodies and set it on fire, to no effect. Some of the dead Arabs were still wearing ammunition bandoliers and the bullets started to explode and fly in all directions, but the bodies were only scorched. The sight was

horrible, as was the smell. Zettler must have realized the bad impression such a spectacle in the center of the village would create, and ordered his men to clear the bodies from the main street. They refused. Zettler drew a gun threateningly, but Barzilai calmed him down, telling him that a personal example would work better. The two pulled a body from the pile, but its arm came off in Barzilai's hand. Barzilai vomited and that was the end of the attempt to lead by example. There were other

Fig. 45 Moshe Barzilai, Lehi's intelligence officer

efforts to burn bodies. Some of the bodies were carried by wheelbarrows and dumped into a burning house. Others were put onto pyres of blazing wood. The main effort, however, was attempted in one of the quarries to the east of the village, north of the road. Etzel's men carried dozens of bodies into the quarry, poured gasoline over them, and set them on fire. The results were the same, the bodies were only scorched. The pile of partially burned bodies in the bottom of the quarry would later fuel the story of executions having been carried out there.[13]

One of the more bizarre allegations was the claim that the attackers threw 150 bodies into a well, more specifically the Jawza well, and then sealed it with concrete to conceal their crime. The story sprouted from de Reynier's words to Khalidi that 150 bodies were thrown into some sort of an excavation (which de Reynier admitted he had not witnessed), which Khalidi interpreted as referring to a well. His interpretation later developed into the "corpses in the well" accusation and even came to be believed by some of the survivors. The real basis for this accusation seems to have been the bodies carried into the quarry and burned there. One of the survivors conflated the accounts and said that the attackers threw the bodies into a well, poured gasoline over them and set them on fire. Regardless, it seems from testimonies of Haganah men later engaged in burying the dead that a few bodies were in fact thrown into wells. In any case, on Monday, 12 April, when the Haganah was supposed to take over the village, the dead were still unburied.[14]

THE BRITISH PLAN REPRISALS

High Commissioner Cunningham believed that what had happened in Deir Yassin "is far the worst to which the present communal clashes have so far given rise." At first, he was cautious, stating only that "Arab allegations of Jewish atrocities such as the lining up and shooting with automatic weapons of unarmed men, women and children now seem to contain some truth." However, several days later he reported, without reservation, to his minister that "women and children were stripped, lined up, photographed and then slaughtered by automatic fire," a description that was forwarded verbatim by the British to the United Nations. He also apprised the minister of Arab "sharp criticism" of the British "for their failure immediately to intervene or to punish the criminals." Cunningham's perception of the affair was common to many British officials who accepted the massacre narrative at face value. The attackers had "indulged" in massacring the villagers, their children and even their cattle, an army newsletter reported. The government radio called Deir Yassin a second Lidice (alluding to the Czech village whose inhabitants had been liquidated by the Nazis), while Chief Secretary Gurney wrote in his diary that the atrocities committed there "are too horrible for words and [Bergen] Belsen pales beside them." He also mentioned the shock of the British journalists at the British failure to retaliate.[15]

In the British House of Commons, Colonial Minister Arthur Creech-Jones had to face questions regarding the affair. All he could do was repeat the details given by Etzel and Lehi at their press conference, and express "the horror with which His Majesty's Government regard such barbarous action." This answer did not satisfy the MPs. "Do the Government propose to take any other steps than that of expressing regret," he was asked. He answered that the army was doing its best considering its limited resources and the fact that it was in a process of withdrawal. Members of the House understood that the minister had actually given up hope of arresting the perpetrators. A suggestion by one MP to ask for the assistance of the Jewish Agency was rejected by the minister outright as useless since the Haganah was involved too.[16]

When Cunningham realized that the army was not going to intervene, he asked the Air Officer Commanding, Vice Marshal Dawson, to bomb the village from the air. This would be their chance to settle accounts with Etzel and Lehi, most of whose combatants in Jerusalem were presently concentrated in the village. The latter agreed to attack them with rockets, but informed Cunningham that in the framework of the withdrawal, the last squadron of light bombers had been sent the day before to Egypt and their rockets to Iraq and it would take 24 hours to get the them back. Cunningham asked him to do so and it was decided to attack the village on Wednesday, 14 April. On the morning of 13 April, RAF 249 squadron, stationed in Habbaniyya air base in Iraq, got an instruction to prepare a detachment of rocket firing Tempest planes for an air strike against Deir Yassin. By 4:50 p.m. three armed Tempests arrived at Ramat David air base, followed by a Ventura plane carrying rocket warheads and engines. Urgent instructions were issued to Spitfire 208 squadron to photograph the location. The plan was to start the attack early in the morning with the Spitfires and to continue with the Tempests. Two additional Tempests arrived the next day, but by then it was already too late.[17]

Etzel and Lehi quickly learned of the British plans. An agent of Lehi in the Jerusalem's post office eavesdropped on a call between Shaltiel and the British, in which the former stated that only "dissidents" were present in Deir Yassin and not the Haganah. The British informed him that they intended to bomb the village. An informer from Bayt Jala told Lehi that British forces in Atarot airfield were planning an attack on Deir Yassin. Etzel also received intelligence that the British intended to settle their old accounts with them by means of an air attack. In fact, following the British decision to attack, Richard Stubbs, the director of the government public information office, hinted that the RAF was about to bomb the village unless the attackers withdrew. Etzel and Lehi in any case were not interested in garrisoning the village after taking it, and as early as Friday, Kaufman had asked Shaltiel to take over the village. However, at this point, it became urgent for them to evacuate the village, which they did on Monday, being replaced by the Haganah (see below).[18]

The Jewish Agency lost no time in informing the British of the Etzel and Lehi withdrawal and that the village was now under Haganah control, and a British officer sent to Deir Yassin confirmed the new situation. Following these developments, on Tuesday morning, 13 April, Cunningham and Dawson met again and decided that there was no point in continuing with the air strike. In a telegram to London, Cunningham explained that he decided to cancel the attack for three reasons: since the perpetrators had left, there would be no element of punishment, if they nevertheless continued with the strike making the Jews leave, they would have to send ground troops to occupy the village, of whom they did not have enough to spare. Finally, the Arabs, in any case, were unlikely to return, so a British attack would yield no compensation for them. An hour later Stubbs released the news and at noon the government radio made it public. In an official statement, the government announced that, "An air strike against the Jewish dissidents in the village of Deir Yassin was arranged and was suspended when it became clear that the dissidents had left."[19]

Cunningham was very upset. "We have missed the bus," he said to his military assistant. The latter, too, thought it was a pity that the attack had to be called off, as both sides needed "a salutary lesson of what we can do." Jerusalem's British appointed mayor, Richard Graves, wrote in his diary that the British security forces had missed "a heaven-sent opportunity of getting their own back." In parliament, Minister of State Hector McNeil delivered a further statement on behalf of the colonial minister, admitting that the authorities could not conduct an investigation of their own in Deir Yassin, since the Haganah was heavily guarding the approaches to the village. They wanted to punish the perpetrators, but since a ground operation was liable to be very costly in British life, they preferred to arrange an air strike. This too was canceled when it became clear beyond doubt that the perpetrators had left. "It must be realised that with the progressively reduced strength of our armed forces as our withdrawal proceeds intervention in every instance of violence between Arab and Jew is not practicable," he concluded.[20]

Fig. 46   Last Salute: High Commissioner, General Alan Cunningham, leaving Palestine for good five weeks after the affair

THE HAGANAH TAKES OVER

After the battle, Kaufman met with Shaltiel in Givat Shaul, updated him about the situation and requested that the Haganah take over the village. Shaltiel answered that he had no forces in reserve to replace them, and therefore the departure of the underground forces would open the western suburbs of the city to Arab attack. Kaufman insisted that his men were not suitable for garrisoning the village and told Shaltiel that he was determined to withdraw them. Shaltiel sent Schiff and Zion Eldad (Shaltiel's operations officer) to accompany Kaufman back into the village and assess the size of the force needed to occupy it. When they returned to Givat Shaul, Eldad told Shaltiel that a company of Gadna (Youth Battalions, the youth movement associated with the Haganah) would suffice. Schiff, however, shocked by the sight of the bodies he had seen in the village, some of which had been crushed under the debris, told Shaltiel that it was wrong to let the youngsters see such horrors. Shaltiel therefore made the burial of the bodies a precondition for the Haganah to take over the village. As related earlier, Kaufman reluctantly agreed, but his men could not accomplish the burial. Kaufman phoned Shaltiel to say that they intended to evacuate the village the next morning. Shaltiel begged him to stay at least until Sunday, and it was agreed that they would remain in the village for an additional 48 hours and then be replaced by the Haganah.[21]

Exhausted, on Friday evening Etzel's combatants started to leave the village. Kaufman and Lapidot also left, while Goldschmidt remained behind. Lehi undertook to guard the village on Friday night and Saturday morning. A reserve unit coming from Jerusalem, though, replaced most of those who had participated in the battle. Fearing an Arab counter-attack, Lehi's combatants prepared fortified defensive positions, especially in the direction of 'Ayn Karm. During Saturday, some of Etzel's combatants returned, with more arriving on Sunday. On Saturday, the combatants had a visitor, Eliyahu Arbel, an operations officer in the Etzioni brigade, sent by Shaltiel to tour the village and see the bodies. On Sunday, they had two more visitors, de Reynier, the Red Cross representative, and Yitzhak Levy, the commander of the Haganah intelligence in Jerusalem. The latter had been sent by Shaltiel to convince them to bury the dead before leaving; however, he was unsuccessful. At this point, information was received about the impending British air strike. By now it was clear that they could no longer remain in the village. Kaufman and Selivansky went to the headquarters of the Michmash battalion in Beit ha-Kerem and demanded from Schiff that the Haganah should keep its word and replace them.[22]

Earlier, Shaltiel had summoned Yaakov Shapira, an officer in the Michmash battalion, and asked him to take over the village, in order to prevent its reoccupation by Arab irregulars once the "dissidents" had left. He promised to place two military police squads and two Gadna platoons at his disposal, totaling about 80 men. At the same time, Shaltiel instructed Yehoshua Arieli, commander of the Gadna in Jerusalem, to take his cadets to Deir Yassin, to defend it from a possible Arab attack from 'Ayn Karm. When Shapira, Schiff and some other officers visited the village to prepare for their arrival, they discovered that the bodies were still there. Schiff phoned Shaltiel, but the latter insisted that the Gadna should enter the village, being the only force available (the other forces were engaged in Operation Nahshon). It was during the graduation ceremony of the Jerusalem Hebrew Gymnasium, late in the morning of 11 April, that Gadna sergeant Yair Tzaban got a note to gather all his fellow Gadna members who were pupils at the school for an operation. The ceremony was cut short by a Gadna commander, who announced to the surprised parents that their children were "as of this moment" fully mobilized. They all drove to a hostel in Beit ha-Kerem, where they were joined by

Fig. 47 David Shaltiel inspecting a Gadna soldier

a number of Gadna instructors under the command of Tzvi Ankori, all of whom had traveled from their base in the deserted Arab village of Sheikh Badr. New Czech rifles were divided among them and the next morning they set out for Deir Yassin.[23]

At 8:00 p.m., on Sunday, Shaltiel summoned Shapira urgently, apprising him that Etzel and Lehi intended to leave the village without burying the dead. Their attempt to burn the corpses had been unsuccessful. He asked him to prevent their departure until they buried the dead, and if they refused, he should disarm them. Subsequently, Shapira instructed the military police at his disposal to take up positions on both sides of the road to Deir Yassin with two machine guns. At 10:00 p.m., a group of Lehi tried to leave the village. Shapira conveyed Shaltiel's instructions to their commander, who refused to obey and threatened to attack. The military police released the safety catches of their firearms, Lehi's commander said something to the effect of needing to avoid war between brothers, and eventually Lehi's men returned to the village. Shapira went to sleep, to discover by the morning that Lehi had succeeded in leaving the village after they had detonated a mine in front of the military police (by accident, according to a Lehi man). The military policemen, being awake for the entire night, did not consider themselves capable of stopping two trucks full of armed combatants and they too left.[24]

Etzel and some Lehi commanders were still in the village several hours later when the Gadna youths arrived. Kaufman, Lapidot and their men were awaiting them in a row, ready to leave the village. Arieli, the Gadna's commander, asked Ankori to tell the "dissidents" that they had "smeared the name of the Jewish people." Ankori did so with gusto. He wanted to show his men that they were actually expelling the "dissidents." He told them, in front of the Etzel fighters, that Etzel and Lehi were nothing more than bandits, who brought shame on the Jewish people. In their barbarous acts, they proved to be a bunch of murderers, not warriors. "You are expelled," he concluded, turning to Etzel's men. The Gadna's culture officer (that is, *politruk*), Shlomo Dinur, added a few derogatory words in the same spirit. It was too much. "Go away! I am unwilling even to talk to you," Kaufman responded. "We will leave when we wish." Some of his men cocked their Stens. "Stop your men," Ankori shouted to him. "You caused it," Kaufman replied. At that point, Etzel's reinforcements started to arrive from Givat Shaul, followed by some exchanges of blows

Figs. 48 and 49   Etzel prepares to leave Deir Yassin (Kaufman inspecting his men), while the Haganah prepares to take over

148

between the parties. Arieli insisted that they were not going to leave before burying the bodies, and as if to corroborate his words, one of his men pointed an MG 34 machine gun at the Etzel combatants. Etzel's Yehoshua Gorodenchik, a hefty person, grabbed the machine gun from his hands and aimed it at the Gadna. Lapidot ordered him to return the weapon, which restored some calm.[25]

A short while after the Gadna's arrival, Schiff with some of his men entered the village. He met Zettler and told him that they were "a bunch of swine"; this was no way to fight. He radioed Shaltiel to inform him of the situation, and he responded by ordering Schiff to disarm Etzel and Lehi. Should they resist, Shaltiel went on, Schiff should open fire on them. Schiff refused, asserting that he could not shoot Jews. "Do not tell me what you can or what you cannot do, those are your orders," Shaltiel said. Schiff responded he just could not do it, and if Shaltiel were going to force him, it would stain Shaltiel's name forever. "Jewish history will never forgive you." Shaltiel thought it over and finally allowed Schiff to use his discretion. Everyone involved realized that it had gone too far and the Gadna commanders eventually gave up and let Etzel and the rest of the Lehi men leave the village without burying the dead.[26]

In accordance with its original objective, the Gadna spread over the village to organize its defense against an Arab attack. Some were sent to the southern slopes of the village, to forestall an attack from 'Ayn Karm. Arab snipers were shooting at them from afar, without hitting anyone. At this point, Shaltiel told Shapira that they had to bury the dead. The Red Cross was about to return and they had to finish the burial before that. He instructed Shapira to leave two combatants at each position, and the rest would bury the dead. A similar instruction was delivered to Arieli. In order to spare the cadets the sight of the dead, Arieli decided to employ only the instructors in burying the bodies; even some of them vomited, got dizzy and asked to be relieved of the duty. The smell was horrible. Handkerchiefs to cover their faces, along with gloves, were brought from Jerusalem. Pairs of instructors removed the bodies, either dragging them by hand or carrying them on the few stretchers that were available. They started late in the afternoon, worked through the night and finished by the morning. Soon they realized that it would take days to dig graves in the rocky ground. Instead, they put the bodies downhill of the terraces and rolled the terraces' stones over them. Some of the bodies they dragged into the quarry, added to those brought there by Etzel, and covered with earth (apparently ineptly, as de Reynier saw them when he visited the village the next day). Other bodies were hard to extricate from the houses, and Arieli asked permission to blow up two houses over the bodies. Haganah sappers arrived in the morning and blew up the houses. On some of the burial sites the Gadna put signs reading "Holy place. Do not enter."[27]

The Gadna remained in Deir Yassin about a month. On their second day there, they found a young girl alive, who had hidden in a cellar for five days. She was taken to Jerusalem and delivered to the police, being the last Arab to be evacuated from Deir Yassin.[28]

Chapter 9

The Posters War

THE HAGANAH REPORTS THE BATTLE

Palmach commander Yaakov Weg was the only Haganah man to visit Deir Yassin while the battle was going on and subsequently to write a report about it (his deputy, Moshe Vachman, only gave testimonies years later). In his report, written on 11 April and addressed to Shaltiel, Weg described the Palmach's intervention in Deir Yassin, emphasizing that Shaltiel had approved it in principle. He explained why they had to enter the village, but his description of the actual activities of the Palmach in the village was minimal. Nothing in his report suggested a massacre or referred to the killing of non-combatants; he actually referred to the attackers as "brave fighters."[1]

The second Haganah man to enter the village and write a report was the regional intelligence officer, Mordechai Gicherman, who arrived at Deir Yassin at about 3:00 p.m., after the fighting had already ended. Therefore, although he saw the results of the battle, he did not witness its actual progress. The day after, at the request of Meir Pilavsky, a former head of a Haganah unit that had operated against the "dissidents," he prepared a report covering the events from 7 to 10 April. It reviewed some of the preparations for the attack and detailed the attackers' manpower and weaponry (his figures were totally inaccurate). Gicherman concisely described the attack itself, analyzing its faults: disorder, lack of discipline, no advance intelligence, no coordination between the forces, and no previous training in this kind of fighting. According to him, the Arab males taken prisoner, were paraded in Jerusalem and then returned to the village and shot to death (which he clearly could not have witnessed personally). The overall number of the dead was about 200. He also mentioned the assistance rendered by the Haganah, most notably the Spandau fire from the Sharafa ridge (which he himself was responsible for), and concluded with a recommendation: "There is an urgent need to exploit this for a widespread propaganda campaign to undermine confidence in the dissidents, both with regard to their military ability and moral stature."[2]

While he was visiting Deir Yassin, Gicherman did not see the next Haganah man who came on the scene and who would also write a report. This was Pilavsky himself, because the latter only arrived at 4:00 p.m., after Gicherman had already left. According to his own words, Pilavsky only stayed in the village for an hour. In his report, addressed to Shaltiel, he, too, emphasized the disorder among the attackers and the lack of discipline. He described them as looking like armed rioters. "Each one of the dissidents was walking covered with blood and proud of the number of people he killed; it was apparent that they lacked the education and intelligence of our [Haganah] soldiers." In a section titled "The Pogrom Results," he stated the village to be full of the bodies of Arabs, which, in his opinion, had been lined up against walls to be shot and had not been killed in battle. He also stated that he saw the bodies of five Arabs whom the attackers had paraded in Jerusalem, lying dead in a quarry. While he was there, the attackers were looting the village. They also intended to kill all the prisoners they had captured, though in the evening he learned that they released them (actually, when Pilavsky visited the village, the prisoners had already arrived in Arab Jerusalem). A copy of the report, with photo negatives of the dead, was sent to Yisrael Galili, the Haganah's chief of staff, who in turn showed it to Ben-Gurion.[3]

Perhaps on Gicherman's recommendation, all three reports (of Weg, Gicherman, and Pilavsky), were assembled into a briefing booklet, distributed on 12 April by the intelligence officer of the Haganah's operations branch. Titled "The Lesson from Operation Deir Yassin," it was addressed to the Haganah soldiers, but also reached journalists.[4]

On 12 and 13 April, Yitzhak Levy sent a series of reports about Deir Yassin to the political department of the Haganah's intelligence service, with copies to Shaltiel. The reports were mainly based on two sources, "Ram," (Pilavsky's code name), and "Esther," (Shimon Moneta's code name). While Pilavsky was a staunch opponent of the "dissidents," Moneta, as will be recalled, was a Haganah agent inside Lehi. While he remained faithful to his operators, he nevertheless came to at least partially identify with Lehi. The difference between the reports based on Pilavsky and those based on Moneta was obvious. While a report based on the former was titled "The Atrocities of the Dissidents in Operation Deir Yassin," the reports based on Moneta were titled "A Joint Operation of the Dissidents in Jerusalem" and "The Dissidents' Operation in Deir Yassin." The report based on Pilavsky concentrated on various allegedly unjustified killings committed by Etzel and Lehi. In contrast, the reports based on Moneta gave a fair description of the events (and accurate figures),

Fig. 50 Shimon Moneta, the Haganah's spy inside Lehi

with an emphasis on Lehi's doings. A Moneta based report, for obvious reasons, presented Lehi in a more favorable light than Etzel. It mentioned the defective weaponry brought by Etzel and that the disorder in the ranks of Etzel was greater than in Lehi. It claimed that Etzel treated the prisoners barbarously, while Lehi tried to attend to the issue of burial. It also claimed that Lehi felt deceived by Etzel on various occasions during the attack.[5]

Levy also compiled a report summing up the affair based on all the sources in his possession, including both "Ram" and "Esther."

While the report emphasized the faults of the attack ("chaos," lack of intelligence, lack of proper training and shortage of ammunition), it pointed out that the performance of Lehi was more efficient than Etzel's. It repeated the claim that Lehi was bitter about Etzel's inadequate performance. Yet the report also adopted Pilavsky's words regarding the various Arabs killed and the cruelty of the conquest. "Whole families were killed, women, the elderly and children; piles of dead people were stacked up." A copy of the report was sent to Shaltiel (and to Pilavsky).[6]

HAGANAH VERSUS ETZEL AND LEHI

In the midst of battle, at 11:50 a.m., Etzel radioed an announcement about the progress of the fighting to its headquarters in Tel Aviv, forwarded by Saturday to the Jewish press and broadcast on Sunday by *Kol Zion ha-Lohemet*, Etzel's broadcasting station. It mentioned two Palmach units having joined the battle, news that astounded the Haganah's headquarters in Tel Aviv. On midnight Saturday, Arnan Azaryahu, Galili's adjutant, cabled Shaltiel asking for details of Palmach participation. "It will be denied," Azaryahu stressed. By then, Shaltiel already knew the number of dead, and apparently dismayed by the implications, wanted to dissociate himself from the affair. The next morning he answered Galili and Azaryahu that he had tried to dissuade the "dissidents" from launching the attack, offering them Qalunya or 'Ayn Karm instead as targets, to the benefit of Operation Nahshon. They had refused, got into difficulties and subsequently begging the Haganah to save their wounded, which it did. However, "Our forces did not attend the village nor took part." Shaltiel further reported that the "dissidents" fought incompetently, massacred children, women and old people, and paraded prisoners in the city, scoffing at them (the Haganah delivered them to the British). Etzel left the village after looting it. Lehi was still there. Shaltiel repeated this statement to journalists, claiming that the Haganah had no advance knowledge of the attack, which did not integrate into the overall plan for Jerusalem's defense. Lehi informed the press that the Haganah were aware. The Haganah in

Tel Aviv vehemently denied the participation of any Palmach units in the attack.[7]

The Haganah decided to publish an official statement about the affair. Eliyahu Sasson, director of the Arab section of the Jewish Agency's political department, prepared a draft in which he suggested not just to rebuke the "dissidents" for their disgraceful act, inconsistent with the tradition of the Jewish people, but to permit the villagers to return and resettle. The Haganah would undertake to defend the returning villagers from any further evil and thus rectify the injustice done to them. He, in effect proposed reestablishing the village. Sasson's draft was not adopted. On 12 April, the Haganah issued a statement, posted throughout Jerusalem, in which it explained that it had to replace Etzel and Lehi in Deir Yassin after they had fled, because their actions exposed Jerusalem to a new front. The actions of the "dissidents" had not been a real military operation, amounting to nothing more than a propaganda exercise. Had they sought to make a real contribution, they would have attacked the Arab irregulars operating around Jerusalem, and not a peaceful village. "For the whole day Etzel and Lehi were engaged in the slaughter of women and children, and also men, not in battle, but intentionally and clearly for the sole purpose of massacre and murder." They had also looted the village. Their claim that two Palmach units fought with them was false; the Haganah only assisted in first aid operations to save their wounded. Looking for cheap success, the "dissidents" revealed their military incompetence and barbarism. It was left for the Haganah to bury the dead and to look after the property left, in order to return it to its owners in due course.[8]

The Haganah's statement astounded Etzel and Lehi. Immediately they posted a counter statement, denouncing Shaltiel's "distortion" and the "agitation" carried out by the "hypocrites." They insisted that Deir Yassin was a hostile village of a strategic value, which had frequently attacked Jerusalem's western suburbs. Taking the village had freed the western suburbs from the threat of the Arab irregulars that had used it as a base and who had also endangered the Jerusalem-Tel Aviv road. Shaltiel himself had understood the necessity of conquering the village, which he confirmed in a letter he had written to them. It had been a fierce battle. They had been fired on from almost every house, as attested to by the high number of casualties they had suffered. In order to minimize loss of life, they had used a loudspeaker in advance of the attack to warn the villagers to evacuate, thus sacrificing the element of surprise. Only those who did not heed the warning were injured or killed during the fighting. One hundred and fifty prisoners had been transferred to security zone C, and the Haganah's claim to have carried it out was a lie. They expressed their regret that women and children had suffered, but it had not been their fault. The poster reminded the Haganah "hypocrites" of similar attacks they had carried out, without any advance warning, which ended up with the death of women and children. Shaltiel was motivated by nothing more than blindness and jealousy.[9]

Etzel and Lehi quickly issued a further poster, which included a photo of Shaltiel's letter of 7 April, which unequivocally proved that he knew about the attack, and in which he stated, "the capture and holding of Deir Yassin forms one phase of our general plan." Kaufman erased the last words of Shaltiel's letter, about the plan to build an airstrip, adding a handwritten remark: "The last words were erased out of security considerations relating to the entire [Jewish] community." In addition to the letter, the poster reiterated the claim that capturing Deir Yassin released Jerusalem's western suburbs from the threat of attack from Arab irregulars that found shelter there. Furthermore, at the Haganah's request on the eve of the battle, they coordinated the attack with the recapture of Qastal by the Haganah. The capture of Deir Yassin frightened the Arabs in the nearby villages into fleeing, thus loosening the siege of Jerusalem. The poster also explained the reasons for Etzel's and Lehi's withdrawal from the village. Firstly, they were a combat force, needed for further operations, and not a garrison unit. Secondly, the British intended to exploit the opportunity to launch an air strike on them, as had been stated by the government radio. As to the looting charge raised by the Haganah, the Haganah and Solel Boneh did a much better job of robbing the village when they replaced them.[10]

Etzel's headquarters in Tel Aviv also issued a poster containing Shaltiel's letter, titled "Hypocrisy Should be Denounced." Following

רק כד

הודעה על פרשת דיר-יאסין

תשובה לכרוז הצהוב (על משקל הטלאי הצהוב) של ה„הגנה".

את הנמקים הצבאיים שחייבו את החזקת דיר יאסין הסברנו.

אנו מביאים בזה לידיעת הצבור את המכתב של ה„הגנה" במחוז ירושלים (ממ"ז) ללא פירושים נוספים:

אל: א.צ.ל

מאת: פס"ז.

נודע לי שאתם מתכונים לבצע .פעולה על דיר-יאסי'.

ברצוני להעיר את תשומת-לבכם לעובדה, שתפיסת דיר-יאסין
והחזקתה הנם שלב אחד בתכנית כללית. אין לי כל התנגדות שאתם
תבצעו את הפעולה בתנאי שיש בכחכם להחזיק בו. אם אין לאל ידכם לעשות
זו, הריני מזהיר אתכם מפני פיצוץ הכפר, אשר בעקבותיו יביא לעזיבתו ע"י
התושבים ותפיסת החרבות והגנים העזובים ע"י כוחות זרים. מצב כזה כנגד
במקרה להכל על הערכה הכללית וכיבוש שני של המקום יהיה כרוך בקרב'/ענות
גדולים של אנשינו.

בימוק נוסף שנרצוני להביא לפניכם הוא, שאם יישכנו לספוק כוחות
זרים, יהיה בזה פסום הפרעה לתכנית הקמת ~~תכנית~~
7.4.48

לאחר שכבשנו את הכפר דיר-יאסין והחזקנו בו שלשה ימים רצופים, הגשמנו את המטרות שהצבנו לעצמנו במלואן:

א. השמדנו את כוחות הפושעים הערבים שהתבצרו במקום ואיימו על השכונות המערביות של ירושלים העברית.

ב. הזרמנו את כל הנשק והתחמושת שבכפר והעברנום לרשות האומה הלוחמת.

ג. הראינו שע"י כוח עב"י לוחם קטן ביחס, אפשר לבצע פעולה צבאית אסטרטגית ממדרגה ראשונה—אם הכוח העברי הזה פועל לפי תכנית נועזת ומחושבת לפרטיה.

...

א. ביום ח' בח' אדר ב' בערב, פנו אלינו אנשי ה„הגנה" בבקשה, שנתאים את שעת קרב הכבוש שלנו עם שעת קרב הכבוש של תקפסל מחדש המבוצע על יד**ם. ואכן, שתי פעולות אלו בוצעו בעת ובשונה אחת.**

...

האצ"ל הצבאי הלאומי
בארץ ישראל

ניסן תש"ח

the letter were several sharply worded statements: "It is clear now that (a) the Haganah's commander consciously lied when he stated following the conquest of Deir Yassin that this operation was contrary to the 'general plan'; (b) the truth is that conquering Deir Yassin was part of his own plan." Actually, Etzel and Lehi did the job for the Haganah, at a high price of 4 dead and 32 wounded, probably saving the Haganah similar losses. Etzel's radio station broadcast the contents of Shaltiel's letter and accused him of "lying, cowardice and disgusting hypocrisy." It claimed that the conquest of Deir Yassin had changed the strategic position of Jerusalem "with one blow." Etzel and Lehi had conquered the village as requested and had delivered it to the Haganah as promised, and it was only after the fact that Shaltiel began abusing and vilifying them. It further suggested that Shaltiel was doing so at the command of his party (*Mapai*, Ben-Gurion's center-left party) and the Jewish Agency.[11]

As usual in such cases, Haganah members started to tear down Etzel's posters, which in some cases led to exchanges of blows. Meir Pilavsky hastened to publish an article in *ba-Mahane*, the Haganah's countrywide organ, in which he defended Shaltiel, accusing Etzel and Lehi of aggravating their crime by the publication of Shaltiel's letter. The man responsible for Jerusalem's defense had to waste his time in negotiating and corresponding with the "dissidents." He further claimed that the Haganah only killed rioters when attacking Arab villages, and if women and children were killed, it was unintentionally. In contrast to the "dissidents," the Haganah did not carry out "a massacre for the sake of massacre." Etzel and Lehi "disgraced the Hebrew weapon."[12]

The Haganah leadership, however, was genuinely puzzled. In an urgent cable, Galili demanded to know if Shaltiel was corresponding with Etzel and if he had written to them about Deir Yassin. He wanted to see a copy of the 7 April letter. He demanded an end to any correspondence with Etzel. Shaltiel answered that he actually did not want to meet with them at all and warned them that if they could not hold the village it would complicate the situation and endanger the plan to build an airstrip. He promised Galili to cease any written or oral contact with them, pending further instructions. He would also try to curb their activities so much as possible. The publication of the 7 April letter seriously damaged Shaltiel's credibility. *Mapam* (United Workers Party), the far-left partner of Ben-Gurion's center-left *Mapai* (Land of Israel Workers Party), and especially its *ha-Shomer ha-Tzair* (Youth Guard) wing, demanded Shaltiel's dismissal for his cooperation with the "dissidents." Shaltiel countered that such operations were within his discretion. In any case, Ben-Gurion did not intend to fire him. It seems that, at some point, Ben-Gurion made his own inquiries. Many years later, two notes written by him were found. In the first, he wrote, "A Haganah (Palmach) force participated in Deir Yassin (without my authorization)." In the second, he wrote, "The Haganah did not initiate the operation and at first did not take part. But the 'unit' that was there did more than just 'rescuing' the rioters."[13]

OTHER JEWISH RESPONSES

On 11 April, in a meeting of the executive of the Jewish Agency in Tel Aviv, Ben-Gurion noted that Leo Kohn asked their permission to denounce the "dissidents" in a press conference. Permission was granted. In the evening, the executive issued a statement of its own regarding Deir Yassin, expressing its "horror and disgust" at the "barbarous" behavior of Etzel and Lehi. Nonetheless, it noted the many barbarities committed by Arabs (murdering civilians, killing the wounded, mutilating the dead, and refusing to take prisoners), which had never been condemned by any of the Arab leaders. Still, similar brutalities committed by Jews were "utterly repugnant" to the spirit of the Jewish community. Since armed conflict in Palestine seemed inevitable, the Jewish Agency was asking all parties involved at least to follow "the rules of civilised warfare." The Agency, for its part, would scrupulously observe these principles. The statement was broadcast the next day by the Haganah's radio in Arabic, which pointed out that the Arabs were proud of their crimes against the Jews, making the Jews retaliate. Although the perpetrators of the tragedy in Deir Yassin were irresponsible people, and the Jews felt ashamed by their deeds, they would be glad to see Arab leaders reacting similarly to atrocities committed by Arabs. Had they done so, the Deir Yassin crime would never have happened and the situation in Palestine would not have reached its present crisis.[14]

On 12 April, the Jewish Agency decided to send a message to 'Abdallah, king of Transjordan, to clarify its position regarding the affair. The message, written by Eliyahu Sasson, was an abstract of the previous day's statement, condemning the incident, and defining it as barbarous and contradicting the spirit of the Jewish people. It stressed that the perpetrators belonged to "dissident" groups. The Agency called on all parties to manage the conflict in a civilized manner and according to the rules of war. Sending the message seemed odd to many, including the British ambassador in Amman (no other Arab leader got such a message). The most widely believed explanation was that Ben-Gurion feared that the affair would put pressure on 'Abdallah to refrain from reaching an understanding with him. It might drive Transjordan into war with the nascent Jewish state. He therefore tried to appease 'Abdallah, which could also benefit Jewish diplomacy in the United Nations, proving that a non-belligerent solution was still possible. However, on the very same day, Samir al-Rifa'i, chief of the Royal Bureau, answered in 'Abdallah's name, that everyone knew that the Agency was in control of everything concerning the Zionists and that no Jew would act against its will – in other words, it could not shirk responsibility. While such an incident might prevent the possibility of truce, nevertheless the Agency's abhorrence of it was appreciated. The Agency should do everything required to prevent atrocities. Etzel and the like should also reflect upon the grave consequences of their savage actions.[15]

The Chief Rabbinate, too, issued a proclamation, signed by the two chief rabbis, denouncing the affair. It was the deed of an irresponsible minority, contradicting the basic principles of mankind and Jewish moral heritage. The perpetrators brought shame on the Jewish community and cast a slur on its struggle for survival. They were praying that a Spirit from on High would cleanse the hearts of those Jews, frenzied into such acts by Jewish miseries. The proclamation did not include an excommunication of the attackers, as was later claimed. Zettler was deeply offended by it and went to the Sephardi chief rabbi, Rabbi Ben-Zion Uziel, to protest, only to learn, according to Zettler, that the rabbi did not even know about the proclamation he was supposed to have signed. (In an earlier testimony, Zettler said that Rabbi Uziel did sign the proclamation but was ready to disclaim it.) Following Rabbi Uziel's advice, Zettler also went to the Ashkenazi chief rabbi, Rabbi Isaac Herzog, suggesting to him that he meet with some of Lehi's combatants to hear their version of the story. He told him that, in order to avoid unnecessary bloodshed they had brought a car with a loudspeaker, thus risking their own life. No Arab would do something like that, nor any Christian. However, they were shot at from everywhere and had no choice but to shoot back. Rabbi Herzog was not convinced.[16]

While Etzel's leader, Menachem Begin, considered the conquest of Deir Yassin a great, heroic achievement, and congratulated his combatants, the opinions among Lehi's leaders were divided. Israel Scheib, Lehi's ideologist, later wrote that without Deir Yassin the state of Israel would have no chance to exist. Nathan Friedman-Yellin, at the time sick in Tel Aviv, believed the massacre narrative and contemplated publicly denouncing the affair, which he did not do because of the agitation carried out against Lehi by the Haganah and the "apologies" cable sent to 'Abdallah. (Many of Lehi's members were infuriated by this telegram.) He did though send a private letter to Zettler, sharply condemning the operation, for both its ferocity and the cooperation with Etzel without prior permission from Lehi's central command. Friedman-Yellin complained to Scheib that it was Zettler's "independence" which caused all this.[17]

Despite the turbid relations, in mid-May Etzel's Jerusalem branch resumed cooperation with the Haganah, in face of the invading Arab Legion; Lehi preferred to continue to operate independently. The Haganah completed the planned airstrip, but since it was exposed to both enemy shells from Nabi Samwil and strong winds, it was hardly used. Actually, only a single light airplane dared to frequent it. The deserted quarries south of it also constituted a risk, and finally, after the Burma Road had been opened at the beginning of the first truce, relieving Jerusalem of the siege, the runway was abandoned.

Today it constitutes Givat Shaul's ruler-straight main road, Kanfei Nesharim.[18]

Amidst the war, several members of the tiny *Ihud* (Union) association (which believed in a bi-national state for Jews and Arabs in Palestine), headed by Martin Buber, demanded that the Jewish Agency publish a report on Deir Yassin, as it had been done in similar cases of atrocities against Jews. Describing the affair as "degraded hooliganism" of the worst kind against peaceful neighbors, they demanded either an objective detailed report, if possible, or at least the setting up of an official inquiry commission with a preset timetable. They also recommended compensating the families of the casualties. No one bothered to answer them. A year later, when the Israeli government intended to settle the village with new immigrants, Buber, Ernst Simon and some others appealed to Ben-Gurion asking him to refrain from this step. They claimed that the wound was too fresh; hundreds of innocent people had been killed there, which had stained the honor the Jewish nation. Perhaps in the future something might be done there to demonstrate the Jewish will for justice and fraternity with the Arabs. For the time being, however, the village should be left alone, uncultivated and unpopulated. Settling the place a year after the crime, would mean approving the mass murder. Ben-Gurion did not bother to answer, nor answer two reminders, and when Buber pressed, Ben-Gurion's secretary answered that he could not find the time to read their letter.[19]

In the summer of 1948, representatives of both the Israeli government and the Jewish Agency visited Deir Yassin to examine its suitability for resettlement. The conclusion was that the village was suitable for farmers and artisans. The houses did not need much renovating and the village had public facilities like schools. In early 1949, it was decided to resettle the village with new immigrants from Eastern Europe. Several hundred immigrants were brought there, bus service resumed, phones were connected, and a grocery, a clinic and a synagogue were opened. The village was renamed Givat Shaul B in a public ceremony, attended by ministers, the mayor of Jerusalem and the chief rabbis. President Weizmann sent his congratulations. The village did not prove to be a success, and was turned over to the ministry of health, which in 1951 opened a mental hospital there (the last of the immigrants left by 1959). The hospital, "Kfar Shaul," still operates today and makes use of many of the village's old houses; though since the 1980s it has been surrounded by the new Jewish neighborhood of Har Nof.[20]

In 1951, four former members of Etzel, who had been wounded in Deir Yassin, demanded to receive the appropriate benefits from the state, as given to other veterans. The officer in charge consulted Ben-Gurion and the answer was negative. According to the law, only people involved in organized operations against Arab irregulars or the invading Arab armies, from 30 November 1947 to the end of 1948, could be considered as having served in the army. Ben-Gurion, in his capacity as security minister, "could not see the possibility" to define the attack on Deir Yassin as an organized operation against Arab irregulars. The veterans lodged an appeal against the decision. The trial lasted a year. Besides the appellants themselves, also Kaufman, Cohen and some others who had been involved in the events gave testimonies. Shaltiel's letter of 7 April turned out to be the main evidence in favor of the appellants. While Kaufman encountered some difficulties in tracing it, the army authorities located the outgoing copy. When reading it, they realized that their case was lost. It clearly stated that the Haganah itself intended to conquer Deir Yassin and proved that Shaltiel did not oppose the operation. They further found Gicherman's report of 10 April, in which he detailed some of the Haganah's assistance to the operation. They concluded that the operation had, indeed, been coordinated with the Haganah. On 24 May 1953, the judges unanimously accepted the appeal. Based on the evidence provided, they stated the conquest of Deir Yassin to fall within the definitions of the law. For the first time, the battle over Deir Yassin was officially recognized.[21]

Chapter 10

The Arab Reactions

THE PALESTINIAN COMMUNITY

On Sunday, the American consul-general, Thomas Wasson, visited Husayn al-Khalidi, who "trembling with rage," avowed that the Jews were using the "worst Nazi tactics." Dana Adams Schmidt, the correspondent of the *New York Times*, visited Khalidi too, finding him in a similar mood. It was a terrorist act, he said, intended to panic the Arabs. In the evening Khalidi convened a press conference, attended by more than forty correspondents, foreign and local. Khalidi felt that, in order to pressure the Arab states to intervene and to strengthen the Palestinian *sumud* (resistance), he had to exaggerate. Khalidi was going to commit a grave, fatal mistake, which he did not realize at the time. Much of his statement in the conference was reasonably accurate. He spoke about the non-belligerency agreement between Deir Yassin and the Jews, he related how the British had turned him down when he was asking for help, which obliged him to turn to the Red Cross, and he reported de Reynier's findings and the attempts to bury the dead. The main bulk of his speech, however, dealt with the "massacre." The Jews, living among the Arabs for 1,300 years (and one million Jews were still living among them, he noted), were exercising

165

against the Arabs the same methods the Nazis had used against the Jews. Two hundred and fifty Arabs had been killed, among them 25 pregnant women, 50 breast-feeding mothers and 60 other women and girls, all "slaughtered like sheep." Although Khalidi believed the 250 death toll to be an accurate accounting, the other numbers were simply an invention.[1]

At 9:30 p.m., the Jerusalem radio broadcast Khalidi's statement. At its end, Khalidi promised to issue a detailed communiqué shortly.

Fig. 52 Husayn Fakhri al-Khalidi, secretary of the Arab Higher Committee

He instructed Hazim Nusayba, the Arabic news editor of the Palestine Broadcasting Service, to give the affair "the utmost propaganda possible." "We are forced to give a picture – not what is actually happening – but we had to exaggerate a little bit so that maybe the Arab countries would become enthusiastic to come and assist us," he told him. He issued Nusayba a strongly worded communiqué to broadcast, alleging the rape of pregnant women, murder of children, mutilation of bodies and numerous other atrocities. The idea was to broadcast it without prior screening by the British censorship. The impact of the broadcast was overwhelming, as will be described below.[2]

However, this was not enough. Khalidi was one of the first to visit the refugees from Deir Yassin arriving in Jerusalem. He summoned some of them to his headquarters to convince them to exaggerate their accounts of the affair. "We want you to say that the Jews slaughtered people, committed atrocities, raped and stole gold," he told them, overriding any objection. This was the only way to make the Arab armies free Palestine. Some of the refugees obeyed, sending telegrams to that effect to the Arab kings and governments. An Arab physician treating a bruise on a child's forehead asked his mother what else the attackers had done. They "put the children on the road and put the mothers in a truck and drove over the children" she answered. Perhaps some of the impressions gathered by Assistant Inspector-General Catling (see above) could also be attributed to statements conforming to these instructions. Some of the refugees were photographed for propaganda purposes. Rumors also spread that an Arab photographer took pictures in Deir Yassin of mutilated bodies. When the Arab Higher Committee published such photos, a Haganah intelligence man identified the bodies as actually being Jewish victims of mutilation by Arabs.[3]

At the end of his statement, Khalidi pointed out that he had already informed 'Abdallah and other Muslim and Christian leaders of the "outrage" committed in Deir Yassin. A report was also sent to the Arab League. The next day, Khalidi left Jerusalem for Amman, to recount the details to 'Abdallah in person and apprise him of the delicate situation of Arab Jerusalem. After his meeting with 'Abdallah, Khalidi continued to Damascus to meet with President Shukri al-Quwwatli for the same purpose. He then continued to Beirut and Egypt. Khalidi would be absent from Palestine until the end of the war, except for a period during the first truce. In later life he would develop quite a significant political career, appointed to various offices in Jordan, including twice serving as foreign minister (in 1953 and 1955) and for ten days prime minister (in April 1957).[4]

The two Arab dailies appearing in Palestine at the time, *al-Difa'* and *Filastin*, played a key role in spreading the story. Under the headline "The Jews committed a savage crime in Deir Yassin," *al-Difa'* related to its readers how the Jews had stripped the women of Deir Yassin naked as well as torturing women and children, the sick and the elderly. Under the headline "The blood curdles at the hideous Jewish atrocities in Deir Yassin," the newspaper related how children lost their parents, women suffered torture and degradation, and men were killed and maimed. The newspaper also reported Khalidi's press conference in detail, under the title "The Jewish criminals slew 250 victims, most of them women and children, in the barbarous massacre of innocents in the village of Deir Yassin." *Filastin* wrote of houses being blown up over their occupants, unarmed men killed

with cold steel and the mutilation of bodies. The women who survived were stripped and paraded naked through Jerusalem. It headed
the article, "O Arabs! The Jews have driven away your women and
children; hereafter, there should be neither forbearance nor tolerance
toward this kind of cowardly gutless people." In another article, titled
"Crocodile tears," it blamed the Jewish Agency for connivance with
the attackers. *Filastin* also brought the story of Fahima Zaydan (see
above), presented as a proof for the massacre narrative, again repeating the stripping of the women allegation (adding that they had been
photographed naked).[5]

When the released prisoners from Deir Yassin arrived in Arab
Jerusalem, two organizations took it upon themselves to supply
them with food, clothing and shelter, the National Committee and
the social affairs department of the Arab Higher Committee. The
mandatory government's social welfare department also assisted. In
addition to the two hundred released prisoners, there were a further
seven hundred other refugees, mainly in 'Ayn Karm, to attend to.
Some of the latter were employed in the preparation of coffins for
the dead (which no one was going to use). It was clear that the first,
urgent task was to gather all the refugees into one location. Trucks
and buses were sent to 'Ayn Karm and other villages in the vicinity
to collect the survivors and bring them to Jerusalem. The refugees'
first stop was a hotel near Jaffa Gate, where for the first time, they
could try to find out which of their relatives had survived the attack.
Their first concern was to bury their family members who had been
killed, but appeals to the British army and police to facilitate these
efforts were ignored. The National Committee and the Arab Higher
Committee were looking after a total of 730 refugees, a number too
great to be accommodated inside the walls of the Old City. Therefore, the refugees were dispersed to other locations, many of them
(over 200) to the village of Silwan, where local families temporarily
hosted them. Others were sent to Arab neighborhoods outside the
walls, such as Qatamon.[6]

Providing for the refugees was very costly and the National
Committee did not have the necessary funds. It estimated that a
minimum of 146 Palestine pounds per day was needed to provide for

the needs of the refugees. Some suggested awarding each refugee a cash grant of at least ten pounds, to make them feel they had received something substantial. The Committee started a fund-raising campaign, setting up a special subcommittee to handle this, and applied to various institutions for help. Ahmad Hilmi 'Abd al-Baqi, owner of the Arab National Bank, donated 1,000 Palestine pounds. The Arab Bank also donated, as did its workers individually, along with the Arab workers of the postal service. The Supreme Muslim Council donated 200 Palestine pounds. Sums of money were collected daily, both in Jerusalem and in remote cities such as Haifa and Jaffa. In addition to the fundraising, schools collected large quantities of clothing for the refugees, delivering them to the National Committee. The local women's union decided to set up subcommittees to assist the refugees and buy food and clothing for the children, as well as see to it that pregnant women and the wounded received medical treatment and were hospitalized where necessary. The union and the schools helped the National Committee in distributing the aid; a mission on behalf of the union visited Silwan to investigate the needs of the refugees.[7]

A special project in this regard was the establishment of an orphanage by Hind al-Husayni, a cousin of 'Abd al-Qadir. On her way to a meeting with Anwar al-Khatib, the acting mayor of Arab Jerusalem, she saw children wandering the street. When she warned them to go home, lest stray bullets might injure them, one of them answered that they had no home, as they were refugees from Deir Yassin. In the meeting, she apprised the attendees of what she had seen. Khatib retorted that there was no point in going into specifics and anyhow there were more refugees than they could provide for. She realized that it was up to her to cope with the issue and during the following week gathered more than fifty orphans, first lodging them in two rented rooms and later in her own family mansion. The orphanage, called *Dar al-Tifl al-'Arabi* (the house of the Arab child), expanded over the years, developing into a school, which still exists to this very day.[8]

However, there also were other reactions, of a different nature. The Palestinian Arab Party issued a communiqué to the mukhtars of the villages around Jerusalem calling on them to admit outside combatants into their villages, citing the fate of Deir Yassin, which had refused to do so. An instruction was given to kill any Jew without exception instead of taking prisoners. Fawzi al-Qawuqji, the commander of the Rescue Army, then besieging the Jewish settlement of Mishmar ha-Emek, was asked to slaughter all the settlement's occupants "without mercy." Qawuqji could not do so, since his forces in Mishmar ha-Emek were defeated. However, on Saturday evening an artillery battery, sent by him earlier to assist the Arabs in the battle over Qastal, was tasked to shell the western Jewish suburbs causing some damage. One Jew was killed.[9]

On 13 April, a much more serious incident took place. The Arabs attacked a Jewish convoy on its way to Hadassah hospital, killing 78 people (20 of them women), most of them medical staff. Many, including senior British officials, the High Commissioner among them, interpreted the attack as a reprisal for Deir Yassin. While some of the assailants did shout "Remember Deir Yassin!" and "Avenge Deir Yassin!" it appears that the attack would have been carried out anyhow. The Arabs believed that Haganah combatants were exploiting the convoy to reach Mount Scopus and operate from the hospital and the university against them. The same applied to the attack a month later on Kfar Etzion, bringing about the death of 127 Jews (21 of them women), after they had surrendered. Some of the Arab attackers shouted "Deir Yassin, Deir Yassin," but the attack would have taken place anyway because of the settlement's strategic location. It might be that the Deir Yassin affair aggravated the outcomes of these attacks but it did not cause them.[10]

THE IMPACT ON THE PALESTINIAN FLIGHT

"The other villages started to leave one after the other, without resistance, out of fear and apprehension of another similar massacre," Yunus Radwan, a survivor from Deir Yassin, wrote five years later. It happened, he continued, "because of a mistake committed by our leaders and those responsible for the spreading of rumors who overstated the crimes of the Jews." They did it in order to awaken the Arab League and armies to defeat the Jews, but instead they buried the Palestinian determination. "By spreading these rumors, that the Jews committed savage and atrocious crimes," they sowed fear in the hearts of Palestinians, who left their houses and property for the Jews. "These rumor spreaders committed the gravest political mistake," most of the Palestinians falling victim to their error, he concluded. It was "the most stupid misguided policy." Yunus Radwan was not alone in this conviction. Actually, 'Adil Yahya, a Palestinian researcher who interviewed many refugees in the late 1990s, reached the conclusion that most of them clearly stated that "the Deir Yassin affair was the main cause for the 1948 exodus."[11]

As related above, Khalidi, the senior Arab political authority in Jerusalem at the time, was of the opinion that only by exaggerating the affair and adding atrocities, would the Arab states be persuaded to intervene militarily and prevent "a catastrophe." He also hoped that it would strengthen the Palestinian resistance. He had instructed Nusayba, of the Palestine Broadcasting Service, to give it "the utmost propaganda possible," and issued him a communiqué stating rapes, murders, mutilation of bodies and other atrocities, soon broadcast repeatedly all over Palestine. "This was a decisive moment," Nusayba related. "This particular strong communiqué when I think about it now was one of the main reasons for the collapse of the armed resistance in Palestine. We did not understand the mentality of our own Palestinian people." "This turned [out] to be the highest, most expensive mistake that we made." "It had a traumatic effect." Until this point, the villages had been willing to defend themselves, but now they were panicked and demoralized. It triggered the mass exodus. "Dr Hussein Fakhri Al-Khalidi was the one who caused the catastrophe," Muhammad Mahmud Radwan, another survivor, declared. "Instead of working in our favour, the propaganda worked in favour of the Jews. Whole villages and towns fled because what they heard had happened in Deir Yassin." Other survivors concurred. As one Palestinian researcher summed it up "The Palestinian people paid dearly for a communiqué issued without a sober estimate of the situation."[12]

Many believe that the major factor driving the Palestinians to flee was the rape allegation. Nusayba said it "touched a raw nerve in the Palestinian psyche." The moment the Palestinians heard about rapes they started to leave, refusing to remain and defend their villages. One of the mukhtars told him: "We are not afraid of death, but we will not accept that our women be raped. We cannot survive if our women are raped." Everyone believed that women and girls were raped in Deir Yassin. Amin al-Majjaj, a physician in Jerusalem at the time, related that they heard that "most of the women of Deiryassin from the ages of six to seventy were raped." He said that it was the rape of women, rather than the other alleged atrocities, which caused the Palestinian exodus. The impact of the fear of rapes was overwhelming, as attested to by many Palestinian refugees, both men and women. A refugee woman told an interviewer that the Arabs of Haifa left because of this. Another refugee woman related that she heard that girls were raped in front of their families and then murdered. Since they did not want the same to happen to them, they fled. Another woman related that her father wanted to fight. However, since he was afraid about their honor (*'ird*), he decided that they should leave instead.[13]

The attack on Deir Yassin coincided with the recapture of Qastal by the Jews (which temporarily broke the Arab siege of Jerusalem), the death of 'Abd al-Qadir al-Husayni, and the later defeat of Qawuqji in Mishmar ha-Emek. Arab morale was at its nadir, while the Jews were gaining their first military successes. Entire villages evacuated without a single shot out of fear of the advancing Jewish forces. Many Arab sources claimed that the Jews actually exploited the Deir Yassin affair in order to drive the Palestinians out. Some claimed that Etzel and Lehi deliberately let Arab survivors leave the village, in order that they would spread the story. Others blamed the Jewish mainstream, which ostensibly condemned the affair, for using all kinds of media to disseminate the rumors, in order to scare the Palestinians away. One accusation was that Haganah vehicles with loudspeakers were driving through the streets of Jerusalem's Arab neighborhoods, warning the residents "unless you leave your homes, the fate of Deir Yassin will be your fate" and advising them that the road to Jericho was still open. There is hardly any corroborating evidence for this from Haganah sources. Actually, only one report relating to Khirbat 'Azzun recounted that Haganah men told the villagers that one could not guarantee that "another Deir Yassin would not occur here as well," as an argument why they should leave. It seems therefore, that if such a phenomenon existed, it was not part of a coordinated campaign but the result of initiatives by local commanders.[14]

In a poster Etzel and Lehi circulated after the affair they boasted that "the conquest of Deir Yassin frightened and terrified the Arabs in all the nearby villages; Maliha, Qalunya and Bayt Iksa began to stampede," which facilitated the resumption of transportation to Jerusalem. "With one blow we changed the strategic position of our capital," Etzel's broadcasting station added. Begin reiterated this in his memories, adding that the horror propaganda about Deir Yassin also facilitated the conquest of Tiberias and Haifa. Kaufman and Zettler shared his opinion, both defining the battle over Deir Yassin as a turning point in the 1948 war. Historian Meir Pa'il (formerly Pilavsky), sought to minimize the role played by Etzel and Lehi in the war. He examined the behavior of the Arab villages within a radius of ten kilometers around Deir Yassin, and concluded that the taking of Deir Yassin was worthless from the military perspective. He claimed that no one fled from the advancing Jewish forces due to Deir Yassin. Although it was true that the Haganah captured some places relatively easily, in other places it encountered serious difficulties. In some places, there was a heavy fighting and in Nabi Samwil and Bayt Surik, the Haganah failed. Therefore, Pa'il concluded, the argument that Deir Yassin caused the Arabs to flee was "real garbage."[15]

It seems that Pa'il's concept was fundamentally flawed. The question was not whether Arab combatants continued to withstand the Jewish forces, but whether the civilian population run away as a result of the rumors about Deir Yassin. In cases where the civilians fled, the fact that armed combatants continued to defend the villages was to a certain extent irrelevant. In any case, the records reveal a different picture than that portrayed by Pa'il. Starting on Friday, many of 'Ayn Karm's inhabitants, especially women and children, left. The village was captured in mid-July without a fight. Some of the old women who remained told a visitor that the flight was the result of the events in Deir Yassin. Qalunya was conquered on 11 April almost without resistance. Its inhabitants fled to Arab Jerusalem. Many of Suba's inhabitants also fled there in April, despite the Haganah attacks on it having failed up to this point, it was conquered in mid-July without a battle. The Haganah took Saris in mid-April without resistance, its inhabitants fleeing to Arab Jerusalem. Maliha's inhabitants started to leave in mid-April (almost all of the women and children within one week). The village was completely evacuated only in mid-July after a fierce battle. Bayt Iksa's inhabitants, too, started to leave in mid-April, though the village eventually remained beyond the armistice line. The villages of Biddu and Bayt Surik, captured by the Haganah on 20 April, also remained beyond the line of Jewish control. Other villages in the vicinity, Jura, Sataf and Walaja, were conquered at a later stage of the war.[16]

While many of the refugees from the surrounding villages flocked to Jerusalem, many Arab families from the new city left for the Old City or planned to leave the country altogether. Hala al-Sakakini, living in Qatamon, wrote in her diary that since the massacre in Deir Yassin they seriously considered leaving Jerusalem. They heard hideous stories from survivors. "Pregnant women and children were tortured to death, young women were stripped naked, humiliated and driven through the Jewish quarters to be spit upon by the crowds." As the Jews were liable to repeat such acts, they might have to leave their home soon. In Talbiya Arabs were so terrified by the Deir Yassin stories, that they left their meal on the table and fled when the Jewish forces arrived. An Arab from Musrara related that "news of the massacre there sent shivers of fear into the hearts of every Palestinian, man, woman and child." A woman from Abu Dis said, "This massacre scared the *whole* population of Palestine. Everyone talked about the massacre in Deir Yassin."[17]

The impact of Deir Yassin went far beyond Jerusalem and the surrounding villages and spread all over Palestine, causing fear and driving people to leave. A woman from Safad related hearing of the rapes and killings in Deir Yassin. Another refugee woman attributed the flight from Haifa to the fear of what the Jews were going to do to women, as they heard that women and girls were raped in Deir Yassin and the bellies of pregnant women were slashed. "What do you want? Do you want them to come and open my belly?" a pregnant woman from Nazareth asked her husband. A native of Haifa updated an acquaintance of his about Deir Yassin, citing Khalidi's stories, including the slaughter "like sheep" of 25 pregnant women, 50 breast-feeding mothers and 60 other women and girls. A great fear was also noticed in the villages near Haifa, like Yajur or Furaydis. The residents of the former left in the second half of April, while those of the latter approached the Haifa's National Committee for help (about a week before the fall of Haifa itself). Khirbat 'Azzun in the coastal plain evacuated in mid-April to avoid Deir Yassin's fate. Demoralization partly attributed to Deir Yassin was also noticed in Jaffa. A native of the city wrote to an acquaintance in Egypt that the Jews used axes in Tiberias and Deir Yassin to chop off hands and legs of men and children, and did "awful things" to women. Deir Yassin was also "a main topic" in mid-April in Gaza and its environs.[18]

In contrast to Pa'il's view, Israeli intelligence estimated the following in June 1948, when analyzing the causes for the Palestinian flight:

> The action of Deir Yassin, especially, greatly affected the thinking of the Arab; not a little of the immediate flight during our attacks, especially in the central and southern areas … was due to this factor, which can be described as a decisive accelerating factor.[19]

The Haganah's official history also admitted that the rumors about Deir Yassin intensified the process of Arab flight from mixed cities and from villages adjacent to Jewish settlements. It defined the Deir Yassin operation as "an ancillary factor in the collapse of the Arab rear." Even left wing *Mapam*'s leaders considered Deir Yassin as one of two key events in the exodus of the Palestinian Arabs (the other one, in their opinion, was the fall of Haifa).[20]

A month after the events Emil al-Ghuri, secretary-general of the Palestinian Arab Party and a member of the Arab Higher Committee, maintained that the Arab siege of Jerusalem failed because of Deir Yassin. "The Arab volunteers abandoned the front and ran back to their villages to save their families," he stated. Anwar Nusayba, secretary of Jerusalem's National Committee, also defined the Deir

Yassin affair as a "turning point" in the war, causing people everywhere to start leaving the moment they heard about it. 'Abd al-Rahman 'Azzam Pasha, secretary-general of the Arab League, used the same phrase. Deir Yassin, he declared, was "the turning point of the Palestinian war," implanting fear in the Palestinians and making them run away, letting their military effort crumble. A similar view was held by 'Abdallah al-Tall, the commander of the Arab Legion on the Jerusalem front, by Cunningham and his staff, and by Jacques de Reynier.[21]

Tens of thousands of Arabs left Palestine before the Deir Yassin affair, but the numbers increased dramatically after it. One estimate spoke of a first wave of 60,000 refugees up to 9 April, and then a second wave of 350,000 refugees from 9 April to 15 May (the establishment of the state of Israel), with an average of about 10,000 refugees per day.[22] It is impractical to identify the exact reason causing each individual Palestinian to flee, and there were other reasons for them to feel fear and demoralization, such as Qawuqji's defeat in Mishmar ha-Emek, to mention only one. The available evidence, however, makes it clear that Deir Yassin was a major factor in the flight, which should not be underestimated.

The Palestinian refugees scattered all over the West Bank, the Gaza Strip, the neighboring Arab states and beyond, with those from Deir Yassin among them. A few remained in the Old City while many settled in the neighboring villages of Silwan, Abu Dis, al-Tur, 'Ayzariyya, 'Anata, Shu'afat and Bayt Hanina. Others went further, to Ramallah and its surrounding villages, such as Bira, Baytin, Baytuniyya and 'Ayn Yabrud. Some settled in Jericho and Hebron, while others left Palestine altogether, to Jordan (Amman, Zarqa and Salt), Lebanon (Tyre), Syria (Damascus), Kuwait and the United States. Fifty years later, the overall number of the Deir Yassin refugees and their descendants was estimated at 4,345.[23]

THE ARAB WORLD

Khalidi sent the gist of his 11 April statement to King 'Abdallah and other Arab leaders, as did some of the Deir Yassin refugees, asking for their help. The Arab League was also apprised of the event.

'Abdallah was the first to respond, sending the refugees 500 pounds through the Transjordanian consulate-general in Jerusalem, who he instructed to assist the refugees. He also ordered a fundraising campaign in Transjordan on the refugees' behalf, headed by the chief of the Royal Bureau.[24]

But this was not enough for him. He approached the British ambassador to Amman, Alec Kirkbride, asking permission from the British government for Arab Legion forces to enter into Palestine to defend the Arab regions from the recurrence of such attacks. He emphasized that he did not intend to attack Jewish settlements, just to protect the Arab regions or regain regions formerly in Arab hands, like Qastal and Deir Yassin. Kirkbride advised him not to forward such a request to the British government. Even if it had wanted to, Britain was unable to let an Arab army operate independently in Palestine before the end of the mandate. In any case, he added, there were so many Arab villages liable to be attacked by Jews, that the whole Arab Legion would not be enough to protect them. Instead, Kirkbride suggested that Glubb, the Arab Legion's commander, would check with General MacMillan the possibility that forces of the Arab Legion already in Palestine under MacMillan's command, would participate in the defense of the Arab regions. 'Abdallah was satisfied with this suggestion.[25]

'Abdallah also approached the Arab League with the suggestion to employ the Arab Legion to protect the Palestinian Arabs. The League's political committee welcomed the idea and sent Isma'il Safwat, nominal supreme commander of the Rescue Army (Qawuqji was its field commander), to discuss with him ways to prevent similar massacres. Nothing came of the meeting ('Abdallah did not think well of Safwat). 'Abdallah, for his part, escalated his expressions regarding the Deir Yassin affair, calling it a Jewish declaration of war on Transjordan and the rest of the Arab world. In a telegram to Cunningham, copied to the British Foreign Office, 'Abdallah warned that the "outrages" committed in Deir Yassin and elsewhere caused serious anger among the Transjordanians. Finally, after his army had invaded Palestine, 'Abdallah explained to the secretary-general of the United Nations, that he had to invade, in order to defend the Palestinians from massacres like that of Deir Yassin. Later, his commander of the Jerusalem front, 'Abdallah al-Tall, would excuse his refusal to allow the evacuation of the wounded from the Jewish quarter of the Old City, arguing that the Arab thirst for revenge for Deir Yassin made it difficult for the Arab Legion to permit it.[26]

The Syrian government held a special meeting in the presidential palace, in the presence of the president, to discuss Deir Yassin, and decided to approach the Security Council of the United Nations and the governments of Britain and the United States. The Syrian Red Crescent also discussed the subject, deciding to protest to the various foreign legations in Damascus, to the United Nations and to the Red Cross. The students of Damascus' university and high schools held a one-day protest strike. An American diplomat declared that the Syrian press "went wild" over the matter. The Damascus radio warned that similar tragedies were expected. In Beirut, an orderly demonstration took place in protest against the "atrocities" at Deir Yassin in the presence of the Lebanese president and the chairman of the parliament, both of whom addressed the crowd. The shops in the city center closed during the demonstration. Stormy protests also took place in Baghdad, with thousands of students marching and condemning the deeds of the Jews in Deir Yassin and calling for an independent Arab Palestine. When they reached the government house, the prime minister came out and addressed them. The Iraqi parties published a joint communiqué condemning the "repugnant" acts. The Iraqi foreign minister sent a memorandum to the British, conveying his government's concern about the Zionists' "foul attacks" on Deir Yassin and elsewhere, and threatening to take "the necessary measures" to prevent the impending disaster for the Palestinian Arabs.[27]

The political committee of the Arab League issued a communiqué condemning the massacre of the "peaceful nonfighting inhabitants" of Deir Yassin. There and elsewhere, the Zionists disregarded internationally accepted conventions and practices of war and callously ignored the principles of honor and humanity. It was becoming clear that the Zionists intended to annihilate the Arabs, had they been able to. However, their deeds "shall only strengthen the Arab states in their determination to act by all the means at their disposal to save their Arab brethren of Palestine." Several weeks later, after the invasion of the Arab armies into Palestine, 'Azzam Pasha, the League's secretary-general, maintained that Deir Yassin "was to a great extent the cause of the wrath of the Arab countries and the most important factor for sending the Arab armies." He was not sure that the Arab states could be so unified, if not for the impact of Deir Yassin.[28] The Arab states and 'Abdallah in particular, had many reasons to invade Palestine, among them being the pressure exerted on them by their peoples to invade and save the Palestinians. They could not ignore the wrath of their peoples and the Deir Yassin affair was a major factor in creating these pressures.

Chapter 11

From Propaganda to Bookshelf

EXAGGERATIONS AND HORROR PROPAGANDA

Besides the horror narratives related below, the stories spread about Deir Yassin included various exaggerations about the battle, especially with regard to the manpower and weaponry possessed by the attackers. While radio Beirut reported that 300 Jews took part in the attack (a number adopted by the Palestinian Encyclopedia), *Filastin* raised it to 500 (adopted by several writers), Anwar Nusayba to 1,000, and one of the refugees insisted on several occasions that they numbered 3,000.[1] According to Cunningham and some foreign news agencies, Lehi's armored car turned into eight armored cars. Fifteen cars, an Arab author wrote. A tank, some Arab survivors insisted. Two (Sherman!) tanks, another Arab author elaborated. Fifteen tanks, 'Arif and many Arab writers who followed him, believed. These tanks were supposed to cross the trenches in front of the village with the help of movable bridges brought by the attackers, according to a couple of Arab writers. According to *Filastin* and many survivors, the attackers were also assisted by heavy guns, an airplane (which dropped seven bombs, according to 'Arif and his followers), and even missiles, according to one survivor.[2]

Some of the Arab survivors and writers also exaggerated in the extreme the Jewish losses. They put it at 100 Jews killed (an Arab woman told 'Arif that she herself carried 80 Jewish corpses), or even 700 according to one version. According to 'Arif, 'Ali Qasim killed ten Jews, while a member of the Sammur family killed nine Jews.[3] The number of Arabs killed in Deir Yassin has already been discussed in detail earlier. Formerly it was believed that their number reached about 250. However, some of those who accepted this number interpreted it in a twisted manner. John Bagot Glubb, the Arab Legion's commander-in-chief, claimed that the attackers killed all those found in the village, without exception, totaling 250 people. A TASS commentator remarked after the Sabra and Shatila massacre that it was not the first time in Begin's biography he had committed a massacre, blaming him for the carnage of all the 250 inhabitants of Deir Yassin "by knives and bayonets."[4]

The main accusation against the attackers, according to the massacre narrative, was that they lined up whole families against walls and shot them, men, women, children and babies alike. Some added that they tied the hands of the victims before slaughtering them. However, the descriptions went further. A booklet about Deir Yassin asserted, "They killed them and mutilated them, ripping bellies open, slashing hands, legs and breasts, gouging out eyes, amputating noses and shattering skulls." An Egyptian propaganda booklet elaborated, "Some were dismembered, while the bellies of others were split open before they were finished off" (the same booklet bemoaned that exaggerated descriptions "portraying much more than really happened" had caused the Palestinian exodus). Collins and Lapierre brought a survivor's testimony that an Arab had been cut in two from head to foot. A resident of Jaffa related that the Jews used axes in Deir Yassin to chop off hands and legs. A former Haganah commander noted that he saw "amputated genitals." A survivor testified that he saw "children with their throats cut open." A woman related that they "put the children on the road and put the mothers in a truck and drove over the children." A survivor averred that the baker's son had been thrown into the oven alive. Others said that both the baker and his son had been incinerated. Finally, there was an unbelievable story about Ariel Sharon taking part in the massacre and beheading a Palestinian (his alleged actions "surpassed Hitler's slaughters").[5]

The fate of Deir Yassin's women received a special treatment in the horror propaganda. Many cited Khalidi's numbers that 25 pregnant women, 50 breast-feeding mothers and 60 other women and girls were "slaughtered like sheep." However, the propaganda did not end there. Accounts of the women's fate concentrated on four topics: rapes, brutal looting of valuables, being paraded naked and gender-oriented killings. The Arab Higher Committee was primarily responsible for spreading the rape stories. The alleged rape of Safiyya 'Atiyya, graphically described in *O Jerusalem!* by Collins and Lapierre and cited by many, had already been mentioned. According to an Arab physician from Jerusalem, "Most of the women of Deir yassin from the ages of six to seventy were raped," A refugee woman said that girls were raped in front of their families. Two hundred of them, she added. Collins and Lapierre also claimed that the attackers brutally tore off earrings, tearing the women's earlobes. If needed, "they would cut the arm to take the bracelet or cut the finger to take a ring," a survivor added. The attackers extracted the gold teeth of an old lady, another survivor related. After being robbed, the women and girls were stripped of their clothes, put naked in open trucks, and taken by the Jews all around the western side of Jerusalem. Some added that the naked women were photographed, by either the Jewish combatants or the bystanders (no such photos have ever been presented).[6]

The horror propaganda paid special attention to the fate of the pregnant women. The Egyptian propaganda booklet reported that twenty-five pregnant women were killed, "their bellies split open while they were still alive." The Libyan news agency was to explain many years later that "The ripping open of pregnant women," in Deir Yassin was a prelude to what later happened in every Palestinian town and village. "They ripped open the bellies of all women they found," a survivor testified, while others claimed that the attackers liked to shoot pregnant women at close range. Ariel Sharon starred in this regard, reported to have tied up pregnant women and then merrily opened their bellies with his own hands, explaining that from his viewpoint he was killing future terrorists. Many sources brought the story of pregnant Salihiyya 'Id (most of them distorting her first name in one way or another), whose stomach was allegedly torn apart with a knife – "sideways and then upwards" – after she had been shot to death. In fact, her body was lying in the house where the prisoners were confined, which belonged to her father-in-law, and no one witnessed anything resembling such a scene. Other pregnant women were also mentioned in this regard, like the two pregnant Zaynabs of the Zahran family. A Gadna commander, who took part in the burial operation, later testified that she saw a dead woman with a large torn apart belly, which does not seem impossible, given the widespread use of hand grenades and explosives during the battle.[7]

It seems, however, that the most incredible story in the framework of the horror propaganda regarding the pregnant women appeared in 1950 in the Egyptian magazine *Proche-Orient*:

> As a climax of cruelty certain Jewish terrorists laid wagers on the sex of the unborn babies of expectant mothers. The wretched women were cruelly disembowelled alive, their wombs drawn out and searched for the evidence which would determine the winner.

The story has repeatedly been cited since, recently by the Egyptian Muslim preacher Yusuf al-Qaradawi.[8] With such stories widely believed at the time among the Palestinians, it is not surprising that they compared the Deir Yassin affair to Lidice. The government radio, made the same comparison, while some British officials went even further, to describe it as a "beastly Holocaust" (Bernard de Bunsen, director of the education department) or to maintain that "[Bergen] Belsen pales,"

Fig. 53 Chief Secretary Henry Gurney;
compared Deir Yassin with Bergen Belsen
(in favor of the latter)

beside it (Gurney). Glubb explained that most of the "terrorists" came from Eastern Europe, either slaughtered by the Nazis or exiled by the Soviets to Siberia. This fact made him conclude that "They meted out to their Arab victims the same treatment as they had suffered from their persecutors." The Arab Office in London exploited the opportunity not just to compare the Deir Yassin affair to the "highlights" of Nazi atrocities, but also to attack the movement that begot it, Zionism, for which violence and terrorism were inherent in its nature.[9]

MEIR PA'IL'S TESTIMONY

Interviews and testimonies given by Col. (res.) Meir Pa'il (formerly Pilavsky), from the early 1970s until the late 2000s, constituted one of the major bases for the adherents of the massacre narrative. Pa'il, a former Haganah officer, claimed to have been in Deir Yassin from the beginning of the battle, to have seen the massacre with his own eyes, reported it to his superiors and taken pictures. Many challenged his claims, stating that he had not been present during the battle. It was therefore of the utmost importance for the adherents of the massacre narrative to prove Pa'il's credibility.[10] His words also served as a basis for some of the Arab accounts, including those of survivors, presenting the massacre narrative, especially with regard to the alleged executions in the quarries. The fact that a senior Israeli officer supported this narrative was highly significant for them.[11]

Meir Pilavsky arrived at Deir Yassin at 4:00 p.m., after the battle was already over. He brought with him a photographer, who belonged to Haganah intelligence in Jerusalem, to take pictures. The photographer, Shraga Stahl (later Peled), brought a German Leica camera and a subminiature Minox "spy" camera with him, with two rolls of film. Both reported that they had seen the convoy of prisoners passing through the streets of Jerusalem, which occurred shortly before 4:00 p.m. (which means that they had not yet reached the village by that time). After about an hour in the village they returned to Jerusalem and Pilavsky asked his assistant to develop the negatives of the films, which he did and duly delivered them to his superior, Yehezkel Rabi'. Pilavsky wrote a report about his time in the village, which he delivered the next day to Shaltiel. He later related that he had opened the report with several lines from a poem written by the Hebrew poet Bialik after the Kishinev pogrom. The report and the photos were sent to Tel Aviv to Yisrael Galili, the Haganah's chief of staff, who in turn showed them to Ben-Gurion.[12]

In his report, Pilavsky stated, explicitly, that he had arrived in the village at 4:00 p.m. and stayed for an hour. The content of the report was detailed above, in the section discussing the Haganah's reports of the battle. It is clear from the report, however, that Pilavsky arrived after the battle had already ended. He reported the "dissident" combatants' claim that they had finished their job and wanted to go home. He reported a chat with a Lehi commander, who spoke about the battle in the past tense. With regard to the dead Arabs, he wrote, "It is apparent that the Arabs were not killed in battle, but lined up against a wall." That is an inference he was making, he did not claim to have seen such an event with his own eyes. He also claimed to have seen the bodies of five Arabs in a quarry, Arabs he previously had seen being paraded in Jerusalem. While one may doubt that he would be able to identify scorched bodies, this claim clearly demonstrates that he arrived at the village no earlier than 4:00 p.m. Pa'il later denied that he wrote the available printed version of the report, a claim that is difficult to evaluate due to the absence of the original handwritten version. He claimed that his original report had been altered in order to conceal the fact that a Haganah man had been present at the battle. It is possible that the printed version, included in a booklet distributed by the Haganah to its soldiers, was an edited and abridged one (for example, it did not include Bialik's poem), like the slightly censored Gicherman report that was also included in the booklet. It is, however, highly unlikely that someone falsified the timing of his arrival in order to conceal his presence, taking into account that the booklet also included Weg's report, which recounted the entire participation of the Palmach in the battle.[13]

Although one of the major components in Pa'il's later testimonies was that he met with the Palmach force that came to assist the attackers, and had a talk with its commander, Yaakov Weg, there was no mention of Weg in his report, nor of his in Weg's report.

Furthermore, Moshe Vachman, Weg's deputy, explicitly testified that he saw no other Palmach personnel in the village besides their force (Pa'il belonged to the Palmach).[14] Shraga Peled, the photographer, also denied that they arrived at the village during the battle and had witnessed a massacre. He arrived after the battle, he said, and photographed bodies. Pa'il claimed that they saw the executions in the quarries and took photos from above, but Peled insisted that he was not there when it happened. While he saw the bodies in the quarry and photographed them, it did not seem to him that they had been rounded up there for execution. People who saw the photos in the IDF archives, which have not yet been released to the public, have confirmed that they showed dead bodies but not a massacre or executions taking place. At a later interview Pa'il contended that Peled's superior, Rabi', came with him to the village, but Rabi', too, denied this and said that he only arrived after the battle.[15]

In his report, Pilavsky claimed that one of Lehi's commanders invited him to visit the occupied village. Later on, when Pa'il adhered to the version that he attended the village throughout the battle, he claimed that it was Lehi's Moshe Edelstein, a past member of the Palmach, who informed him of the upcoming attack. Edelstein vehemently denied this, insisting that Pa'il was not present during the battle. In a conference in Bar-Ilan University attended by both, Edelstein publicly shouted on Pa'il: "You were not in Deir Yassin!" Pa'il blushed but kept silent. Other Lehi men who knew Pa'il but denied his presence included Zettler, Selivansky and Barzilai, as well as Etzel's Kaufman and Lapidot.[16] Gicherman, the first Haganah man to arrive in the village after the battle, also did not see Pa'il, nor Peled, nor any other Haganah personnel there when he arrived. It was only the day after that he met Pa'il, and at his request prepared a detailed report about the affair.[17]

A week after the battle, Pilavsky published an article in *ba-Mahane*, the Haganah's paper, titled "Deir Yassin and Its Disgrace," in which he explained the differences between the attack on Deir Yassin and similar attacks carried out by the Haganah. The Haganah was only killing rioters, he wrote, and if innocent women and children were occasionally killed, it was unintentionally. The Haganah did not parade women and children after battles. It did not carry out "a massacre for the sake of massacre." Etzel and Lehi, on the other hand, "disgraced the Hebrew weapon."[18] For the next 23 years, Pa'il served in the IDF in various positions, during which he referred no more in public to the Deir Yassin affair.

In May 1971, a few months before his release from the army, Pa'il gave testimony to the Haganah archives in which he presented most of the components of his narrative for the first time. He related that he arrived at the village in the morning, accompanied by a colleague, after Edelstein had apprised him of the attack. Nobody noticed them. They joined an Etzel unit. Shots from the mukhtar's house stalled the attack. At a certain point, he noticed Weg and his men attacking the house with machine guns and a mortar and taking it. No house was blown up during the attack. After the Palmach had gone, Etzel and Lehi started a massacre, moving from house to house and killing the occupants, mostly women, children and aged people, with automatic weapons fire. They caught 15 to 20 unarmed men, paraded them in Jewish Jerusalem, returned them to a nearby quarry and there murdered them. He saw all this with his own eyes. He tried to find the commanders to stop the killing, but one of them told him to mind his own business. They rounded up the remaining women and children in the school, some suggesting blowing up the building over them, but eventually they transferred them to Arab Jerusalem. When he left the village, Etzel and Lehi were looting it. That night he wrote a letter to Galili comparing it to Lidice, although later he assessed that it was not a premeditated massacre, but a spontaneous response to the losses the attackers had suffered.[19]

Following his release from the army, Pa'il taught military history in Tel Aviv University. In 1972, one of his students, a journalist in *Yedi'ot Aharonot*, published Pa'il's version of events at Deir Yassin together with those of Kaufman (by then Raanan) and Zettler. Pa'il stressed that the Arab fire had been light, except for the mukhtar house, and that after the Palmach had left, Etzel and Lehi started a cleansing operation, shooting and throwing explosives into the houses. Pa'il, though, brought forward a new component, that some residents from the Jewish suburbs joined him in begging the commanders to stop the shooting. In this article, he spoke of 25 men paraded in Jerusalem before being returned to the quarry and shot to death. Since Pa'il felt that this article only painted a partial picture of the events, two weeks later he published an article of his own in *Yedi'ot Aharonot*, adding further details. He asserted that the Palmach (20 to 25 men) finished the conquest of the village after Etzel and Lehi had failed, despite only facing light resistance. He stressed that no Arab was killed as a result of the blowing up of houses and that an indiscriminate massacre took place, people being lined up against walls. He also mentioned photographic evidence of the massacre and the executions in the quarry.[20]

Pa'il's next testimony was deposited during the 1970s in the Jabotinsky archives (belonging to his political opponents), while he was a member of Knesset (the Israeli parliament). According to this document, the Arabs did not have any automatic weapons, yet, armed with only 10 to 12 rifles, they managed to block the attack by Etzel and Lehi forces. Subsequently, 10 to 15 Palmach men arrived and easily captured the mukhtar's house. He further maintained that Weg had told him that he had returned from a raid on 'Ayn Karm (no such raid ever took place that night), when he was approached by a Lehi man, formerly a Palmach member, who asked for Weg's help. Pa'il urged Weg to leave the village, and after the Palmach

Fig. 54 MK Meir Pa'il
(picture taken in the 1970s)

had left the "pogrom" began. Etzel and Lehi men then entered the houses and killed everyone. They ran amuck, "murdering, killing and looting." The rampage only stopped when Jews from Givat Shaul entered the village and remonstrated with them and also prevented them from blowing up their prisoners. In this testimony, too, Pa'il mentioned the executions in the quarry and the photos allegedly taken there.[21]

During the 1980s Pa'il was interviewed by several journalists and authors, repeating the basic components of his version, with some variations. In an interview in the journal *Monitin*, he emphasized the issue of the photos, 36 of them, according to him, following which the journalist subtitled the article "Show Us the Photos." "I saw the whole attack. I even saw the massacre," he told the British author Lynne Reid Banks, and explained that he joined the attack in order to assess the military capabilities of the underground organizations, which proved to be on the lowest level. Twenty-five Palmach combatants, on the other hand, conquered the western part of the village within minutes. The Arabs were killed by shooting or by hand grenades, "thrown into the building *after* the village had been conquered." In an interview conducted by Begin's biographer, Eric Silver, he described what happened as a "disorganized massacre." He heard the cries of the victims but could do nothing. "Their eyes were glazed," he said about the attackers. "It was as if they were drugged, mentally poisoned, in ecstasy."[22]

In the 1990s Pa'il continued to be interviewed about Deir Yassin, especially toward the 50th anniversary of the affair, in newspapers, for books, in a TV series, and finally online. In an interview for Daniel McGowan, Pa'il related that he entered the village with Lehi (contrary to former statements in which he referred to Etzel). Ultimately, the village was conquered by the Palmach (18 combatants) within fifteen minutes. After they had left, the massacre began. "It was like a bunch of pogromists." He believed that the massacre was spontaneous rather than premeditated and denied the usage of knives and rapes. Pa'il elaborated about the role of Givat Shaul's Jews in stopping the massacre. Five hundred of them entered the village shouting at the attackers, "What are you doing, you bastards, you murderers." In a TV series in 1998 Pa'il went further to assert that the Jews coming from Givat Shaul were ultra-Orthodox, which he repeated in a testimony posted that year on the Internet, that included most of the components of his version. It is highly unlikely that a short while before the beginning of the Jewish Sabbath, hundreds of ultra-Orthodox Jews would flock into a war zone to save the people of whom they were afraid. In any case, none of these hundreds has ever come forward to corroborate the story.[23]

Advanced in years, Pa'il persisted in expressing his opinions about the affair into the 2000s. In a lengthy interview available in the Yad Tabenkin archives, he repeated all the elements of his narrative in an orderly account. The number of Arabs executed in the quarry rose to 25–30 in this version. The description of the ultra-Orthodox coming to stop the massacre was more graphic (they entered "with their side locks and hats") and their shouts were in Yiddish. In a later interview given to the historian Norman Rose, the ultra-Orthodox ("appearing from nowhere") were now described as Hasidic. He characterized the attackers to Rose as "full of lust for murder," while in a book he published with a partner he portrayed them as "beasts of prey," shooting at anything moving. Finally, in a filmed joint interview with Peled and Rabi' in 2008, despite the fact that in his presence both of them denied that they attended a massacre (both also denied that Deir Yassin was a peaceful village, as claimed by him), he insisted on his version. He remembered things differently.[24]

Pa'il's account of the Deir Yassin affair became a cornerstone for the adherents of the massacre narrative. His version, however, evolved during the years, bolstering the parallel reality he created with various new components, many of them no more than figments of his imagination. While most of the components were present throughout, he was not always consistent in his accounts. Thus, for example, in some of his accounts he joined the Etzel force, while in others the Lehi force. In some of the testimonies, he tried to convince the attackers' commanders to stop the carnage, while in others he said he could do nothing. The number of Arabs allegedly executed in the quarry, according to him, increased from 5 in his 1948 report to 30 in later accounts. Likewise, the number of Palmach men operating in the village fluctuated. Some elements appeared later, like the Jews from Givat Shaul, who first appeared in the 1970s, became ultra-Orthodox in the 1990s and graduated to become Yiddish-speaking Hasidim in the 2000s. Pa'il claimed for years to have been in Deir Yassin when the massacre took place, but the evidence indicates otherwise. Why did he make such claims? It seems that, from the beginning, Pa'il knew a lot about the affair and collected more information over the years. As with others who were involved in the controversy, he became committed to his version. He evidently believed, that his version of the affair was the true one, whether he was there or not. It was not.

THE HISTORIOGRAPHY

In 1969, the information division of Israel's foreign ministry published a booklet titled *Background Notes on Current Themes: Dir Yassin*, in which it essentially adopted Etzel and Lehi's version of the affair. It described the battle as an integral part of the campaign to relieve Jerusalem from the Arab siege, like the battle over Qastal, insisted that Iraqi soldiers also defended the village, and emphasized the advance warning that was given, saving the lives of many. It was a fierce battle in which the attackers suffered considerable casualties. When the battle was over, many civilians had been killed side by side with the Arab combatants. The fault for these deaths lay with the Arab fighters, since they had not evacuated the non-combatants to a safe place. The affair had been exploited by the Arabs as a propaganda tool against the Jews ever since, but the truth, the booklet concluded, was that under the existing circumstances the death of the non-combatants was inevitable and definitely unintentional. Ostensibly, it looked as if the Israeli government, that is, the Jewish mainstream, at last accepted the version of Etzel and Lehi.[25]

It turned out, however, that the story was more complex. It was the days of the national unity government following the Six Day War. Minister without portfolio Menachem Begin had just returned from a tour abroad in which he encountered Arab propaganda regarding Deir Yassin. He asked the information division of the foreign ministry to issue counter materials. Begin supplied the data while Yaakov Morris, a foreign ministry official (and father of the historian Benny Morris), wrote the booklet. The booklet remained unnoticed until 1971, when Begin referred to it in one of his articles in the daily *Ma'ariv*. He described a tour in the United States, in which the booklet made it easier for him to explain Deir Yassin since the foreign ministry had "reported the true facts." Apparently, he added, the foreign ministry had also reached the conclusion that the internal "incitement" by "certain circles" was harmful to Israel; Arab propaganda based itself on what "Jews said about Jews." The article incensed the Haganah veterans. Yitzhak Levy wrote Begin a personal letter, copied to many, warning him against the dissemination of his "untrue version." Others directly approached foreign minister Abba Eban, reprimanding him for the publication of the booklet. Bewildered Eban immediately issued instructions to cease circulating the booklet, explaining to Galili that it was no fundamental research, just information material to rebut propaganda abroad. Begin's party, *Herut*, however, continued to circulate the booklet independently of the foreign ministry.[26]

The foreign ministry booklet had one thing in common with most of the other publications written about Deir Yassin; it too was ideologically motivated, or, in other words, agenda-driven. Most of the publications written about Deir Yassin for the last seventy years were biased or politically motivated in one way or another. Laying blatant propaganda aside, one could roughly divide the publications discussing Deir Yassin into six groups. The first group comprised books written by former Etzel and Lehi members. The second comprised researches consciously positive toward Etzel and Lehi, trying to vindicate them from the guilt of massacre. The third included publications by Haganah members, insisting that there was a massacre. The fourth consisted of books by Arab writers, heavily based on survivor testimonies. The fifth was publications by Westerners, trying to establish a massacre. The sixth was objective researches by professional historians.

Several former Etzel and Lehi members, when writing their memoirs, devoted a significant portion of their books to discussing the Deir Yassin affair and demonstrating that no massacre took place there. Among the first of them were Etzel's Yehoshua Ofir's, *On the Walls* (1961 in Hebrew), and Lehi's Ezra Yakhin's, *The Story of Elnaqam* (1977 in Hebrew). The best of this genre, however, were the two almost identical volumes written by Yehuda Lapidot, a retired biochemistry professor of the Hebrew University and the deputy commander of Etzel's force in Deir Yassin. While he wrote the former volume,

On Your Walls (1992 in Hebrew), in the first person as memoirs, he used many documents for the latter, *In the Flame of Revolt* (1996 in Hebrew), in order to turn it into some sort of a history book.[27]

Yardena Golani, *The Myth of Deir Yassin* (1976 in Hebrew) was the first research based publication about Deir Yassin that declared positive approach toward the assailants. Actually, it was so one-sided that even a Lehi member, Baruch Nadel, sharply criticized it in a book review he wrote, accusing the author of distorting the facts. Furthermore, the book was also replete with factual errors, to the point that even Etzel member Lapidot considered it unreliable. (For example, according to Golani, cited by many, the so-called "mukhtar house" – Mahmud Salah's house – was not captured until Saturday.)[28]

Uri Milstein published the most recent book of this genre, *Blood Libel in Deir Yassin* (2007 in Hebrew). Only the book's first chapter deals with Deir Yassin. The second addresses the attack on the Hadassah convoy, in order to prove that it was actually the Arabs who committed massacres in 1948. The third deals with the attack on 'Ayn Zaytun, in order to prove that the Haganah were the Jewish forces who carried out massacres in 1948. The other chapters examined sundry security issues, unrelated to the book's subject entirely. Furthermore, the first chapter was almost a verbatim citation of the respective chapter in Milstein's, *History of the War of Independence* (1991 in Hebrew and 1998 in English). There were, however, some differences between the two versions. While Milstein slightly updated his 2007 chapter with new information that had appeared up to the date of publication, he omitted some paragraphs from it that had appeared in the 1991 chapter. For example, he omitted a quotation of Zettler, saying prior to the attack, that the Arabs of Deir Yassin had been "good Arabs, quiet Arabs" (1998, p. 351). Milstein also completely disqualified all Arab evidence, considering it the fruit of Arab imagination (2007, p. 69). In 2012, Milstein published an English translation of his 2007 book. Titled, *The Birth of a Palestinian Nation*, he added a new afterword trying to prove that the Deir Yassin myth was a foundation stone in the formation of the Palestinian nation. Furthermore, he argued, since Meir Pa'il wove the blood libel, this made him the father of the Palestinian nation (2012, pp. 242–243).

Many things can be thought about Col. (res.) Pa'il, but it seems that titles such as "father of the Palestinian nation" would be better reserved for Amin al-Husayni, Yasir 'Arafat and the like.[29]

It was Morton Klein, however, national president of the Zionist Organization of America, who published the most striking publication in the effort to exonerate the fighters of Etzel and Lehi (in practice, written by several researchers on his behalf). The booklet, titled *Deir Yassin: History of a Lie* (1998), was mainly based on Milstein's discoveries, but it also included a comprehensive survey of the literature written about Deir Yassin in the West. More than 160 publications arguing that a massacre took place were analyzed for several months by the researchers of the organization, convincingly proving how shallow and unreliable they were. This publication was destined to attract much fire from the adherents of the massacre narrative (see below).[30]

Most studies written by former Haganah members adopted the stand that Etzel and Lehi committed a massacre in Deir Yassin. This accusation began with a few sentences by Netanel Lorch, founder of the IDF historical branch, in his *The Edge of the Sword* (1961), and continued with a broader description in the official *History of the Haganah* (1972 in Hebrew), which stated there had been executions and a massacre. It culminated in a critical study of the affair, based on Haganah documents (presenting large portions of Gicherman's report), made by the former commander of the Haganah's intelligence in Jerusalem, Yitzhak Levy, in his *Nine Measures* (1986 in Hebrew).[31]

'Arif al-'Arif (1956) was the first to establish that the toll of Arabs killed in Deir Yassin was 110, based on survivor testimonies, but his figures were ignored for years, with the rest of the world clinging to the number 254. In 1978, the Palestinian historian and journalist, 'Arafat Hijazi, was the first to publish a full-length book in Arabic wholly devoted to the affair. Its title attested to the writer's approach: *Deir Yassin: The Roots and the Dimensions of the Crime in Zionist Thought*. Hijazi cited all the massacre components in his book, inter alia, the intentional killing of women and children, ripping open the bellies of pregnant women, and even the story of gambling on the sex of the embryos and disemboweling the mothers to determine the winners.

It was, however, Kana'na and Zaytawi's 1986 research which constituted a milestone in the historiography of Deir Yassin, diminishing the number of the dead. For the first time, the authors managed to produce a reliable list of names of 107 people killed. This time the scholarly community accepted the number. Yet the two only devoted a few pages of their research to what happened in April 1948; the rest was an anthropological account of various aspects of the village.[32]

A far more comprehensive study of the affair from the Arab viewpoint was Walid Khalidi, *Deir Yassin: Friday, 9 April 1948* (1999 in Arabic), originally published as a series of articles in *al-Hayat* (London) and *al-Ayyam* (Ramallah). Khalidi based his research primarily on some thirty testimonies by Arab eyewitnesses, the most comprehensive collection of survivor testimonies available. He, too, brought a list of the dead (100 names), but also a map of all the houses in the village (numbering them), with an exact list of all the families which inhabited them. In each of the testimonies he cited, he indicated (by referencing the map) to which houses they referred. It proved to be an invaluable resource for this present book. The Palestinian researcher Fadi Salayima also published a comprehensive book about Deir Yassin (2008 in Arabic), but of a somewhat more popular nature, including some bizarre stories, such as Ariel Sharon taking part in the massacre (Salayima himself doubted this). It should be noted, though, that such unlikely tales also existed on the other side. The equivalence is a claim made by a Jewish author that "Yasser Arafat was highly likely one of the Muqadass officers in Deir Yassin."[33]

The first Westerner to write extensively on Deir Yassin was the American journalist and writer Dan Kurzman, in his *Genesis 1948* (1970). His description of the affair was balanced and impressively well informed. This contrasted starkly with the next Western work examining the affair, *O Jerusalem!* (1972), a collaboration by the American writer Larry Collins and the French writer Dominique Lapierre. They based their book on many interviews conducted in the late 1960s in Israel (most of them deposited in the Special Collections Research Center of Georgetown University). While they tried to do justice to both sides of the conflict, and their description of the Jewish mainstream effort was generally in the positive, their chapter about Deir Yassin was replete with all kinds of imaginary rapes and atrocities.[34]

However, the staunchest adherents of the massacre narrative among the Westerners were Daniel McGowan, Matthew Hogan and Marc Ellis. All belonged to Deir Yassin Remembered, an association founded by McGowan in order to build a memorial in Deir Yassin to commemorate the massacre, in a location facing Yad Vashem, Israel's national Holocaust memorial, which could posit some sort of equivalency between the two. This equation recurred in their writings, where argued that describing the massacre "as false, exaggerated, or in dispute" was tantamount to Holocaust denial. Hogan and McGowan first published "Anatomy of a Whitewash" (1998) as an attempt to refute Klein's *Deir Yassin: History of a Lie*. In an improved version published a year later under the title *The Saga of Deir Yassin*, they defined Klein's "tract" as "fraudulent revisionism," which the critical reader should dismiss without further research. McGowan and Ellis published *Remembering Deir Yassin* (1998), a collection of essays that also included an interview with Meir Pa'il and a short summary of the affair, repeating the accusations of lining people up against the wall to be shot and the cutting of a pregnant woman's stomach. Hogan also published "The 1948 Massacre at Deir Yassin Revisited" (2001), an article arguing that the massacre was accompanied by rapes and other atrocities. He mainly used secondary sources for corroborating the allegations, but was nevertheless convinced that his evidence "put to rest any serious questioning of whether there was or was not a massacre at Deir Yassin" (p. 330). "There is no doubt," McGowan stated, "that what occurred in Deir Yassin was not a battle; it was unequivocally a massacre" (*Remembering*, p. 4). The people of Deir Yassin were "deliberately massacred" and "intentionally killed," he and Hogan concluded. It is interesting to note, though, that several of the survivors and their descendants apparently disapproved of McGowan and his association, feeling that he was appropriating their agony. "He exploits our name and blood for making money," some of them said.[35]

Not many wrote about Deir Yassin objectively. Among the few, one may count the historians Benny Morris and Yoav Gelber. Morris published "The Historiography of Deir Yassin" (2005), an article surveying the literature written about Deir Yassin by Israelis and Arabs. He devoted three pages of the article to a description of the affair itself, mainly based on Haganah documents. Morris concisely dealt with the affair in some of his other works, about the refugee problem and the 1948 war, establishing that it "had the most lasting effect of any single event of the war in precipitating the Palestinian exodus" (2004, p. 237). A fair description of the affair also appeared in Yoav Gelber, "Propaganda as History: What Happened at Deir Yassin?" (2006). It included some very important insights. He opens the article with, "A wide gap separates what happened in the village from the stories that spread at the time and persist to the present" (p. 307). He concludes it with, "The massacre at Deir Yassin, if what happened in the village deserves this definition, was an almost inevitable outcome of circumstances" (p. 318). In between, he argues that the fact that the civilian population did not realize that the attackers had come to conquer the village for good, and therefore remained in the village during the battle, was the cause for the high number of casualties (pp. 310–311). His most important historiographical insight is that the testimonies of the survivors correspond to those of the attackers (p. 314). Still, the main flaw of both Morris and Gelber was that they relied too much on Haganah records, whose authors were not present at the battle, rendering their accounts of secondary quality when compared to those of Etzel and Lehi's fighters and the Arabs who were there.[36]

Both Morris and Gelber used Haganah documents closed to the public. They were able to do so, because in the mid-1990s, the IDF archives opened the Deir Yassin documents to the public for more than a decade, but then reconsidered and closed them again. For years, the IDF archives refused demands by researchers and others to release the 'forbidden' documents and photos. Finally, in 2007, the daily *ha-Aretz* and a student from Bezalel Academy of Arts and Design jointly petitioned the Israeli High Court of Justice to order the IDF archives to show them the documents and the photos. The state responded that the release of the documents and photos might jeopardize Israel's foreign relations and was liable to damage the ongoing negotiations with the Palestinians. It could also compromise Israel's relations with its Arab minority. The state's answer attested to the continued relevance of the affair. In May 2010, after examining the materials in question, the court ruled to accept the state's position. The documents and the photos remained closed.[37] One might wonder whether the court would have issued the same ruling if it had been apprised of the fact that the documents had already been available for more than a decade, and therefore any resourceful researcher could find a way to view them.

Conclusions

Deir Yassin was a tragedy caused by both the attackers' miscalculations and the defenders' basic misunderstanding of the nature of the event. Etzel and Lehi expected it to be an easy win. It was not. The villagers "expected the fighting to last two or three hours, after which they [the attackers] would retreat."[1] They were wrong. Deir Yassin was one of the first Arab villages in the 1948 war that the Jews conquered and held for good. It was a new phenomenon. The inhabitants did not realize that the purpose of the attack differed from similar attacks carried out earlier, on other villages. They believed it to be another hit-and-run raid and that after blowing up several houses the assailants would retreat. Therefore, from their viewpoint, it seemed sensible to try to hold out until the attackers retreated. It was a tragic mistake. Etzel and Lehi were determined to take the village. "The moment the inhabitants of Deir Yassin resolved to fight, they determined their fate," Lehi's commander in Jerusalem, Yehoshua Zettler, stated.[2]

Plan D of the Haganah, framed in early March 1948, which served as guideline for Operation Nahshon and for the Haganah's countrywide offensive in April, required the taking of Arab villages within or close to its defensive lines in order to prevent their use by hostile forces. Villages the Haganah could not occupy permanently were to be destroyed. The inhabitants of villages that offered resistance were to be expelled after any armed resistance was overcome.

Villages that surrendered were to be garrisoned, with the inhabitants allowed to remain.[3] Within this framework, it was not surprising that David Shaltiel, the Haganah's district commander of Jerusalem, told the commanders of Etzel and Lehi in Jerusalem in his 7 April letter, that he considered the taking of Deir Yassin as, "one phase in our general plan."

Contrary to later claims, the relations between Deir Yassin and its Jewish neighbors were problematic from the outset. They knew ups and downs. Deir Yassin was not the peaceful village some sought to portray. There were, however, some more substantial reasons for Etzel and Lehi to attack it than intermittent hostile acts. Conquering the village meant completing Jewish continuity in western Jerusalem. It was seen as a potential strategic base for hostile forces, since it over-looked the Jerusalem-Tel Aviv road. Etzel and Lehi rightly assessed that the British would not intervene, as the village was far from their routes of evacuation. They wrongly assessed that it would be easy prey. "They did not realize the intensity of the fire they were going to face," a Haganah intelligence man was later to say. "Had they known they would face [such] a strong resistance, they would not have started it," Zalman Mart, the commander of the Moriah battalion, surmised. On earlier occasions, in Lifta, in Sheikh Badr, it had been easy. "We did not shoot a single shot," Moneta related. Lapidot elaborated:

> We didn't expect any specific problems. We didn't expect the strong resistance we met, and we didn't dream that our ammunition supply would end. We didn't expect them to be prepared, they were. We didn't expect so many people; and the worst part we didn't anticipate a house to house battle.

An Arab taken prisoner by the attackers, who later escaped, con-firmed this attitude of the attackers. He asked his captors why they had done it. They answered that they had no advance intention of doing it. "On the contrary," they said. "We were confident in our ability to conquer the village without any bloodshed whatsoever."[4]

On one side were Etzel and Lehi's fighters, who mostly lacked training in both urban and open area combat, and were definitely

inexperienced in a house-to-house fighting. They had never participated in a full-scale battle, or even in a field operation. They had no
experience in the conquest of populated areas and did not have the
slightest idea how to conquer an Arab village efficiently. On the other
side were the Arab combatants, determined to defend the village and
withstand the attack, not realizing that the attackers would continue
to fight until victory. The attackers outnumbered the defenders, but
not significantly. About 120 attackers fought 70 to 80 defenders, with
the defenders possessing the advantage of fighting from within the
houses, while the attackers were in the open, exposed to Arab fire.
During the preceding months, the defenders had trained in field
exercises, shooting and first aid, and more than a dozen firing positions had been prepared in the village. The initial number of firearms was also similar, the Arabs bringing a large share of their arms
from Egypt just five days before the attack. It resulted in a stalemate
between the two sides for several hours, with neither succeeding in
tipping the balance. About 30 percent of the attackers were hit, most
injured but some killed.

However, while the Arabs were running out of ammunition,
the attackers kept receiving additional ammunition from the Haganah
(Ben-Sasson, Azulay and Shaltiel), and later from the Palmach, who
had sent combatants with mortars to assist them. Vachman's squad
definitely did more than just evacuating the wounded. During its
short visit to Deir Yassin, it fought no less than Etzel and Lehi. The
Haganah also delivered some weapons, while a Haganah Spandau
machine gun, posted on the Sharafa ridge in the morning, assisted
the attackers by shooting at the southern slopes and the western part
of the village. Furthermore, the attackers discovered several arms
depots in the village, which meant that the defenders did not use all
the arms they had, and this share of their own weapons was subsequently turned against them. Although the Arab defenders fought
"from house to house and from street to street," "to the last bullet,"[5]
defending the village was beyond their abilities. Unlike the attackers,
they were neither resupplied, nor reinforced, and eventually could
no longer withstand the attackers and the balance tipped. Etzel and
Lehi accomplished their mission. However, unlike other villages later

conquered by the Haganah, many non-combatants failed to leave Deir Yassin before the attack, resulting in the battle for Deir Yassin taking place in the presence of a significant number of civilians, leading inevitably to the high number of casualties among them.

Etzel and Lehi were utterly convinced before the attack that the village was packed with foreign soldiers, mainly Iraqis. Since they believed in it, they also 'saw' them or found 'proofs' of their presence. There is no reason to doubt their testimonies, but men dressed in khaki or wearing red-and-white checkered *keffiyeh*s, even the presence of helmets or Iraqi military insignia, did not denote Iraqi soldiers. Arab combatants in Deir Yassin were local, with no external support. No one came to help them. Not the Rescue Army, camping in 'Ayn Karm about two kilometers away, not the fighters of the Army of Sacred Jihad, engaged at the time in the funeral of 'Abd al-Qadir al-Husayni in Jerusalem. Not even the inhabitants of 'Ayn Karm or other villages in the vicinity came to their aid. The British, too, received strict orders from General MacMillan not to interfere under any circumstances.

Deir Yassin was a paradigm of why the Palestinian Arabs failed in the 1948 war. The villagers fortified the village, set up patrols and purchased arms, but did everything alone. Their horizon was limited to the precincts of their own village. Prior to the attack, they did not seek the help of the Arab Higher Committee nor of 'Abd al-Qadir al-Husayni. They did not even have substantial contacts with the village closest to them, 'Ayn Karm, which, when the time came, did not help them at all. Countrywide activity, of the type 'Abd al-Qadir al-Husayni tried to conduct, was the exception. While the Jewish fighters were part of countrywide frameworks, the villagers faced them alone, and therefore doomed to failure. While the Jewish community was relatively unified, there was no coherent Arab society facing it, only scattered independent villages fighting alone a lost war.[6]

When Husayn al-Khalidi reported the results of the battle, he went one-step too far, fabricating outrages against women. He did so in order to prevent a catastrophe, but instead created one. He wanted the Arab states to intervene, but his fabrications soon became one of the major incentives for the Palestinian flight. "Dr Hussein Fakhri Al-Khalidi was the one who caused the catastrophe," a refugee survivor was to say.[7] There were no rapes in Deir Yassin, or gender-oriented atrocities. The impact of these things that did not happen was, however, overwhelming, boomeranging on the Palestinians. Following the rule of *al-'ird qabla al-ard* (women's honor before land), the moment the Palestinians heard about rapes they started to leave. Whole families decided to leave. Although tens of thousands of Arabs had left Palestine before the Deir Yassin affair, their numbers dramatically increased after it. While it is impossible to identify the exact reasons that caused each of them to flee, and other factors definitely contributed to the exodus, the available evidence makes it clear that the stories of Deir Yassin significantly contributed to the flight in a way that cannot be dismissed or underestimated. A Palestinian researcher interviewing a couple from Deir Yassin, who vehemently denied the rape allegations, clearly figured out what had happened: "So the Israelis are acquitted on this charge, but the Palestinians lost their lands."[8]

The testimonies of both Etzel and Lehi's combatants and the Arab survivors were surprisingly similar, sometimes almost identical. Actually, this should not be surprising, as both were there when it happened. A remarkable example for this appeared in the memoirs of former Knesset member and minister, Yehoshua Matza (published in 2014). He was among the Lehi combatants following the loudspeaker car and being shot at by the guards standing on the roof of Ahmad Radwan's house. One of Lehi's combatants was killed and others were injured. When the guards ran out of ammunition they escaped to the western part of the village, except for Radwan As'ad Radwan, Ahmad's brother. Injured, he descended from the roof into the house and continued to shoot through a window. Lehi's combatants threw a hand grenade and broke in. Radwan thought to feign sleeping, hiding his rifle beneath the bed, but he was identified as one of the shooters and shot to death. The story, with some variations, appeared in both Matza's memoirs and in testimonies by Radwan's niece, Naziha. For Matza, they killed an Arab who had shot at them, possibly injuring or killing his comrades. For Naziha, Lehi's combatants killed her uncle. Doubtlessly, none of the two read the other's narrative, but definitely, they described the same episode.[9]

However, the narratives of both the attackers and the defenders could not prevail over the narratives offered by the Jewish and Palestinian mainstreams, both having their own interests in describing the affair differently. The Jewish mainstream, and later the Israeli Left, exploited the affair to defame the "dissidents," and later the Israeli Right, as murderers who blackened Israel's name in the world. The Palestinian establishment created the massacre narrative with descriptions that contradicted the express testimony of the survivors, doing so because it believed it served the Palestinian interest. Yet their decision to exaggerate events led to disastrous results, and it was precisely their realization of their responsibility for the calamity that made them justify the results by clinging to the narrative that the Jews created the Palestinian refugee problem by their murderous acts, such as the Deir Yassin massacre. The Haganah poster distributed after the affair and the Jewish Agency's condemnation only assisted the Arabs in establishing the massacre allegation. Since then, the massacre narrative has only "improved," exploited by Palestinian and Arab propagandists to smear Israel's name for its alleged inhumanity.[10]

Seventy percent of the about 1,000 inhabitants of Deir Yassin managed to escape the attack (because the attackers let them escape), twenty percent were taken prisoner and later released, and ten percent were killed. As was shown above, the ratio between Arabs killed and injured (about 100 of each) did not suggest massacre. Even more indicative is the fact that double the number of Arabs were taken prisoner as were killed. This is an even better metric, because the decision to take individuals prisoner was an intentional act on the part of the captors (unlike when injuring people). Finally, the very fact that the overwhelming majority, ninety percent, survived the attack is the clearest refutation of the accusation of a massacre. Sixty-one people out of the 84, whose circumstances of death were ascertained, were killed in battle conditions even if they themselves were not all active combatants. "I believe that most of those who were killed were among the fighters and the women and children who helped the fighters," one of the survivors stated.[11] Forty-two percent of the people killed were males of an age fit for fighting. Twenty-four of the people killed were combatants. Relatively, many heads of families remained alive, while their families were killed (Jum'a Zahran and 'Ali Mustafa Zaydan, to mention two salient examples). It was precisely because they were armed combatants that they had the ability and skills to succeed in escaping.

As mentioned above, the battle for Deir Yassin took place in the presence of a civilian population. Combatants and non-combatants were present in the same houses. In many instances, heads of families, with their sons or other relatives, would shoot at the attackers from within the houses with the rest of their families with them. The attackers responded with a three-phase method of using explosives, hand grenades and automatic fire, successively, when bursting into the houses. The occupants did not stand much of a chance to survive it. Some of the adherents of the massacre narrative claim that the events took place in two stages, asserting that, after the battle had ended and the Palmach had left, Etzel and Lehi staged a full-scale massacre. The available evidence negates this allegation. Most of the people killed in the village were killed during the battle and under battle conditions and not in a subsequent deliberate massacre. Generally speaking, when the battle ended, the killing stopped.

There were no incidents of families being lined up against walls and shot in Deir Yassin. While it was said about six people at most, four of them combatants, that they were killed in the quarries, no survivor reported seeing this with his own eyes. The closest story to the lining up of a family against the wall was the incident of the Zaydan family. When they came out of their house, an Etzel combatant standing nearby holding a Bren opened fire on them, killing eleven and injuring others, apparently as a revenge for a friend being severely wounded near that house shortly before. Many in the village saw the incident. Furthermore, an Associated Press correspondent later interviewed Fahima Zaydan, one of the injured, in the government hospital about the incident. The story soon spread worldwide, constituting the basis for the "lining up against the walls" allegations and the massacre narrative of the affair.

"This is war; whoever gets a bullet drops dead" (Muhammad 'Ayish Zaydan, a survivor, 1997).[12] There is a substantial difference between people killed during fighting and a massacre. Except for the specific incidents listed above, people in Deir Yassin were killed, not massacred.

Notes

NOTES FOR CHAPTER I

I. Sharif Kana'na and Nihad Zaytawi, *Dayr Yasin* (Birzeit, 2nd rep. 1987), p. 6; Sharif Kana'na, "Madhbahat Dayr Yasin: Qira'a Jadida," in *Al-Shatat al-Filastini: Hijra am Tahjir?* (Bira, 2000), pp. 166–167; Walid al-Khalidi, *Dayr Yasin: Al-Jum'a, 9 Nisan/Abril 1948* (Jerusalem, 1999), p. 7; Fadi Salayima, *Dayr Yasin: Al-Qarya al-Shahida* (Damascus, 2008), p. 58; "Dayr Yasin (Qarya)," *Al-Mawsu'a al-Filastiniyya* (Damascus, 1984), al-Qism al-'Amm, vol. 2, p. 432; Salman H. Abu-Sitta, *The Palestinian Nakba 1948: The Register of Depopulated Localities in Palestine* (London, 1998), p. 44, and *Atlas of Palestine 1948* (London, 2004), p. 19, both based on Palestine Government, *Village Statistics of 1944* (Jerusalem, 1945); Walid Khalidi (ed.), *All That Remains: The Palestinian Villages Occupied and Depopulated by Israel in 1948* (Washington DC, [1992] rep. 2006), pp. 289–290; Basheer K. Nijim and Bishara Muammar, *Toward the De-Arabization of Palestine/Israel 1945–1977* (Dubuque IA, 1984), p. 139; Ruth Kark and Michal Oren-Nordheim, *Jerusalem and its Environs: Quarters, Neighborhoods, Villages 1800–1948* (Jerusalem and Detroit, 2001), p. 239; "Welcome to Dayr Yasin," www.palestineremembered.com/Jerusalem/Dayr-Yasin/index. html; YTA 12-4/16/6: "Hativat Har'el – Modi'in (Kfarim): Ha-Kfar Dir Yasin" n.d.; Yardena Golani, *Ha-Mitos shel Dir Yasin* (Tel Aviv, 1976), p. 12. The Israel State Archives contain many files referring to lands that the British defined as belonging to Deir Yassin, which are clearly located in Givat Shaul (most of these files are available in ISA containers M-854 to M-858). For example, there is a file about a possible property transfer in Deir Yassin of two synagogues and a mikveh (Jewish ritual bath). Self-evidently, these facilities were located in Givat Shaul (ISA M-30/20).

Notes for Chapter 1

2. JA K4-10/1: testimony by Ben-Zion Cohen; JA K4-10/9: testimony by same during the benefits trial, 5 January 1953; also Etzel member Yehoshua Ofir, *'Al ha-Homot* (Tel Aviv, 1961), p. 54, put it at 400; Jacques de Reynier, *A Jerusalem un drapeau flottait sur la ligne de feu* (Neuchâtel, 1950), p. 74; Jacques Derogy and Edouard Saab, *Les deux Exodes* (Paris, 1968), p. 142; Dan Kurzman, *Genesis 1948: The First Arab-Israeli War* (New York, 1970), p. 148, said that according to Jewish sources 400 people lived there, while Arab sources gave a figure of 1,000.

3. YTA 12-4/16/6: "Hativat Har'el – Modi'in (Kfarim): Ha-Kfar Dir Yasin" n.d.; *New York Times*, 12 April 1948, p. 9 (citing Husayn Fakhri al-Khalidi); Husayn Fakhri al-Khalidi, *Wa-Mada 'Ahd al-Mujamalat: Mudhakkirat Husayn Fakhri al-Khalidi* (Amman, 2014), vol. 2, p, 260; IDFA 59/500/48: "Tzror Yedi'ot 'Araviyot Musmakhot," 11 April 1948; IDFA 355/2644/49: "Tzror Yedi'ot 'Araviyot," 12 April 1948; IDFA 2/2605/49: Hashmona'i to Moriah, "Nispahim le-Rikuz Yedi'ot No. 162," 12 April 1948; Staughton Lynd, Sam Bahour and Alice Lynd (eds.), *Homeland: Oral History of Palestine and Palestinians* (New York, 1994), p. 22 (interviewing Ahmad 'Ayish Khalil); PACE 237: interview with Wahid and Ibtisam Zaydan; "The Struggle: Survivor of Deir Yassin," 5 October 2013, 10:01, www.youtube.com/watch?v=OcfRSe7ayoo (interview with Da'ud Ahmad As'ad Radwan); CO 733/477/5: tel. 933, Alan Cunningham (Jerusalem) to Secretary of State for the Colonies (London), 10 April 1948.

4. Abu Sitta, *Nakba*, p. 44, and *Atlas*, p. 77, using *Village Statistics of 1944*.

5. Khalidi, *Dayr Yasin*, pp. 3, 124; Idem, *All That Remains*, p. 290; Kana'na and Zaytawi, *Dayr Yasin*, p. 6; Kana'na, "Madhbahat," p. 154; Salayima, *Dayr Yasin*, p. 57; 'Arif al-'Arif, *Nakbat Filastin wal-Firdaws al-Mafqud 1947–1952* ([Sidon, 1956]), vol. 1, p. 169; Bahjat Abu Gharbiyya, *Fi Khidamm al-Nidal al-'Arabi al-Filastini: Mudhakkirat al-Munadil Bahjat Abu Gharbiyya 1916–1949* (Beirut, 1993), p. 220; BUPA: Muhammad Mahmud As'ad [Radwan] 'Aql, "Haqa'iq Waqi'iyya min Majzarat Dayr Yasin al-Basila (1948)," www.awraq. birzeit.edu/sites/default/files/PDF_153.; "Abu Mahmud ma Zala Shahidan 'ala Majzarat Dayr Yasin," *al-Safir*, 8 April 2001, p. 8 (interview with same); "Qadiyya wa-Hiwar: Dayr Yasin ... al-Dhakira al-Hayya" (Qanat al-Hiwar), 1 May 2012, 22:59, www.youtube.com,watch?v=1cpTx4rbcRo (interview with Mustafa Mahmud); PACE 240: interview with 'Ayish Muhammad 'Ayish Zaydan; PACE 241: interview with Muhammad 'Ayish Zaydan; 'Awni Farsakh, "Majzarat Dayr Yasin fi Dhikraha al-Sittin," 12 April 2008, www.arabs48. com/?mod=articles&ID=53368; JA K4-10/2: "Parashat Dir Yasin" [1949]; LC 3/29: DLP [Dominique Lapierre], "Deir Yassin," n.d., p. 1. I wish to thank Jacob Jaffe of Georgetown University for his help with the Larry Collins papers. The survivor Yunus Ahmad As'ad Radwan put it at 900. Yunus Ahmad As'ad, "Al-Dhikra al-Khamisa li-Majzarat Dayr Yasin Yaktabuha Ahad Abna'iha," *al-Urdunn*, 9 April 1953, p. 3.

6. Kurzman, *Genesis*, p. 139; 'Arafat Hijazi, *Dayr Yasin: Judhur wa-Ab'ad al-Jarima fil-Fikr al-Sahyuni* ([Amman?], 1978), p. 56; Yoav Gelber, "Propaganda as History: What Happened at Deir Yassin?" in idem, *Palestine 1948: War, Escape and the Emergence of the Palestinian Refugee Problem* (Brighton, 2006), p. 309 (Gelber though doubted the 1,200 figure); Uri Milstein, *History of Israel's War of Independence* (Lanham MD, 1998), vol. 4, p. 351, and *The Birth of a Palestinian Nation: The Myth of the Deir Yassin Massacre* (Jerusalem and New York, 2012), p. 31.

7. IDFA 978/100001/57: letter, Social Affairs Committee of the Jerusalem National Committee (Jerusalem) to Head of the General Affairs Department of the Arab Higher Committee, 20 April 1948; Kana'na and Zaytawi, *Dayr Yasin*, pp. 18–23 (although the authors themselves, on p. 6, put the number at 750).

8. Ibid., pp. 16–23; Khalidi, *Dayr Yasin*, pp. 10, 72, 74, 152–158; LC 3/29: DLP, "Deir Yassin," pp. 1–2.

9. Khalidi, *Dayr Yasin*, p. 7 (for the quarries and crushers, see also map between pages 10 and 11); Idem, *All That Remains*, p. 289; Kana'na and Zaytawi, *Dayr Yasin*, pp. 28, 46; 'Abbas Nimr, *Dayr Yasin fi Atun al-Ma'raka* ([Ramallah?], n.d.), pp. 11–12; Lynd, Bahour and Lynd, *Homeland*, pp. 22 (interviewing Ahmad 'Ayish Khalil), 24 (interviewing 'Ayisha Jum'a Zaydan); PACE 240: interview with 'Ayish Muhammad Zaydan; YTA 12-4/16/6: "Hativat Har'el – Modi'in (Kfarim): Ha-Kfar Dir Yasin" n.d.; Salim Tamari (ed.), *Jerusalem 1948: The Arab Neighbourhoods and Their Fate in the War* (Jerusalem and Bethlehem, 1999), p. 79; Meron Benvenisti, *Sacred Landscape: The Buried History of the Holy Land Since 1948* (Berkeley CA, 2002), p. 115. For the economic ties with the Jews, see also Khadija Hassuna, "Al-'Alaqat bayna al-'Arab wal-Yahud qabla 'Am 1948 – Dayr Yasin: Dirasat Hala," *al-Turath wal-Mujtama'*, 41 (2005), pp. 116–118.

10. Kana'na and Zaytawi, *Dayr Yasin*, pp. 27–30; Khalidi, *Dayr Yasin*, pp. 7, 9, 148; Idem, *All That Remains*, p. 290; Salayima, *Dayr Yasin*, pp. 27, 30; Nimr, *Dayr Yasin*, p. 12; LC 3/29: DLP, "Deir Yassin," p. 4. Benvenisti, *Landscape*, p. 115.

11. Yitzhak Shweki, "Shkhunat Giv'at Sha'ul," www.shimur.org; *Hashqafa*, 2 November 1906, p. 2; Avraham Binyamin, "Ha-Bor shel Saba," *'Olam Qatan*, 442, 28 March 2014, pp. 8–9 (based on Yosef Tzvi Goldschmidt's memoirs); Zehava Cohen, Letter to the Editor, *Ma'ariv*, 19 May 1974, p. 25 (Cohen was a daughter of Yosef Tzvi Goldschmidt); CZA L4/739: report 66 JM (Jerusalem), 16 May 1920; Golani, *Mitos*, p. 90.

12. YTA 12-3/9/3: letter, Committee of Givat Shaul Neighborhood to the Executive of the City Committee of the Jews of Jerusalem, 19 October 1927; *Davar*, 8 November 1927, p. 4; Ben-Zion Dinur and others (eds.), *Sefer Toldot ha-Haganah* (Tel Aviv, 1954–1972), vol. 2, pt. 1, pp. 354–355; David Ben-Gurion, *Zikhronot* (Tel Aviv, 1971), vol. 1, p. 346; HA 95.3: testimony by Akiva Azulay;

Soli Sharvit, *Akiva Azulay Ish Yerushalayim* ([Jerusalem, 1987]), p. 68; Golani, *Mitos*, p. 90; Yitshaq Ben-Ami, *Years of Wrath, Days of Glory: Memoirs from the Irgun* (New York, 2nd ed. 1983), p. 439, mentioning assistance to the villagers of Qalunya in isolating the Jewish settlement Motza.

13. Tzvi Bar'el and Eli Shay, "Be-Hazara le-Dir Yasin," *Kol ha-'Ir*, 1 May 1981, p. 23 (interviewing Muhammad 'Arif Sammur); Kana'na and Zaytawi, *Dayr Yasin*, pp. 46–50; Salayima, *Dayr Yasin*, pp. 59–61; Nimr, *Dayr Yasin*, p. 14; YTA 12-4/16/6: "Hativat Har'el – Modi'in (Kfarim): Ha-Kfar Dir Yasin" n.d.; Golani, *Mitos*, p. 90.

14. Kana'na and Zaytawi, *Dayr Yasin*, p. 46; Salayima, *Dayr Yasin*, p. 59 (testimony by Khumays Zaydan); Ben-Ami, *Years*, pp. 439–440; CZA S25/2966: A[vraham] L[utzqi], "Kruzey Harga'a 'Arviyim u-Britot Shalom" [September 1937]; HA 15.31: testimony by Nahum Diamant (a Haganah member who commanded the Jewish supernumerary police in Givat Shaul until 1940); Khalidi, *Dayr Yasin*, p. 11; Idem, *All That Remains*, p. 290; Nimr, *Dayr Yasin*, p. 14.

15. Khalidi, *Dayr Yasin*, pp. 11–12 (testimony by Da'ud Husayn Zaydan); Hijazi, *Dayr Yasin*, p. 56; LC 3/29: DLP, "Deir Yassin," p. 6; Umar Igbariyyeh, "The 60th Anniversary of the Deir Yassin Massacre," 17 April 2008, www.palestineremembered.com/Jerusalem/Dayr-Yasin/Story9373.html; IDFA 16/2504/49: 24 December 1947; IDFA 6/2605/49: 29 December 1947 and 8 January 1948; Aryeh Yitzhaqi, *Latrun: Ha-Ma'arakha 'al ha-Derekh li-Yerushalayim* (Jerusalem, 1982), vol. 1, p. 17, citing an order issued by the Palmach headquarters, 8 December 1947. For the Army of Sacred Jihad, see Eliezer Tauber, *Military Resistance in Late Mandatory Palestine: The Activities of the Jewish and Arab Military Organizations as Reflected in the Reports of High Commissioner General Sir Alan Cunningham* (Ramat Gan, 2012), pp. 29–31.

16. Kana'na and Zaytawi, *Dayr Yasin*, p. 51; Khalidi, *Dayr Yasin*, p. 14 (testimonies by Ahmad Khalil Muhammad 'Id and Khalil Muhammad Sammur); [Elias Zananiri], "Interviews: 50th Anniversary of Deir Yassin Massacre," *ArabicNews.com*, 10 April 1998, www.arabicnews.com/ansub/Daily/Day/980410/1998041030.html (interviewing Abu Tawfiq); YTA 12-3/9/3: Mordechai Gichon, "Parashat Dir Yasin Tashah," enclosed with letter by Gichon, 29 December 1992; IDFA 56/500/48: Hashmona'i [intelligence officer, Etzioni brigade] to Ben-Yehuda, "Doh le 11–12.1.48"; IDFA 61/500/48: Tzadiq [intelligence officer] to Mathen and Hashmona'i, "Doh le-Yom 11.1.48"; IDFA 16/2504/49: 25 and 26 December 1947, and 4 and 12 January 1948; IDFA 6/2605/49: 26 December 1947 and 4 January 1948; IDFA 520/4944/49: Tzadiq to Mathen and Hashmona'i, "Doh le-Yom 14.1.48–15.1.48"; Ben Yechiel, "Jerusalem Letter (January 1948)," *The New Judaea* (January–February 1948), pp. 64–65.

17. HA 105/72: "Tna'ey ha-Heskem beyn Dir Yasin ve-Givat Shaul," [20 January 1948] (the agreement); IDFA 520/4944/49: Tzadiq to Mathen and Hashmona'i, "Doh le-Yom 22.1.48"; IDFA 810/100001/57: "Yedi'ot Tene (A) [Intelligence

Service, Arab Department]," 25 January 1948; IDFA 35/500/48: testimony by
Yitzhak Levy; Yitzhak Levy, *Tish'a Qabin: Yerushalayim bi-Qravot Milhemet ha-
'Atzma'ut* ([Tel Aviv], 1986), p. 340; Sharvit, *Akiva*, p. 70; Gelber, "Propaganda,"
p. 308; YTA 16-12/52/81: interview with Meir Pa'il; Meir Pail and Ami Isseroff,
"Deir Yassin: Meir Pail's Eyewitness Account," 1 October 1998, www.ariga.com/
peacewatch/dy/dypail.htm; MEC GB165-0282/2/4: "Dir Yasin" – interviewee
not named [later referred to as Abu M.]; Muhammad 'Aql, "'Alaqat Ahali Dayr
Yasin al-Tayyiba bil-Yahud lam Tamna' al-Madhbaha," 1 April 2010, www.
arabs48.com/?mod=articles&ID=69887; Robert John and Sami Hadawi, *The
Palestine Diary* (New York, 1970), vol. 2, p. 328.

18. IDFA 35/500/48: testimony by Yitzhak Levy; Bar'el and Shay, "Hazara," p. 25
(interviewing Yoel Kimhi); Avraham Vered, *Yerushalayim zo Hazit ha-Merkaz*
(Tel Aviv, 1998), p. 71, citing a report by Meir [Yehoshua Zettler], March 1948;
Ha-Ma'as, 78, March 1948, copied in *Lohamey Herut Yisra'el – Ktavim* (Tel
Aviv, 1959), vol. 2, p. 972; IDFA 20/446/48: Hashmona'i to Shadmi [Zalman
Mart], 2 February 1948; IDFA 16/2504/49: 1 February 1948, 4 February 1948,
and "Tzror Yedi'ot," 4 February 1948; HA 105/72: 02104 [a source from Givat
Shaul] to Tene (A), 1 February 1948; *Al-Difa'*, 12 April 1948, *New York Herald
Tribune*, 12 April 1948, and *Palestine Post*, 12 April 1948, all citing Khalidi; *The
Jewish Agency's Digest of Press and Events*, no. 219 (Jerusalem), 18 April 1948, p. 16.

19. Sharvit, *Akiva*, p. 70; Shuki Ben-Ami, "Dir Yasin – Petza' she-lo Higlid," *'al
ha-Mishmar*, 8 April 1983, Saturday's supplement, p. 4; Kurzman, *Genesis*, p. 139;
'Arif, *Nakbat*, vol. 1, p. 171; IDFA 61/500/48: Tzadiq to Hashmona'i, "Tzror
Yedi'ot," 21 January 1948, Tzadiq to Mathen and Hashmona'i, "Doh le-Yom
23.1.48," 23 January 1948, same to same, "Doh le-Yom 28.1.48," 28 January 1948,
same to same, "Doh le-Yom 29.1.48," 29 January 1948, same to same, "Doh
le-Yom 30.1.48," 30 January 1948, and "Yedi'ot," [25 February 1948]; IDFA
16/2504/49: 26 December 1947, 28 January 1948, 29 January 1948, 30 January
1948, "Dir Yasin," 3 February 1948, "Dir Yasin," 15 February 1948, "Dir Yasin,"
24 February 1948, "Dir Yasin," 26 February 1948, and "Dir Yasin," 29 February
1948; IDFA 6/2605/49: 4 January 1948, 21 January 1948, "Dir Yasin" 25 February 1948, Eliezer [Mordechai Gicherman] to Tzadiq, Bernhard and Gold, "Dir
Yasin," 3 March 1948, and same to same, "Dir Yasin," 4 March 1948; IDFA
520/4944/49: Tzadiq to Mathen and Hashmona'i, "Doh le-Yom 22.1.48," 22
January 1948, same to same, "Doh le-Yom 26.1.48," 26 January 1948, same to
same, "Doh le-Yom 3.2.48," 3 February 1948, and same to same, "Doh le-Yom
15.2.48," 15 February 1948.

20. IDFA 61/500/48: Tzadiq to Mathen and Hashmona'i, "Doh le-Yom 28.1.48,"
28 January 1948; IDFA 56/500/48: Hashmona'i to David, "Doh le-Yom
27–28.1.48"; IDFA 20/446/48: Hashmona'i to Shadmi, 2 and 6 February 1948;
IDFA 16/2504/49: 1 February 1948, "Tzror Yedi'ot," 4 February 1948, "Dir Yasin,"
6 February 1948, and "Yahasey Dir Yasin le-'Abd al-Husayni," 6 February 1948;
IDFA 6/2605/49: 4 February 1948 and 27 February 1948; HA 105/72: 02104 to

Tene (A), 1 February 1948, and Yavne [Yitzhak Levy] to Tene (A), 29 February 1948; IDFA 35/500/48: appendix to letter 229/41/6, 11 September 1952, re the Deir Yassin trial; Benny Morris, *The Birth of the Palestinian Refugee Problem Revisited* (Cambridge, 2004), p. 97; Milstein, *History*, vol. 4, p. 351, and *Myth*, p. 31. For the Rescue Army, see Tauber, *Military Resistance*, pp. 31–34.

21. JA K4-10/9: testimony by Arnold Spaer during the benefits trial, 11 August 1952; Khalidi, *Dayr Yasin*, pp. 13–14 (testimonies by Da'ud Zaydan and Khalil Sammur); Kana'na and Zaytawi, *Dayr Yasin*, p. 51.

22. IDFA 18/446/48: Hashmona'i to Moriah, "Rikuz Yedi'ot No. 128," 31 March 1948, and "Nispahim le-Rikuz Yedi'ot No. 128," 31 March 1948; IDFA 6/2605/49: "Dir Yasin," 24 March 1948, and "Dir Yasin," 3 April 1948; IDFA 2/2605/49: Hashmona'i to Moriah, "Nispahim le-Rikuz Yedi'ot No. 139," 7 April 1948; 355/2644/49: "Tzror Yedi'ot 'Arviyot," 3 April 1948; IDFA 75/5254/49: Yavne to District Commander, "Tzror Yedi'ot 'Arviyot Dhufot," 3 April 1948; HA 105/216a: Yavne to Tene, 30 March 1948; IDFA 810/100001/57: "Yedi'ot Tene (A)," 9 April 1948; YTA 12-3/9/3: Gichon, "Parashat Dir Yasin Tashah"; Milstein, *History*, vol. 4, p. 352, and *Myth*, pp. 32, 34 (Milstein interviewed Gichon); Yehuda Lapidot, *Be-Lahav ha-Mered: Ma'arkhot ha-Etzel bi-Yerushalayim* ([Tel Aviv], 1996), p. 307, and *'Al Homotayikh: Zikhronot Lohem Etzel* ([Tel Aviv], 1992), pp. 148–149; Idem, "Ha-'Uvdot Kvar Yedu'ot," *ha-Aretz*, 18 May 1993, p. 16; JA K4-10/1: testimony by Reuven Greenberg; Walter Lever, *Jerusalem Is Called Liberty* (Jerusalem, 1951), p. 161. Lever was a native of Manchester who taught English literature in the Hebrew University in 1948. In his memoirs he took for a fact that an advance force of Iraqis entered the village in early April and fortified its approaches.

23. *Davar*, 4 April 1948, p. 2; *Ha-Tzofe*, 4 April 1948, p. 4; *Mishmar*, 4 April 1948, p. 4; Lever, *Jerusalem*, p. 161; Aviezer Goldstein, *Lehavot bi-Shmey Yerushalayim* (Tel Aviv, 1949), p. 105; Yehuda Avner, "The Ghosts of Deir Yassin," *Jerusalem Post*, 8 April 2007, p. 13; Lapidot, *Lahav*, p. 308; JA 'EG-28/2: testimony by David Gottlieb; JA K4-10/1: testimony by Reuven Greenberg; Milstein, *History*, vol. 4, p. 353, and *Myth*, p. 34; Gelber, "Propaganda," p. 308; IDFA 520/4944/49: "Nispah le-Doh mi-Yom 5/6.4.48 sa'if 8"; Mordechai Gichon, *Mate Mordechai* ([Reut], 2010), p. 248.

24. IDFA 29/500/48: Yavne to District Commander, "Tzror Yedi'ot 'Arviyot Dhufot," 7 April 1948; IDFA 355/2644/49: "Tzror Yedi'ot 'Arviyot," 7 April 1948; YTA 12-3/9/3: letter, Yitzhak Levy (Jerusalem) to Menachem Begin, 12 April 1971; Khalidi, *Dayr Yasin*, p. 15 (testimony by Khalil Sammur who participated in the battle); Kana'na and Zaytawi, *Dayr Yasin*, p. 51; Nimr, *Dayr Yasin*, p. 15; PACE 240: interview with 'Ayish Muhammad Zaydan; CO 537/3857: CID, Headquarters, the Palestine Police Force (Jerusalem), "Summary of Events," 9 April 1948; Golani, *Mitos*, p. 13; Lapidot, *Lahav*, p. 306, and *Homotayikh*, p. 148.

25. Hijazi, *Dayr Yasin*, p. 58; Khalidi, *Dayr Yasin*, p. 15 (testimony by Khalil Sammur); Kana'na and Zaytawi, *Dayr Yasin*, p. 52; *Filastin*, 11 April 1948; LC 3/29: DLP, "Deir Yassin," pp. 5–6; Bar'el and Shay, "Hazara," p. 25 (interviewing Muhammad 'Arif Sammur); Rim 'Ubaydu, "Khamsun 'Aman 'ala al-Nakba – Qaryat Dayr Yasin Sarat Mustashfa lil-Majanin al-Yahud," *al-Nahar*, 16 May 1998, p. 15 (interview with Zaynab Muhammad Isma'il 'Atiyya); BUPA: 'Aql, "Haqa'iq Waqi'iyya"; Zananiri, "Interviews" (interviewing Muhammad Mahmud As'ad Radwan); Ahron Bregman and Jihan al-Tahri, *The Fifty Years War: Israel and the Arabs* (London, 1998), p. 29 (interview with same); "Abu Mahmud," p. 8; Sahera Dirbas, "Deir Yassin Village and Massacre" (Sahera Production), 15 December 2012, 2:38, www.youtube.com/watch?v=k4YLmBv Q4XQ&noredirect=1 (interview with same); BUPA: Shafiqa 'Iyad, "Shuhud 'Iyan min Madhbahat Dayr Yasin," www.awraq.birzeit.edu/sites/default/files/ PDF_154. (testimony by Umm 'Aziz [wife of Jamil 'Isa 'Id]).

26. *Filastin*, 14 April 1948.

27. Wadi' 'Awawda, *Dhakira la Tamutu* ([Haifa], 2000), p. 88 (testimony by 'Abd al-Qadir Zaydan); Idem, "Isra'il Tarfadu Fath Milaff Dayr Yasin," *al-Jazira Net*, 8 April 2011, www.palestineremembered.com/Jerusalem/Dayr-Yasin/Story19755. html (interview with same); PACE 240: interview with 'Ayish Muhammad Zaydan; PACE 237: interview with Wahid Zaydan (a baby at the time); JA K4-10/1: testimony by Ben-Zion Cohen; JA K4-10/9: testimony by same during the benefits trial, 5 January 1953; Uri Milstein, "Dir Yasin," *ha-Aretz*, 30 August 1968, p. 17, also believed it to be 60.

28. 'Arif, *Nakbat*, vol. 1, p. 171; Muhammad Fa'iz al-Qusari, *Harb Filastin 'Am 1948* (Damascus, 1962), vol. 2, p. 128; Salayima, *Dayr Yasin*, p. 108; Farsakh, "Majzarat"; BUPA: 'Aql, "Haqa'iq Waqi'iyya"; "Abu Mahmud," p. 8.

29. Lapidot, *Lahav*, p. 325; Lynd, Bahour and Lynd, *Homeland*, p. 23 (interview with Ahmad 'Ayish Khalil); Gelber, "Propaganda," p. 312.

30. As'ad, "Dhikra," p. 3; CO 733/477/5: tel. 933, Cunningham to Secretary of State for the Colonies, 10 April 1948.

31. Kana'na and Zaytawi, *Dayr Yasin*, pp. 50–51; Khalidi, *Dayr Yasin*, pp. 12 (testimony by Da'ud Zaydan), 53; Salayima, *Dayr Yasin*, pp. 94, 109; Hijazi, *Dayr Yasin*, p. 56 ; LC 3/29: DLP, "Deir Yassin," p. 6; PACE 237: interview with Ibtisam Zaydan; Zananiri, "Interviews" (interviewing Abu Tawfiq); Lynd, Bahour and Lynd, *Homeland*, p. 24 (interview with 'Ayisha Jum'a Zaydan); Bregman and Tahri, *Fifty Years*, p. 29 (interview with Muhammad Mahmud Radwan); Igbariyyeh, "60th Anniversary" (testimony by 'Abd al-Qadir Zaydan).

32. Bar'el and Shay, "Hazara," p. 25 (quoting Anwar Nusayba); "Qadiyya wa-Hiwar," 6:10 (interview with Mustafa Mahmud); MEC GB165-0282/2/4: "Dir Yasin" – interviewee not named; Daniel A. McGowan and Marc H. Ellis (eds.),

Remembering Deir Yassin: The Future of Israel and Palestine (New York, 1998), pp. 36 (interview with Meir Pa'il), 47; LC 3/29: DLP, "Deir Yassin," p. 6; Larry Collins and Dominique Lapierre, *O Jerusalem!* (Jerusalem, 1972), p. 272; PACE 237: interview with Wahid Zaydan; IDFA 35/500/48: testimony by Yitzhak Levy.

33. Khalidi, *Dayr Yasin*, pp. 12–13 (testimonies by Da'ud Zaydan and Husayn Muhammad 'Atiyya); Hijazi, *Dayr Yasin*, p. 56 (testimony by 'Abd al-'Aziz Sammur); Kana'na and Zaytawi, *Dayr Yasin*, p. 50; Salayima, *Dayr Yasin*, p. 92 (testimony by same); "'Aql Yakshifu Tafasil Murawwi'a 'an Madhbahat Dayr Yasin," *Ida'a*, 15 April 2013, eda2a.com/news/3/35534 (interview with 'Uthman ['Atiyya] 'Aql); Zananiri, "Interviews" (interviewing Abu Tawfiq); Paul Holmes, "Deir Yassin a casualty of guns and propaganda" (Jerusalem: [Reuters], [6 April 1998]), radiobergen.eu/palestine/deir-02.html; Bar'el and Shay, "Hazara," p. 25 (interviewing Muhammad 'Arif Sammur); Bregman and Tahri, *Fifty Years*, p. 30 (interview with Muhammad Mahmud Radwan). Hasan As'ad Radwan related that during the battle he used a British rifle brought from Egypt with some 30 5-round magazines. Khalidi, *Dayr Yasin*, p. 54.

34. Itamar Raday, *Ha-Kohot ha-Bilti Sdirim ve-ha-Hit'argenut ha-'Arvit be-Ezor Yerushalayim me-Reshit Detzember 1947 'ad ha-19 be-May 1948* (MA thesis, Hebrew University, 2002), p. 98; Lynd, Bahour and Lynd, *Homeland*, p. 22 (interview with Ahmad 'Ayish Khalil); 'Arif, *Nakbat*, vol. 1, p. 171; Salayima, *Dayr Yasin*, p. 108; MEC GB165-0346/2/24: interview with Ezra Yakhin; Ezra Yakhin, *Sipuro shel Elnaqam* (Tel Aviv, 1977), p. 257; IDFA 16/2504/49: "Dir Yasin," 16 February 1948, and "Dir Yasin," 21 February 1948; IDFA 520/4944/49: Tzadiq to Mathen, Hasmona'i and Shadmi, "Doh le-Yom 16.2.48," 16 February 1948, and Tzadiq to Mathen and Hasmona'i, "Doh le-Yom 17.2.48," 17 February 1948; Golani, *Mitos*, pp. 36, 53, 67–68; David Niv, *Ma'arkhot ha-Irgun ha-Tzva'i ha-Le'umi* (Tel Aviv, 1980), vol. 6, p. 84; Lapidot, *Lahav*, p. 325; Ben-Ami, *Years*, p. 441; Milstein, "Dir Yasin," p. 19; JA K4-10/1: testimony by Yehoshua Gorodenchik; Milstein, *History*, vol. 4, p. 363, and *Myth*, p. 58 (interview with Yehoshua Gorodenchik); JA K4-10/9: testimonies by Mordechai Kaufman, [30 June 1952], and by Ben-Zion Cohen, 5 January 1953, during the benefits trial; MEC GB165-0346/3/5: interview with Ben-Zion Cohen; Interview with Yehuda Lapidot (Jerusalem), 24 August 2010; Ilan Kfir, "Shalosh Girsot 'al Parashat Dir Yasin," *Yedi'ot Aharonot*, 4 April 1972, p. 3 (interview with Yehoshua Zettler); 'Awawda, *Dhakira*, p. 88 (testimony by 'Abd al-Qadir Zaydan); "Al-Dhikra 58 'ala Madhbahat Dayr Yasin wa-Dhikra Istishhad 'Abd al-Qadir al-Husayni," 8 April 2006, www.arabs48.com/?mod=articles&ID=35979 (speech by same); "Abu Mahmud," p. 8.

35. 'Arif, *Nakbat*, vol. 1, p. 171; Salayima, *Dayr Yasin*, pp. 108–109; Nimr, *Dayr Yasin*, p. 15; Qusari, *Harb*, vol. 2, p. 128; Abu Gharbiyya, *Khidamm*, p. 220 (Abu Gharbiyya indicated that the villagers had considerable quantities of ammunition available to them); PACE 240: interview with 'Ayish Muhammad

Zaydan; Lynd, Bahour and Lynd, *Homeland,* p. 22 (interview with Ahmad 'Ayish Khalil). For the Jewish sources see former note.

36. Hassida Pa'il, "Parashat Dir Yasin, Yom Shishi 9/4/48, Ra'ayonot 'im Anshey Shay 60 Shana Aharey," [2008], pt. 2, 2:56, www.meirpail.co.il (interview with Shraga Peled); HA 95.3: testimony by Akiva Azulay.

37. IDFA 16/2504/49: 26 December 1947, Eliezer [Gicherman] to Tzadiq and Bernhard, "'Amadot be-Dir Yasin," 1 February 1948, and "Dir Yasin," 29 February 1948; IDFA 6/2605/49: 26 December 1947 and 30 December 1947; YTA 12-3/41/14: interview with Moshe Edelstein; JA K4-10/1: testimonies by Yehoshua Gorodenchik and Yehuda Marinburg; "Jacob Shafrir – Deir Yassin Massacre," 2 June 2010, pt. 1, 6:40, www.youtube.com; MEC GB165-0346/3/19: interview with Yair Tzaban; Lever, *Jerusalem,* p. 170; "Dir Yasin – Kol ha-Emet," *Ma'oz,* 18, October 1970, p. 16; Khalidi, *Dayr Yasin,* p. 49 (testimonies by Da'ud Jabir Mustafa Jabir and Husayn 'Atiyya).

38. Ibid., pp. 12–13 (interview with Khalil Sammur and testimony by Mahfuz 'Abd al-'Aziz Sammur – for the location of the trench, see map between pages 10 and 11); Kana'na and Zaytawi, *Dayr Yasin,* p. 51; Dawud A. Assad, *Palestine Rising: How I Survived the 1948 Deir Yasin Massacre* ([Bloomington IN], [2010] 2nd rep. 2011), pp. 103, 105 (he also published his memoirs in Arabic, with alterations, amendments, and additions, Da'ud Ahmad As'ad, *Filastin Tashu: Ahdath wa-Masir – Kayfa Najawtu min Madhbahat Dir Yasin,* [Bloomington IN], 2012); Zananiri, "Interviews" (interviewing Abu Tawfiq and Muhammad Mahmud Radwan); Sharvit, *Akiva,* p. 70.

39. For a short history of the Jewish military organizations that operated in Palestine during that period, see Tauber, *Military Resistance,* pp. 19–26.

40. About the relations between Kaufman and Zettler, and Shaltiel, see respectively J. Bowyer Bell, *Terror Out of Zion: The Fight for Israeli Independence* (New Brunswick NJ and London, 1996), p. 291, and Hadas Regev-Yarkoni and Ofer Regev, *Lohem Herut Yerushalayim: Zikhronotav shel Yehoshu'a Zetler* (Tzur Yigal, 2007), p. 139 . About the strained relations between Shaltiel and Galili, see Yoram Nimrod, "Dir Yasin o Mishmar ha-'Emeq? Shtey Astrategyot Menugadot be-Milhemet ha-Shihrur," in idem, *Mifgash be-Tzomet: Yehudim ve-'Aravim be-Eretz Yisra'el – Dorot Aharonim, Pirqey Mehqar ve-Hora'a* (Haifa University-Oranim, 1985), pp. 124–125, and *Breyrat ha-Shalom ve-Derekh ha-Milhama: Hithavut Dfusim shel Yahasey Yisra'el-'Arav, 1947–1950* (Givat Haviva, 2000), p. 128; Eli Tzur, *Shomer le-Yisra'el: Pirqey Hayav shel David Sha'alti'el* (n.p., 2001), pp. 170–171.

41. Ofir, *Homot,* p. 15; Lapidot, *Lahav,* pp. 277, 300; Niv, *Ma'arkhot,* vol. 6, p. 231; Levy, *Tish'a,* pp. 335–336; LC 3/29: testimonies by Amnon [should be Yehuda] Lapidot, Yehoshua Zettler and Zalman Mart; IDFA 290/922/75: testimony 32 by same; phone conversation with Ben-Zion Cohen, 15 February 2015; JA

H13-3/48/2: case against Nathan Friedman-Yellin and Matityahu Shmuelevitz in the special military court, Protocol II, 14 December 1948, p. 257 (testimony by Nathan Friedman-Yellin); JA H13-3/48/4: same, Protocol IV, 7 January 1949, p. 1398 (testimony by David Shaltiel); Nechemia Ben-Tor, *Sefer Toldot Lohamey Herut Yisra'el (Lehi)* (Jerusalem, 2010), vol. 4, p. 436; Israel Eldad, *Ma'aser Rishon: Pirkey Zikhronot u-Musar Haskel* (Tel Aviv, 3rd ed. 1975), p. 333; Vered, *Yerushalayim,* pp. 70–71.

42. IDFA 290/922/75: testimony 33 by Eliyahu Arbel; E[liyahu] Arbel, "Hayiti Qtzin ha-Haganah she-Siyyer be-Dir Yasin le-Mohorat ha-Pe'ula," *Yedi'ot Aharonot,* 2 May 1972, p. 20.

43. HA 58.49: testimony by Zalman Mart; LC 3/29: testimony by same; IDFA 290/922/75: testimony 32 by same; Regev-Yarkoni and Regev, *Lohem,* pp. 132–133, 139; JA H13-3/48/4: case against Nathan Friedman-Yellin and Matityahu Shmuelevitz in the special military court, Protocol IV, 7 January 1949, pp. 1400–1403 (testimony by David Shaltiel); Milstein, *History,* vol. 4, pp. 345–346, and *Myth,* p. 20 (interview with Yehoshua Zettler); IDFA 1/446/48: Tzadiq to Hashmona'i, Moriah and Yarkoni, "Doh 'al Pe'ulat Lehi ba-Qatamon be-Leyl 13.3.48," 14 March 1948; FO 816/117: tel. 644, Cunningham to Secretary of State for the Colonies, 15 March 1948; 'Arif, *Nakbat,* vol. 1, pp. 117, 133.

44. LC 3/29: testimony by Yehoshua Zettler; Regev-Yarkoni and Regev, *Lohem,* p. 133; YTA 12-3/41/14: interview with Moshe Edelstein; Yosef Shapira (ed.), *David Sha'alti'el: Yerushalayim Tashah* (Tel Aviv, 1981), p. 143; Tzur, *Shomer,* pp. 170–171; Nimrod, "Dir Yasin," p. 125.

45. There are many sources for the battle over Qastal. For the Jewish version, see *Sefer Toldot ha-Hagana,* vol. 3, pt. 2, pp. 1561–1563. For the Arab version, see 'Arif, *Nakbat,* vol. 1, pp. 156–158, 162–165.

46. IDFA 290/922/75: testimony 31 by Yeshurun Schiff; LC 3/29: testimony by same [No. 2]; Levy, *Tish'a,* p. 341.

47. JA K4-10/1: Mordechai Raanan [Kaufman], "Mikhtav Galuy le-Mar David Shalti'el, le-she-'Avar Mefaqed ha-Hagana bi-Yerushalayim ba-Tqufa she-beyn Detzember 1947 – September 1948"; JA 'ER-12/1: testimony by Mordechai Raanan; JA 'ER-12/5: interview with same; Lapidot, *Lahav,* pp. 301, 303, and *Homotayikh,* p. 147; Kfir, "Shalosh," p. 2 (interview with Mordechai Raanan); Kurzman, *Genesis,* p. 140.

48. IDFA 149/5254/49: letter to the Haganah's commander in the Jerusalem district, 4 April 1948, and letter to Lehi's commander in the Jerusalem district, 4 April 1948; JA H13-3/48/4: case against Nathan Friedman-Yellin and Matityahu Shmuelevitz in the special military court, Protocol IV, 7 January 1949, p. 1402 (testimony by David Shaltiel); JA 'ER-12/5: interview with Mordechai Raanan; Kfir, "Shalosh," p. 2 (interview with Yehoshua Zettler); Lapidot, *Lahav,*

pp. 303–304, and *Homotayikh*, p. 147; *Lehi – Ktavim*, vol. 2, pp. 967–968 (Lehi's poster explaining the failure of the negotiations, April 1948).

49. JA 'ER-12/1: testimony by Mordechai Raanan; JA 'ER-12/5: interview with same; JA K4-10/9: testimony by same during the benefits trial, [30 June 1952]; Ofir, *Homot*, p. 50; Lapidot, *Lahav*, p. 304, and *Homotayikh*, p. 147; Kfir, "Shalosh," p. 2 (interviews with Mordechai Raanan and Yehoshua Zettler); Kurzman, *Genesis*, p. 140.

50. JA 'ER-12/1: testimony by Mordechai Raanan; JA 'ER-12/5: interview with same; Ofir, *Homot*, p. 50; Idem, *Tirat al-'Amawi* (Givatayim, 1987), p. 273; Meir Hovav, *Gal – Dmuto shel Lohem: Hayav u-Ma'asav shel Lohem ha-Etzel Yehush'a Yeruham Goldshmid* (Tel Aviv, 1990), pp. 76–77; Lapidot, *Lahav*, p. 304, and *Homotayikh*, p. 147; Ben-Tor, *Sefer*, vol. 4, p. 455; Milstein, *History*, vol. 4, p. 350, and *Myth*, p. 25 (interview with Shimon Moneta). Several days earlier, a Lehi unit under the command of Shimon Moneta had patrolled near Shu'afat. Moneta was a Haganah agent planted in Lehi. When he reported this to his operator in the Haganah, the latter warned him that the strong British forces still there would butcher the Lehi men if they attacked the village. Ibid.

51. JA 'ER-12/5: interview with Mordechai Raanan; Ofir, *Homot*, p. 50; Idem, *Tirat*, p. 273; Nahum Barnea, "'Amos Qeynan: Ha-Shanim ha-Shhorot," *Koteret Rashit*, 108, 26 December 1984, p. 30; YTA 12-3/41/14: interview with Moshe Edelstein.

52. Hovav, *Gal*, pp. 76–78; Ofir, *Homot*, pp. 49, 51; Idem, *Tirat*, p. 273; Binyamin, "Bor," p. 9; Yosef Waxman, "Mefaqdey ha-Etzel le-she-'Avar Hitkansu be-Lishkato shel Rosh ha-Memshala," *Ma'ariv*, 18 June 1979, p. 4 (citing Yehuda Lapidot); Lapidot, *Lahav*, p. 304, and *Homotayikh*, p. 147; JA K4-10/1: testimonies by Yehuda Lapidot and Reuven Greenberg, and Mordechai Raanan, "Mikhtav Galuy le-Mar David Shalti'el"; JA 'ER-12/3: testimony by Mordechai Raanan; JA 'ER-12/5: interview with same; JA K4-10/9: testimony by same during the benefits trial, [30 June 1952]; Kfir, "Shalosh," p. 2 (interview with same); JA 'EB-30/5: interview with Kalman Bergman; LC 3/29: testimony by Yehoshua Zettler; MEC GB165-0346/3/5: interview with Ben-Zion Cohen; YTA 12-3/41/14: interview with Moshe Edelstein; JA 'EG-28/1: testimony by David Gottlieb; ISA P-2878/5: interview with Shimon Moneta; JA K4-13/8: broadcast of *Kol Zion ha-Lohemet*, Etzel's broadcasting station, 11 April 1948; *New York Times*, 10 April 1948; Nathan Yellin-Mor, *Lohamey Herut Yisra'el* (Jerusalem, 1974), p. 470; Idem, "Refuting a Libel," *New Outlook*, 12:4 (1969), p. 64; Menachem Begin, *The Revolt* (Tel Aviv, [1952]), p. 162; Golani, *Mitos*, pp. 16–18; Lever, *Jerusalem*, p. 161; Kurzman, *Genesis*, p. 140; IDFA 291/922/75: testimony 72 by Yitzhak Levy. It is interesting to note that also Yitzhak Levy admitted that Deir Yassin had "certain" strategic importance. Levy, *Tish'a*, p. 340. One of the Arab survivors, too, was of the opinion that Deir Yassin

was attacked because it was "the key to Jerusalem." PACE 241: interview with Muhammad 'Ayish Zaydan.

53. Hovav, *Gal*, p. 76; Milstein, "Dir Yasin," p. 17; Holmes, "Deir Yassin" (citing Yehuda Lapidot); David Shipler, *Arab and Jew: Wounded Spirits in a Promised Land* (London, 1988), p. 38; 'Awawda, *Dhakira*, p. 89 (citing Muhammad Mahmud Radwan); Eric Silver, *Begin: A Biography* (London, 1984), pp. 90–91 (citing Yehuda Lapidot); JA 'EB-30/6: interview with Kalman Bergman; MEC GB165-0346/2/14: interview with Shimon Moneta; Shimon Moneta, *Gam Ele Toldot: Asufat Dapim* (Jerusalem, 2011), p. 61; Kati Marton, *A Death in Jerusalem* (New York, 1996), p. 29 (citing Baruch Nadel). For Meir Pa'il's interpretation of this (the Abu Gosh option), see MacGowan and Ellis, *Remembering*, p. 37.

54. JA K4-10/1: testimony by Yehuda Lapidot; Kana'na, "Madhbahat," p. 169; Shimon Moneta, "Kavana Re'uya, Aval Shiqul Mut'e," *ha-Aretz, Tarbut ve-Sifrut* supplement, 1 May 2009, p. 4; Idem, *Toldot*, pp. 60–61; ISA P-2878/5: interview with Shimon Moneta; MEC GB165-0346/2/14: interview with same; Ofir, *Tirat*, p. 274.

55. JA 'EB-30/5: interview with Kalman Bergman; JA K4-10/1: unidentified testimony [Ben-Zion Cohen]; JA 'EG-28/1: testimony by David Gottlieb; Golani, *Mitos*, p. 15; 'Awawda, *Dhakira*, p. 89 (citing Muhammad Mahmud Radwan); Kana'na, "Madhbahat," p. 169.

56. Dov Joseph, *The Faithful City* (New York, 1960), p. 71; IDFA 54/500/48: Yavne to Tene (D) [Intelligence Service, Political Department], "Pe'ulat Etzel ve-Lehi be-Dir Yasin," 12 April 1948; LC 3/29: testimony by Yeshurun Schiff [no. 2]; Silver, *Begin*, p. 89; Kana'na, "Madhbahat," p. 168; Lynne Reid Banks, *Torn Country: An Oral History of the Israeli War of Independence* (New York, 1982), p. 55 (testimony by Meir Pa'il); Meir Pa'il and Pinchas Yurman, *Mivhan ha-Tnu'a ha-Tziyonit 1931–1948: Marut ha-Hanhaga ha-Medinit mul ha-Porshim* (Tel Aviv, [2003]), p. 329; Motti Golani, *Hanhagat ha-Yishuv u-Sh'elat Yerushalayim be-Milhemet ha-'Atzma'ut, Detzember 1947 – May 1948* (MA thesis, Hebrew University, 1988), p. 124; YTA 12-3/41/14: interview with Moshe Edelstein.

57. Nimrod, "Dir Yasin," p. 123; Idem, *Breyrat*, p. 127; Silver, *Begin*, p. 89; Marton, *Death*, p. 29 (citing Baruch Nadel). See also Lapidot, *Homotayikh*, p. 149, for Kaufman's views.

NOTES FOR CHAPTER 2

1. Milstein, *History*, vol. 4, p. 356 (citing Shimon Moneta); Regev-Yarkoni and Regev, *Lohem*, p. 134; Eliahu Amikam, "Ha-Hagana Hiskima me-Rosh le-Kibush Kfar Dir Yasin," *Yedi'ot Aharonot*, 19 August 1960, *7 Yamim* Saturday's supplement, p. 3; IDFA 54/500/48: Etzioni [David Shaltiel] to Hillel [Yisrael

Galili] and Diqi [Arnan Azaryahu, Galili's adjutant], 11 April 1948; JA H13-3/48/4: case against Nathan Friedman-Yellin and Matityahu Shmuelevitz in the special military court, Protocol IV, 7 January 1949, pp. 1399–1400 (testimony by David Shaltiel); IDFA 291/922/75: testimonies 75 by same and 53 by Zion Eldad; Shapira, *David*, p. 139; Meir Avizohar, *Moriya bi-Yerushalayim be-Tashah: Gdud ha-Hish ha-Rishon bi-Qravot Yerushalayim* (Lod, 2002), p. 90; Yaakov Orenstein, "Aluf David Sha'alti'el: Ha-Kni'a Hayta be-Nigud le-Hora'otay," *Hed ha-Hagana*, 11 (October 1960), pp. 88–89; IDFA 35/500/48: testimony by Yitzhak Levy; Joseph, *City*, p. 71; YTA 15-34/13/5: testimony by Meir Pa'il, "Dir Yasin"; JA 'EP-19/1: testimony by same; Pail and Isseroff, "Deir Yassin"; Banks, *Country*, pp. 55–56 (testimony by Meir Pa'il); Avner Avrahami, "Ruhot ha-Refa'im shel Dir Yasin," *Ma'ariv* of Sukkot, 11 October 1992, p. 29 (interview with same); LC 3/29: testimony by Zalman Mart; Silver, *Begin*, p. 91 (citing Yehuda Lapidot).

2.   IDFA 35/500/48: District Commander [David Shaltiel] to Yitzhak Shapira [Zettler's code name for the Haganah], 7 April 1948 (the letter was afterward made public when Etzel and Lehi incorporated it in posters they disseminated – see below); LC 3/29: Arye Levavi Files, p. 90; Shapira, *David*, p. 139; Kurzman, *Genesis*, pp. 140–141; Pail and Isseroff, "Deir Yassin." It is interesting to note that in a recent interview Meir Pa'il argued that the attack was sanctioned not just by the Jerusalem command but also by the supreme command of the Haganah. Pa'il, "Ra'ayonot Anshey Shay," pt. 1, 4:34. There is no corroborating evidence for this.

3.   IDFA 105/5254/49: [Meir] Batz and Nimrod [Eliahu Arbel] to [Zion] Eldad and Yarkoni, "Sdot ha-Te'ufah," 9 April 1948; Goldstein, *Lehavot*, p. 105; Golani, *Mitos*, pp. 13–14; Silver, *Begin*, p. 89.

4.   YTA 15-34/13/5: testimony by Meir Pa'il, "Dir Yasin"; YTA 16-12/52/81: interview with same; JA 'EP-19/1: testimony by same; Pail and Isseroff, "Deir Yassin"; Avrahami, "Ruhot," p. 29 (interview with Meir Pa'il); Y. Dvir [Shay Gefen], "Dir Yasin: Ha-Sipur ha-Male," *ha-Shavu'a*, parashat Tazri'a-Metzora', April 1998, p. 20 (citing Yehuda Lapidot); Milstein, *History*, vol. 4, pp. 354–355, and *Myth*, p. 39 (interview with Moshe Edelstein); BBC, "The 50 Years War: Israel and the Arabs," 15 March 1998, 11:05 (interview with Meir Pa'il); Bregman and Tahri, *Fifty Years*, p. 29.

5.   IDFA 35/500/48: testimony by Yitzhak Levy; IDFA 291/922/75: testimony 72 by same; Levy, *Tish'a*, p. 341.

6.   Milstein, *History*, vol. 4, p. 357, and *Myth*, p. 45; YTA 15-46/183/2: Eliezer [Gicherman] to Tzadiq, Bernhard, Yarkoni and Avraham [Meir Pilavsky], "Doh Kibush Dir Yasin," 10 April 1948; Interview with Yehuda Lapidot, 24 August 2010.

7. Milstein, *History*, vol. 4, p. 356, and *Myth*, pp. 42–43 (interviews with Moshe Barzilai, Moshe Edelstein, Yehoshua Zettler and Petahya Selivansky); Ben-Tor, *Sefer*, vol. 4, p. 456; Kfir, "Shalosh," p. 3 (interview with Yehoshua Zettler); Amikam, "Hagana," p. 3 (citing same); Ofir, *Homot*, p. 51; Lapidot, *Lahav*, p. 306, and *Homotayikh*, p. 148; Avraham Vered, *Ari'ela: Le'a Prizant, Lohemet Herut Yisra'el* (Tel Aviv, 2001), p. 112; YTA 12-3/41/14: interview with Moshe Edelstein.

8. YTA 15-46/183/2: Eliezer to Tzadiq, Bernhard, Yarkoni and Avraham, "Doh Kibush Dir Yasin," 10 April 1948; Milstein, *History*, vol. 4, pp. 356, 358, and *Myth*, pp. 42, 46–47 (interviews with Petahya Selivansky and others); JA K4-10/1: testimony by Yehuda Lapidot; CO 733/477/5: tel. 933, Cunningham to Secretary of State for the Colonies, 10 April 1948; WO 275/64: "Fortnightly Intelligence Newsletter No. 66" (HQ Palestine), by HQ British Troops in Palestine, 21 April 1948; HA 95.3: testimony by Akiva Azulay; Sharvit, *Akiva*, p. 68; Rachel Yanait, Yitzhak Avrahami and Yerah Etzion (eds.), *Ha-Hagana bi-Yerushalayim: 'Eduyot ve-Zikhronot mi-Pi Haverim* (Jerusalem, 1975), vol. 2, p. 125 (testimony by Azulay); Ben-Tor, *Sefer*, vol. 4, p. 457.

9. Goldstein, *Lehavot*, pp. 105–106; Lever, *Jerusalem*, p. 169; Milstein, *History*, vol. 4, pp. 356, 358, and *Myth*, pp. 41, 47 (interviews with Yehuda Lapidot and Mordechai Gichon); YTA 15-46/183/2: Eliezer to Tzadiq, Bernhard, Yarkoni and Avraham, "Doh Kibush Dir Yasin," 10 April 1948; Avizohar, *Moriya*, p. 90. It is interesting to note that in a "top secret" document prepared by the IDF for the benefits trial, the author indicated that all the above proved that there was "certain coordination" between the Haganah and the organizations regarding the attack. See IDFA 35/500/48: appendix to letter 229/41/6, 11 September 1952, re the Deir Yassin trial.

10. JA K4-10/1: supplements to unidentified testimony [Ben-Zion Cohen]; LC 3/29: testimony by [Yehuda] Lapidot; JA 'ER-12/5: interview with Mordechai Raanan; Regev-Yarkoni and Regev, *Lohem*, pp. 134–135; Lapidot, *Lahav*, p. 310, and *Homotayikh*, p. 151; Golani, *Mitos*, p. 19; Ben-Tor, *Sefer*, vol. 4, pp. 455, 457.

11. JA K4-10/1: testimony by Yehuda Lapidot and unidentified testimony [Ben-Zion Cohen]; JA 'EB-30/5: interview with Kalman Bergman; JA 'EB-30/6: interview with same; Avner, "Ghosts," p. 14; Regev-Yarkoni and Regev, *Lohem*, p. 134; MacGowan and Ellis, *Remembering*, p. 37 (interview with Meir Pa'il); Silver, *Begin*, p. 90 (citing Yehuda Lapidot and Meir Pa'il); Interview with Yehuda Lapidot, 24 August 2010; Golani, *Mitos*, p. 19; Sharvit, *Akiva*, p. 71; Ben-Ami, "Dir Yasin," p. 4; MEC GB165-0346/3/5: interview with Ben-Zion Cohen; MEC GB165-0346/2/24: interview with Ezra Yakhin.

12. Milstein, *History*, vol. 4, pp. 354, 357, and *Myth*, pp. 37, 45; Idem, "Dir Yasin," p. 17; YTA 15-46/183/2: Eliezer to Tzadiq, Bernhard, Yarkoni and Avraham, "Doh Kibush Dir Yasin," 10 April 1948; Lapidot, *Homotayikh*, pp. 149–150;

Interview with Yehuda Lapidot, 24 August 2010; JA 'EB-30/5: interview with Kalman Bergman.

13. JA K4-10/1: unidentified testimony [Ben-Zion Cohen] and testimonies by same and Yehoshua Gorodenchik; MEC GB165-0346/3/5: interview with Ben-Zion Cohen; Lapidot, *Lahav*, pp. 308–309, and *Homotayikh*, p. 150; LC 3/29: testimony by [Yehuda] Lapidot; JA 'ER-12/5: interview with Mordechai Raanan; Milstein, *History*, vol. 4, p. 357, and *Myth*, p. 45; YTA 12-3/42/29: interview with Yitzhak Lumbroso; YTA 15-46/183/2: Eliezer to Tzadiq, Bernhard, Yarkoni and Avraham, "Doh Kibush Dir Yasin," 10 April 1948; Nurith Gertz, *'Al Da'at 'Atzmo: Araba'a Pirqey Hayim shel 'Amos Qeynan* (Tel Aviv, 2008), pp. 183–186; Barne'a, "'Amos," p. 30.

14. Interview with Yehuda Lapidot, 24 August 2010; IDFA 58/900/52: "Yedi'ot Tene – Taqtzir Yomi," 18 April 1948; Ben-Tor, *Sefer*, vol. 4, p. 457; Hovav, *Gal*, p. 78; YTA 12-3/42/29: interview with Yitzhak Lumbroso.

15. Banks, *Country*, p. 59 (testimony by Ezra Yakhin); Moneta, "Kavana," p. 4; Idem, *Toldot*, pp. 60–61; MEC GB165-0346/2/14: interview with Shimon Moneta; Bregman and Tahri, *Fifty Years*, p. 28 (interviews with Ezra Yakhin and Shimon Moneta); ISA P-2878/5: interview with same; phone conversation with same, 7 August 2014.

16. JA H13-3/48/2: case against Nathan Friedman-Yellin and Matityahu Shmuelevitz in the special military court, Protocol II, 14 December 1948, p. 257 (testimony by Nathan Friedman-Yellin); JA H13-3/48/7: case against Nathan Friedman-Yellin and Matityahu Shmuelevitz in the special military court – the Verdict, 10 February 1949, pp. 4–5; Kurzman, *Genesis*, p. 141; Yalin-Mor, "Refuting," p. 64; Eldad, *Ma'aser*, p. 335; Milstein, *History*, vol. 4, p. 348, and *Myth*, p. 28.

17. Lapidot, *Lahav*, p. 329, and *Homotayikh*, p. 165; Dvir, "Dir Yasin," p. 20 (citing Yehuda Lapidot); RH MSS. Brit. Emp. s. 527/10/2: interview with Shmuel Katz; Ned Temko, *To Win or to Die: A Personal Portrait of Menachem Begin* (New York, 1987), pp. 111–112, 114, 367, 369 (based on interviews with Yehuda Lapidot, Mordechai Raanan and Yaakov Amrami); Amos Perlmutter, *The Life and Times of Menachem Begin* (Garden City NY, 1987), p. 215; Frank Gervasi, *The Life and Times of Menahem Begin: Rebel to Statesman* (New York, 1979), p. 232.

18. JA 'ER-12/5: interview with Mordechai Raanan; MEC GB165-0346/3/5: interview with Ben-Zion Cohen; Lapidot, *Lahav*, pp. 309–310, and *Homotayikh*, pp. 150–151; Idem, Letter to the Editor, *ha-Aretz*, 2 February 1998, p. B6; Hovav, *Gal*, p. 78; JA K4-10/1: unidentified testimony, "Kibush Dir Yasin"; JA 'EB-30/6: interview with Kalman Bergman; Bar'el and Shay, "Hazara," p. 23 (interviewing Yoel Kimhi); Ben-Ami, *Years*, p. 441; Golani, *Mitos*, pp. 21–22.

19. JA K4-10/9: testimony by Ben-Zion Cohen, 5 January 1953, during the benefits trial; JA K4-10/1: unidentified testimony [by same] and supplements to

unidentified testimony; MEC GB165-0346/3/5: interview with same; JA 'ER-12/5: interview with Mordechai Raanan; IDFA 372/5254/49: Yavne to Tene (D), "Pe'ula Meshutefet shel ha-Porshim bi-Yerushalayim," 12 April 1948; YTA 15-46/183/2: Eliezer to Tzadiq, Bernhard, Yarkoni and Avraham, "Doh Kibush Dir Yasin," 10 April 1948; *Ha-Boqer*, 11 April 1948, p. 1; Lapidot, *Lahav*, p. 310, and *Homotayikh*, p. 152; Y[hoshua] Ofir, "Dir Yasin – Az ve-ha-Yom," *Herut*, 5 April 1957, p. 5; Ofir, *Homot*, p. 57; Bar'el and Shay, "Hazara," p. 23 (interviewing Yoel Kimhi); Golani, *Mitos*, p. 22; Gervasi, *Life*, p. 232.

20. Yakhin, *Sipuro*, pp. 250–251; MEC GB165-0346/2/24: interview with Ezra Yakhin; Banks, *Country*, p. 59 (testimony by same); Gertz, *Da'at*, pp. 187–188; Kfir, "Shalosh," p. 3 (interview with Yehoshua Zettler); Ben-Tor, *Sefer*, vol. 4, p. 457; Yehoshua Matza, *Shney Eqdahim: Praqim me-Havayot Politiyot* (Tel Aviv, 2014), p. 48; Kurzman, *Genesis*, p. 139.

21. IDFA 372/5254/49: Yavne to Tene (D), "Pe'ula Meshutefet shel ha-Porshim bi-Yerushalayim," 12 April 1948, and same to same, "Pe'ulat ha-Porshim be-Dir Yasin," 13 April 1948; HA 95.3: testimony by Akiva Azulay; Sharvit, *Akiva*, pp. 68–69; *Ha-Hagana bi-Yerushalayim*, vol. 2, p. 125 (testimony by Azulay); Gertz, *Da'at*, pp. 188–189; Amikam, "Hagana," p. 3 (citing Petahya Selivansky); JA K4-10/1: testimony by Ezra Yakhin; Banks, *Country*, p. 59 (testimony by same); Yakhin, *Sipuro*, p. 251; Matza, *Shney Eqdahim*, p. 48; Lapidot, *Lahav*, p. 310, and *Homotayikh*, p. 152; Milstein, *History*, vol. 4, p. 358, and *Myth*, pp. 46–47; Ben-Tor, *Sefer*, vol. 4, pp. 457–458.

22. Hijazi, *Dayr Yasin*, p. 58; Nimr, *Dayr Yasin*, p. 15; Sharvit, *Akiva*, p. 71; Milstein, *History*, vol. 4, p. 358, and *Myth*, p. 47 (Milstein interviewed Ben-Sasson).

23. *Filastin*, 10 April 1948; *New York Herald Tribune*, 10 April 1948; CO 537/3857: CID, "Summary of Events," 9 April 1948; CO 733/477/5: tel. 928, Cunningham to Secretary of State for the Colonies, 10 April 1948; NARA RG 84, Jerusalem Consulate General Classified Records, 1948 – 800 Political Affairs, 6: tel. 433, [Thomas C.] Wasson (Jerusalem) to Secretary of State (Washington), 14 April 1948; IDFA 54/500/48: Etzioni [Shaltiel] to Hillel and Diqi, 11 April 1948. It is interesting to note that several hours after Cunningham had reported his overestimation, he sent a revised, underestimation of 100 attackers. CO 733/477/5: tel. 933, Cunningham to Secretary of State for the Colonies, 10 April 1948. *New York Times*, 10 April 1948, p. 6, also reported 100.

24. E.g. Milstein, *History*, vol. 4, p. 358, and *Myth*, p. 46; Matthew Hogan, "The 1948 Massacre at Deir Yassin Revisited," *The Historian*, 63:2 (2001), p. 316; Morton A. Klein, *Deir Yassin: History of a Lie* (The Zionist Organization of America, 9 March 1998), p. 8; Benny Morris, "The Historiography of Deir Yassin," *The Journal of Israeli History*, 24:1 (2005), p. 86.

25. E.g. IDFA 372/5254/49: Yavne to Tene (D), "Pe'ulat Etzel ve-Lehi be-Dir Yasin," 12 April 1948; YTA 12-3/9/3: letter, Levy to Begin, 12 April 1971; *Sefer Toldot ha-Hagana*, , vol. 3, pt. 2, p. 1547; Shapira, *David*, p. 140.

26. JA 'ER-12/5: interview with Mordechai Raanan; Kfir, "Shalosh," p. 2 (interview with same); JA K4-10/1: testimony by Ben-Zion Cohen; MEC GB165-0346/3/5: interview with same; Interview with Yehuda Lapidot, 24 August 2010; E-mails from same to the author, 7 and 9 March 2014; Lapidot, *Lahav*, p. 309, and *Homotayikh*, p. 150; JA 'EA-3/2: testimony by Yosef Avni. Avni (then Danoch) was a commander of a ten-combatant squad in Lapidot's platoon.

27. JA K4-10/1: testimony by Ezra Yakhin; IDFA 372/5254/49: Yavne to Tene (D), "Pe'ula Meshutefet shel ha-Porshim bi-Yerushalayim," 12 April 1948, and same to same, "Pe'ulat ha-Porshim be-Dir Yasin," 13 April 1948 (both based on "Esther"); MEC GB165-0346/2/14: interview with Shimon Moneta; Moneta, *Toldot*, p. 61; Yellin-Mor, *Lohamey*, p. 469.

28. JA 'EG-28/1: testimony by David Gottlieb; IDFA 58/900/52: "Yedi'ot Tene – Taqtzir Yomi," 18 April 1948; IDFA 372/5254/49: Yavne to Tene (D), "Pe'ulat Etzel ve-Lehi be-Dir Yasin," 12 April 1948, same to same, "Pe'ula Meshutefet shel ha-Porshim bi-Yerushalayim," 12 April 1948, and same to same, "Pe'ulat ha-Porshim be-Dir Yasin," 13 April 1948; Temko, *Win*, p. 112 (interviewing Raanan and Lapidot); Gervasi, *Life*, p. 232; Ben-Ami, *Years*, p. 440; Golani, *Mitos*, p. 19; E-mail from Yehuda Lapidot to the author, 7 March 2014.

29. JA 'EA-3/2: testimony by Yosef Avni; Milstein, *History*, vol. 4, p. 357, and *Myth*, p. 46; Idem, "Dir Yasin," p. 17; Hovav, *Gal*, p. 79; E-mail from Yehuda Lapidot to the author, 7 March 2014.

30. JA 'ER-12/1: testimony by Mordechai Raanan; JA 'ER-12/3: testimony by same; JA 'ER-12/5: interview with same; JA K4-10/1: testimonies by Ben-Zion Cohen and Yehuda Marinburg; MEC GB165-0346/3/5: interview with Ben-Zion Cohen; E-mail from Yehuda Lapidot to the author, 6 March 2014; Lapidot, *Lahav*, p. 325 (Lapidot mentioned some 50 Sten guns, but when calculating the number of Stens delivered to the squads, this figure seems too high); Interview with Yehuda Lapidot, 24 August 2010; YTA 12-3/41/14: interview with Moshe Edelstein; Kfir, "Shalosh," p. 2 (interview with Mordechai Raanan); IDFA 372/5254/49: Yavne to Tene (D), "Pe'ula Meshutefet shel ha-Porshim bi-Yerushalayim," 12 April 1948; Milstein, *History*, vol. 4, p. 358, and *Myth*, p. 46; JA K4-10/9: testimony by Ben-Zion Cohen during the benefits trial, 5 January 1953; Bregman and Tahri, *Fifty Years*, p. 28 (interview with same); HA 20/253: Avraham [Meir Pilavsky] to District Commander [Shaltiel], "Pe'ulat ha-Porshim be-Dir Yasin," 10 April 1948; Golani, *Mitos*, pp. 18–20; Ben-Tor, *Sefer*, vol. 4, pp. 457, 463; Gertz, *Da'at*, p. 189.

31. YTA 15-46/183/2: Eliezer to Tzadiq, Bernhard, Yarkoni and Avraham, "Doh Kibush Dir Yasin," 10 April 1948; Golani, *Mitos*, pp. 20–21; Lever, *Jerusalem*, p. 170.

NOTES FOR CHAPTER 3

1. Khalidi, *Dayr Yasin*, pp. 48–49 (testimony by Isma'il Muhammad 'Atiyya); Salayima, *Dayr Yasin*, pp. 109 (testimony by same), 136 (testimony by Zaynab 'Atiyya); Hijazi, *Dayr Yasin*, p. 58 (testimony by Isma'il Muhammad 'Atiyya); Dirbas, "Deir Yassin," 3:26 (interview with Maryam ['Atiyya] 'Aql); Kana'na and Zaytawi, *Dayr Yasin*, p. 52; Bar'el and Shay, "Hazara," p. 23 (interviewing Muhammad 'Arif Sammur); BUPA: 'Aql, "Haqa'iq Waqi'iyya."

2. JA K4-10/9: testimonies by Ben-Zion Cohen, 5 January 1953, and Moshe Nahum Mizrahi, 12 May 1952, during the benefits trial; MEC GB165-0346/3/5: interview with Ben-Zion Cohen; JA K4-10/1: testimony by same and supplements to unidentified testimony [by same]; Milstein, *History*, vol. 4, p. 358, and *Myth*, pp. 47–48 (interview with same); Bregman and Tahri, *Fifty Years*, p. 29 (interview with same); Lapidot, *Lahav*, p. 310, and *Homotayikh*, p. 152; JA 'ER-12/5: interview with Mordechai Raanan; Kfir, "Shalosh," p. 3 (interview with same); Golani, *Mitos*, pp. 24–25; Regev-Yarkoni and Regev, *Lohem*, p. 135; Gervasi, *Life*, p. 233; "Dir Yasin – Kol ha-Emet," p. 15; Ofir, *Homot*, p. 57; Lever, *Jerusalem*, p. 170.

3. Kurzman, *Genesis*, p. 141; Salayima, *Dayr Yasin*, pp. 136, 138–139 (testimony by Zaynab 'Atiyya); Zananiri, "Interviews" (interviewing Muhammad Mahmud Radwan); "37 'Aman 'ala al-Majzara: Shuyukh Dayr Yasin Yatadhakkaruna," *Sawt al-Bilad*, 40 (1985), p. 11 (testimony by Maryam Barakat); JA K4-10/9: testimony by Ben-Zion Cohen during the benefits trial, 5 January 1953; Hovav, *Gal*, p. 79; Ofir, *Homot*, p. 57; 'Awawda, *Dhakira*, p. 88 (testimony by 'Abd al-Qadir Zaydan); Idem, "Isra'il Tarfadu" (interview with same).

4. YTA 15-46/183/2: Eliezer to Tzadiq, Bernhard, Yarkoni and Avraham, "Doh Kibush Dir Yasin," 10 April 1948; JA 'EA-3/2: testimony by Yosef Avni; JA K4-10/1: testimonies by Yehuda Lapidot and Ben-Zion Cohen and unidentified testimony [by same]; JA K4-10/9: testimony by same during the benefits trial, 5 January 1953; MEC GB165-0346/3/5: interview with same; Milstein, *History*, vol. 4, p. 359, and *Myth*, p. 48 (interview with Michael Harif); Lapidot, *Lahav*, p. 311, and *Homotayikh*, pp. 152–153; LC 3/29: testimony by [Yehuda] Lapidot; Amikam, "Hagana," p. 3 (citing Mordechai Raanan); "Dir Yasin – Kol ha-Emet," p. 16; Ofir, *Homot*, pp. 59–60; Golani, *Mitos*, p. 35.

5. IDFA 372/5254/49: Yavne to Tene (D), "Pe'ulat Etzel ve-Lehi be-Dir Yasin," 12 April 1948; Milstein, *History*, vol. 4, p. 362, and *Myth*, p. 52; Banks, *Country*,

p. 62 (testimony by Ezra Yakhin); E-mail from same to the author, 30 March 2014; Amikam, "Hagana," p. 3 (citing Mordechai Raanan); JA 'EA-3/2: testimony by Yosef Avni; MEC GB165-0346/3/5: interview with Ben-Zion Cohen; "Dir Yasin – Kol ha-Emet," p. 16; Ben-Tor, *Sefer*, vol. 4, p. 464; Golani, *Mitos*, p. 33; Lapidot, *Lahav*, p. 311, and *Homotayikh*, p. 152; YTA 12-3/43/45: interview with Gideon Sarig; 'Awawda, *Dhakira*, p. 88 (testimony by 'Abd al-Qadir Zaydan). For some obscure reason, all the Jewish sources called Salah's house "the mukhtar's house," which it definitely was not. Muhammad Isma'il Sammur's house was located in the eastern part of the village.

6.   JA K4-10/1: testimonies by Yehoshua Gorodenchik and Yehuda Marinburg; JA K4-10/9: testimony by Ben-Zion Cohen during the benefits trial, 5 January 1953; MEC GB165-0346/3/5: interview with same; LC 3/29: testimony by [Yehuda] Lapidot; Lapidot, *Lahav*, p. 311, and *Homotayikh*, p. 153; Banks, *Country*, p. 62 (testimony by Ezra Yakhin); Golani, *Mitos*, pp. 36, 53, 67; Milstein, *History*, vol. 4, p. 363, and *Myth*, p. 58 (interviews with Yonah Ben-Sasson, Yehuda Lapidot and Yehoshua Gorodenchik); Idem, "Dir Yassin," p. 19; HA 95.3: testimony by Akiva Azulay; Sharvit, *Akiva*, p. 69.

7.   LC 3/29: testimony by [Yehuda] Lapidot; IDFA 26/70/2004: letter, Avichai Yehudayof (Tel Aviv) to *Yedi'ot Aharonot*, 22 August 1960; JA K4-10/1: unidentified testimony [Ben-Zion Cohen]; YTA 15-34/13/5: testimony by Moshe Vachman, "Dir Yasin"; Lapidot, *Lahav*, p. 311, and *Homotayikh*, p. 152; Milstein, *History*, vol. 4, pp. 362–363, and *Myth*, pp. 53, 56; Idem, "Dir Yassin," p. 19; Golani, *Mitos*, pp. 48–50; Kana'na and Zaytawi, *Dayr Yasin*, p. 54; BUPA: 'Aql, "Haqa'iq Waqi'iyya"; 'Arif, *Nakbat*, vol. 1, p. 172 (citing Zaynab Ahmad Musa); Salayima, *Dayr Yasin*, p. 144; "37 'Aman," pp. 10–11 (testimony by Fatima Hamida); Ghanim Habib Allah, "Majzarat Dayr Yasin fil-Fikr wal-Mumarasa al-Sahyuniyya," *Kan'an*, 3 (1991), p. 70 (based on testimonies of survivors); Khalidi, *Mudhakkirat*, vol. 2, p. 263, citing report by Anwar Nusayba (National Committee, Jerusalem), 10 April 1948 (a photo of the original report is available ibid., vol. 3, p. 354).

8.   YTA 15-46/183/2: Eliezer to Tzadiq, Bernhard, Yarkoni and Avraham, "Doh Kibush Dir Yasin," 10 April 1948; JA K4-10/1: testimonies by Yehoshua Gorodenchik and Ben-Zion Cohen and unidentified testimony [by same]; *Ha-Hagana bi-Yerushalayim*, vol. 2, p. 124 (testimony by Yerah Etzion); Golani, *Mitos*, pp. 20, 38–39; Lapidot, *Lahav*, pp. 311–312, and *Homotayikh*, pp. 153–154; Ben-Tor, *Sefer*, vol. 4, p. 457; Salayima, *Dayr Yasin*, p. 108; PACE 241: interview with Muhammad 'Ayish Zaydan.

9.   YTA 12-3/43/45: interview with Gideon Sarig; JA 'ER-12/1: testimony by Mordechai Raanan; JA 'ER-12/3: testimony by same; JA 'ER-12/5: interview with same; LC 3/29: testimony by [Yehuda] Lapidot; Milstein, *History*, vol. 4, pp. 360, 362, and *Myth*, pp. 49, 52; "Dir Yasin – Kol ha-Emet," p. 16; Kfir, "Shalosh," p. 3 (interview with Mordechai Raanan); Ofir, *Homot*, p. 60; Golani, *Mitos*,

p. 46; Gervasi, *Life*, p. 233; Kurzman, *Genesis*, p. 145. Oyserman's film did not survive. Although it reached IDFA, it was already in unusable condition by the 1970s. Phone conversation with Yaakov Gross, 23 March 2014.

10. Amikam, "Hagana," p. 3 (citing Petahya Selivansky); "Dir Yasin – Kol ha-Emet," p. 15; Sharvit, *Akiva*, pp. 68–69; Khalidi, *Dayr Yasin*, pp. 49–50 (testimonies by Husayn 'Atiyya and Jum'a Muhammad Zahran).

11. IDFA 372/5254/49: Yavne to Tene (D), "Pe'ulat ha-Porshim be-Dir Yasin," 13 April 1948 (based on "Esther" – Shimon Moneta); Milstein, *History*, vol. 4, p. 358, and *Myth*, p. 47 (testimony by Petahya Selivansky and interview with Shimon Moneta); phone conversation with same, 1 April 2014; Bar'el and Shay, "Hazara," p. 23 (interviewing Muhammad 'Arif Sammur); ISA P-2878/5: interview with Shimon Moneta; MEC GB165-0346/2/14: interview with same; Moneta, "Kavana," p. 4; Idem, *Toldot*, p. 61; Vered, *Yerushalayim*, p. 113; Amikam, "Hagana," p. 3 (citing Petahya Selivansky); Khalidi, *Dayr Yasin*, pp. 50–51 (testimonies by Husayn 'Atiyya, and Jum'a Zahran, and interview with and testimony by Khalil Sammur), 71.

12. ISA P-2878/5: interview with Shimon Moneta; Milstein, *History*, vol. 4, p. 361, and *Myth*, p. 50 (testimony by Petahya Selivansky and interviews with same and Shimon Moneta); Ben-Tor, *Sefer*, vol. 4, p. 463; Golani, *Mitos*, pp. 28, 31; Amikam, "Hagana," p. 3 (citing Petahya Selivansky); IDFA 372/5254/49: Yavne to Tene (D), "Pe'ulat ha-Porshim be-Dir Yasin," 13 April 1948; MEC GB165-0346/2/14: interview with Shimon Moneta; Moneta, *Toldot*, p. 61; Vered, *Yerushalayim*, p. 113.

13. Ben-Tor, *Sefer*, vol. 4, p. 464; Amikam, "Hagana," p. 3; MEC GB165-0346/2/14: interview with Shimon Moneta; IDFA 372/5254/49: Yavne to Tene (D), "Pe'ulat ha-Porshim be-Dir Yasin," 13 April 1948; ISA P-2878/5: interview with Shimon Moneta; Vered, *Yerushalayim*, p. 113; Golani, *Mitos*, pp. 29, 43.

14. LC 3/29: testimony by [Yehuda] Lapidot; Lapidot, *Lahav*, pp. 310, 329, and *Homotayikh*, p. 165; Interview with Yehuda Lapidot, 24 August 2010; YTA 12-3/41/14: interview with Moshe Edelstein; MEC GB165-0346/2/24: interview with Ezra Yakhin; Regev-Yarkoni and Regev, *Lohem*, p. 134; IDFA 372/5254/49: Yavne to Tene (D), "Pe'ula Meshutefet shel ha-Porshim bi-Yerushalayim," 12 April 1948; IDFA 54/500/48: same to same, "Pe'ulat Etzel ve-Lehi be-Dir Yasin," 12 April 1948; Shapira, *David*, p. 139; JA H13-3/48/4: case against Nathan Friedman-Yellin and Matityahu Shmuelevitz in the special military court, Protocol IV, 7 January 1949, p. 1403 (testimony by David Shaltiel).

15. "Dir Yasin – Kol ha-Emet," p. 15; JA 'ER-12/5: interview with Mordechai Raanan; JA 'EG-28/1: testimony by David Gottlieb; Yakhin, *Sipuro*, pp. 253–254 (Yakhin accompanied the armored car); MEC GB165-0346/2/24: interview with Ezra Yakhin; Sharvit, *Akiva*, p. 69 (citing same); Gertz, *Da'at*, p. 190 (interview with same); Banks, *Country*, p. 60 (testimony by same); Milstein,

History, vol. 4, p. 359, and *Myth*, p. 48 (interview with same); E-mail from same to the author, 30 March 2014; Bregman and Tahri, *Fifty Years*, p. 30 (interviews with same and Abu Tawfiq); "60 Sha'ot be-Dir Yasin (Sipuro shel ha-Lohem Ya'aqov)" [the code name of Yissachar Huberman, who sat in the car], in Baruch Oren [Nadel], *Ba-Matzor: Emet Yerushalayim* (Tel Aviv, 1949), p. 34 (also in *Mivraq*, 19 April 1948); Khalidi, *Dayr Yasin*, p. 50 (testimony by Husayn 'Atiyya); Assad, *Palestine*, p. 105; Zananiri, "Interviews" (interviewing Abu Tawfiq and Muhammad Mahmud Radwan); Bar'el and Shay, "Hazara," pp. 23 (interviewing Yoel Kimhi), 25; YTA 12-3/41/14: interview with Moshe Edelstein; JA K4-10/1: testimony by Yehuda Marinburg and unidentified testimony [Ben-Zion Cohen]; YTA 15-34/13/5: testimony by Moshe Vachman, "Dir Yasin"; YTA 16-12/52/8: testimony by same; JA K4-13/8: broadcast of *Kol Zion ha-Lohemet*, 11 April 1948; *Ha-Boqer*, 11 April 1948, p. 1; *Palestine Post*, 11 April 1948, p. 1; Kfir, "Shalosh," p. 3 (interview with Yehoshua Zettler); Lapidot, *Lahav*, p. 310, and *Homotayikh*, p. 152; Regev-Yarkoni and Regev, *Lohem*, p. 135; Hovav, *Gal*, p. 80; Lever, *Jerusalem*, p. 170; Kurzman, *Genesis*, p. 142.

16.   JA 'ER-12/3: testimony by Mordechai Raanan; JA K4-10/1: testimony by Ezra Yakhin; JA 'EG-28/1: testimony by David Gottlieb; JA 'EG-28/2: testimony by same; Ben-Ami, *Years*, p. 441; Golani, *Mitos*, p. 25; Haim Oded, "Oto Mifne," *Herut*, 2 March 1951, p. 6; Avner, "Ghosts," p. 14; Gervasi, *Life*, p. 233; Lever, *Jerusalem*, pp. 170, 172; Kurzman, *Genesis*, p. 142; "Dayr Yasin (Madhbaha – 1948)," *Al-Mawsu'a al-Filastiniyya* (Damascus, 1984), al-Qism al-'Amm, vol. 2, p. 434; Avi Katzman, "Ha-Mitos be-Lav Hakhi Ma'afil 'al ha-'Uvdot," *ha-Aretz*, 25 April 1993, p. B9; ISA P-2878/5: interview with Shimon Moneta; phone conversation with same, 1 April 2014; Regev-Yarkoni and Regev, *Lohem*, p. 135; Gertz, *Da'at*, p. 192 (interview with Zaynab ['Atiyya] and Maryam 'Aql). Bar'el and Shay, "Hazara," p. 23 (interviewing Muhammad 'Arif Sammur); Zananiri, "Interviews" (interviewing Abu Tawfiq and Muhammad Mahmud Radwan); Bregman and Tahri, *Fifty Years*, p. 30 (interview with same); PACE 237: interview with Ibtisam Zaydan. Haganah member Daniel Spicehandler, present at the time near Deir Yassin, also testified that he heard the loudspeaker's warnings. Ralph G. Martin, *Golda – Golda Meir: The Romantic Years* (New York, 1988), p. 329.

17.   Khalidi, *Dayr Yasin*, pp. 68–69 (testimonies by Naziha Ahmad As'ad Radwan and Husayn 'Atiyya); PACE 237: interview with Ibtisam Zaydan; Dirbas, "Deir Yassin," 7:08 (interview with Muhammad Mahmud Radwan); Kurzman, *Genesis*, p. 142; Lapidot, *Lahav*, pp. 310–311, and *Homotayikh*, p. 152; Gervasi, *Life*, p. 233; Katzman, "Mitos," p. B9; Golani, *Mitos*, pp. 26–27; Gertz, *Da'at*, pp. 190–192 (interviews with Ezra Yakhin and Amos Kenan); Yakhin, *Sipuro*, pp. 254–256; MEC GB165-0346/2/24: interview with Ezra Yakhin; JA K4-10/1: testimony by same; Banks, *Country*, pp. 60–62 (testimony by same); E-mails from same to the author, 30 March and 1 April 2014; "60 Sha'ot," p. 34 (Huberman was Ben-Uziyahu's Bren-gunner).

18. Avrahami, "Ruhot," p. 29 (citing Yehuda Lapidot); JA K4-10/1: testimony by same; LC 3/29: testimony by same; Interview with same, 24 August 2010; ISA P-2878/5: interview with Shimon Moneta; MEC GB165-0346/2/14: interview with same; IDFA 372/5254/49: Yavne to Tene (D), "Pe'ulat Etzel ve-Lehi be-Dir Yasin," 12 April 1948; Temko, *Win*, pp. 112, 368 (interviewing Mordechai Raanan and Yehuda Lapidot); Ben-Ami, *Years*, p. 442; Avner, "Ghosts," p. 14; phone conversation with Ben-Zion Cohen, 15 February 2015. Although some Lehi fighters had undergone field exercises, these had taken place in the coastal plain, and they therefore had no understanding of fighting in mountainous terrain, such as the Jerusalem hills. See Vered, *Ari'ela*, p. 113.

19. Avner, "Ghosts," p. 14; ISA P-2878/5: interview with Shimon Moneta.

20. IDFA 1/150/86: [Yosef] Ben-Nun, "Tizkoret," 9 April 1948; YTA 15-46/183/2: Eliezer to Tzadiq, Bernhard, Yarkoni and Avraham, "Doh Kibush Dir Yasin," 10 April 1948; IDFA 372/5254/49: Yavne to Tene (D), "Pe'ulat Etzel ve-Lehi be-Dir Yasin," 12 April 1948, and same to same, "Pe'ulat ha-Porshim be-Dir Yasin," 13 April 1948; IDFA 58/900/52: "Yedi'ot Tene – Taqtzir Yomi," 18 April 1948; JA 'EA-3/2: testimony by Yosef Avni; JA K4-10/1: testimony by Ben-Zion Cohen; Vered, *Ari'ela*, p. 113; Milstein, *History*, vol. 4, p. 360, and *Myth*, p. 49; Golani, *Mitos*, p. 23; Niv, *Ma'arkhot*, vol. 6, p. 83; Hovav, *Gal*, pp. 79, 81 (citing Yehuda Lapidot).

21. Kfir, "Shalosh," p. 3 (interview with Mordechai Raanan); Temko, *Win*, p. 112 (interviewing same); JA 'ER-12/3: testimony by same; JA 'ER-12/5: interview with same; Lapidot, *Lahav*, pp. 311, 325, and *Homotayikh*, pp. 153, 161; Holmes, "Deir Yassin" (citing Yehuda Lapidot); Interview with same, 24 August 2010; *New York Times*, 10 April 1948, p. 6; *Ha-Boqer*, 11 April 1948, p. 4; Golani, *Mitos*, pp. 46, 60; Ben-Ami, *Years*, p. 442; Milstein, *History*, vol. 4, p. 362, and *Myth*, p. 52; Gervasi, *Life*, pp. 233–234; Kurzman, *Genesis*, p. 145; "Dir Yasin – Kol ha-Emet," p. 16 (mentioning 25 blown up houses).

22. JA 'ER-12/3: testimony by Mordechai Raanan; JA 'ER-12/5: interview with same; LC 3/29: DLP, "Deir Yassin," p. 10 (citing Shafiqa Muhammad Sammur, the mukhtar's daughter); Lynd, Bahour and Lynd, *Homeland*, p. 24 (interview with 'Ayisha Jum'a Zaydan); Sharvit, *Akiva*, p. 71; YTA 15-46/183/2: testimony by Isser Halamish; Ben-Ami, *Years*, p. 442; Golani, *Mitos*, pp. 28, 31, 46; Gervasi, *Life*, p. 234 (Gervasi wrote that the warnings were transmitted from the loudspeaker car; this could not be true both because the loudspeaker malfunctioned and because the car was stuck far away from Etzel's field of operation); Kfir, "Shalosh," p. 3 (interview with Yehoshua Zettler); Amikam, "Hagana," p. 3 (mentioning 20 blown up houses); IDFA 372/5254/49: Yavne to Tene (D), "Pe'ulat ha-Porshim be-Dir Yasin," 13 April 1948 (based on "Esther" – Shimon Moneta).

23. Hogan, "1948 Massacre," pp. 321–322; MacGowan and Ellis, *Remembering*, p. 39 (interview with Meir Pa'il); JA 'EP-19/1: testimony by same; Meir Pa'il, "Ha-Emet ha-Hatzuya be-Farashat Dir Yasin," *Yedi'ot Aharonot*, 20 April 1972, p. 14; Arbel, "Hayiti," p. 20. See also LC 3/29: testimony by Menachem Adler. Gelber, "Propaganda," p. 310, also believed that "contrary to some testimonies, the houses were not blown up on their residents."

24. *Filastin*, 10 and 11 April 1948; 'Arif, *Nakbat*, vol. 1, p. 173; Walid Yasin, *Dayr Yasin Abadan Tatamarradu 'ala al-Nisyan* (Jerusalem, 1984), p. 35; Derogy and Saab, *Exodes*, p. 142; Kana'na and Zaytawi, *Dayr Yasin*, p. 52; Khalidi, *Mudhakkirat*, vol. 2, pp. 261–262, citing report by Nusayba, 10 April 1948; PACE 241: interview with Muhammad 'Ayish Zaydan; "Qadiyya wa-Hiwar," 22:20 (interview with Mustafa Mahmud); WO 275/117: letter CS725/2, Vivian Fox-Strangways (Chief Secretary Office, Jerusalem) to HQ British Troops in Palestine, 16 April 1948; CO 537/3857: CID, "Summary of Events," 9 April 1948; CO 733/477/5: tel. 928, Cunningham to Secretary of State for the Colonies, 10 April 1948; YTA 12-3/9/3: Gichon, "Parashat Dir Yasin Tashah"; YTA 15-34/13/5: testimony by Moshe Vachman, "Dir Yasin"; Avner, "Ghosts," pp. 13–14. Collins and Lapierre, *O Jerusalem!*, p. 275, claimed that 15 houses were dynamited, including that of the mukhtar (while actually this house was not destroyed – see below).

25. Tom Segev, *1949: The First Israelis* (New York, 1986), pp. 86–87; Survey of Israel, photo 5114, sortie DEV7, 25 January 1946, and photo 8334, sortie P/56, 23 November 1951. The photos are of a very high resolution. When magnified, one can clearly pick out all the houses. See also Khalidi, *Dayr Yasin*, map between pages 10 and 11, and list of house owners, ibid., pp. 145–148.

26. JA 'ER-12/3: testimony by Mordechai Raanan; Hovav, *Gal*, p. 80; Ben-Tor, *Sefer*, vol. 4, p. 463; *New York Times*, 10 April 1948, p. 6; Interview with Yehuda Lapidot, 24 August 2010; Gertz, *Da'at*, pp. 192–193 (interview with Amos Kenan); JA 'EB-30/5: interview with Kalman Bergman; Katzman, "Mitos," p. B9; Kana'na and Zaytawi, *Dayr Yasin*, p. 55 (citing Fahima 'Ali Mustafa Zaydan); Hijazi, *Dayr Yasin*, p. 61 (citing same); Salayima, *Dayr Yasin*, p. 132 (citing same); Nawaf al-Zaru, *Min Dayr Yasin ila Mukhayyam Jinin* (Amman, 2002), p. 28.

27. JA K4-10/9: testimony by Ben-Zion Cohen during the benefits trial, 5 January 1953; MEC GB165-0346/3/5: interview with same; Bregman and Tahri, *Fifty Years*, pp. 30–31 (interviews with same and Muhammad Mahmud Radwan); BBC, "50 Years," 12:48 (interviews with both); LC 3/29: testimony by [Yehuda] Lapidot; Interview with same, 24 August 2010; JA K4-10/1: testimonies by Eliyahu Levi, Ezra Yakhin and Yehuda Marinburg; JA 'EB-30/6: interview with Kalman Bergman; Avichai Yehudayof, "Dir Yasin," *ba-Sa'ar*, 11 March 1949, p. 11; IDFA 26/70/2004: letter, same to *Yedi'ot Aharonot*, 22 August 1960; MEC GB165-0346/2/24: interview with Ezra Yakhin; Banks, *Country*, p. 62 (testimony by same); JA 'EG-28/1: testimony by David Gottlieb; JA 'EG-28/2: testimony

by same; YTA 12-3/41/14: interview with Moshe Edelstein; Niv, *Ma'arkhot*, vol. 6, pp. 83–84; Golani, *Mitos*, pp. 31, 33; Kurzman, *Genesis*, p. 142; Lever, *Jerusalem*, p. 173; Khalidi, *Dayr Yasin*, pp. 75–76 (testimonies by Zaynab 'Atiyya and 'Aziza Isma'il 'Atiyya); Salayima, *Dayr Yasin*, p. 116 (testimony by Muhammad Mahmud Radwan); Assad, *Palestine*, p. 117; MEC GB165-0282/2/4: "Dir Yasin" – interviewee not named.

28. Milstein, *History*, vol. 4, p. 361, and *Myth*, p. 50 (testimony by and interview with Petahya Selivansky). See also JA K4-10/1: unidentified testimony, "Kibush Dir Yasin" (an Etzel fighter describing the blowing up of a position, throwing two hand grenades into the building, and shooting with Stens).

NOTES FOR CHAPTER 4

1. Khalidi, *Dayr Yasin*, pp. 48–49, 52–53 (testimonies by Isma'il Muhammad 'Atiyya and 'Azmi Isma'il 'Atiyya); Salayima, *Dayr Yasin*, pp. 109, 136 (testimonies by Isma'il Muhammad 'Atiyya and Zaynab 'Atiyya); Hijazi, *Dayr Yasin*, p. 58 (testimony by Isma'il Muhammad 'Atiyya); Fayha' 'Abd al-Hadi, "Majzarat Dayr Yasin: Shahadat man Shahidu al-Majzara," *Dawriyyat Dirasat al-Mar'a*, 3 (2005), pp. 10, 12 (testimony by Zaynab ['Atiyya] 'Aql); Dirbas, "Deir Yassin," 3:26 (interview with Maryam 'Aql); Assad, *Palestine*, p. 121 (testimony by 'Uthman 'Aql); "'Aql Yakshifu" (interview with same); BUPA: 'Aql, "Haqa'iq Waqi'iyya"; JA K4-10/9: testimony by Moshe Nahum Mizrahi during the benefits trial, 12 May 1952; MEC GB165-0346/3/5: interview with Ben-Zion Cohen; Kurzman, *Genesis*, p. 141; Golani, *Mitos*, pp. 24–25.

2. Khalidi, *Dayr Yasin*, pp. 48–50, 68–69 (testimonies by Da'ud Jabir, Husayn 'Atiyya and Naziha Radwan); Assad, *Palestine*, pp. 104–107, 119 (testimony by same); "Survivor," 13:30 (interview with Da'ud Radwan); Kana'na and Zaytawi, *Dayr Yasin*, p. 53; Bregman and Tahri, *Fifty Years*, p. 30 (interview with Abu Tawfiq); BUPA: 'Aql, "Haqa'iq Waqi'iyya"; "Abu Mahmud," p. 8; Matza, *Shney Eqdahim*, p. 50; Gervasi, *Life*, p. 233; Golani, *Mitos*, pp. 25–28.

3. Khalidi, *Dayr Yasin*, pp. 50–52 (testimony by Jum'a Zahran, and interview with and testimony by Khalil Sammur).

4. PACE 240: interview with 'Ayish Muhammad Zaydan; PACE 237: interview with Ibtisam Zaydan; Nimr, *Dayr Yasin*, p. 16; Khalidi, *Dayr Yasin*, p. 53; Salayima, *Dayr Yasin*, p. 117 (testimony by Zaynab Ahmad Musa); 'Arif, *Nakbat*, vol. 1, p. 172; BUPA: 'Aql, "Haqa'iq Waqi'iyya"; Bregman and Tahri, *Fifty Years*, p. 30 (interview with Muhammad Mahmud Radwan); Kana'na and Zaytawi, *Dayr Yasin*, p. 53; YTA 15-46/183/2: Eliezer to Tzadiq, Bernhard, Yarkoni and Avraham, "Doh Kibush Dir Yasin," 10 April 1948; Golani, *Mitos*,

pp. 38–39; Yakhin, *Sipuro*, p. 257; Banks, *Country*, p. 62 (testimony by Ezra Yakhin); "60 Sha'ot," p. 35.

5. Zananiri, "Interviews" (interviewing Abu Tawfiq); Khalidi, *Dayr Yasin*, pp. 53–55, 65 (testimony by Hasan As'ad Radwan, and interview with and testimony by Khalil Sammur); Dirbas, "Deir Yassin," 5:12 (interview with Muhammad Mahmud Radwan); Interview with Yehuda Lapidot, 24 August 2010.

6. 'Awawda, *Dhakira*, pp. 86, 88 (testimonies by Mustafa Hamida and 'Abd al-Qadir Zaydan); Idem, "Isra'il Tarfadu" (interview with same); "Dhikra 58" (speech by same); Salayima, *Dayr Yasin*, p. 117 (testimony by Zaynab Ahmad Musa); PACE 240: interview with 'Ayish Muhammad Zaydan; "Qadiyya wa-Hiwar," 25:10 (interview with Mustafa Mahmud); Abu Gharbiyya, *Khidamm*, p. 221; 'Arif, *Nakbat*, vol. 1, p. 172; Kana'na and Zaytawi, *Dayr Yasin*, p. 53; Nimr, *Dayr Yasin*, p. 16; As'ad, "Dhikra," p. 3; "Abu Mahmud," p. 8; Holmes, "Deir Yassin" (citing Muhammad Mahmud Radwan); Amikam, "Hagana," p. 3 (citing Petahya Selivansky); MEC GB165-0346/2/24: interview with Ezra Yakhin; JA K4-10/9: testimony by Mordechai Kaufman during the benefits trial, [30 June 1952]; Lever, *Jerusalem*, p. 170; "Dir Yasin – Kol ha-Emet," p. 16; IDFA 26/70/2004: letter, Yehudayof to *Yedi'ot Aharonot*, 22 August 1960; Silver, *Begin*, p. 92. Apparently, the villagers were well aware of their limited ammunition and received strict orders not to shoot unless in danger. See Bregman and Tahri, *Fifty Years*, p. 30 (interview with Muhammad Mahmud Radwan).

7. For Etzel, see e.g. MEC GB165-0346/3/5: interview with Ben-Zion Cohen; Bar'el and Shay, "Hazara," p. 23 (interviewing Yoel Kimhi); Ben-Ami, *Years*, p. 441 (also mentioning a Muslim colonel from Yugoslavia and several Britons); Niv, *Ma'arkhot*, vol. 6, p. 84; Golani, *Mitos*, pp. 34, 37, 41, 62. For Lehi, see e.g. ISA P-2878/5: interview with Shimon Moneta; JA K4-10/1: testimony by Yehuda Marinburg; Stanley Goldfoot, "I Was There," *The Times of Israel*, 23 April 1970, p. 11; Gertz, *Da'at*, pp. 185, 188; Yellin-Mor, *Lohamey*, p. 471.

8. Golani, *Mitos*, pp. 57, 60, 62; Yakhin, *Sipuro*, p. 255; MEC GB165-0346/2/24: interview with Ezra Yakhin; Banks, *Country*, p. 61 (testimony by same); Lapidot, *Homotayikh*, p. 153; Dvir, "Dir Yasin," p. 19 (citing Yehuda Lapidot); Milstein, *History*, vol. 4, p. 359, and *Myth*, p. 48 (interview with Michael Harif); Amikam, "Hagana," pp. 3–4 (also mentioning a Yugoslavian captain); Harry Levin, *Jerusalem Embattled: A Diary of the City under Siege, March 25th, 1948 to July 18th, 1948* (London, 1950), p. 59 (citing a Haganah photographer); MEC GB165-0346/3/5: interview with Ben-Zion Cohen; JA K4-10/9: testimonies by same, 5 January 1953, and Moshe Nahum Mizrahi and Yehoshua Sari,12 May 1952, during the benefits trial; "Dir Yasin – Kol ha-Emet," p. 16.

9. JA K4-10/9: testimony by Mordechai Kaufman during the benefits trial, [30 June 1952]; Amikam, "Hagana," p. 4.

10. Interview with Yehuda Lapidot, 24 August 2010; Temko, *Win*, p. 113 (interviewing same); Milstein, *History*, vol. 4, p. 361, and *Myth*, p. 50 (testimony by and interview with Petahya Selivansky); YTA 12-3/43/45: interview with Gideon Sarig; "60 Sha'ot," pp. 36–37; Golani, *Mitos*, p. 38; Orenstein, "Aluf," p. 89; IDFA 372/5254/49: Yavne to Tene (D), "Pe'ulat Etzel ve-Lehi be-Dir Yasin," 12 April 1948; Kana'na, "Madhbahat," p. 167; Gelber, "Propaganda," p. 311; Hogan, "1948 Massacre," p. 321; Matthew C. Hogan and Daniel A. McGowan, "Anatomy of a Whitewash: A Critical Examination and Refutation of the Historical Revisionist 'Deir Yasin: History of a Lie', Issued by the Zionist Organization of America (March 8, 1998)," www.deiryassin.org/op0005.html.

11. Salayima, *Dayr Yasin*, p. 117 (testimony by Zaynab Ahmad Musa); 'Arif, *Nakbat*, vol. 1, pp. 172–173; 'Awawda, *Dhakira*, p. 86 (testimony by Mustafa Hamida); PACE 240: interview with 'Ayish Muhammad Zaydan; Khalidi, *Dayr Yasin*, p. 79 (testimonies by Da'ud Zaydan and wife of Muhammad Mustafa 'Id); BUPA: 'Iyad, "Shuhud 'Iyan" (testimony by wife of Jamil 'Id); Fa'iza 'Abd al-Majid, "Sutur min Kifah Filastin: Shahidat Dayr Yasin Hayat Salim al-Balbisi," *al-'Arabi*, 65 (1964), pp. 118, 121–122; *Al-Difa'*, 11 April 1948, p. 4 (an announcement on Balabsa's death); Hijazi, *Dayr Yasin*, pp. 37, 60, 77–78 (on the latter page there is a list of all those killed in battle – 59 names, including 18 women); LC 3/29: DLP, "Deir Yasin," pp. 4, 7; MacGowan and Ellis, *Remembering*, p. 30; Ofir, *Homot*, pp. 60, 66; Idem, "Dir Yasin," p. 5; E-mail from Ezra Yakhin to the author, 30 March 2014; Golani, *Mitos*, p. 62; JA K4-10/1: unidentified testimony, "Kibush Dir Yasin," and testimony by Reuven Greenberg.

12. Zananiri, "Interviews" (interviewing Abu Tawfiq and Muhammad Mahmud Radwan); Gelber, "Propaganda," p. 314; MEC GB165-0346/3/19: interview with Yair Tzaban; Silver, *Begin*, p. 93 (interview with same); Yakhin, *Sipuro*, p. 256; Banks, *Country*, p. 62 (testimony by Ezra Yakhin); MEC GB165-0346/2/24: interview with same; E-mail from same to the author, 30 March 2014; MEC GB165-0346/3/5: interview with Ben-Zion Cohen; Yoel Kimhi, "Sin'a 'Iveret le-Irguney ha-Mahteret," *Yedi'ot Aharonot*, 2 May 1972, p. 21; Golani, *Mitos*, pp. 33, 58–60; Milstein, *History*, vol. 4, p. 381, and *Myth*, p. 86; Interview with Yehuda Lapidot, 24 August 2010; Ofir, *Homot*, p. 60; Amikam, "Hagana," p. 3; Ben-Ami, *Years*, p. 441; JA K4-10/1: testimony by Yehoshua Gorodenchik. The latter testimony is posted in a censored form on the Internet site of the archives, without the paragraph explaining the shooting of women. It appears fully in the original document, as well as in its copy in JA 'EG-8/1.

13. Khalidi, *Dayr Yasin*, pp. 75–77 (testimonies by Zaynab 'Atiyya and 'Aziza 'Atiyya); Salayima, *Dayr Yasin*, p. 138 (testimony by Zaynab 'Atiyya); 'Ubaydu, "Khamsun," p. 15 (interview with same); 'Abd al-Hadi, "Majzarat," pp. 11–12 (interview with same); Assad, *Palestine*, pp. 115–116, and p. 120 in the Arabic version (testimony by same); LC 3/29: DLP, "Deir Yasin," pp. 9–10; "37

'Aman," pp. 10–11 (testimony by Fatima Hamida). As'ad, *Filastin*, pp. 114, 122, 127, indicated that they were guarded by Jewish women.

14. Khalidi, *Dayr Yasin*, pp. 69–71 (testimony by Naziha Radwan), 97; Assad, *Palestine*, pp. 107–109, 119–120 (testimony by same); "Survivor," 8:22 and 12:54 (interview with Da'ud Radwan); Salayima, *Dayr Yasin*, p. 137 (testimony by Zaynab 'Atiyya); PACE 241: interview with Muhammad 'Ayish Zaydan; "37 'Aman," p. 11 (testimony by same); Anton La Guardia, *War Without End: Israelis, Palestinians, and the Struggle for a Promised Land* (New York, [2001] updated ed. 2003), p. 199 (interview with 'Ayish Muhammad 'Ayish Zaydan).

15. Goldstein, *Lehavot*, p. 107; Kurzman, *Genesis*, p. 143; Gervasi, *Life*, p. 233; Lever, *Jerusalem*, pp. 170, 173.

16. Khalidi, *Dayr Yasin*, p. 78 (testimony by Sakina Mahmud As'ad Radwan); Kana'na and Zaytawi, *Dayr Yasin*, pp. 52, 56; Lynd, Bahour and Lynd, *Homeland*, pp. 22–24 (interviews with Ahmad 'Ayish Khalil and 'Ayisha Jum'a Zaydan); MEC GB165-0282/2/4: "Dir Yasin" – interviewee not named; Felicia Langer, *Be-Darki sheli* (Tel Aviv, 1991), p. 77; La Gwardia, *War*, p. 199 (interview with 'Ayish Muhammad 'Ayish Zaydan); PACE 240: interview with same; "37 'Aman," pp. 11–12 (testimonies by Maryam Barakat and Muhammad Darwish [Hamida]); LC 3/29: DLP, "Deir Yassin," p. 7; Silver, *Begin*, p. 94 (citing Muhammad 'Arif Sammur); Bar'el and Shay, "Hazara," p. 23 (interviewing same); Igbariyyeh, "60th Anniversary" (testimony by 'Abd al-Qadir Zaydan); JA K4-10/2: "Parashat Dir Yasin"; Ben-Tor, *Sefer*, vol. 4, p. 464; Milstein, *History*, vol. 4, p. 365, and *Myth*, p. 62.

17. Hogan, "1948 Massacre," p. 316; 'Arif, *Nakbat*, vol. 1, p. 173; Kana'na, "Madhbahat," p. 174; LC 3/29: testimony by Eliyahu [should be Yehoshua] Arieli; Kurzman, *Genesis*, p. 146; MacGowan and Ellis, *Remembering*, pp. 43, 48 (interview with Meir Pa'il and testimony by Jamil Ahmad 'Alya); Salayima, *Dayr Yasin*, p. 147 (testimony by same); Banks, *Country*, p. 62 (testimony by Ezra Yakhin); MEC GB165-0346/2/24: interview with same; "37 'Aman," p. 11 (testimony by Maryam Barakat); Zananiri, "Interviews" (interviewing Abu Tawfiq); Igbariyyeh, "60th Anniversary" (testimony by 'Abd al-Qadir Zaydan); 'Awawda, *Dhakira*, p. 88 (testimony by same); Idem, "Isra'il Tarfadu" (interview with same); BUPA: 'Aql, "Haqa'iq Waqi'iyya"; LC 3/29: DLP, "Deir Yassin," p. 7; JA K4-10/9: testimony by Mordechai Kaufman during the benefits trial, [30 June 1952].

18. YTA 15-46/183/2: Eliezer [Gicherman] to Tzadiq, Bernhard, Yarkoni and Avraham, "Doh Kibush Dir Yasin," 10 April 1948; YTA 12-3/9/3: Gichon, "Parashat Dir Yasin Tashah"; Milstein, *History*, vol. 4, pp. 362, 365, and *Myth*, pp. 57, 62 (interview with Mordechai Gichon); Regev-Yarkoni and Regev, *Lohem*, p. 136; Lapidot, *Lahav*, p. 311, and *Homotayikh*, p. 153; JA K4-13/8: broadcast of *Kol Zion ha-Lohemet*, 11 April 1948; *Ha-Boqer*, 11 April 1948, p. 1.

19. 'Arif, *Nakbat*, vol. 1, p. 172; Nimr, *Dayr Yasin*, pp. 15–16; Kurzman, *Genesis*, p. 144; Khalidi, *Dayr Yasin*, p. 65 (interview with and testimony by Khalil Sammur); BUPA: 'Aql, "Haqa'iq Waqi'iyya"; Kana'na and Zaytawi, *Dayr Yasin*, p. 61, claiming the number of soldiers in 'Ayn Karm to be 600; Zananiri, "Interviews" (interviewing Abu Tawfiq); Farsakh, "Majzarat"; Wadi' 'Awawda, "Majzarat Dayr Yasin Tuthiru al-Jadal bayna al-Isra'iliyyin," *al-Jazira Net*, 9 April 2008, www.palestineremembered.com/Jerusalem/Dayr-Yasin/Story9261. html (interview with Zaynab Muhammad Jabir); Musa Budeiri, "A Chronicle of a Defeat Foretold: The Battle for Jerusalem in the Memoirs of Anwar Nusseibeh," *Jerusalem Quarterly File*, 11–12 (2001), p. 44 (citing the memoirs' manuscript, p. 119); Abu Gharbiyya, *Khidamm*, p. 221; PACE 240: interview with 'Ayish Muhammad Zaydan (who believed that if 20 to 30 warriors would have come to assist Deir Yasin, the battle would have ended differently); PACE 237: interview with Ibtisam Zaydan; *Filastin*, 11 April 1948.

20. Khalidi, *Dayr Yasin*, p. 65 (interview with Khalil Sammur and testimony by Fatima Isma'il Sammur); 'Arif, *Nakbat*, vol. 1, p. 172; Abu Gharbiyya, *Khidamm*, p. 221; Farsakh, "Majzarat"; PACE 237: interview with Ibtisam Zaydan; 'Awawda, *Dhakira*, p. 89 (testimony by 'Ali Jabir); Pa'il, "Ra'ayonot Anshey Shay," pt. 2, 3:48 (interview with Yehezkel Rabi'); Gelber, "Propaganda," p. 310; *Al-Difa'*, 13 April 1948, p. 3.

21. Kurzman, *Genesis*, p. 144; Khalidi, *Dayr Yasin*, p. 65 (testimony by Ahmad Khalil 'Id and interview with and testimony by Khalil Sammur); IDFA 355/2644/49: "Tzror Yedi'ot 'Arviyot," 9 April 1948; IDFA 18/446/48: Hashmona'i to Moriah, "Rikuz Yedi'ot No. 148," 10 April 1948, and "Nispahim le-Rikuz Yedi'ot No. 148," 10 April 1948; Farsakh, "Majzarat"; Gelber, "Propaganda," pp. 308, 310. For the role of the national committees, see Tauber, *Military Resistance*, pp. 28–29.

22. IDFA 6/2605/49: "Ein Karm," 9 April 1948; IDFA 355/2644/49: "Tzror Yedi'ot 'Arviyot," 9 April 1948, and "Tzror Yedi'ot 'Arviyot," 10 April 1948; IDFA 75/5254/49: Yavne to District Commander, "Tzror Yedi'ot 'Arviyot Dhufot," 9 April 1948, and same to same, "Tzror Yedi'ot 'Arviyot Dhufot," 10 April 1948; IDFA 2/2605/49: Hashmona'i to Beit Horon, "Rikuz Yedi'ot No. 147," 10 April 1948, and "Nispahim le-Rikuz Yedi'ot No. 147," 10 April 1948; Khalidi, *Mudhakkirat*, vol. 2, p. 267; IDFA 1/150/86: Hashmona'i to David [Shaltiel], "Doh No. 135 le-Yom 12–13 April 1948," 13 April 1948; Ehud Amir, *Gadna' Yerushalayim be-Tashah* (n.p., 2003), p. 49.

23. Khalidi, *Mudhakkirat*, vol. 2, pp. 265–266; *Ha-Boqer*, 11 April 1948, p. 4; *Al-Difa'*, 12 April 1948, p. 1, *Palestine Post*, 12 April 1948, p. 2, and *New York Times*, 12 April 1948, p. 9, all citing Khalidi; R[ichard] M. Graves, *Experiment in Anarchy* (London, 1949), p. 179 (entry for 15 April 1948).

24. Khalidi, *Mudhakkirat*, vol. 2, pp. 265–266; *Al-Difa'*, 12 April 1948, p. 1 (citing Husayn al-Khalidi); LC 3/29: testimonies by Alan Cunningham, James Pollock,

Splosh Jones and [Gordon] MacMillan; IDFA 6/2605/49: "Dir Yasin," 9 April 1948; IDFA 355/2644/49: "Tzror Yedi'ot 'Arviyot," 9 April 1948; 18/446/48: Hashmona'i to Moriah, "Nispahim le-Rikuz Yedi'ot No. 148," 10 April 1948; RH MSS. Brit. Emp. s. 527/10/2: interview with Gordon MacMillan; MEC GB165-0282/1/19: interview with Horatius Murray.

25. WO 275/117: letter CS725/2, Fox-Strangways to HQ British Troops in Palestine, 16 April 1948; IDFA 6/2605/49: "Dir Yasin," 9 April 1948; IDFA 355/2644/49: "Tzror Yedi'ot 'Arviyot," 9 April 1948; 18/446/48: Hashmona'i to Moriah, "Nispahim le-Rikuz Yedi'ot No. 148," 10 April 1948; Khalidi, *Mudhakkirat*, vol. 2, p. 266; *Palestine Post*, 12 April 1948, p. 2, and *New York Times*, 12 April 1948, p. 9 (citing Husayn al-Khalidi); LC 2/1: Jacques de Reynier, "Mission C.I.C.R. en Palestine" [de Reynier's diary], 11 April 1948, p. 83; ACICR B G 59/I/GC, file 17: letter JdR/JM 29, J[acques] de Reynier (Jerusalem) to Comité International de la Croix-Rouge (Geneva), 13 April 1948.

26. *New York Times*, 12 April 1948, p. 9; FBIS, FRB-48-290, 15 April 1948, p. II4: Arabic radio from Jerusalem, 13 April 1948, 14:00; WO 275/117: letter CS725/2, Fox-Strangways to HQ British Troops in Palestine, 16 April 1948; *Daily Telegraph*, 12 April 1948, p. 1; *New York Herald Tribune*, 12 April 1948; MEC GB165-0072/4/1: "Minutes of Security Conference," 16 April 1948; MEC GB165-0072/3/3: tel. 956, High Commissioner for Palestine to Secretary of State, 13 April 1948; LC 3/29: testimony by Alan Cunningham; Motti Golani, *Ha-Natziv ha-Aharon: Ha-General Seyr Elen Gordon Qaningham, 1945–1948* (Tel Aviv, 2011), p. 258.

NOTES FOR CHAPTER 5

1. HA 95.3: testimony by Akiva Azulay; *Ha-Hagana bi-Yerushalayim*, vol. 2, pp. 125–126 (testimony by same); Sharvit, *Akiva*, pp. 68–69; Milstein, *History*, vol. 4, p. 363, and *Myth*, p. 58 (interview with Yonah Ben-Sasson); IDFA 290/922/75: testimony 32 by Zalman Mart.

2. YTA 12-3/9/3: Gichon, "Parashat Dir Yasin Tashah"; YTA 15-46/183/2: Eliezer [Gicherman] to Tzadiq, Bernhard, Yarkoni and Avraham, "Doh Kibush Dir Yasin," 10 April 1948; Gichon, *Mate*, p. 249; Avizohar, *Moriya*, p. 90; Milstein, *History*, vol. 4, p. 362, and *Myth*, p. 57 (interview with Mordechai Gichon); Idem, "Dir Yasin," p. 19.

3. Idem, *History*, vol. 4, pp. 359, 363, and *Myth*, pp. 55–57; Avizohar, *Moriya*, p. 90; Bregman and Tahri, *Fifty Years*, p. 29; YTA 12-3/9/3: Gichon, "Parashat Dir Yasin Tashah"; JA K4-13/8: broadcast of *Kol Zion ha-Lohemet*, 11 April 1948; IDFA 290/922/75: testimony 32 by Zalman Mart; HA 58.49: testimony by same; IDFA 291/922/75: testimony 53 by Zion Eldad; JA K4-10/1: testimonies

by Yehoshua Gorodenchik and Yehuda Marinburg; JA K4-10/9: testimony by Ben-Zion Cohen during the benefits trial, 5 January 1953; Ofir, "Dir Yasin," p. 5; JA H13-3/48/4: case against Nathan Friedman-Yellin and Matityahu Shmuelevitz in the special military court, Protocol IV, 7 January 1949, p. 1403 (testimony by David Shaltiel); *Sefer Toldot ha-Hagana*, vol. 3, pt. 2, p. 1547; Hovav, *Gal*, p. 80.

4. Kfir, "Shalosh," p. 3 (interview with Mordechai Raanan); YTA 12-3/9/3: Gichon, "Parashat Dir Yasin Tashah"; phone conversation with Mordechai Gichon, 21 May 2014; Rami Rozen, "Kol Ehad ve-ha-Tashah shelo," *ha-Aretz*, supplement, 19 April 1991, p. 47; Milstein, *History*, vol. 4, p. 377, and *Myth*, p. 82 (interview with Mordechai Gichon); JA 'ER-12/1: testimony by Mordechai Raanan; JA 'ER-12/5: interview with same; JA K4-10/9: testimony by same during the benefits trial, [30 June 1952]; Ofir, *Homot*, pp. 60–61.

5. YTA 12-3/41/14: interview with Moshe Edelstein; YTA 16-12/52/8: testimony by Moshe Vachman-Eran; YTA 15-46/183/2: testimony by Isser Halamish; YTA 12-3/41/34: interview with Yosef Barkai; YTA 12-3/43/45: interview with Gideon Sarig; E-mail from Ezra Yakhin to the author, 30 March 2014; JA 'EB-30/5: interview with Kalman Bergman; Amikam, "Hagana," p. 3; "Dir Yasin – Kol ha-Emet," p. 16; Milstein, *History*, vol. 4, p. 363, and *Myth*, p. 59; Lapidot, *Lahav*, p. 311, and *Homotayikh*, p. 153; Niv, *Ma'arkhot*, vol. 6, p. 84; JA 'EG-28/2: testimony by David Gottlieb; Ben-Tor, *Sefer*, vol. 4, p. 464.

6. IDFA 584/4944/49: Company Commander (4th Company, 6th Battalion) to Jerusalem's District Commander, "Doh Dir Yasin," 11 April 1948; YTA 15-34/13/5: testimony by Moshe Vachman, "Dir Yasin"; YTA 12-3/43/16: interview with same; YTA 16-12/52/8: testimony by same; YTA 12-3/41/14: interview with Moshe Edelstein; Milstein, *History*, vol. 4, pp. 363–364, and *Myth*, p. 59; "Dir Yasin – Kol ha-Emet," p. 16; E-mail from Ezra Yakhin to the author, 30 March 2014; YTA 15-34/13/5: letter, Uri Brenner (Maoz Haim) to Ehud Marioz, 25 June 1974; JA H13-3/48/4: case against Nathan Friedman-Yellin and Matityahu Shmuelevitz in the special military court, Protocol IV, 7 January 1949, p. 1403 (testimony by David Shaltiel); IDFA 291/922/75: testimonies 75 by same and 72 by Yitzhak Levy; YTA 12-4/48/3: testimony by Yosef Tabenkin; YTA 15-22/4/9: letter, [same] to [Yitzhak] Ben-Aharon, 3 November [1969?]; Yosef Tabenkin, *Ha-Mifne be-Milhemet ha-'Atzma'ut: Mitqefet Gdud Palmah "ha-Portzim" be-Mivtze'ey Nahshon ve-Har'el* (Ramat Efal, 1989), p. 102; YTA 15-46/183/2: note [by David Ben-Gurion]; *Sefer Toldot ha-Hagana*, vol. 3, pt. 2, p. 1547.

7. YTA 16-12/52/8: testimony by Moshe Vachman-Eran; YTA 15-34/13/5: testimony by same, "Dir Yasin"; YTA 12-3/43/16: interview with same; YTA 15-46/183/2: testimony by Isser Halamish; IDFA 584/4944/49: Company Commander to District Commander, "Doh Dir Yasin," 11 April 1948; YTA 12-3/41/14: interview with Moshe Edelstein; YTA 12-3/41/34: interview with Yosef Barkai; YTA 12-3/43/45: interview with Gideon Sarig; *Ha-Hagana bi-Yerushalayim*, vol. 2, p. 125; Bregman and Tahri, *Fifty Years*, p. 31 (citing Moshe Vachman).

8. YTA 12-3/41/14: interview with Moshe Edelstein; JA K4-10/9: testimony by Ben-Zion Cohen during the benefits trial, 5 January 1953; HA 95.3: testimony by Akiva Azulay; "Dir Yasin – Kol ha-Emet," p. 16; IDFA 584/4944/49: Company Commander to District Commander, "Doh Dir Yasin," 11 April 1948; YTA 15-34/13/5: testimony by Moshe Vachman, "Dir Yasin."

9. JA 'ER-12/1: testimony by Mordechai Raanan; JA 'ER-12/5: interview with same; JA K4-10/1: testimonies by Yehuda Marinburg, Yehuda Lapidot, Ben-Zion Cohen and Yehoshua Gorodenchik; YTA 12-4/48/3: testimony by Yosef Tabenkin; YTA 16-12/52/8: testimony by Moshe Vachman-Eran; YTA 15-34/13/5: testimony by same, "Dir Yasin"; ISA P-2878/5: interview with Shimon Moneta; MEC GB165-0346/2/14: interview with same; Bregman and Tahri, *Fifty Years*, p. 31 (citing same); phone conversation with same, 7 August 2014; Moneta, "Kavana," p. 4; Idem, *Toldot*, p. 62; YTA 15-46/183/2: testimony by Isser Halamish; IDFA 584/4944/49: Company Commander to District Commander, "Doh Dir Yasin," 11 April 1948; IDFA 290/922/75: testimony 32 by Zalman Mart; Kfir, "Shalosh," p. 3 (interview with Yehoshua Zettler); Vered, *Yerushalayim*, p. 113; Lapidot, *Lahav*, p. 311, and *Homotayikh*, p. 153; Amikam, "Hagana," p. 3; "Dir Yasin – Kol ha-Emet," p. 16; Golani, *Mitos*, p. 54; Katzman, "Mitos," p. B9; Bar'el and Shay, "Hazara," p. 23 (interviewing Muhammad 'Arif Sammur); Tamari, *Jerusalem*, p. 138 (citing Salih 'Abd al-Jawad of Birzeit University). Also *Palestine Post*, 11 April 1948, p. 1, reported that some of the Arabs were injured by mortar bombs.

10. YTA 15-34/13/5: testimony by Moshe Vachman, "Dir Yasin"; YTA 12-3/43/16: interview with same; YTA 16-12/52/8: testimony by same; Milstein, *History*, vol. 4, pp. 364–365, and *Myth*, p. 61 (interviews with same and Kalman Rosenblatt); JA 'EG-28/2: testimony by David Gottlieb; YTA 12-3/43/45: interview with Gideon Sarig; Khalidi, *Dayr Yasin*, p. 65 (interview with and testimony by Khalil Sammur).

11. YTA 12-3/43/16: interview with Moshe Eran (Vachman); YTA 16-12/52/8: testimony by same; YTA 15-34/13/5: testimony by same, "Dir Yasin"; IDFA 584/4944/49: Company Commander to District Commander, "Doh Dir Yasin," 11 April 1948; HA 95.3: testimony by Akiva Azulay; Sharvit, *Akiva*, p. 69; YTA 12-3/32/39: interview with Yaakov Giron; YTA 15-34/13/5: letter, Brenner to Marioz, 25 June 1974; LC 3/29: testimony by [Yehuda] Lapidot.

12. Golani, *Mitos*, pp. 37, 60; Khalidi, *Dayr Yasin*, pp. 54–55 (testimony by Hasan Radwan); Kana'na and Zaytawi, *Dayr Yasin*, p. 53; Salayima, *Dayr Yasin*, p. 111 (testimony by Muhammad Mahmud Radwan); Bregman and Tahri, *Fifty Years*, p. 31 (citing same); JA K4-10/1: unidentified testimony, "Kibush Dir Yasin," and unidentified testimony [Ben-Zion Cohen]; JA K4-10/9: testimony by same during the benefits trial, 5 January 1953; ISA P-2878/5: interview with Shimon Moneta; MEC GB165-0346/2/14: interview with same; YTA 12-3/41/14:

interview with Moshe Edelstein; Katzman, "Mitos," p. B9; "60 Sha'ot," p. 35; "Dir Yasin – Kol ha-Emet," p. 14.

13. Khalidi, *Dayr Yasin*, p. 65 (interview with and testimony by Khalil Sammur); JA 'ER-12/1: testimony by Mordechai Raanan; JA K4-10/1: testimonies by Yehoshua Gorodenchik and Reuven Greenberg and unidentified testimony, "Kibush Dir Yasin"; Interview with Yehuda Lapidot, 24 August 2010; LC 3/29: testimony by [Yehuda] Lapidot; Lapidot, *Lahav*, p. 312, and *Homotayikh*, p. 153; Golani, *Mitos*, pp. 54, 65–66 (Golani's claim, cited by others, that the house was only conquered on Saturday, 10 April, is wrong); Ofir, "Dir Yasin," p. 5; Idem, *Homot*, p. 60; Ben-Tor, *Sefer*, vol. 4, p. 464; Kurzman, *Genesis*, p. 146; IDFA 372/5254/49: Yavne to Tene (D), "Pe'ulat ha-Porshim be-Dir Yasin: Ha-Bduta 'al Ramqol," 12 April 1948; "Dir Yasin – Kol ha-Emet," p. 14; Avner, "Ghosts," p. 13; Lever, *Jerusalem*, p. 171.

14. Kana'na and Zaytawi, *Dayr Yasin*, pp. 53–54; Awawda, *Dhakira*, p. 88 (testimony by 'Abd al-Qadir Zaydan – he was one of the remaining nine); "Dhikra 58" (speech by same); As'ad, "Dhikra," p. 3; PACE 240: interview with 'Ayish Muhammad Zaydan; 'Arif, *Nakbat*, vol. 1, p. 172; Salayima, *Dayr Yasin*, p. 117 (testimony by Zaynab Ahmad Musa); "Qadiyya wa-Hiwar," 7:00 and 25:22 (interview with Mustafa Mahmud); Yakhin, *Sipuro*, p. 257; Banks, *Country*, p. 62 (testimony by Ezra Yakhin); Lapidot, *Homotayikh*, p. 153; Golani, *Mitos*, p. 61; IDFA 372/5254/49: Yavne to Tene (D), "Pe'ulat ha-Porshim be-Dir Yasin: Ha-Bduta 'al Ramqol," 12 April 1948.

15. JA 'EA-3/2: testimony by Yosef Avni. See also www.izkor.gov.il/HalalKorot.aspx?id=8118.

16. YTA 15-46/183/2: Eliezer to Tzadiq, Bernhard, Yarkoni and Avraham, "Doh Kibush Dir Yasin," 10 April 1948; Lapidot, *Lahav*, p. 312, and *Homotayikh*, p. 154; Golani, *Mitos*, p. 38. See also www.izkor.gov.il/HalalKorot.aspx?id=44206.

17. JA 'EA-3/2: testimony by Yosef Avni; "Dir Yasin – Kol ha-Emet," p. 16; Lapidot, *Lahav*, pp. 311, 329–330, and *Homotayikh*, pp. 152, 165–166; Golani, *Mitos*, pp. 48, 51. See also www.izkor.gov.il/HalalKorot.aspx?id=7471.

18. Golani, *Mitos*, p. 104; *Davar*, 14 April 1948, p. 2. See also www.izkor.gov.il/HalalKorot.aspx?id=88407.

19. JA K4-10/1: testimony by Yehuda Marinburg; Banks, *Country*, p. 60 (testimony by Ezra Yakhin); Golani, *Mitos*, pp. 28, 105. See also www.izkor.gov.il/HalalKorot.aspx?id=8462.

20. YTA 12-3/9/3: letter, Levy to Begin, 12 April 1971; *New York Times*, 30 November 1948, p. 5, citing Kaufman's speech. Morris, "Historiography," p. 86, mentioned about a dozen seriously wounded, pointing out that the figures of 30 to 40 injured were "surely an exaggeration." Yet in his later book, *1948: A History of the First Arab-Israeli War* (New Haven and London, 2008), p. 126, he was

already speaking about several dozens of injured. In a letter to *Yedi'ot Aharonot*, 22 August 1960 (available in IDFA 26/70/2004), Avichai Yehudayof, describing himself as a simple Etzel soldier who had participated in the operation from beginning to end, also claimed that the number of injured was close to 50.

21. IDFA 54/500/48: Yavne [Levy] to Tene (D), "Pe'ulat Etzel ve-Lehi be-Dir Yasin," 12 April 1948; JA K4-10/9: testimony by Mordechai Kaufman during the benefits trial, [30 June 1952]; JA K4-13/8: broadcast of *Kol Zion ha-Lohemet*, 11 April 1948, citing Etzel's announcement at 19:00; JA K4-10/4: "Tuqa' ha-Tzvi'ut," a poster by Etzel, April 1948; *Ha-Boqer*, 11 April 1948, p. 1; *Palestine Post*, 11 April 1948, p. 1; *Ha-Mashqif*, 11 April 1948, p. 1; *Davar*, 11 April 1948, p. 1; *Jewish Agency's Digest*, p. 16; Interview with Yehuda Lapidot, 24 August 2010. See also JA K4-10/1: unidentified testimony, "Kibush Dir Yasin," and JA K4-10/2: "Parashat Dir Yasin."

22. Begin, *Revolt*, p. 163; JA K4-10/1: testimony by Ben-Zion Cohen; MEC GB165-0346/3/5: interview with same; BBC, "50 Years," 12:23 (interview with same); Ofir, *Homot*, p. 60; LC 3/29: testimony by [Yehuda] Lapidot; Avizohar, *Moriya*, p. 90; *New York Times*, 10 April 1948, p. 6. See also "Dir Yasin – Kol ha-Emet," p. 14.

23. JA K4-10/1: testimony by Yehuda Lapidot; Moneta, "Kavana," p. 4; Idem, *Toldot*, pp. 60–62; ISA P-2878/5: interview with Shimon Moneta; MEC GB165-0346/2/14: interview with same; Bregman and Tahri, *Fifty Years*, pp. 28, 32 (citing same); Lapidot, *Homotayikh*, p. 168; YTA 12-3/41/14: interview with Moshe Edelstein; JA K4-10/1: testimony by Yehoshua Gorodenchik; YTA 15-46/183/2: Eliezer to Tzadiq, Bernhard, Yarkoni and Avraham, "Doh Kibush Dir Yasin," 10 April 1948, and "Tosefet" by [Yosef] Ben-Nun; IDFA 372/5254/49: Yavne to Tene (D), "Ha-Shalal she-Nilqah bi-F'ulat Dir Yasin," 12 April 1948; IDFA 54/500/48: same to same, "Pe'ulat Etzel ve-Lehi be-Dir Yasin," 12 April 1948; YTA 15-34/13/5: testimony by Moshe Vachman, "Dir Yasin"; YTA 12-3/43/45: interview with Gideon Sarig; YTA 12-3/32/39: interview with Yaakov Giron; HA 20/253: Avraham to District Commander, "Pe'ulat ha-Porshim be-Dir Yasin," 10 April 1948; Khalidi, *Mudhakkirat*, vol. 2, pp. 263–264, citing report by Nusayba, 10 April 1948; "37 'Aman," pp. 10–11 (testimony by Fatima Hamida); As'ad, *Filastin*, p. 127 (testimony by Naziha Radwan); MEC GB165-0282/2/4: "Dir Yasin" – interviewee not named; Lynd, Bahour and Lynd, *Homeland*, p. 25 (interview with 'Ayisha Jum'a Zaydan); Kana'na and Zaytawi, *Dayr Yasin*, p. 54; Khalidi, *Dayr Yasin*, p. 86 (testimony by Naziha Radwan); 'Ubaydu, "Khamsun," p. 15 (interview with Zaynab 'Atiyya); *Filastin*, 14 April 1948; LC 3/29: DLP, "Deir Yassin," p. 10; Zananiri, "Interviews" (interviewing Abu Tawfiq).

24. JA K4-10/1: testimony by Yehuda Marinburg; WO 275/64: "Fortnightly Intelligence Newsletter No. 66," by HQ British Troops in Palestine, 21 April 1948; YTA 15-46/183/2: Eliezer to Tzadiq, Bernhard, Yarkoni and Avraham, "Doh Kibush Dir Yasin," 10 April 1948; YTA 12-3/43/45: interview with Gideon

Sarig; Lapidot, *Homotayikh,* p. 168; MEC GB165-0346/3/5: interview with Ben-Zion Cohen; IDFA 1/5440/49: tel., Yavne to Tene, 14 April 1948; HA 20/253: Avraham to District Commander, "Pe'ulat ha-Porshim be-Dir Yasin," 10 April 1948; IDFA 372/5254/49: Yavne to Tene (D), "Ha-Shalal she-Nilqah bi-F'ulat Dir Yasin," 12 April 1948; YTA 15-46/183/2: testimony by Shoshana Winkler; Hadassah Avigdori-Avidov, *"Ba-Derekh she-Halakhnu...": Mi-Yomana shel- Melavat Shayarot* (Tel Aviv, 1988), p. 91; JA K4-10/4: identical posters by Etzel and Lehi, "Hoda'a 'al Parashat Dir Yasin," [14] April 1948.

25.   Lapidot, *Lahav,* p. 313; Interview with Yehuda Lapidot, 24 August 2010; JA 'EG-28/1: testimony by David Gottlieb; Milstein, "Dir Yasin," p. 19; *Ha-Boqer,* 11 April 1948, p. 4; *Ha-Mashqif,* 11 April 1948, p. 3; *Al-Difa',* 13 April 1948, p. 3; *New York Times,* 10 April 1948, p. 6 (article by Dana Adams Schmidt); *New York Herald Tribune,* 10 April 1948 (article by Fitzhugh Turner); *Times,* 10 April 1948; LC 3/29: testimony by Dana Adams Schmidt; Dana Adams Schmidt, *Armageddon in the Middle East* (New York, 1974), p. 4; JA 'EB-30/5: interview with Kalman Bergman; JA 'EB-30/6: interview with same; CO 793/48, file 75156/151A/12, entry 9; FO 371/68504/E4827: Draft Parliamentary Question and Answer for Written Reply (by Minister of State Hector McNeil), 16 April 1948; CO 733/477/5: tel. 933, Cunningham to Secretary of State for the Colonies, 10 April 1948; NARA RG 84, Jerusalem Consulate General Classified Records, 1948 – 800 Political Affairs, 6: tel. 433, Wasson to Secretary of State, 14 April 1948; Khalidi, *Mudhakkirat,* vol. 2, p. 265 (the correspondent of the Associated Press reported the contents of the press conference to Khalidi).

26.   *New York Times,* 10 April 1948, p. 6; *New York Herald Tribune,* 10 April 1948; LC 3/29: testimony by Dana Adams Schmidt; Schmidt, *Armageddon,* pp. 4–5; CO 733/477/5: tels. 928 and 933, Cunningham to Secretary of State for the Colonies, 10 April 1948; CO 537/3869: tel. 937, same to same, 10 April 1948; Khalidi, *Mudhakkirat,* vol. 2, p. 265; Lapidot, *Lahav,* p. 313; JA 'EB-30/5: interview with Kalman Bergman; *Ha-Mashqif,* 11 April 1948, pp. 1, 3; *Davar,* 11 April 1948, p. 1; *Times,* 10 April 1948; NARA RG 84, Jerusalem Consulate General Classified Records, 1948 – 800 Palestine, 4: tel. 431, Wasson to Secretary of State, 13 April 1948; NARA RG 84, Jerusalem Consulate General Classified Records, 1948 – 800 Political Affairs, 6: tel. 433, same to same, 14 April 1948.

NOTES FOR CHAPTER 6

1.   JA 'EB-30/6: interview with Kalman Bergman; Interview with Yehuda Lapidot, 24 August 2010; CO 733/477/5: tel. 933, Cunningham to Secretary of State for the Colonies, 10 April 1948; MEC GB165-0128/1/1: Henry Gurney, *Palestine Postscript: A Short Record of the Last Days of the Mandate,* entry for 10 April 1948; NARA RG 84, Jerusalem Consulate General Classified Records, 1948 – 800 Political Affairs, 6: tel. 433, Wasson to Secretary of State, 14 April

1948; *Ha-Boqer*, 11 April 1948, p. 4; *Ha-Mashqif*, 11 April 1948, p. 3; *Times*, 10 April 1948; *New York Times*, 10 April 1948, p. 6; *New York Herald Tribune*, 10 April 1948; *Filastin*, 11 April 1948; Milstein, *History*, vol. 4, p. 369, and *Myth*, p. 80 (interview with Mordechai Raanan); Golani, *Hanhagat*, p. 213 (testimony by same); Lapidot, *Lahav*, p. 329, and *Homotayikh*, p. 165; Holmes, "Deir Yassin" (citing Yehuda Lapidot).

2. Lapidot, *Lahav*, p. 315, and *Homotayikh*, p. 156; JA K4-13/8: broadcast of *Kol Zion ha-Lohemet*, 11 April 1948, citing the report of 19:00; *Ha-Boqer*, 11 April 1948, p. 1; *Ha-Mashqif*, 11 April 1948, p. 1; La Guardia, *War*, p. 198.

3. Abu Gharbiyya, *Khidamm*, pp. 221–220; Khalidi, *Dayr Yasin*, p. 95; *Al-Difa'*, 12 April 1948, p. 1; *Filastin*, 13 April 1948; *New York Times*, 12 April 1948, pp. 1, 9, and 13 April 1948, p. 7; *New York Herald Tribune*, 12 April 1948; *Palestine Post*, 12 April 1948, p. 1; Kana'na, "Madhbahat," p. 162; "50 'Aman 'ala Madhbahat Dayr Yasin – Mu'arrikh Isra'ili: Madhabih Afza' lam Tudhkar!," *al-Safir*, 7 April 1998, p. 12. In his report to Geneva, de Reynier communicated figures similar to those he orally told Khalidi. See ACICR B G 59/I/GC, file 17: letter JdR/ JM 29, de Reynier to Comité International de la Croix-Rouge, 13 April 1948.

4. See e.g. WO 261/574: "Diary of Events" (HQ Palestine), May 1948; Graves, *Experiment*, p. 179; Edgar O'Ballance, *The Arab-Israeli War 1948* (London, 1956), p. 58; Christopher Sykes, *Cross Roads to Palestine* (London, 1965), p. 417; Salih Sa'ib al-Juburi, *Mihnat Filastin wa-Asraruha al-Siyasiyya wal-'Askariyya* (Beirut, 1970), p. 154; John and Hadawi, *Palestine*, vol. 2, p. 327; Levy, *Tish'a*, p. 342.

5. See e.g. NARA RG 84, Jerusalem Consulate General Classified Records, 1948 – 800 Palestine, 4: tel. 431, Wasson to Secretary of State, 13 April 1948; Arthur Koestler, *Promise and Fulfilment: Palestine 1917–1949* (New York, 1949), p. 160; John Kimche, *Seven Fallen Pillars: The Middle East, 1915–1950* (London, 1950), p. 217; Akram Zu'aytar, *Al-Qadiyya al-Filastiniyya* (Cairo, 1955), p. 210; John Bagot Glubb, *A Soldier with the Arabs* (London, 1957), p. 81; Muhammad 'Izzat Darwaza, *Al-Qadiyya al-Filasiniyya fi Mukhtalif Marahiliha* (Sidon and Beirut, [1960]), vol. 2, p. 129; Wizarat al-Irshad al-Qawmi – Al-Hay'a al-'Amma lil-Isti'lamat, *Dayr Yasin: Ramz Falsafat al-Sahyuniyya, al-Saytara bil-Satw wal-Tahakkum bil-Irhab, 9 Abril 1948 – 9 Abril 1969* ([Cairo, 1969]), p. 5; Pa'il, "Emet," p. 14; *Sefer Toldot ha-Hagana*, vol. 3, pt. 2, p. 1547; Michael Bar-Zohar, *Ben-Gurion* (Tel Aviv, 1977), vol. 2, p. 701; "Dayr Yasin (Madhbaha)," *Mawsu'a*, al-Qism al-'Amm, vol. 2, p. 434.

6. Kana'na and Zaytawi, *Dayr Yasin*, pp. 57–60; Khalidi, *Dayr Yasin*, p. 124; 'Arif, *Nakbat*, vol. 1, p. 173; Abu Gharbiyya, *Khidamm*, p. 222; "Abu Mahmud," p. 8; Holmes, "Deir Yassin" (citing Muhammad Mahmud Radwan); 'Awawda, *Dhakira*, p. 89 (citing same); Assad, *Palestine*, pp. 203–207, and pp. 207–213 in the Arabic version; Bar'el and Shay, "Hazara," p. 23 (interviewing Muhammad 'Arif Sammur); Silver, *Begin*, pp. 95–96 (citing same); "Min Mudhakkirat Khalil

Sammur bi-Khatt Yadihi Ya'uddu fiha Ba'd Asma' al-Shuhada' fil-Madhbaha," www.palestineremembered.com/OralHistoryMP3/Jerusalem/Dayr-Yasin/ Muhammad-Sammur/docs/Picture002.jpg; "37 'Aman," p. 10 (testimony by Khumays Zaydan); Kana'na, "Madhbahat," p. 160 (citing Mahfuz Sammur); Catrina Stewart, "A massacre of arabs masked by state of national amnesia," *The Independent,* 10 May 2010, www.independent.co.uk/news/world/middle-east/a-massacre-of-arabs-masked-by-state-of-national-amnesia-1970018.html (citing 'Abd al-Qadir Zaydan); PACE 240: interview with 'Ayish Muhammad Zaydan; La Guardia, *War,* p. 200 (citing same); PACE 241: interview with Muhammad 'Ayish Zaydan.

7. Milstein, *History,* vol. 4, pp. 376–377, and *Myth,* pp. 77, 82 (interviews with Mordechai Gichon, Yonah Feitelson and Yehoshua Arieli); IDFA 6/2605/49: "Dir Yasin," 10 April 1948; IDFA 75/5254/49: Yavne to District Commander, "Tzror Yedi'ot 'Arviyot Dhufot," 10 April 1948; IDFA 355/2644/49: "Tzror Yedi'ot 'Arviyot," 10 April 1948; IDFA 2/2605/49: Hashmona'i to Beit Horon, "Rikuz Yedi'ot No. 151," 11 April 1948, and "Nispahim le-Rikuz Yedi'ot No. 151," 11 April 1948; IDFA 372/5254/49: Yavne to Tene (A), "Totz'ot Dir Yasin," 12 April 1948; Rozen, "Kol," p. 47 (interviewing Uri Milstein and Yehoshua Arieli); Silver, *Begin,* p. 96 (citing same); JA 'EA-37/1: interview with same; LC 3/29: testimony by same.

8. "Dahaya al-I'tida' al-Ijrami bi-Dayr Yasin," *al-Difa',* 12 April 1948, pp. 1, 4; Yizhar Be'er, "Ha-Kfarim ha-Smuyim min ha-'Ayin," *Kol ha-'Ir,* 25 November 1988, p. 36 (citing Sharif Kana'na).

9. "Asma' al-Shuhada' Alladhina Istashhadu fi Ta'rikh 9.4.1948," www.palestineremembered.com/OralHistoryMP3/Jerusalem/Dayr-Yasin/Muhammad-Sammur/docs/Picture002.jpg.

10. 'Arif, *Nakbat,* vol. 6: *Sijl al-Khulud – Asma' al-Shuhada' Alladhina Istashhadu fi Ma'arik Filastin 1947–1952,* pp. 17–94 ('Arif's statement re Deir Yassin on p. 97).

11. Hijazi, *Dayr Yasin,* pp. 77–78.

12. "37 'Aman," p. 12. The journal was issued by al-Fatah.

13. BUPA: "Haqa'iq 'an Asma' Shuhada' Qaryat Dayr Yasin 'Am 9/4/1948," www.awraq.birzeit.edu/sites/default/files/PDF_158.

14. Kana'na and Zaytawi, *Dayr Yasin,* pp. 57–60; Kana'na, "Madhbahat," pp. 158–160; Be'er, "Kfarim," p. 36 (citing Sharif Kana'na).

15. Walid al-Khalidi (ed.), *Kay la Nansa: Qura Filastin Allati Dammaratha Isra'il Sanat 1948 wa-Asma' Shuhada'iha* (Beirut, [1997]), pp. 784–785.

16. Khalidi, *Dayr Yasin,* pp. 127 (and note 8 on p. 141), 150, and family trees on pp. 72, 74, 152–158.

17. Nimr, *Dayr Yasin*, pp. 19–21.

18. 'Awawda, *Dhakira*, pp. 91–93.

19. Eitan Bronstein, *Zokhrot et Dir Yasin* (Tel Aviv, 2006), pp. 21–22.

20. Salayima, *Dayr Yasin*, pp. 154–158. There also exists an online list made by a certain "Abu Mu'tazz," which is completely identical to that of Salayima, excluding names 32, 61, 77 and 80 of Salayima's list. See Abu Mu'tazz, "Shuhada' Majzarat Dayr Yasin 1948," *Shabakat al-Quds lil-Hiwar*, elqudos.com/vb/showpost.php?p=146840&postcount=1.

21. Assad, *Palestine*, pp. 203–207, and pp. 207–213 in the Arabic version.

22. Hogan and McGowan, "Anatomy"; Kana'na and Zaytawi, *Dayr Yasin*, p. 61. In a later publication Hogan and McGowan admitted that the number of injured could be as high as 50, but still held to their original claim. See Daniel A. McGowan and Matthew C. Hogan, *The Saga of Deir Yassin: Massacre, Revisionism and Reality* (Geneva NY, 1999), pp. 11–13, www.deiryassin.org/pdf/SAGAA4.pdf. In yet another publication, Hogan was even willing to admit 70 injured, but still insisted that the proportion attested to "systematic killing." See Hogan, "1948 Massacre," pp. 324, 330.

23. CO 733/477/5: tel. 933, Cunningham to Secretary of State for the Colonies, 10 April 1948, and tel. 941, same to same, 11 April 1948; CO 537/3857: CID, "Summary of Events," 9 April 1948, and appendix B to "Summary of Events," 10 April 1948; *Palestine Post*, 11 April 1948, p. 1; *New York Times*, 11 April 1948, p. 18; *Al-Difa'*, 11 April 1948, pp. 1, 4, and 13 April 1948, p. 1; Khalidi, *Dayr Yasin*, p. 124; BUPA: 'Aql, "Haqa'iq Waqi'iyya"; Hillel Cohen, "'Amutat Zekher Dir Yasin Tehapes et Gufot Harugey ha-Tevah be-1948 mi-tahat le-Migrash ha-Rusim," *Kol ha-'Ir*, 29 April 1998, p. 31; 'Ubaydu, "Khamsun," p. 15; Salayima, *Dayr Yasin*, p. 207; "Qadiyya wa-Hiwar," 33:15 (interview with Mustafa Mahmud); *Filastin*, 10 April 1948; Kana'na and Zaytawi, *Dayr Yasin*, pp. 56–57; Dani Rubinstein, "Ha-She'ela eyna Kama, Ela Lama," *ha-Aretz*, 28 January 1998, p. B2; IDFA 355/2644/49: "Tzror Yedi'ot 'Arviyot," 10 April 1948.

24. ACICR B G 59/I/GC, file 17: letter JdR/JM 29, de Reynier to Comité International de la Croix-Rouge, 13 April 1948; LC 2/1: de Reynier's diary, 11 April 1948, p. 85; JA 'EG-28/1: testimony by David Gottlieb; JA 'EG-28/2: testimony by same; Derogy and Saab, *Exodes*, p. 144; Hogan, "1948 Massacre," p. 330; Abu Sitta, *Atlas*, p. 62; BUPA: 'Aql, "Haqa'iq Waqi'iyya"; Khalidi, *Dayr Yasin*, p. 53; *Filastin*, 10 and 14 April 1948; 'Abd al-Majid, "Sutur," p. 121; MEC GB165-0346/2/24: interview with Ezra Yakhin; Kana'na and Zaytawi, *Dayr Yasin*, p. 56; *Al-Difa'*, 11 April 1948, p. 4; IDFA 978/100001/57: letter, Social Affairs Committee of the Jerusalem National Committee to Head of the General Affairs Department of the Arab Higher Committee, 20 April 1948.

25. Silver, *Begin*, p. 94 (citing Muhammad 'Arif Sammur); Milstein, *History*, vol. 4, p. 361, and *Myth*, p. 50 (testimony by and interview with Petahya Selivansky); MEC GB165-0346/2/24: interview with Ezra Yakhin; MEC GB165-0346/3/5: interview with Ben-Zion Cohen; PACE 241: interview with Muhammad 'Ayish Zaydan. Two doctors, who visited the village three days later, confirmed that all the bodies checked were of people killed by bullets or "bombs" (a general term that could imply wounds caused by charges, gelignite sticks, petards, or hand grenades). See IDFA 54/500/48: Z[alman] Avigdori and A. Druyan, "Doh 'al ha-Biqur be-Dir Yasin be-Yom 12.4.1948" (Jerusalem), 18 April 1948.

26. Awawda, *Dhakira*, p. 88 (testimony by 'Abd al-Qadir Zaydan); "Dhikra 58" (speech by same); MEC GB165-0346/2/24: interview with Ezra Yakhin; MEC GB165-0346/2/14: interview with Shimon Moneta; Gelber, "Propaganda," p. 311; La Guardia, *War*, p. 200 (citing 'Ayish Muhammad 'Ayish Zaydan); JA K4-10/1: unidentified testimony [Ben-Zion Cohen]; Kfir, "Shalosh," p. 3 (interview with Yehoshua Zettler).

27. Kana'na and Zaytawi, *Dayr Yasin*, p. 54; Habib Allah, "Majzarat," p. 70; Collins and Lapierre, *O Jerusalem!*, p. 274; Zananiri, "Interviews" (interviewing Abu Tawfiq); PACE 240: interview with 'Ayish Muhammad Zaydan; Salayima, *Dayr Yasin*, p. 116 (testimony by Muhammad Mahmud Radwan, claiming that 28 people were burned to death by a bomb thrown into the house); Khalidi, *Dayr Yasin*, pp. 50–51 (testimony by Jum'a Zahran); MEC GB165-0282/2/4: "Dir Yasin" – interviewee not named.

28. *Filastin*, 14 April 1948 (testimony by Fahima Zaydan); Hijazi, *Dayr Yasin*, pp. 61–62 (testimony by same); Kana'na and Zaytawi, *Dayr Yasin*, p. 55 (testimony by same); Salayima, *Dayr Yasin*, pp. 132–133 (testimony by same); MEC GB165-0282/2/4: "Dir Yasin" – interviewee not named; Kfir, "Shalosh," p. 3 (interview with Mordechai Raanan); Interview with Yehuda Lapidot, 24 August 2010. Some of the sources that presented the Arab side of the story, citing Fahima Zaydan, distorted her name to Fahmiyya, and some went even further to turn her into a boy called Fahmi. Among the latter one may find Collins and Lapierre, *O Jerusalem!*, pp. 274–275, Bronstein, *Zokhrot*, pp. 15–16, and Zaru, *Dayr Yasin*, pp. 33–34.

29. Kfir, "Shalosh," p. 3 (interview with Mordechai Raanan); Interview with Yehuda Lapidot, 24 August 2010; Yellin-Mor, *Lohamey*, p. 471 (denying the entire incident); Khalidi, *Dayr Yasin*, p. 73 (testimony by Zaynab 'Atiyya); Assad, *Palestine*, p. 115 (testimony by same); Salayima, *Dayr Yasin*, p. 136 (testimony by same); 'Ubaydu, "Khamsun," p. 15 (interview with same); 'Abd al-Hadi, "Majzarat," p. 10 (testimony by same); Habib Allah, "Majzarat," p. 70; MEC GB165-0282/2/4: "Dir Yasin" – interviewee not named; *Filastin*, 14 April 1948; *Al-Misri*, 12 April 1948, cited in Raday, *Kohot*, p. 103; Kana'na and Zaytawi, *Dayr Yasin*, p. 61.

30. See e.g. McGowan and Hogan, *Saga*, p. 18, and Ami Isseroff, "Deir Yassin: The Conflict as Mass Psychosis," 10 April 2005, www.mideastweb.org/log/archives/00000350.htm. Yehoshua Gorodenchik's testimony is available in JA K4-10/1 and JA 'EG-8/1.

31. Lapidot once asked Gorodenchik about his testimony, and the latter answered that it was distorted. Since he has since passed away, no further explanation can be supplied. E-mail from Yehuda Lapidot to the author, 20 April 2012.

32. JA K4-10/1: testimonies by Yehoshua Gorodenchik and Yehuda Marinburg and unidentified testimony, "Kibush Dir Yasin"; Baruch Nadel, "Siluf History mul Siluf History," *Yedi'ot Aharonot, Tarbut, Sifrut, Amanut* supplement, 30 July 1976, p. 2; Derogy and Saab, *Exodes*, p. 144; IDFA 372/5254/49: Yavne to Tene (D), "Ma'asy ha-Zva'a shel ha-Porshim bi-F'ulat Dir Yasin," 12 April 1948; Bar'el and Shay, "Hazara," p. 23 (interviewing Yoel Kimhi); Zananiri, "Interviews" (interviewing Abu Tawfiq and Muhammad Mahmud Radwan); 'Awawda, "Isra'il Tarfadu" (interview with 'Abd al-Qadir Zaydan); 'Ubaydu, "Khamsun," p. 15 (interview with Zaynab 'Atiyya); Kana'na, "Madhbahat," p. 164; Kana'na and Zaytawi, *Dayr Yasin*, p. 54; Salayima, *Dayr Yasin*, p. 131 (testimony by Muhammad 'Arif Sammur); Silver, *Begin*, p. 94 (citing same); Langer, *Darki*, p. 77; YTA 15-46/183/2: Eliezer [Gicherman] to Tzadiq, Bernhard, Yarkoni and Avraham, "Doh Kibush Dir Yasin," 10 April 1948.

33. Kana'na, "Madhbahat," p. 173; Kana'na and Zaytawi, *Dayr Yasin*, p. 54; 'Arif, *Nakbat*, vol. 1, p. 173; Bregman and Tahri, *Fifty Years*, p. 31 (citing Muhammad Mahmud Radwan); BBC, "50 Years," 13:23 (interview with same); Zananiri, "Interviews" (interviewing same); BUPA: 'Aql, "Haqa'iq Waqi'iyya"; MEC GB165-0282/2/4: "Dir Yasin" – interviewee not named; "Abu Mahmud," p. 8; Salayima, *Dayr Yasin*, pp. 146–147 (testimony by Jamil Ahmad 'Alya); MacGowan and Ellis, *Remembering*, p. 48 (testimony by same); La Guardia, *War*, p. 200 (citing 'Ayish Muhammad 'Ayish Zaydan); BUPA: 'Iyad, "Shuhud 'Iyan" (testimony by wife of Jamil 'Id); 'Ubaydu, "Khamsun," p. 15 (interview with Zaynab 'Atiyya); Bar'el and Shay, "Hazara," p. 23 (interviewing Muhammad 'Arif Sammur); "50 'Aman," p. 12; 'Awawda, *Dhakira*, p. 86 (testimony by Mustafa Hamida); YTA 15-46/183/2: Eliezer to Tzadiq, Bernhard, Yarkoni and Avraham, "Doh Kibush Dir Yasin," 10 April 1948; IDFA 372/5254/49: Yavne to Tene (D), "Ma'asy ha-Zva'a shel ha-Porshim bi-F'ulat Dir Yasin," 12 April 1948; YTA 12-3/9/3: letter, Levy to Begin, 12 April 1971; Kfir, "Shalosh," p. 3 (interview with Mordechai Raanan); Milstein, *History*, vol. 4, p. 379, and *Myth*, p. 93 (interview with Yonah Ben-Sasson); Interview with Yehuda Lapidot, 24 August 2010.

34. Zananiri, "Interviews" (interviewing Muhammad Mahmud Radwan, 'Ali Jabir and Abu Tawfiq); YTA 12-3/43/45: interview with Gideon Sarig.

35. YTA 12-3/43/16: interview with Moshe Eran (Vachman); YTA 15-34/13/5: testimony by same, "Dir Yasin"; YTA 16-12/52/8: testimony by same; YTA 15-46/183/2: testimony by Isser Halamish; Bregman and Tahri, *Fifty Years*, p. 31 (citing Muhammad Mahmud Radwan).

36. LC 3/29: DLP, "Deir Yassin," p. 7; Khalidi, *Dayr Yasin*, p. 79.

37. Ibid., pp. 51, 86; Assad, *Palestine*, pp. 116–117.

38. Khalidi, *Dayr Yasin*, pp. 69–70; Salayima, *Dayr Yasin*, p. 136; Assad, *Palestine*, pp. 109, 119; "Survivor," 8:22.

39. MacGowan and Ellis, *Remembering*, p. 48.

40. Khalidi, *Dayr Yasin*, p. 52; Salayima, *Dayr Yasin*, p. 139; Assad, *Palestine*, p. 122; 'Arif, *Nakbat*, vol. 1, p. 173.

41. Khalidi, *Dayr Yasin*, p. 53; Salayima, *Dayr Yasin*, pp. 109, 136; Hijazi, *Dayr Yasin*, p. 58; Dirbas, "Deir Yassin," 3:26; 'Abd al-Hadi, "Majzarat," pp. 10, 12; "37 'Aman," p. 11.

42. YTA 12-4/16/6: "Hativat Har'el —— Modi'in (Kfarim): Ha-Kfar Dir Yasin" n.d.; Khalidi, *Dayr Yasin*, pp. 52–53; Salayima, *Dayr Yasin*, pp. 136, 139; Assad, *Palestine*, pp. 121–122; "'Aql Yakshifu"; 'Ubaydu, "Khamsun," p. 15.

43. Khalidi, *Dayr Yasin*, p. 75; Salayima, *Dayr Yasin*, p. 138; 'Ubaydu, "Khamsun," p. 15; 'Abd al-Hadi, "Majzarat," p. 12; Gertz, *Da'at*, pp. 203–204; "37 'Aman," p. 11; Assad, *Palestine*, p. 116.

44. Khalidi, *Dayr Yasin*, p. 53; Zananiri, "Interviews"; 'Ubaydu, "Khamsun," p. 15.

45. Khalidi, *Dayr Yasin*, p. 53; 'Abd al-Hadi, "Majzarat," p. 12.

46. Khalidi, *Dayr Yasin*, p. 79; Salayima, *Dayr Yasin*, p. 143; Hijazi, *Dayr Yasin*, pp. 37, 60; 'Abd al-Majid, "Sutur," p. 122; MacGowan and Ellis, *Remembering*, p. 30.

47. Khalidi, *Dayr Yasin*, p. 76.

48. Ibid.

49. *Al-Difa'*, 12 April 1948, p. 4.

50. BUPA: 'Iyad, "Shuhud 'Iyan"; LC 3/29: DLP, "Deir Yassin," p. 6; 'Arif, *Nakbat*, vol. 6, p. 62.

51. BUPA: 'Iyad, "Shuhud 'Iyan"; Kana'na and Zaytawi, *Dayr Yasin*, p. 54; LC 3/29: DLP, "Deir Yassin," p. 6.

52. Zananiri, "Interviews"; BUPA: 'Iyad, "Shuhud 'Iyan."

53. 'Arif, *Nakbat*, vol. 1, p. 173; Kana'na and Zaytawi, *Dayr Yasin*, p. 54; Salayima, *Dayr Yasin*, p. 128; "37 'Aman," p. 11.

54. BUPA: 'Iyad, "Shuhud 'Iyan"; Zananiri, "Interviews"; LC 3/29: DLP, "Deir Yassin," p. 6; Hijazi, *Dayr Yasin*, p. 59.

55. 'Arif, *Nakbat*, vol. 1, p. 173; Kana'na and Zaytawi, *Dayr Yasin*, p. 54; Salayima, *Dayr Yasin*, p. 128; "37 'Aman," p. 11.

56. Kana'na and Zaytawi, *Dayr Yasin*, p. 54; Salayima, *Dayr Yasin*, p. 131; Habib Allah, "Majzarat," p. 70.

57. 'Awawda, *Dhakira*, p. 89; LC 3/29: DLP, "Deir Yassin," p. 7; "37 'Aman," p. 12.

58. Kana'na and Zaytawi, *Dayr Yasin*, p. 54; Zananiri, "Interviews"; Assad, *Palestine*, pp. 116–117.

59. "37 'Aman," p. 12; Zananiri, "Interviews"; Assad, *Palestine*, pp. 116–117.

60. *Al-Difa'*, 12 April 1948, p. 4; Salayima, *Dayr Yasin*, p. 137.

61. Hijazi, *Dayr Yasin*, p. 59; Kana'na and Zaytawi, *Dayr Yasin*, p. 54; 'Arif, *Nakbat*, vol. 6, p. 45; Assad, *Palestine*, pp. 116–117.

62. "37 'Aman," p. 12; Zananiri, "Interviews"; Assad, *Palestine*, pp. 116–117.

63. 'Arif, *Nakbat*, vol. 1, p. 172; Salayima, *Dayr Yasin*, p. 117; 'Awawda, *Dhakira*, p. 86; "37 'Aman," p. 12; PACE 240: interview with 'Ayish Muhammad Zaydan.

64. 'Arif, *Nakbat*, vol. 1, p. 172; Salayima, *Dayr Yasin*, p. 117; 'Awawda, *Dhakira*, p. 86; 'Abd al-Majid, "Sutur," p. 121; "37 'Aman," p. 12; BUPA: 'Iyad, "Shuhud 'Iyan"; Hassuna, "'Alaqat," p. 121; PACE 240: interview with 'Ayish Muhammad Zaydan.

65. 'Arif, *Nakbat*, vol. 1, p. 172; Kana'na and Zaytawi, *Dayr Yasin*, p. 54; Salayima, *Dayr Yasin*, p. 117; 'Awawda, *Dhakira*, p. 86.

66. Assad, *Palestine*, p. 115.

67. Kana'na and Zaytawi, *Dayr Yasin*, p. 54.

68. Hijazi, *Dayr Yasin*, p. 59.

69. Ibid.

70. Ibid.

71. Khalidi, *Dayr Yasin*, p. 77; Hijazi, *Dayr Yasin*, p. 59; Salayima, *Dayr Yasin*, p. 118.

72. Hijazi, *Dayr Yasin*, p. 59.

73. Khalidi, *Dayr Yasin*, p. 69; Assad, *Palestine*, pp. 106–107, 117, 119; "Survivor," 13:30; Matza, *Shney Eqdahim*, p. 50; "Abu Mahmud," p. 8.

74. Khalidi, *Dayr Yasin*, pp. 69–70; Assad, *Palestine*, pp. 104, 109, 119–120; "Survivor," 8:22.

75. Kanaʻna and Zaytawi, *Dayr Yasin*, p. 54; Zananiri, "Interviews"; Barʼel and Shay, "Hazara," p. 25; IDFA 372/5254/49: Yavne to Tene (D), "Maʻasy ha-Zvaʻa shel ha-Porshim bi-Fʻulat Dir Yasin," 12 April 1948.

76. LC 3/29: DLP, "Deir Yassin," p. 9.

77. Khalidi, *Dayr Yasin*, p. 76.

78. PACE 240: interview with ʻAyish Muhammad Zaydan.

79. Khalidi, *Dayr Yasin*, p. 76.

80. Ibid., p. 77.

81. Ibid., p. 76.

82. Ibid., p. 75.

83. Ibid.; Salayima, *Dayr Yasin*, p. 27 (according to him, killed by a hand grenade); "37 ʻAman," p. 11.

84. Kanaʻna and Zaytawi, *Dayr Yasin*, p. 54.

85. LC 3/29: DLP, "Deir Yassin," p. 11.

86. ACICR B G 59/I/GC, file 17: letter JdR/JM 29, de Reynier to Comité International de la Croix-Rouge, 13 April 1948; LC 2/1: de Reynier's diary, 11 April 1948, p. 86; LC 3/29: testimony by Jacques de Reynier; Khalidi, *Dayr Yasin*, pp. 70, 97; Salayima, *Dayr Yasin*, p. 197; Assad, *Palestine*, p. 118.

87. LC 3/29: DLP, "Deir Yassin," p. 11.

88. Khalidi, *Dayr Yasin*, p. 50.

89. Ibid.; Kanaʻna and Zaytawi, *Dayr Yasin*, p. 54.

90. ʻAwawda, *Dhakira*, p. 91.

91. Kanaʻna and Zaytawi, *Dayr Yasin*, p. 54; LC 3/29: DLP, "Deir Yassin," p. 6; Igbariyyeh, "60th Anniversary."

92. Kanaʻna and Zaytawi, *Dayr Yasin*, p. 55; Hijazi, *Dayr Yasin*, p. 62; Salayima, *Dayr Yasin*, p. 132; Assad, *Palestine*, p. 115.

93. Ibid.

94. Salayima, *Dayr Yasin*, p. 132; Silver, *Begin*, p. 94; PACE 240: interview with ʻAyish Muhammad Zaydan.

95. Kanaʻna and Zaytawi, *Dayr Yasin*, p. 54; Zananiri, "Interviews"; PACE 240: interview with ʻAyish Muhammad Zaydan.

96. Asʻad, *Filastin*, p. 120.

97. Kana'na and Zaytawi, *Dayr Yasin*, p. 54; Hijazi, *Dayr Yasin*, p. 62; Salayima, *Dayr Yasin*, p. 132; Assad, *Palestine*, p. 115.

98. YTA 12-4/16/6: "Hativat Har'el – Modi'in (Kfarim): Ha-Kfar Dir Yasin" n.d.; Assad, *Palestine*, p. 115.

99. *Filastin*, 14 April 1948.

100. Hijazi, *Dayr Yasin*, pp. 61–62.

101. Kana'na, "Madhbahat," p. 174. See also Hogan, "1948 Massacre," p. 330.

102. 'Arif, *Nakbat*, vol. 1, p. 173.

103. Actually, the survivor 'Ayish Muhammad 'Ayish Zaydan (also not an eyewitness; he fled at an early stage), gave exactly that number to the British journalist and writer Anton La Guardia. See La Guardia, *War*, p. 200. La Guardia also cited Kana'na giving data similar to the ones brought here, i.e., 20 to 30 combatants killed and about 60 women, children, and the elderly. Ibid., p. 198.

104. Collins and Lapierre, *O Jerusalem!*, pp. 275–276, based on file 179/110/17/GS: reports, Richard C. Catling to Henry Gurney, 13, 15 and 16 April 1948 (the reports are unavailable in Larry Collins papers at Georgetown University, but Lilly Rivlin, Collins and Lapierre's assistant in the late 1960s, believes that they got them – e-mail from Lilly Rivlin to the author, 22 November 2013); IDFA 372/5254/49: Yavne to Tene (D), "Pe'ulat ha-Porshim be-Dir Yasin," 13 April 1948. See also Katzman, "Mitos," p. B9.

105. Khalidi, *Dayr Yasin*, p. 71 (testimony by Naziha Radwan); Assad, *Palestine*, p. 120 (testimony by same). Idem, *Filastin*, pp. 114, 122, 127, indicated that Jewish women guarded the Arab women and children who had been captured.

106. MEC GB165-0346/4/5: interview with Hazem Nusseibeh; Bregman and Tahri, *Fifty Years*, pp. 32–33 (citing same and Muhammad Mahmud Radwan); BBC, "50 Years," 14:37 (interview with Hazim Nusayba) and 15:10 (interview with Muhammad Mahmud Radwan); Zananiri, "Interviews" (interviewing 'Ali Jabir); PACE 240: interview with 'Ayish Muhammad Zaydan; "50 'Aman," p. 12.

107. MEC GB165-0346/4/5: interview with Hazem Nusseibeh; Bregman and Tahri, *Fifty Years*, p. 33 (citing same); BBC, "50 Years," 15:22 (interview with same); RH MSS. Brit. Emp. s. 527/10/2: interview with Amin Majaj; 'Abd al-Hadi, "Majzarat," pp. 8–9, 15–16 (bringing many testimonies of Palestinian refugee women about this issue). See also Frances S. Hasso, "Modernity and Gender in Arab Accounts of the 1948 and 1967 Defeats," *International Journal of Middle East Studies*, 32:4 (2000), pp. 497–498, and Isabelle Humphries and Laleh Khalili, "Gender of Nakba Memory," in Ahmad H. Sa'di and Lila Abu-Lughod (eds.), *Nakba: Palestine, 1948, and the Claims of Memory* (New York, 2007), p. 212.

108. MEC GB165-0346/4/5: interview with Hazem Nusseibeh; Bregman and Tahri, *Fifty Years*, p. 33, citing same (It is interesting to note, that pro-Etzel and Lehi Golani, *Mitos*, p. 99, brought the same argument as the Nusaybas, why it was impossible for Etzel and Lehi to commit rapes); Zananiri, "Interviews" (interviewing 'Ali Jabir and Muhammad Mahmud Radwan); Holmes, "Deir Yassin" (citing same); 'Awawda, "Majzarat" (interview with same); Silver, *Begin*, p. 95 (citing Muhammad 'Arif Sammur); PACE 241: interview with Muhammad 'Ayish Zaydan; PACE 240: interview with 'Ayish Muhammad Zaydan; PACE 237: interview with Ibtisam Zaydan; Raday, *Kohot*, p. 104 (citing Umm Khalid); 'Abd al-Hadi, "Majzarat," p. 15 (interview with Bahjat Abu Gharbiyya); Bar'el and Shay, "Hazara," p. 25 (citing Anwar Nusayba).

109. Milstein, *History*, vol. 4, p. 371, and *Myth*, p. 70 (interview with Alfred Engel); IDFA 54/500/48: Avigdori and Druyan, "Doh 'al ha-Biqur be-Dir Yasin be-Yom 12.4.1948," 18 April 1948.

110. Hogan, "1948 Massacre," p. 326; Hogan and McGowan, "Anatomy." Also Michael Palumbo, *The Palestinian Catastrophe: The 1948 Expulsion of a People from Their Homeland* (London, [1987] 1989), p. 57, cast doubts regarding the Arab denials of rapes, for the same reasons.

NOTES FOR CHAPTER 7

1. JA 'EB-30/5: interview with Kalman Bergman; JA 'EB-30/6: interview with same; Avner, "Ghosts," p. 14; Silver, *Begin*, p. 90 (citing Yehuda Lapidot); Lapidot, *Lahav*, pp. 309–310, and *Homotayikh*, p. 151; Idem, Letter to the Editor, *ha-Aretz*, 2 February 1998, p. B6; Hovav, *Gal*, p. 78; JA K4-10/1: unidentified testimony, "Kibush Dir Yasin"; MEC GB165-0346/2/24: interview with Ezra Yakhin; Yakhin, *Sipuro*, p. 251; Matza, *Shney Eqdahim*, p. 48; Kurzman, *Genesis*, p. 139.

2. BUPA: 'Aql, "Haqa'iq Waqi'iyya"; Khalidi, *Dayr Yasin*, pp. 71, 77, 86–87 (testimonies by Naziha Radwan, 'Aziza 'Atiyya and Zaynab 'Atiyya); BUPA: 'Iyad, "Shuhud 'Iyan" (testimony by wife of Jamil 'Id); Kana'na and Zaytawi, *Dayr Yasin*, p. 55; Salayima, *Dayr Yasin*, p. 144; "37 'Aman," pp. 10–11 (testimony by Fatima Hamida); Khalidi, *Mudhakkirat*, vol. 2, pp. 263–264, citing report by Nusayba, 10 April 1948; JA 'ER-12/5: interview with Mordechai Raanan; JA 'ER-12/3: testimony by same; Kfir, "Shalosh," p. 3 (interview with same); ISA P-2878/5: interview with Shimon Moneta; Milstein, *History*, vol. 4, p. 366, and *Myth*, p. 63 (interview with Yaffa Badian); JA 'EB-30/5: interview with Kalman Bergman; Interview with Yehuda Lapidot, 24 August 2010; Bar'el and Shay, "Hazara," p. 25 (interviewing Yoel Kimhi); LC 3/29: DLP, "Deir Yassin," p. 10; *Filastin*, 14 April 1948; 'Ubaydu, "Khamsun," p. 15 (interview with Zaynab 'Atiyya); Assad, *Palestine*, pp. 110, 116 (testinony by same), 120 (testimony by

Naziha Radwan); Idem, *Filastin*, p. 127 (testimony by same); Derogy and Saab, *Exodes*, pp. 146–147; Gervasi, *Life*, p. 234.

3. JA 'EB-30/5: interview with Kalman Bergman; MEC GB165-0346/2/14: interview with Shimon Moneta; Bregman and Tahri, *Fifty Years*, p. 32 (citing same); Milstein, *History*, vol. 4, p. 366, and *Myth*, p. 64 (interview with same); JA K4-10/1: testimony by Yehuda Marinburg; Gertz, *Da'at*, p. 198 (interview with Amos Kenan); Levin, *Jerusalem*, p. 57; Kimhi, "Sin'a," p. 21; Banks, *Country*, p. 63 (testimony by Ezra Yakhin); Ben-Ami, "Dir Yasin," p. 5; BUPA: 'Iyad, "Shuhud 'Iyan" (testimony by wife of Jamil 'Id); Khalidi, *Dayr Yasin*, p. 87 (testimony by 'Aziza 'Atiyya); 'Ubaydu, "Khamsun," p. 15 (interview with Zaynab 'Atiyya); Assad, *Palestine*, pp. 110, 116 (testinony by same), 120 (testimony by Naziha Radwan), 123 (testimony by 'Abd al-'Aziz ['Atiyya] 'Aql); *Al-Difa'*, 12 April 1948, p. 1 (citing Husayn al-Khalidi); *Daily Telegraph*, 12 April 1948, p. 1 (citing same); Khalidi, *Mudhakkirat*, vol. 2, p. 261; IDFA 2062/100001/57: letter, Muhsin [surname illegible] (Haifa) to Muhammad Qasim Zuhdi, 18 April 1948; 'Abd al-Hadi, "Majzarat," p. 12 (testimony by Zaynab ['Atiyya] 'Aql); LC 3/29: DLP, "Deir Yassin," p. 10. Yellin-Mor, *Lohamey*, p. 472, theorized that perhaps the ultra-Orthodox Jews of Mea Shearim were the ones to shout at the trucks, in protest against the transgression of the Jewish Sabbath. This could not be the case, both because the trucks did not pass through Mea Shearim but south of it, and because the trucks reached their destination more than an hour before the beginning of the Sabbath.

4. YTA 15-46/183/2: Eliezer [Gicherman] to Tzadiq, Bernhard, Yarkoni and Avraham, "Doh Kibush Dir Yasin," 10 April 1948; Kfir, "Shalosh," p. 3 (interview with Yehoshua Zettler); Banks, *Country*, p. 63 (testimony by Ezra Yakhin); Kimhi, "Sin'a," p. 21; YTA 12-3/45/69: interview with Tzvi Sinai; IDFA 1/150/86: Ben-Nun, "Tizkoret," 9 April 1948; JA 'EB-30/5: interview with Kalman Bergman; Avizohar, *Moriya*, p. 91; Ben-Ami, "Dir Yasin," p. 5; Levin, *Jerusalem*, p. 57; Collins and Lapierre, *O Jerusalem!*, p. 279; YTA 16-12/52/82: interview with Shraga Peled; Pa'il, "Ra'ayonot Anshey Shay," pt. 1, 7:00, (interview with same); Shraga Peled (Stahl), *Sipurim min ha-Arkhiyon* (Tel Aviv, 2006), p. 137; 'Abd al-Hadi, "Majzarat," p. 15 (interview with Bahjat Abu Gharbiyya); IDFA 372/5254/49: letter, S[himon] Shershevski (Bikkur Cholim Hospital, Jerusalem) to Headquarters (Jerusalem), 11 April 1948; Golani, *Mitos*, pp. 63, 87; Milstein, *History*, vol. 4, p. 366, and *Myth*, p. 64; Gabriel Stern, "Ani mi-Dir Yasin," *al ha-Mishmar*, 4 August 1982, p. 8; JA 'ER-12/5: interview with Mordechai Raanan; CO 537/3857: CID, "Summary of Events," 9 April 1948; MEC GB165-0128/1/1: Gurney, *Palestine*, entry for 10 April 1948; Goldstein, *Lehavot*, p. 107; "37 'Aman," p. 11 (testimony by Fatima Hamida); Khalidi, *Mudhakkirat*, vol. 2, p. 264, citing report by Nusayba, 10 April 1948; 'Arif, *Nakbat*, vol. 1, p. 174; Salayima, *Dayr Yasin*, p. 147; LC 3/29: DLP, "Deir Yassin," p. 10.

5.   Kanaʿna and Zaytawi, *Dayr Yasin*, p. 55; Salayima, *Dayr Yasin*, p. 147; JA ʿER-12/3: testimony by Mordechai Raanan; JA ʿER-12/5: interview with same; CO 537/3857: CID, "Summary of Events," 9 April 1948; IDFA 6/2605/49: "Dir Yasin," 9 April 1948; IDFA 355/2644/49: "Tzror Yediʿot ʿArviyot," 9 April 1948; IDFA 18/446/48: Hashmonaʾi to Moriah, "Nispahim le-Rikuz Yediʿot No. 148," 10 April 1948; Abu Gharbiyya, *Khidamm*, p. 222; ʿAbd al-Hadi, "Majzarat," pp. 14–15 (interview with Bahjat Abu Gharbiyya); MEC GB165-0346/4/5: interview with Hazem Nusseibeh; Hazem Zaki Nusseibeh, *Jerusalemites: A Living Memory* (Nicosia, 2009), p. 359; Khalidi, *Mudhakkirat*, vol. 2, pp. 262, 264, citing report by Nusayba, 10 April 1948; "37 ʿAman," p. 11 (testimony by Fatima Hamida); BUPA: ʿAql, "Haqaʾiq Waqiʿiyya"; Ann N. Madsen, *Making Their Own Peace: Twelve Women of Jerusalem* (New York, 2003), pp. 59–60 (citing Hind al-Husayni); Ellen Fleishmann, "Young Women in the City: Mandate Memories," *Jerusalem Quarterly File*, 2 (1998), p. 37 (interview with same); Dirbas, "Deir Yassin," 9:44 (interview with same). One of Husayn al-Khalidi's assertions, later cited in the press, was that the Jews fired over the heads of the released prisoners in order to hurry them to the Arab lines. See *al-Difaʿ*, 12 April 1948, p. 1, *Daily Telegraph*, 12 April 1948, p. 1, and Khalidi, *Mudhakkirat*, vol. 2, p. 261. This story was not corroborated by any of the released prisoners and is highly unlikely, due to the fact they they were released between two British zones.

6.   IDFA 54/500/48: Etzioni [Shaltiel] to Hillel and Diqi, 11 April 1948; Shapira, *David*, p. 140; Paʿil and Yurman, *Mivhan*, p. 333; *Palestine Post*, 11 April 1948, p. 1; *Davar*, 12 April 1948, p. 1; *New York Times*, 11 April 1948, p. 18; *New York Herald Tribune*, 12 April 1948; *Jewish Agency's Digest*, p. 16; Levin, *Jerusalem*, p. 57; JA K4-10/4: identical posters by Etzel and Lehi, "Hodaʿa," April 1948; *Al-Difaʿ*, 11 April 1948, p. 1. For the National Guard, see Tauber, *Military Resistance*, p. 29.

7.   Milstein, *History*, vol. 4, pp. 365–367, and *Myth*, p. 63 (interview with Sarah Peli and testimony by Shimon Moneta); Ben-Tor, *Sefer*, vol. 4, p. 464; YTA 15-46/183/2: Eliezer to Tzadiq, Bernhard, Yarkoni and Avraham, "Doh Kibush Dir Yasin," 10 April 1948; IDFA 372/5254/49: Yavne to Tene (D), "Maʿasy ha-Zvaʿa shel ha-Porshim bi-Fʿulat Dir Yasin," 12 April 1948; Moneta, "Kavana," p. 4; Idem, *Toldot*, p. 63; phone conversation with Shimon Moneta, 7 August 2014; MEC GB165-0346/2/14: interview with same; MacGowan and Ellis, *Remembering*, p. 51; Khalidi, *Mudhakkirat*, vol. 2, p. 264, citing report by Nusayba, 10 April 1948; IDFA 372/5254/49: Yavne to Tene (D), "Peʿulat ha-Porshim be-Dir Yasin," 13 April 1948; Yellin-Mor, *Lohamey*, p. 472 (citing Avraham Ben-Yaakov); CO 537/3857: CID, "Summary of Events," 10 April 1948.

8.   *New York Times*, 10 April 1948, p. 6. See also Khalidi, *All That Remains*, p. 291, and Goldstein, *Lehavot*, p. 107 (78, according to him).

9. JA K4-10/4: identical posters by Etzel and Lehi, "Hoda'a," April 1948; Oren, *Matzor*, p. 51; JA K4-10/1: testimony by Yehuda Marinburg; *Al-Difa'*, 12 April 1948, p. 1 (citing Husayn al-Khalidi); *Daily Telegraph*, 12 April 1948, p. 1 (citing same); John and Hadawi, *Palestine*, vol. 2, p. 328; Khalidi, *Dayr Yasin*, pp. 4, 88; MEC GB165-0128/1/1: Gurney, *Palestine*, entry for 10 April 1948; Hogan, "1948 Massacre," p. 324. In their press conference on Friday evening, the organizations reported 140 prisoners transferred to Arab Jerusalem (see above).

10. JA 'ER-12/3: testimony by Mordechai Raanan; JA 'ER-12/5: interview with same; Abu Gharbiyya, *Khidamm*, p. 222; 'Abd al-Hadi, "Majzarat," p. 14 (interview with Bahjat Abu Gharbiyya). *Filastin*, 11 April 1948, Avizohar, *Moriya*, p. 91, and Gervasi, *Life*, p. 234, also mentioned about 200 prisoners.

11. Interview with Yehuda Lapidot, 24 August 2010. About 120 prisoners were also mentioned by Ofir, *Homot*, p. 60, Hovav, *Gal*, p. 80, Niv, *Ma'arkhot*, vol. 6, p. 85, and Samuel Katz, *Days of Fire* (London, 1968), p. 215.

NOTES FOR CHAPTER 8

1. LC 3/29: testimony by Jacques de Reynier; ACICR B G 59/I/GC, file 17: letter JdR/JM 29, de Reynier to Comité International de la Croix-Rouge, 13 April 1948; LC 2/1: de Reynier's diary, 11 April 1948, pp. 83–84; De Reynier, *Jerusalem*, p. 69; Dominique-D. Junod, *The Imperiled Red Cross and the Palestine–Eretz-Yisrael Conflict 1945–1952* (London and New York, 1996), pp. 128–129, 131; *Al-Difa'*, 12 April 1948, p. 1 (citing Husayn al-Khalidi); *Palestine Post*, 12 April 1948, p. 1 (citing same); *New York Times*, 11 April 1948, p. 18; *New York Herald Tribune*, 12 April 1948; *Filastin*, 13 April 1948; Khalidi, *Mudhakkirat*, vol. 2, p. 266; Hijazi, *Dayr Yasin*, p. 65; JA 'EB-30/5: interview with Kalman Bergman; JA 'EB-30/6: interview with same; Milstein, *History*, vol. 4, pp. 370–371, and *Myth*, p. 69 (interviews with Moshe Barzilai and Alfred Engel); Golani, *Mitos*, pp. 68–69; IDFA 372/5254/49: Nur (City Doctor) to District Commander, "Pe'ulat Hat'anat ha-Gviyot be-Dir Yasin be-Shituf 'im Ba Koah ha-Tzlav ha-Adom ha-beyn Le'umi," 11 April 1948; ISA P-2878/5: interview with Shimon Moneta; Kurzman, *Genesis*, p. 147.

2. ACICR B G 59/I/GC, file 17: letter JdR/JM 29, de Reynier to Comité International de la Croix-Rouge, 13 April 1948; LC 2/1: de Reynier's diary, 11 April 1948, pp. 84–86; LC 3/29: testimony by Jacques de Reynier; De Reynier, *Jerusalem*, pp. 70–72; Milstein, *History*, vol. 4, pp. 370–371, and *Myth*, pp. 68–70 (interviews with Moshe Barzilai, Petahya Selivansky and Alfred Engel); JA 'EB-30/5: interview with Kalman Bergman; JA 'EB-30/6: interview with same; E-mail from Yehuda Lapidot to the author, 24 August 2014; Goldfoot, "I Was There," p. 11; IDFA 372/5254/49: Nur to District Commander, "Pe'ulat Hat'anat ha-Gviyot be-Dir Yasin be-Shituf 'im Ba Koah ha-Tzlav ha-Adom ha-beyn

Le'umi," 11 April 1948, and "Doh shel ha-Rofe she-Yatza le-Dir Yasin," 11 April 1948; *Al-Difa'*, 12 April 1948, p. 1; *Daily Telegraph*, 12 April 1948, p. 1; *New York Herald Tribune*, 12 April 1948; *New York Times*, 12 April 1948, p. 9; Junod, *Red Cross*, p. 129; Ben-Ami, *Years*, p. 443.

3. ACICR B G 59/I/GC, file 17: letter JdR/JM 29, de Reynier to Comité International de la Croix-Rouge, 13 April 1948; LC 2/1: de Reynier's diary, 11 April 1948, p. 86; LC 3/29: testimony by Jacques de Reynier; De Reynier, *Jerusalem*, pp. 73–74; IDFA 372/5254/49: Nur to District Commander, "Pe'ulat Hat'anat ha-Gviyot be-Dir Yasin be-Shituf 'im Ba Koah ha-Tzlav ha-Adom ha-beyn Le'umi," 11 April 1948, and "Doh shel ha-Rofe she-Yatza le-Dir Yasin," 11 April 1948; JA 'EB-30/5: interview with Kalman Bergman; JA 'EB-30/6: interview with same; Khalidi, *Dayr Yasin*, p. 97; Salayima, *Dayr Yasin*, p. 197; Khalidi, *Mudhakkirat*, vol. 2, p. 268; *New York Herald Tribune*, 12 April 1948; International Committee of the Red Cross, *The International Committee of the Red Cross in Palestine* (Geneva, July 1948), p. 12 (a somewhat distorted version made by the president of the Red Cross); Junod, *Red Cross*, pp. 129, 131; Kurzman, *Genesis*, p. 147; Collins and Lapierre, *O Jerusalem!*, p. 278.

4. ACICR B G 59/I/GC, file 17: letter JdR/JM 29, de Reynier to Comité International de la Croix-Rouge, 13 April 1948; LC 2/1: de Reynier's diary, 11 April 1948, p. 86; IDFA 372/5254/49: Nur to District Commander, "Pe'ulat Hat'anat ha-Gviyot be-Dir Yasin be-Shituf 'im Ba Koah ha-Tzlav ha-Adom ha-beyn Le'umi," 11 April 1948; *Al-Difa'*, 12 April 1948, p. 1 (citing Husayn al-Khalidi); Milstein, *History*, vol. 4, p. 371, and *Myth*, p. 69 (interview with Alfred Engel); Lapidot, *Lahav*, p. 313; Interview with Yehuda Lapidot, 24 August 2010; JA 'EB-30/5: interview with Kalman Bergman; ISA P-2878/5: interview with Shimon Moneta; MEC GB165-0346/2/14: interview with same; *New York Times*, 11 April 1948, p. 18; *Palestine Post*, 12 April 1948, p. 1; *Ha-Mashqif*, 11 April 1948, p. 1; CO 537/3857: CID, "Summary of Events," 11 April 1948.

5. ACICR B G 59/I/GC, file 17: letter JdR/JM 29, de Reynier to Comité International de la Croix-Rouge, 13 April 1948; LC 2/1: de Reynier's diary, 11 April 1948, pp. 86–87; De Reynier, *Jerusalem*, p. 74; *Al-Difa'*, 12 April 1948, p. 1 (citing Husayn al-Khalidi); *New York Times*, 12 April 1948, p. 9 (citing same); Khalidi, *Mudhakkirat*, vol. 2, p. 268; JA 'EB-30/5: interview with Kalman Bergman; JA 'EB-30/6: interview with same; Interview with Yehuda Lapidot, 24 August 2010; Graves, *Experiment*, p. 179 (entry for 15 April 1948); Junod, *Red Cross*, p. 131.

6. ACICR B G 59/I/GC, file 17: letter JdR/JM 29, de Reynier to Comité International de la Croix-Rouge, 13 April 1948; LC 2/1: de Reynier's diary, 11 April 1948, pp. 87–88; De Reynier, *Jerusalem*, pp. 74–75; IDFA 372/5254/49: Nur to District Commander, "Pe'ulat Hat'anat ha-Gviyot be-Dir Yasin be-Shituf 'im Ba Koah ha-Tzlav ha-Adom ha-beyn Le'umi," 11 April 1948; Milstein, *History*, vol. 4, p. 372, and *Myth*, p. 71 (interviews with Moshe Barzilai and Shimon Moneta); ISA P-2878/5: interview with same; MEC GB165-0346/2/14: interview

with same; Moneta, *Toldot*, p. 63; Lapidot, *Lahav*, p. 313; Golani, *Mitos*, p. 69; Junod, *Red Cross*, p. 129.

7. IDFA 54/500/48: Avigdori and Druyan, "Doh 'al ha-Biqur be-Dir Yasin be-Yom 12.4.1948," 18 April 1948; Avigdori-Avidov, *Derekh*, p. 90; Lapidot, *Lahav*, pp. 316–317, and *Homotayikh*, pp. 156–157; Interview with Yehuda Lapidot, 24 August 2010; Milstein, *History*, vol. 4, p. 374, and *Myth*, p. 75 (testimony by same); LC 3/29: testimony by same; Regev-Yarkoni and Regev, *Lohem*, p. 137; "Dir Yasin – Kol ha-Emet," p. 18 (citing Petahya Selivansky); Milstein, "Dir Yasin," p. 19; Golani, *Mitos*, p. 69; Shapira, *David*, p. 140; Goldstein, *Lehavot*, p. 107. Etzel and Lehi mentioned Avigdori's words in the identical poster they circulated after the affair. See JA K4-10/4: posters by Etzel and Lehi, "Hoda'a 'al Parashat Dir Yasin," [14] April 1948.

8. LC 2/1: de Reynier's diary, 16 April 1948, p. 92; De Reynier, *Jerusalem*, p. 75; LC 3/29: testimony by Jacques de Reynier; IDFA 148/5254/49: Yeshurun [Schiff] to District Commander, 14 April 1948, and note, 16 April 1948.

9. De Reynier, *Jerusalem*, pp. 75–76; LC 2/1: de Reynier's diary, 16 April 1948, p. 92; Kurzman, *Genesis*, p. 147; Golani, *Mitos*, pp. 70–71; "Dir Yasin – Kol ha-Emet," p. 18 (citing Petahya Selivansky); Ben-Ami, *Years*, p. 443.

10. ACICR B G 59/I/GC, file 17: letter JdR/JM 29, de Reynier to Comité International de la Croix-Rouge, 13 April 1948, and letter 42, D[avid] de Traz to de Reynier, 30 April 1948.

11. YTA 12-3/9/3: Gichon, "Parashat Dir Yasin Tashah"; Gichon, *Mate*, p. 252; Milstein, *History*, vol. 4, pp. 367–369, and *Myth*, pp. 65–66, 68 (interviews with Mordechai Gichon and Mordechai Raanan); LC 3/29: testimony by Yeshurun Schiff [no. 2]; JA 'ER-12/5: interview with Mordechai Raanan; Silver, *Begin*, p. 90 (citing Yehuda Lapidot); Katzman, "Mitos," p. B9; Gervasi, *Life*, p. 234; MacGowan and Ellis, *Remembering*, p. 51.

12. ACICR B G 59/I/GC, file 17: letter JdR/JM 29, de Reynier to Comité International de la Croix-Rouge, 13 April 1948; LC 2/1: de Reynier's diary, 11 April 1948, pp. 86–87; IDFA 372/5254/49: Nur to District Commander, "Pe'ulat Hat'anat ha-Gviyot be-Dir Yasin be-Shituf 'im Ba Koah ha-Tzlav ha-Adom ha-beyn Le'umi," 11 April 1948, and Yavne to Tene (D), "Pe'ulat ha-Porshim be-Dir Yasin," 13 April 1948; MEC GB165-0346/2/14: interview with Shimon Moneta; ISA P-2878/5: interview with same; Milstein, *History*, vol. 4, pp. 370, 372, and *Myth*, p. 71 (interview with same); Moneta, "Kavana," p. 4; Idem, *Toldot*, pp. 62–63; Vered, *Yerushalayim*, p. 113; Lapidot, *Lahav*, p. 313; Interview with Yehuda Lapidot, 24 August 2010; *Al-Difa'*, 12 April 1948, p. 1 (citing Husayn al-Khalidi); *Daily Telegraph*, 12 April 1948, p. 4 (citing same); Khalidi, *Mudhakkirat*, vol. 2, p. 268; IDFA 59/500/48: "Tzror Yedi'ot 'Araviyot Musmakhot," 11 April 1948; IDFA 355/2644/49: "Tzror Yedi'ot 'Araviyot," 12 April

1948; IDFA 2/2605/49: Hashmonaʾi to Moriah, "Nispahim le-Rikuz Yediʿot No. 162," 12 April 1948.

13. Moneta, "Kavana," p. 4; Idem, *Toldot*, p. 63; ISA P-2878/5: interview with Shimon Moneta; MEC GB165-0346/2/14: interview with same; Gertz, *Daʾat*, p. 200 (interview with same); JA K4-10/1: testimony by Yehuda Marinburg; JA ʿEG-28/1: testimony by David Gottlieb; JA ʿEG-28/2: testimony by same; Milstein, *History*, vol. 4, pp. 372–373, and *Myth*, pp. 71–73 (interviews with Moshe Barzilai, Doron Hisday and Baruch Sarel); JA ʿEA-37/1: interview with Yehoshua Arieli; IDFA 54/500/48: Avigdori and Druyan, "Doh ʿal ha-Biqur be-Dir Yasin be-Yom 12.4.1948," 18 April 1948; Golani, *Mitos*, p. 70; Wadiʿ ʿAwawda, "Israʾil Tuwasilu al-Takattum ʿala Majzarat Dayr Yasin," *al-Jazira Net*, 9 April 2008, www.palestineremembered.com/Jerusalem/Dayr-Yasin/Story9260.html; Katzman, "Mitos," p. B9 (citing Doron Hisday); Hassida Paʿil, "Parashat Dir Yasin, Yom Shishi 9/4/48, Raʾayonot ʿim Gadnaʿim 60 Shana Aharey," 2008, pt. 1, 4:38 and 5:52, www.meirpail.co.il (interviews with Eliezer Shmueli and Yair Tzaban); Dalia Karpel, "Zikhronot mi-Dir Yasin," *ha-Aretz*, supplement, 12 August 2011, p. 34 (interview with same); MEC GB165-0346/3/19: interview with same; Amir, *Gadnaʿ*, p. 50; LC 2/1: de Reynier's diary, 16 April 1948, p. 92; LC 3/29: testimony by Jacques de Reynier; Levin, *Jerusalem*, p. 59.

14. *Al-Difaʿ*, 12 April 1948, p. 1 (citing Husayn al-Khalidi), also cited by Kanaʿna and Zaytawi, *Dayr Yasin*, p. 56; *Daily Telegraph*, 12 April 1948, p. 1; *New York Herald Tribune*, 12 April 1948. Among the survivors, one may find Muhammad Mahmud Radwan, ʿAli Jabir and Muhammad ʿAyish Zaydan, the first two in Zananiri, "Interviews," the second also in ʿAwawda, *Dhakira*, p. 89, and the third in PACE 241. Among the authors who brought this story, one may count Hijazi, *Dayr Yasin*, p. 65, ʿAwawda, *Dhakira*, p. 84, Zaru, *Dayr Yasin*, p. 34, Salayima, *Dayr Yasin*, p. 145, *Dayr Yasin: Ramz Falsafat al-Sahyuniyya*, p. 6, and LC 3/29: DLP, "Deir Yassin," p. 1. For the Haganah testimonies, see YTA 12-3/43/45: interview with Gideon Sarig, and Rubinstein, "Sheʾela," p. B2.

15. MEC GB165-0072/3/3: tel. 956, High Commissioner for Palestine to Secretary of State, 13 April 1948, and tel. 1023, same to same, 17 April 1948; UNISPAL: letter, J[ohn] Fletcher-Cooke (United Kingdom Delegation to the United Nations, New York) to Ralph J. Bunche (Principal Secretary to the United Nations Palestine Commission, Lake Success), 20 April 1948; WO 275/64: "Fortnightly Intelligence Newsletter No. 66," by HQ British Troops in Palestine, 21 April 1948; MEC GB165-0128/1/1: Gurney, *Palestine*, entries for 14 and 15 April 1948; Lever, *Jerusalem*, p. 171; Golani, *Natziv*, p. 258; Idem, *The End of the British Mandate for Palestine, 1948: The Diary of Sir Henry Gurney* (Basingstoke, 2009), pp. 105–106.

16. *Hansard* (London), 12 April 1948, cols. 626–630; *Palestine Post*, 13 April 1948, p. 3; *Davar*, 13 April 1948, p. 1; *Al-Difaʿ*, 13 April 1948, p. 1; *Filastin*, 13 April 1948.

17. MEC GB165-0072/3/3: tel. 966, High Commissioner for Palestine to Secretary of State, 13 April 1948, and tel. 1023, same to same, 17 April 1948; LC 3/29: testimonies by Alan Cunningham, [Gordon] MacMillan, Splosh Jones and James Pollock; RH MSS. Brit. Emp. s. 527/10/2: interview with Gordon MacMillan; AIR 23/8350: "Report on the Evacuation of the Royal Air Force from Palestine," by W[alter] L. Dawson (Air Officer Commanding, Levant), [sent on 6 October 1948], pp. 9–10; MEC GB165-0128/1/1: Gurney, *Palestine*, entry for 13 April 1948; Brian Cull, Shlomo Aloni and David Nicolle, *Spitfires over Israel* (London, [1994]), pp. 106–107; Collins and Lapierre, *O Jerusalem!*, p. 279; Golani, *Mitos*, p. 75.

18. YTA 12-3/41/14: interview with Moshe Edelstein; Yakhin, *Sipuro*, p. 259; JA 'EB-30/5: interview with Kalman Bergman; Goldstein, *Lehavot*, p. 109; JA K4-10/4: posters by Etzel and Lehi, "Hoda'a 'al Parashat Dir Yasin," [14] April 1948; JA K4-10/2: "Parashat Dir Yasin"; Lapidot, *Lahav*, p. 314, and *Homotayikh*, p. 155; Niv, *Ma'arkhot*, vol. 6, p. 85.

19. RH MSS. Brit. Emp. s. 527/10/2: interview with Gordon MacMillan; LC 3/29: testimonies by same and James Pollock; AIR 23/8350: "Report on the Evacuation of the Royal Air Force from Palestine," by Dawson, [sent on 6 October 1948], p. 10; IWM 06/43/1: "Diary as M[ilitary] A[ssistant] to HE the High Commissioner of Palestine. Covering the period from 10th April to 14th May, 1948" (Government House, Jerusalem), by Peter F. Towers-Clarck, entry for 13 April 1948; MEC GB165-0072/3/3: tel. 966, High Commissioner for Palestine to Secretary of State, 13 April 1948, and tel. 1023, same to same, 17 April 1948; Goldstein, *Lehavot*, p. 109; JA K4-10/4: posters by Etzel and Lehi, "Hoda'a 'al Parashat Dir Yasin," [14] April 1948; MEC GB165-0128/1/1: Gurney, *Palestine*, entries for 13 and 14 April 1948; *Davar*, 14 April 1948, p. 2; *Jewish Agency's Digest*, p. 16; Cull, Aloni and Nicolle, *Spitfires*, p. 107; Kurzman, *Genesis*, p. 148; Collins and Lapierre, *O Jerusalem!*, p. 279; JA K4-10/2: "Parashat Dir Yasin"; Golani, *Mitos*, p. 75.

20. IWM 06/43/1: "Diary as MA to HE the High Commissioner of Palestine," by Towers-Clarck, entry for 13 April 1948; Graves, *Experiment*, p. 179 (entry for 15 April 1948); FO 371/68504/E4827: Draft Parliamentary Question and Answer for Written Reply (by Hector McNeil), 16 April 1948 [delivered on 19 April 1948].

21. JA 'ER-12/5: interview with Mordechai Raanan; JA 'ER-12/1: testimony by same; Milstein, *History*, vol. 4, pp. 368–369, and *Myth*, pp. 66–68 (interview with same); Kfir, "Shalosh," p. 3 (interview with same); Banks, *Country*, p. 58 (testimony by Meir Pa'il); YTA 15-34/13/5: testimony by same, "Dir Yasin"; JA H13-3/48/4: case against Nathan Friedman-Yellin and Matityahu Shmuelevitz in the special military court, Protocol IV, 7 January 1949, p. 1400 (testimony by David Shaltiel); IDFA 372/5254/49: Yavne to Tene (D), "Pe'ulat Etzel ve-Lehi be-Dir Yasin," 12 April 1948; JA K4-13/8: broadcast of *Kol Zion ha-Lohemet*, 11

April 1948; Golani, *Mitos*, pp. 72–73; Ofir, *Homot*, p. 61; Ben-Tor, *Sefer*, vol. 4, p. 465; Kurzman, *Genesis*, p. 147.

22. IDFA 372/5254/49: Yavne to Tene (D), "Pe'ulat Etzel ve-Lehi be-Dir Yasin," 12 April 1948, and same to same, "Pe'ulat ha-Porshim be-Dir Yasin," 13 April 1948; JA 'ER-12/5: interview with Mordechai Raanan; JA K4-10/1: testimonies by Yehuda Lapidot and Yehoshua Gorodenchik; Lapidot, *Homotayikh*, pp. 153, 155, and *Lahav*, p. 314; Banks, *Country*, p. 62 (testimony by Ezra Yakhin); JA 'EB-30/5: interview with Kalman Bergman; ISA P-2878/5: interview with Shimon Moneta; Moneta, "Kavana," p. 4; Idem, *Toldot*, pp. 62–63; Ofir, *Tirat*, p. 281; Arbel, "Hayiti," p. 20; YTA 15-34/13/5: testimony by Meir Pa'il, "Dir Yasin"; Milstein, *History*, vol. 4, p. 372, and *Myth*, p. 72 (testimony by Petahya Selivansky); Golani, *Mitos*, p. 73.

23. "Jacob Shafrir" [Shapira], pt. 1, 1:16; Yaakov Shafrir, Letter to the Editor, *ha-Aretz*, 9 February 1998, p. B6; JA 'EA-37/1: interview with Yehoshua Arieli; Milstein, *History*, vol. 4, pp. 372–373, and *Myth*, pp. 72–73 (interviews with same and Doron Hisday); MEC GB165-0346/3/19: interview with Yair Tzaban; Pa'il, "Ra'ayonot Gadna'im," pt. 1, 2:10 and 3:00 (interviews with Eliezer Shmueli and Yair Tzaban); Karpel, "Zikhronot," p. 34 (interview with same); Amir, *Gadna'*, pp. 48, 68; David Dayan, *Ken, Anahnu No'ar! Sefer Toldot ha-Gadna'* (Tel Aviv, 1977), p. 120 (testimony by Tzvi Ankori); Pail and Isseroff, "Deir Yassin"; MacGowan and Ellis, *Remembering*, p. 38 (interview with Meir Pa'il); Banks, *Country*, p. 58 (testimony by same); Shapira, *David*, p. 141; Ben-Ami, "Dir Yasin," p. 5.

24. "Jacob Shafrir," pt. 1, 7:52, and pt. 2, 0:01; IDFA 417/2644/49: [Zion] Eldad to District Commander, "Ha-Porshim be-Dir Yasin," enclosing copy of letter from Oded, 12 April 1914, and Yeshurun [Schiff] to Eldad, "Ha-Porshim be-Dir Yasin," April 1948; Milstein, *History*, vol. 4, p. 373, and *Myth*, p. 73 (report by the military police); YTA 12-3/41/14: interview with Moshe Edelstein; JA K4-10/1: testimony by Yehuda Marinburg; "60 Sha'ot," p. 37; *Davar*, 13 April 1948, p. 2; Golani, *Mitos*, p. 73; Ben-Tor, *Sefer*, vol. 4, p. 465.

25. JA 'EA-37/1: interview with Yehoshua Arieli; LC 3/29: testimony by same; Milstein, *History*, vol. 4, pp. 374–375, and *Myth*, pp. 75–76 (interviews with same, Tzvi Ankori, Doron Hisday and Petahya Selivansky); Dayan, *Ken*, p. 121 (testimony by Tzvi Ankori); Pa'il, "Ra'ayonot Gadna'im," pt. 1, 5:03 and 6:25 (interviews with Eliezer Shmueli and Yair Tzaban); Karpel, "Zikhronot," p. 34 (interview with same); MEC GB165-0346/3/19: interview with same; Interview with Yehuda Lapidot, 24 August 2010; LC 3/29: testimony by same; JA K4-10/1: testimony by same; JA 'EB-48/1: interview with Yaffa Badian; IDFA 372/5254/49: Yavne to Tene (D), "Anshey Etzel ve-Lehi ba-Kfar Dir Yasin be-12.4.48," 13 April 1948; Golani, *Mitos*, p. 74; Ben-Ami, *Years*, pp. 442–443; Ben-Tor, *Sefer*, vol. 4, p. 465; Amir, *Gadna'*, p. 48.

26. LC 3/29: testimonies by Yeshurun Schiff [no. 2] and [Yehuda] Lapidot; Milstein, *History*, vol. 4, p. 375, and *Myth*, p. 76 (interview with Yeshurun Schiff); JA K4-10/1: testimony by Yehuda Lapidot; MEC GB165-0346/2/24: interview with Ezra Yakhin; Banks, *Country*, p. 63 (testimony by same); JA 'EB-48/1: interview with Yaffa Badian; Pa'il, "Ra'ayonot Gadna'im," pt. 1, 6:25 (interview with Yair Tzaban); Collins and Lapierre, *O Jerusalem!*, pp. 279–280; Amir, *Gadna'*, p. 49.

27. Ibid., pp. 49–50; MEC GB165-0346/3/19: interview with Yair Tzaban; Pa'il, "Ra'ayonot Gadna'im," pt. 1, 7:38, 8:00, 11:20 and 12:36 (interviews with same and Eliezer Shmueli); JA 'EA-37/1: interview with Yehoshua Arieli; LC 3/29: testimony by same; Yaron London, "Al Tivki America," *Yedi'ot Aharonot*, 14 February 1992, 7 *Yamim* Saturday's supplement, pp. 27, 29 (interview with same); Milstein, *History*, vol. 4, pp. 375–376, and *Myth*, pp. 77–78 (interviews with same and Hillel Politi); "Jacob Shafrir," pt. 2, 3:55; Yaakov Shafrir, Letter to the Editor, *ha-Aretz*, 9 February 1998, p. B6; YTA 12-3/90/8: interview with Shlomo Dinur; Ben-Ami, "Dir Yasin," p. 5 (testimony by Nisan Harpaz); LC 2/1: de Reynier's diary, 16 April 1948, p. 92; *Jewish Agency's Digest*, p. 16.

28. Amir, *Gadna'*, p. 51; MEC GB165-0346/3/19: interview with Yair Tzaban; Pa'il, "Ra'ayonot Gadna'im," pt. 1, 13:57 (interview with same); Gertz, *Da'at*, p. 200 (report by same and interview with Nissim Toucatly); JA 'EA-37/1: interview with Yehoshua Arieli; *Davar*, 14 April 1948, p. 2.

NOTES FOR CHAPTER 9

1. IDFA 584/4944/49: Company Commander (4th Company, 6th Battalion) to Jerusalem's District Commander, "Doh Dir Yasin," 11 April 1948.

2. YTA 15-46/183/2: Eliezer [Mordechai Gicherman] to Tzadiq, Bernhard, Yarkoni and Avraham [Meir Pilavsky], "Doh Kibush Dir Yasin," 10 April 1948; YTA 12-3/9/3: Mordechai Gichon, "Parashat Dir Yasin Tashah," enclosed with letter by Gichon, 29 December 1992; Gichon, *Mate*, p. 253. The report was forwarded, almost verbatim, to the political department of the Haganah's intelligence service by Yitzhak Levy, the commander of Haganah intelligence in Jerusalem: IDFA 372/5254/49: Yavne to Tene (D), "Doh Kibush Dir Yasin," 13 April 1948. A slightly censored version of the report (for example, it lacked the concluding recommendation) was later distributed by the Haganah in a special booklet on the affair it prepared for its soldiers, about which see below.

3. HA 20/253: Avraham [Meir Pilavsky] to District Commander, "Pe'ulat ha-Porshim be-Dir Yasin," 10 April 1948; MacGowan and Ellis, *Remembering*, pp. 40, 44–45 (interview with Meir Pa'il).

4. HA 20/253: The Haganah's Operations Branch – Intelligence Officer, "Ha-Nadon: Leqah Pe'ulat Dir Yasin," 12 April 1948; Yonah Cohen, *Yerushalayim ba-Matzor* (Tel Aviv, 1976), pp. 84–85; Avrahami, "Ruhot," p. 13.

5. IDFA 372/5254/49: Yavne [Yitzhak Levy] to Tene (D), "Ma'asy ha-Zva'a shel ha-Porshim bi-F'ulat Dir Yasin," 12 April 1948 (based on "Ram"), same to same, "Pe'ula Meshutefet shel ha-Porshim bi-Yerushalayim," 12 April 1948 (based on "Esther"), and same to same, "Pe'ulat ha-Porshim be-Dir Yasin," 13 April 1948 (based on "Esther"). See Regev-Yarkoni and Regev, *Lohem*, p. 138, also claiming that while Lehi operated professionally, Etzel "crumbled" at the beginning of the attack, resulting in both organizations being dragged through the mire and Lehi paying for Etzel's "sins."

6. IDFA 372/5254/49: Yavne to Tene (D), "Pe'ulat Etzel ve-Lehi be-Dir Yasin," 12 April 1948 (based on "Esther," "Ram" and "Yigal").

7. JA K4-13/8: broadcast of *Kol Zion ha-Lohemet*, 11 April 1948, and poster summarizing the broadcast; Cohen, *Yerushalayim*, p. 84; IDFA 29/5440/49: tel., Diqi [Arnan Azaryahu] to Etzioni [Shaltiel], 10 April 1948; IDFA 54/500/48: tel., Etzioni to Hillel [Yisrael Galili] and Diqi, 11 April 1948; *Ha-Mashqif*, 11 April 1948, pp. 1, 3; *Ha-Boqer*, 11 April 1948, pp. 1, 4; *Ha-Aretz*, 11 April 1948, pp. 1–2; *Davar*, 12 April 1948, p. 1; *New York Times*, 11 April 1948, p. 18; Shapira, *David*, p. 140; Pa'il and Yurman, *Mivhan*, p. 333; IDFA 291/922/75: testimony 72 by Yitzhak Levy.

8. IDFA 372/5254/49: "Hatza'at Hoda'a be-Qesher le-Dir Yasin," by [Eliyahu] Sasson, n.d.; HA 20/240: "Hoda'at ha-Hagana 'al Parashat Dir Yasin" (Jerusalem), 12 April 1948; JA K4-10/5: same as poster; *Davar*, 12 April 1948, p. 1, and 13 April 1948, p. 2; *Ha-Aretz*, 12 April 1948, p. 1; *Palestine Post*, 13 April 1948, p. 3; *'Iton ha-Magen*, no. 1, 16 April 1948; *Jewish Agency's Digest*, pp. 17–18; *New York Times*, 13 April 1948, p. 7; Pa'il, "Ra'ayonot Gadna'im," pt. 1, 1:35 (interview with Yair Tzaban); MEC GB165-0346/3/19: interview with same. Goldstein, *Lehavot*, p. 108, claimed that Ben-Gurion pressured Shaltiel to issue the statement. It should be noted that most senior British officials were unconvinced by the Haganah denial of its men's participation. See MEC GB165-0072/3/3: tel. 956, High Commissioner for Palestine to Secretary of State, 13 April 1948 ("the usual notices of condemnation which however deceive nobody"); WO 275/64: "Fortnightly Intelligence Newsletter No. 66," by HQ British Troops in Palestine, 21 April 1948; IDFA 355/2644/49: "Tzror Yedi'ot 'Araviyot," 14 April 1948; HA 105/54a: Yavne to Tene, 15 April 1948.

9. JA K4-10/4: identical posters by Etzel and Lehi, "Hoda'a," April 1948 (an original Lehi poster is available in IDFA, large posters collection, no. 15040, and posters collection, no. 3194); "Parashat Dir Yasin," *Esh*, no. 8, 15 April 1948, p. 5; *Jewish Agency's Digest*, p. 18. Etzel and Lehi's broadcasting stations also broadcast the contents of the poster, and the one following it (see below). Ben-Tor, *Sefer*, vol. 4, p. 471.

10. JA K4-10/4: identical posters by Etzel and Lehi, "Hoda'a 'al Parashat Dir Yasin," [14] April 1948 (original Etzel and Lehi posters are available in IDFA, large

posters collection, nos. 15035 and 15043); IDFA 1/5440/49: Yavne to Tene, 14 April 1948; JA 'ER-12/5: interview with Mordechai Raanan. Kaufman used the copy of Shaltiel's letter to Zettler for the poster, which he had in hand (his own copy had already been archived). See "Pe'ulat Dir Yasin Butz'a bi-Yedi'ato shel ha-Aluf Sha'alti'el," *Herut*, 24 April 1953, p. 8.

11. JA K4-10/4: poster by Etzel, "Tuqa' ha-Tzvi'ut," April 1948 (an original Etzel poster is available in IDFA, large posters collection, no. 15034); JA K4-13/8: broadcast of *Kol Zion ha-Lohemet*, 14 April 1948; JA K'E1-222: *Irgun Press*, vol. 1, no. 7, 10 May 1948, p. 3.

12. MEC GB165-0128/1/1: Gurney, *Palestine*, entry for 19 April 1948; Avraham [Meir Pilavsky], "Dir Yasin ve-Herpoteha," *ba-Mahane*, 5–6, 16 April 1948, p. 1.

13. IDFA 37/481/49: tel. "urgent," Hillel to Etzioni, 14 April 1948; IDFA 24/5440/49: tel., Etzioni to Hillel, 15 April 1948; Tzur, *Shomer*, p. 171; Lapidot, *Lahav*, p. 322, and *Homotayikh*, p. 158; Ofir, *Homot*, p. 64; *Ha-Mashqif*, 22 April 1948, p. 4; YTA 15-46/183/2: Yisraelik to Yisrael [Galili], 8 November 1982, enclosing two notes [by Ben-Gurion] (in YTA 15-22/4/9 there is a remark by Yitzhak Ben-Aharon that the notes are in Ben-Gurion's handwriting).

14. CZA S100: protocols of the executive of the Jewish Agency for Palestine, vol. 53, p. 12534 (meeting of 11 April 1948); CZA S25/4150: "Statement Regarding Deir Yassin," 11 April 1948; *Davar*, 12 April 1948, p. 1; *Palestine Post*, 12 April 1948, p. 1; *Daily Telegraph*, 12 April 1948, p. 1; *New York Times*, 12 April 1948, pp. 1, 9; *New York Herald Tribune*, 12 April 1948; *Jewish Agency's Digest*, pp. 16–17; WO 261/574: "Diary of Events" (HQ Palestine), May 1948 (entry for 11 April 1948); FBIS, FRB-48-289, 14 April 1948, pp. II2-II4: Haganah radio in Arabic, 12 April 1948, 13:00.

15. FO 371/68852: letter, Alec Kirkbride (Amman) to B. A. B. Burrows (FO), 15 April 1948; Dan Kurzman, *Ben-Gurion: Prophet of Fire* (New York, 1984), p. 280 (interview with David Ben-Gurion); Bar-Zohar, *Ben-Gurion*, vol. 2, p. 702; Avi Shlaim, *Collusion Across the Jordan: King Abdullah, the Zionist Movement, and the Partition of Palestine* (Oxford, 1988), pp. 164–165; Yoav Gelber, *Jewish-Transjordanian Relations 1921–48* (London, 1997), p. 267; CZA S25/4150: tel. (in Arabic), Jewish Agency to King 'Abdallah (Amman), 12 April 1948; CZA S25/1704: same in Hebrew; CZA S25/9038: tel. (in Arabic), Chief of the Royal Bureau to Jewish Agency (Jerusalem), 12 April 1948; CZA S25/5634: same in Hebrew; *Davar*, 13 April 1948, p. 2, and 15 April 1948, p. 1; *Palestine Post*, 13 April 1948, p. 3; *Jewish Agency's Digest*, p. 17; *Al-Difa'*, 15 April 1948, p. 1; *Filastin*, 15 April 1948; *Al-Jihad*, 17 April 1948; FBIS, FRB-48-290, 15 April 1948, p. II5: radio al-Sharq al-Adna, 14 April 1948, 7:00; FO 816/117: tel. 227, Minister (Amman) to Secretary of State (FO), 16 April 1948; MEC GB165-0072/3/3: tel. 28, same to High Commissioner for Palestine, 16 April 1948; CO 537/3962: "Monthly Situation Report on Transjordan for the Month of April, 1948," by Kirkbride,

4 May 1948. A few days later, 'Abdallah told *al-Ahram* that he considered Deir Yassin a *casus belli* and attached no importance to the Jewish Agency's telegram. Nevertheless, when, in early May, 'Abdallah tried to convince the Palestinians not to leave, he reminded them of the Agency's condemnation of the affair. See Shlaim, *Collusion*, p. 165, Morris, *Revisited*, p. 311, and FBIS, FRB-48-304, 5 May 1948, p. IIı: radio al-Sharq al-Adna, 4 May 1948, 11:00.

16. CZA 25/4147: proclamation by Isaac Herzog and Ben-Zion Uziel, Chief Rabbinate of Palestine (Jerusalem), 12 April 1948; *Palestine Post*, 13 April 1948, p. 3; *Jewish Agency's Digest*, p. 18; *New York Times*, 13 April 1948, p. 7; *Al-Difa'*, 14 April 1948, p. 2; UNISPAL: letter, Fletcher-Cooke to Bunche, 20 April 1948; Regev-Yarkoni and Regev, *Lohem*, p. 136; LC 3/29: testimony by Yehoshua Zettler.

17. Perlmutter, *Life*, pp. 215, 217; Yellin-Mor, *Lohamey*, p. 470; Eldad, *Ma'aser*, pp. 334–335; Marton, *Death*, p. 29 (citing Baruch Nadel).

18. Golani, *Hanhagat*, p. 124; Meir Cohen, "Yerushalayim shel HA," *Bit'on Heyl ha-Avir*, 91 (1973), pp. 75–76; Levy, *Tish'a*, p. 385; Shweki, "Shkhunat."

19. CZA S25/4150: letter, M[artin] Buber, Y[ehoshua] Redler-Feldman (Rabbi Binyamin), D[avid] W[erner] Senator and Y[aakov]. D[avid] Wilhelm (Jerusalem) to the executive of the Jewish Agency, 11 May 1948; ISA G-5559/2: letter, Buber, E[rnst] Simon, Senator and H[aim] Y[ehuda] Roth (Jerusalem) to David Ben Gurion, 6 June 1949, letter, Hannah Baneth (Jerusalem) to secretariat of the prime minister, 27 June 1949, letter, Dorit Rosen (Prime Minister's Bureau) to Baneth, 26 July 1949, letter, Buber to Ben-Gurion (Tel Aviv), 24 July 1949, and letter, Elkana Gali (Secretary to the Prime Minister) to Buber, 1 August 1949.

20. Segev, *1949*, pp. 86–87, 90; CZA S63/51: Z[alman] Mishari (Section for Immigrant Absorption in Settlement) to Settlement Department, "Din ve-Heshbon meha-Matzav ba-Kfar Givat Shaul B (Dir Yasin)," 23 August 1949; Shweki, "Shkhunat"; J[anos A.] Schossberger, "Therapeutic Atmosphere in a Work Village for Mental Patients in Israel," in Jules H. Masserman and J. L. Moreno (eds.), *Progress in Psychotherapy*, vol. 4: *Social Psychotherapy* (New York and London, 1959), pp. 279, 283; MacGowan and Ellis, *Remembering*, p. 49.

21. IDFA 20/1559/52: Nehemia Argov (Military Secretary to the Prime Minister) to M[eir] Kleif (Benefits Officer), 6 February 1951; JA K4-10/9: protocols of the benefits trial (Magistrates Court, Jerusalem), case 89-90-96-92/1951, 1952–1953; IDFA 35/500/48: "Nispah le-Mikhtav 229/41/6 mi-Yom 11.9.52 ba-Nadon: Mishpat Dir Yasin"; IDFA 118/1559/52: Kleif to Michael Avitzur (Bureau Chief of the Chief of the General Staff), 30 September 1952; *Herut*, 1 July 1952, p. 4, 12 August 1952, p. 1, 24 April 1953, p. 4, and 27 May 1953, p. 1.

NOTES FOR CHAPTER 10

1. NARA RG 84, Jerusalem Consulate General Classified Records, 1948 – 800 Palestine, 4: tel. 431, Wasson to Secretary of State, 13 April 1948 (also in *Foreign Relations of the United States, 1948*, Washington DC, 1976, vol. 5, pt. 2, p. 817); LC 3/29: testimony by Dana Adams Schmidt; Schmidt, *Armageddon*, p. 5; Khalidi, *Mudhakkirat*, vol. 2, p. 272; MEC GB165-0346/4/5: interview with Hazem Nusseibeh; *Al-Difa'*, 12 April 1948, p. 1; *Palestine Post*, 12 April 1948, pp. 1–2; *New York Times*, 12 April 1948, pp. 1, 9; *New York Herald Tribune*, 12 April 1948; *Daily Telegraph*, 12 April 1948, pp. 1, 4; *Filastin*, 13 April 1948; *Jewish Agency's Digest*, p. 16.

2. ACICR B G 59/I/GC, file 17: letter JdR/JM 29, de Reynier to Comité International de la Croix-Rouge, 13 April 1948; *Al-Difa'*, 12 April 1948, p. 1; MEC GB165-0346/4/5: interview with Hazem Nusseibeh; Bregman and Tahri, *Fifty Years*, p. 33 (citing same); BBC, "50 Years," 14:37 (interview with same); LC 3/29: testimony by same; "50 'Aman," p. 12; Collins and Lapierre, *O Jerusalem!*, p. 281; Zananiri, "Interviews"; IDFA 355/2644/49: "Tzror Yedi'ot 'Araviyot," 12 April 1948.

3. Bregman and Tahri, *Fifty Years*, pp. 32–33 (citing Muhammad Mahmud Radwan); BBC, "50 Years," 14:18 and 15:10 (interview with same); *Al-Difa'*, 14 April 1948, p. 2; RH MSS. Brit. Emp. s. 527/10/2: interview with Amin Majaj; IDFA 355/2644/49: "Tzror Yedi'ot 'Araviyot," 10 April 1948; IDFA 6/2605/49: "Dir Yasin," 11 April 1948 (mentioning the Arab photographer 'Ali Za'rur); IDFA 372/5254/49: Yavne to Tene (A), "Totz'ot Dir Yasin," 12 April 1948; Hanna Safieh, *A Man and His Camera: Photographs of Palestine 1927–1967* (Jerusalem, 1999), p. 9 (claiming that the photographer Hanna Safiya arrived there the day after); Yoram Nimrod, "Golda Meir beyn Ben-Gurion ve-'Abdallah: Shtey Pgishot Shney Dgeshim Halifiyim," in Yosef Nevo and Yoram Nimrod (eds.), *Ha-'Aravim el mul ha-Tnu'a ha-Tziyonit veha-Yishuv ha-Yehudi 1946–1950* (Oranim, 1987), p. 83. It is highly unlikely that Arabs from the outside would come to Deir Yassin while Etzel and Lehi were still there.

4. *Al-Difa'*, 12 April 1948, p. 1, and 13 April 1948, p. 1; *Palestine Post*, 12 April 1948, p. 1; *Davar*, 13 April 1948, p. 2; *Jewish Agency's Digest*, p. 16; Khalidi, *Mudhakkirat*, vol. 1, p. 42, and vol. 2, pp. 284–286, 290; NARA M1390, Records of the Department of State Relating to Internal Affairs of Palestine, 1945–1949 – 867N.01, roll 14: dispatch A-184, [Robert] Memminger (Damascus) to Secretary of State, 13 April 1948; See also www.khalidilibrary.org/others.html.

5. "Jarima Wahshiyya Yaftariquha al-Yahud fi Dayr Yasin," *al-Difa'*, 11 April 1948, pp. 1, 4; "Faza'i' al-Yahud bi-Dayr Yasin Taqsha'irru li-Bisha'atiha al-Abdan," *al-Difa'*, 11 April 1948, pp. 1, 4; "250 Dahiyya Mu'zamuha min al-Nisa' wal-Atfal Yaftuku biha al-Junat al-Yahud fi Madhbahat al-Abriya' al-Barbariyya bi-Qaryat Dar Yasin," *al-Difa'*, 12 April 1948, p. 1; "Ayyuha al-'Arab: Laqad

Sharrad al-Yahud Nisa'akum wa-Atfalakum fa-la Tasamuha ba'da al-Yawm wa-la Ighda'a ma'a Ashbah al-Rijal al-Ra'adid al-Jubana'," *Filastin*, 11 April 1948; "Dumu' al-Tamasih!?," *Filastin*, 13 April 1948; "Faza'i' al-Barabira fi Dayr Yasin: Kanu Yanhabuna al-Zaytun wa-Yutlifuna wa-Yusawwiruna al-Nisa'!," *Filastin*, 14 April 1948.

6. *Al-Difa'*, 11 April 1948, pp. 1, 4, and 12 April 1948, p. 1; *Filastin*, 11 April 1948; *Davar*, 11 April 1948, p. 1, and 13 April 1948, p. 2; Khalidi, *Mudhakkirat*, vol. 2, p. 264, citing report by Nusayba, 10 April 1948; Kana'na and Zaytawi, *Dayr Yasin*, pp. 56, 62; Salayima, *Dayr Yasin*, p. 147; Khalidi, *Dayr Yasin*, p. 95; IDFA 355/2644/49: "Tzror Yedi'ot 'Araviyot," 10 and 12 April 1948; IDFA 59/500/48: "Tzror Yedi'ot 'Araviyot Musmakhot," 11 April 1948; IDFA 6/2605/49: "Dir Yasin," 12 April 1948; IDFA 2/2605/49: Hashmona'i to Moriah, "Nispahim le-Rikuz Yedi'ot No. 162," 12 April 1948; IDFA 978/100001/57: letter, Social Affairs Committee of the Jerusalem National Committee to Head of the General Affairs Department of the Arab Higher Committee, 20 April 1948; MEC GB165-0346/4/5: interview with Hazem Nusseibeh; Bar'el and Shay, "Hazara," p. 25 (citing Anwar Nusayba); Zananiri, "Interviews" (interviewing 'Ali Jabir); BBC, "50 Years," 14:18 (interview with Muhammad Mahmud Radwan); Bregman and Tahri, *Fifty Years*, p. 32 (citing same); "Survivor," 11:20 (interview with Da'ud Radwan); Lynd, Bahour and Lynd, *Homeland*, p. 24 (interview with 'Ayisha Jum'a Zaydan); Dirbas, "Deir Yassin," 8:45 (interview with Maryam 'Aql); "37 'Aman," pp. 10–12 (testimonies by Khumays Zaydan, Fatima Hamida, Maryam Barakat and Muhammad Darwish); PACE 241: interview with Muhammad 'Ayish Zaydan; BUPA: 'Aql, "Haqa'iq Waqi'iyya"; *New York Herald Tribune*, 12 April 1948; *New York Times*, 12 April 1948, p. 9; *Daily Telegraph*, 12 April 1948, p. 4; Collins and Lapierre, *O Jerusalem!*, p. 276.

7. IDFA 355/2644/49: "Tzror Yedi'ot 'Araviyot," 10 April 1948; IDFA 978/100001/57: letter, Social Affairs Committee of the Jerusalem National Committee to Head of the General Affairs Department of the Arab Higher Committee, 20 April 1948; IDFA 6/2605/49: "Dir Yasin," 11 April 1948; HA 105/257: Yavne – letters, 603, n.d.; 'Arif, *Nakbat*, vol. 1, p. 174; *Filastin*, 11 April 1948; *Al-Difa'*, 11 April 1948, p. 4, 12 April 1948, p. 1, and 14 April 1948, p. 3.

8. Fleishmann, "Women," pp. 37–38 (interview with Hind al-Husayni); Madsen, *Making*, pp. 59–61 (citing same); Dirbas, "Deir Yassin," 9:44 and 13:30 (interviews with same and Maryam 'Aql); Pat McDonnell Twair, "The Surviving Children of Deir Yassin," in MacGowan and Ellis, *Remembering*, pp. 51–52; UNRWA, "The Legacy of Hind al-Husseini," 8 March 2008, unispal.un.org/ UNISPAL.NSF/0/59DC7E2FEDD8D2EB852574080057ACFF; Kana'na and Zaytawi, *Dayr Yasin*, p. 62; 'Arif, *Nakbat*, vol. 1, p. 174; Salayima, *Dayr Yasin*, p. 133 (citing Fahima Zaydan); "37 'Aman," p. 11 (testimony by Maryam Barakat).

9. IDFA 355/2644/49: "Tzror Yedi'ot 'Araviyot," 10 April 1948; IDFA 372/5254/49: Yavne to Tene (A), "Totz'ot Dir Yasin," 12 April 1948; IDFA 810/100001/57: "Yedi'ot Tene (A)," 14 April 1948; CO 537/3857: CID, "Summary of Events," 10 April 1948; CO 733/477/5: tel. 941, Cunningham to Secretary of State for the Colonies, 11 April 1948; MEC GB165-0072/3/3: tel. 966, same to same, 13 April 1948; NARA RG 84, Jerusalem Consulate General Classified Records, 1948 – 800 Political Affairs, 6: tel. 433, Wasson to Secretary of State, 14 April 1948; *Filastin*, 11 April 1948.

10. MEC GB165-0072/3/3: tel. 1023, High Commissioner for Palestine to Secretary of State, 17 April 1948; Milstein, *Myth*, p. 137 (based on IDFA 5/580/56); Levin, *Jerusalem*, p. 71; Pa'il and Yurman, *Mivhan*, p. 336; David Spicehandler, *Let My Right Hand Wither* (New York, 1950), p. 109; Collins and Lapierre, *O Jerusalem!*, pp. 286, 363; *Sefer Toldot ha-Hagana*, vol. 3, pt. 2, pp. 1397, 1439; *Ha-Hagana bi-Yerushalayim*, vol. 2, p. 129; 'Abdallah al-Tall, *Karithat Filastin: Mudhakkirat 'Abdallah al-Tall Qa'id Ma'rakat al-Quds* ([Cairo, 1959], 2nd ed. 1990), p. 18; Tamari, *Jerusalem*, p. 108; O'Ballance, *War*, p. 59. Palumbo, *Catastrophe*, p. 102, claimed that the Arabs learned that some of Etzel's combatants who had been injured in Deir Yassin were in the convoy. Indeed, Yehuda Segal, severely wounded in Deir Yassin, was transferred on 13 April to Hadassah hospital for treatment. His ambulance managed to escape the attack, but because of the rough driving, his stitches opened and he died several days later. See Lapidot, *Lahav*, pp. 329–330, and *Homotayikh*, pp. 165–166.

11. As'ad, "Dhikra," p. 3; PACE 237: interview with Wahid and Ibtisam Zaydan (interviewed by 'Adil Yahya).

12. MEC GB165-0346/4/5: interview with Hazem Nusseibeh; LC 3/29: testimony by same; BBC, "50 Years," 14:37 and 15:22 (interview with same); Bregman and Tahri, *Fifty Years*, p. 33 (citing same and Muhammad Mahmud Radwan); Holmes, "Deir Yassin" (citing same); PACE 240: interview with 'Ayish Muhammad Zaydan; Adel H. Yahya, *The Palestinian Refugees 1948–1998 (An Oral History)* (Ramallah, 1999), p. 60; "50 'Aman," p. 12; Collins and Lapierre, *O Jerusalem!*, p. 281; Izzat Tannous, *The Palestinians: A Detailed Documented Eyewitness History of Palestine under British Mandate* (New York, 1988), pp. 503–504; John Zimmerman, "Radio Propaganda in the Arab-Israeli War 1948," *The Wiener Library Bulletin*, 27, NS nos. 30/31 (1973/4), p. 6; Koestler, *Promise*, p. 160; Matt Rees, "Village of Blood and Lies," *Newsweek* (International ed.), 4 May 1998, p. 29; Farsakh, "Majzarat." Khalidi was well aware of the accusations made against him. Several times in his memoirs, he argued that Deir Yassin was not the cause for the Palestinian flight. He further contended that the Arabs of Palestine did not need his words to know what had happened in Deir Yassin; the survivors disseminated the news. Furthermore, he insisted that he did not exaggerate. He argued that he derived his information from

eyewitness accounts and from reports he received. See Khalidi, *Mudhakkirat,* vol. 2, pp. 262, 264, 276–278.

13. MEC GB165-0346/4/5: interview with Hazem Nusseibeh; BBC, "50 Years," 15:22 (interview with same); RH MSS. Brit. Emp. s. 527/10/2: interview with Amin Majaj; 'Abd al-Hadi, "Majzarat," pp. 8–9, 15–16 (bringing many testimonies of refugee women about this issue); Humphries and Khalili, "Gender," p. 212 (based on interviews with refugees). Hasso, "Modernity," p. 500, explained that the reason that for years sexual assaults were not mentioned as a catalyst for the flight was that defending such values as women's honor was seen as contradicting the modern perceptions of nationalism, which put land before honor. The Palestinian nationalists viewed such concepts of honor as obstacles to national self-determination and therefore avoided discussion of the matter.

14. "50 'Aman," p. 12; Kana'na and Zaytawi, *Dayr Yasin,* p. 57; Yahya, *Refugees,* p. 31; Hijazi, *Dayr Yasin,* p. 70; James Zoghby, "Remembering Deir Yassin," *Al-Ahram Weekly,* 16–22 April 1998, weekly.ahram.org.eg/1998/1948/373_zgby. htm; Salayima, *Dayr Yasin,* pp. 220–221; Yasin, *Dayr Yasin,* p. 8 (arguing that the impact of Deir Yassin prevented the establishment of the Palestinian state, because of the mass exodus); Morris, *Revisited,* pp. 240, 298.

15. JA K4-10/4: posters by Etzel and Lehi, "Hoda'a 'al Parashat Dir Yasin," [14] April 1948; JA K4-13/8: broadcast of *Kol Zion ha-Lohemet,* 14 April 1948; Begin, *Revolt,* pp. 164–165; JA 'ER-12/3: testimony by Mordechai Raanan; Kfir, "Shalosh," p. 3 (interview with Yehoshua Zettler); Morris, *Revisited,* p. 239 (citing Lehi, "Bulitin 'Itonut Yomi No. 33," Tel Aviv, 30 August 1948); Opher Pa'il (ed.), *Meirke – Meir Pa'il: Mefaqed, Mehanekh, Historyon u-Politiqay – Pirqey Hayim u-Ma'amarim* ([Kiryat Ono], 2014), p. 38; Pail and Isseroff, "Deir Yassin"; Pa'il and Yurman, *Mivhan,* p. 336; MacGowan and Ellis, *Remembering,* p. 42 (interview with Meir Pa'il); Banks, *Country,* pp. 67–68 (testimony by same).

16. IDFA 353/2644/49: "Ha-Matzav be-Malha ve-'Eyn Karm," 21 April 1948, and "Beyt Iksa," 15 April 1948; HA 105/257: Yavne to Tene (A), "Me-Hana'ase be-Malha," 15 April 1948, and same to same, "Beyt Iksa," 15 April 1948; IDFA 4/2504/49: 16 April 1948; IDFA 2/2605/49: Hashmona'i to Moriah, "Nispahim le-Rikuz Yedi'ot No. 172," 15 April 1948, and same to Beit Horon, "Nispahim le-Rikuz Yedi'ot No. 174," 16 April 1948; IDFA 978/100001/57: letter, Social Affairs Committee of the Jerusalem National Committee to Head of the General Affairs Department of the Arab Higher Committee, 20 April 1948; WO 275/64: "Fortnightly Intelligence Newsletter No. 66," by HQ British Troops in Palestine, 21 April 1948; Goldstein, *Lehavot,* p. 109; William O. Douglas, *Strange Lands and Friendly People* (New York, 1951), pp. 264–265; Levin, *Jerusalem,* pp. 64–67; Budeiri, "Chronicle," p. 50 (citing the manuscript of Anwar Nusayba's memoirs, p. 122); Khalidi, *All That Remains,* pp. 273, 298, 304–305, 309–310, 316–318, 323.

17. IDFA 810/100001/57: "Yedi'ot Tene (A)," 19 April 1948; Hala Sakakini, *Jerusa-lem and I: A Personal Record* (Jerusalem, 1987), p. 118 (entry for 14 April 1948); Nathan Krystall, "The De-Arabization of West Jerusalem 1947–50," *Journal of Palestine Studies*, 27:2 (1998), p. 11; MacGowan and Ellis, *Remembering*, p. 59; Lynd, Bahour and Lynd, *Homeland*, p. 49 (emphasis in the original).

18. 'Abd al-Hadi, "Majzarat," pp. 8–9 (testimonies by refugee women); Humphries and Khalili, "Gender," p. 214 (interview with refugee woman); Rhoda Kanaaneh and Isis Nusair (eds.), *Displaced at Home: Ethnicity and Gender among Palestin-ians in Israel* (Albany NY, 2010), p. 83 (interviews with Arab women); IDFA 2062/100001/57: letter, Muhsin [surname illegible] (Haifa) to Abu Muhammad Qasim Zuhdi, 18 April 1948; HA 105/257: Hiram to Tene (A), [18 April 1948]; IDFA 23/5942/49: same to Yirmiyahu, "Tzror Yedi'ot Yomi," 15 April 1948; HA 105/31: same to Tene (A), 12 April 1948, and Yovav to Tene (A), 14 April 1948; Morris, *Revisited*, pp. 116, 240, 245; Khalidi, *All That Remains*, pp. 203, 562.

19. "Tnu'at ha-Hagira shel 'Arviyey Eretz Yisra'el ba-Tqufa 1.12.1947-1.6.1948," 30 June 1948, cited in Benny Morris, "The Causes and Character of the Arab Exodus from Palestine: The Israel Defence Forces Intelligence Service Analysis of June 1948," in idem, *1948 and After: Israel and the Palestinians* (Oxford, 1994), p. 90. The document was written by Moshe Sasson (son of Eliyahu), assistant to the director of the Arab department of the Israeli intelligence. The document is available in Ha-Shomer ha-Tzair Archives (Givat Haviva), Aharon Cohen papers, 10.95.13(1) (see ibid., pp. 83–84).

20. *Sefer Toldot ha-Hagana*, vol. 3, pt. 2, pp. 1363, 1548; IDF Historical Branch, *Toldot Milhemet ha-Qomemiyut* (Tel Aviv, [1959] rep. 1978), p. 117; Benny Mor-ris, *The Birth of the Palestinian Refugee Problem, 1947–1949* (Cambridge, [1987] rep. 1994), p. 115. See also *'Iton ha-Magen*, no. 16, 30 July 1948. Yoav Gelber, on the other hand, while acknowledging that the rumors about Deir Yassin drove the Palestinians to flee, nevertheless was of the opinion that "the role of Deir Yassin in the mechanism of Palestinians' mass flight has been highly inflated." See Gelber, "Propaganda," p. 317.

21. Goldstein, *Lehavot*, p. 104 (citing Emil al-Ghuri); Bar'el and Shay, "Hazara," p. 25 (citing Anwar Nusayba); *Ha-Mashqif*, 20 May 1948, p. 1 (citing 'Azzam Pasha); Al-Tall, *Karithat*, p. 18; Morris, *Revisited*, p. 239 (citing Cunningham); IWM 06/43/1: "Diary as MA to HE the High Commissioner of Palestine," by Towers-Clarck, entry for 17 April 1948 ("As a result of the Deir Yassin episode, there is no doubt that the villagers are scared to their wits"); Eliel Dror, "Dir Yasin," *Herut*, 19 May 1950, p. 5 (citing Archer Crust); De Reynier, *Jerusalem*, p. 76.

22. Muhammad 'Isa Salihiyya, "Al-Nuzuh al-Kabir," *Al-Qadiyya al-Filastiniyya fi Arba'in 'Aman – Bayna Darawat al-Waqi' wa-Tumuhat al-Mustaqbal: Buhuth wa-Munaqashat al-Nadwa al-Fikriyya Allati Nazzamatha Jam'iyyat al-Khirrijin*

fil-Kuwayt (Beirut and Kuwait, 1989), pp. 143–144. Nicholas Bethell, *The Pal-estine Triangle: The Struggle between the British, the Jews and the Arabs 1935–48* (London, 1979), p. 355, estimated that the immediate result of the Deir Yassin affair was the flight of about 300,000 Arabs, comprising two-thirds of the Arabs who lived in the area designated for the Jewish state according to the Palestine partition resolution.

23. 'Arif, *Nakbat*, vol. 1, p. 174; Kana'na and Zaytawi, *Dayr Yasin*, pp. 62–63; Habib Allah, "Majzarat," p. 70; 'Awawda, *Dhakira*, pp. 84–85; Lynd, Bahour and Lynd, *Homeland*, p. 25; Derogy and Saab, *Exodes*, p. 145; Abu Sitta, *Nakba*, p. 45; Idem, *Atlas*, p. 77; "Welcome to Dayr Yasin."

24. *Al-Difa'*, 12 April 1948, p. 1, 13 April 1948, p. 4, 14 April 1948, p. 2, and 15 April 1948, p. 1; *Palestine Post*, 12 April 1948, p. 1; *Filastin*, 15 April 1948; *Davar*, 15 April 1948, p. 1; FBIS, FRB-48-290, 15 April 1948, p. II5: radio al-Sharq al-Adna, 14 April 1948, 7:00; IDFA 504/4944/49: "Yedi'ot ha-'Itonut ha-'Aravit," no. 90/48, 15 April 1948; IDFA 75/5254/49: Hashmona'i, "Tzror Yedi'ot 'Arviyot no. 178," 19 April 1948; Yosef Nevo, *'Abdallah ve-'Arviyey Eretz Yisra'el* (Tel Aviv, 1975), p. 76; 'Arif, *Nakbat*, vol. 1, p. 174.

25. FO 816/117: letter, 'Abdallah to Kirkbride, 12 April 1948; FO 371/68852: letter, Kirkbride to B. A. B. Burrows, 15 April 1948. It is interesting to note, that some of the refugees blamed the Arab Legion units in Palestine for spreading the false rumors of rape. See Yahya, *Refugees*, p. 60.

26. FO 816/117: letter, 'Abd al-Rahman 'Azzam (Cairo) to 'Abdallah, 15 April 1948, enclosed with dispatch 23, Kirkbride to [Ernest] Bevin (FO), 22 April 1948, and tel., 'Abdallah to Cunningham, 23 April 1948, enclosed with tel. 244, Minister (Amman) to Secretary of State (FO), 23 April 1948; MEC GB165-0072/3/4: same from 'Abdallah to Cunningham, enclosed with tel. 1186, High Commissioner for Palestine to Minister (Amman), 25 April 1948; *Al-Ahram*, 17 April 1948, cited in Shlaim, *Collusion*, p. 165; CO 537/3962: "Monthly Situation Report on Transjordan for the Month of April, 1948," by Kirk-bride, 4 May 1948; Arab Higher Committee, "Why the Arab States Entered Palestine" (New York), Memorandum to the United Nations Delegates (A/658), p. 8, cited in John and Hadawi, *Palestine*, vol. 2, p. 378; Joseph, *City*, p. 173.

27. *Filastin*, 15 April 1948; *Al-Difa'*, 13 April 1948, p. 4, and 14 April 1948, p. 1; *Davar*, 14 April 1948, p. 2; NARA M1390, Records of the Department of State Relating to Internal Affairs of Palestine, 1945–1949 – 867N.01, roll 14: dispatch A-184, Memminger to Secretary of State, 13 April 1948; Zimmerman, "Radio," p. 6 (citing radio Damascus, 14 April 1948); FO 816/117: tel. 284, Beirut to FO, 16 April 1948; FO 371/68373/E6559: dispatch 145, British Embassy (Baghdad) to Secretary of State (FO), 6 May 1948, enclosing memorandum by Iraqi Minister of Foreign Affairs, n.d.

28. NARA LM163, Confidential U.S. State Department Central Files, Palestine and Israel, Internal and Foreign Affairs 1945–1949 – Political Affairs, Government, reel 1: letter, acting Chargé d'Affaires (Egyptian Embassy, Washington DC) to Robert A. Lovett (Department of State, Washington DC), 16 April 1948, enclosing communiqué by the Political Committee of the Arab League; FO 371/68504/E4820: letter 1119/8-2/3, 'Abd al-Fattah 'Ali 'Amr (Egyptian Embassy, London) to Secretary of State (FO), 16 April 1948, enclosing "Communiqué du Comité Politique de la Ligue Arabe"; *Filastin*, 15 April 1948; FBIS, FRB-48-291, 16 April 1948, p. II5: radio al-Sharq al-Adna, 15 April 1948, 11:00; FBIS, FRB-48-316, 21 May 1948, p. II3: radio al-Sharq al-Adna, 20 May 1948, 11:00 (citing 'Azzam Pasha); *Ha-Mashqif*, 20 May 1948, p. 1 (citing same).

NOTES FOR CHAPTER 12

1. *Davar*, 11 April 1948, p. 1 (citing radio Beirut); *Ha-Mashqif*, 11 April 1948, p. 3 (citing same); "Dayr Yasin (Madhbaha)," *Mawsu'a*, al-Qism al-'Amm, vol. 2, p. 434; *Filastin*, 14 April 1948 (citing Fahima Zaydan); 'Arafat Hijazi, *15 Ayyar 'Am al-Nakba* ([Amman, 1968]), p. 55; "The Deir Yassin Massacres," *Proche-Orient: Near East Monthly Review*, 6:1 (May 1950), p. 35; Khalidi, *Mudhakkirat*, vol. 2, p. 262, citing report by Nusayba, 10 April 1948; Zananiri, "Interviews" (interviewing Muhammad Mahmud Radwan); "Abu Mahmud," p. 8; BUPA: 'Aql, "Haqa'iq Waqi'iyya."

2. CO 733/477/5: tel. 928, Cunningham to Secretary of State for the Colonies, 10 April 1948; *Ha-Mashqif*, 11 April 1948, p. 3; *Davar*, 11 April 1948, p. 1 (citing the *Egyptian Mail*); Qusari, *Harb*, vol. 2, p. 128; Kana'na and Zaytawi, *Dayr Yasin*, pp. 52–53; Zananiri, "Interviews" (interviewing Muhammad Mahmud Radwan); Hijazi, *15 Ayyar*, p. 55; Idem, *Dayr Yasin*, p. 74; 'Arif, *Nakbat*, vol. 1, p. 171; Salayima, *Dayr Yasin*, p. 108; 'Abd al-Majid, "Sutur," p. 121; Salihiyya, "Nuzuh," p. 128; Lynd, Bahour and Lynd, *Homeland*, p. 22 (interview with Ahmad 'Ayish Khalil); *Filastin*, 14 April 1948 (testimony by Fahima Zaydan); PACE 241: interview with Muhammad 'Ayish Zaydan; PACE 240: interview with 'Ayish Muhammad Zaydan; Khalidi, *Mudhakkirat*, vol. 2, p. 262, citing report by Nusayba, 10 April 1948; Farsakh, "Majzarat."

3. 'Arif, *Nakbat*, vol. 1, p. 172 (citing Zaynab Ahmad Musa); Salayima, *Dayr Yasin*, p. 117 (citing same but commenting that she exaggerated); Abu Gharbiyya, *Khidamm*, p. 222; Kana'na and Zaytawi, *Dayr Yasin*, p. 53.

4. Glubb, *Soldier*, p. 81; FBIS, SOV-82-183, 21 September 1982, p. H6: TASS News Agency (Moscow), 20 September 1982, 16:03 GMT.

5. Collins and Lapierre, *O Jerusalem!*, pp. 274–276; Roger Delorme, *Inni Attahimu* (Montreal, 2nd ed. 1983), pp. 52–53; "Dayr Yasin (Madhbaha)," *Mawsu'a*, al-Qism al-'Amm, vol. 2, p. 434; Zaru, *Dayr Yasin*, p. 33; 'Ubaydu, "Khamsun,"

p. 15; MacGowan and Ellis, *Remembering*, p. 48; Langer, *Darki*, p. 77; Cathy Sultan, *Israeli and Palestinian Voices: A Dialogue with Both Sides* (Minneapolis MN, 2nd ed. 2006), p. 196; Yasin, *Dayr Yasin*, p. 23; *Dayr Yasin: Ramz Falsafat al-Sahyuniyya*, pp. 5, 16; Morris, *Revisited*, p. 116; Nahum Barnea, "Dir Yasin Hazarnu Elayikh Shenit," *Davar*, 9 April 1982, p. 13; Amira Howeidy, "It's Difficult to Count," *Al-Ahram Weekly*, 9–15 April 1998, weekly.ahram.org. eg/1998/1948/372_yass.htm (testimony by Mahmud Qasim); RH MSS. Brit. Emp. s. 527/10/2: interview with Amin Majaj; MEC GB165-0282/2/4: "Dir Yasin" – interviewee not named; Assad, *Palestine*, p. 121 (testimony by 'Uthman 'Aql, adding in idem, *Filastin*, p. 128, that the Jews were no better than the Nazis); "'Aql Yakshifu" (interview with same); "Survivor," 16:44 (interview with Da'ud Radwan); Salayima, *Dayr Yasin*, pp. 127 (bringing the story about Sharon), 136. Salayima himself did not believe the story about Sharon, yet cited American consul-general Robert Macatee as the ostensible source of the report of his presence. Macatee could not have made such a report, as he left Jerusalem before the Deir Yassin affair, being replaced by Thomas Wasson.

6. *Al-Difa'*, 11 April 1948, p. 1, and 12 April 1948, p. 1; *New York Herald Tribune*, 12 April 1948; PACE 240: interview with 'Ayish Muhammad Zaydan; Collins and Lapierre, *O Jerusalem!*, p. 275; Delorme, *Inni*, p. 53; RH MSS. Brit. Emp. s. 527/10/2: interviews with Amin Majaj and Shmuel Katz; 'Abd al-Hadi, "Majzarat," pp. 8–9 (testimonies by refugee women); MEC GB165-0282/2/4: "Dir Yasin" – interviewee not named; Langer, *Darki*, p. 77; *Filastin*, 11 and 14 April 1948 (testimony by Fahima Zaydan); "Deir Yassin Massacres," p. 37 (citing same); Khalidi, *Mudhakkirat*, vol. 2, p. 261; *Dayr Yasin: Ramz Falsafat al-Sahyuniyya*, p. 6; Hijazi, *Dayr Yasin*, p. 64; Zaru, *Dayr Yasin*, p. 35; Sakakini, *Jerusalem*, p. 118 (entry for 14 April 1948); Graves, *Experiment*, p. 179 (entry for 15 April 1948); LC 3/29: DLP, "Deir Yassin," p. 10; Derogy and Saab, *Exodes*, p. 146; League of Arab States, Secretariat General, Palestine Department, Political Section, *Israel's Aggression prior to the Israeli Attack of October 29, 1956, on Egypt* (Cairo, 1957), pp. 10–11. Cunningham believed, and it was reported to the United Nations, that "women and children were stripped, lined up, photographed and then slaughtered by automatic fire." See MEC GB165-0072/3/3: tel. 1023, High Commissioner for Palestine to Secretary of State, 17 April 1948; UNISPAL: letter, Fletcher-Cooke to Bunche, 20 April 1948.

7. *Dayr Yasin: Ramz Falsafat al-Sahyuniyya*, p. 5; FBIS, NES-95-195, 10 October 1995, p. 39: JANA News Agency (Tripoli), 8 October 1995, 8:15 GMT; MEC GB165-0282/2/4: "Dir Yasin" – interviewee not named; Kana'na, "Madhbahat," p. 174; 'Abd al-Hadi, "Majzarat," pp. 8, 10–11, 16 (testimonies by refugee women and Zaynab 'Aql); Kanaaneh and Nusair, *Displaced*, p. 83 (interviews with Arab women); Salayima, *Dayr Yasin*, pp. 126, 128, 137; MacGowan and Ellis, *Remembering*, p. 48; Delorme, *Inni*, p. 52; Collins and Lapierre, *O Jerusalem!*, p. 275; Hijazi, *Dayr Yasin*, p. 62; Zaru, *Dayr Yasin*, p. 33; Howeidy, "It's Difficult" (testimony by Mahmud Qasim); Bar'el and Shay, "Hazara," p. 23 (interviewing

Muhammad 'Arif Sammur); "37 'Aman," p. 11 (testimony by Fatima Hamida); Milstein, *History*, vol. 4, p. 376 (interview with Shoshana Shatay). Muhammad Mahmud Radwan claimed that only two pregnant women were killed, one by a bomb and the other by being shot. See 'Awawda, "Majzarat."

8. "Deir Yassin Massacres," p. 35. I wish to thank Ben Rogers, the archivist of Baylor University Collections of Political Materials, for providing me with a copy of this journal, available in the papers of US former congressman Ed Lee Gossett, apparently the only existing copy of this issue of the journal. See also Hijazi, *Dayr Yasin*, p. 64, Tannous, *Palestinians*, p. 503, and Khalid al-Sa'd (ed.), *Khutab al-Shaykh al-Qaradawi* (Cairo, 2003), vol. 5, p. 182.

9. *Al-Difa'*, 14 April 1948, p. 2; *Al-Misri*, 12 April 1948, cited in Raday, *Kohot*, p. 104, and idem, *Beyn Shtey 'Arim: Ha-'Aravim ha-Palestinim bi-Yerushalayim uve-Yafo 1947–1948* (Tel Aviv, 2015), p. 124 (mentioning that the exiled Grand Mufti of Jerusalem, Amin al-Husayni, also compared it to Lidice); Khalidi, *Mudhakkirat*, vol. 2, p. 267; Lever, *Jerusalem*, p. 171; Guy Ottewell, "Deir Yassin: A Forgotten Tragedy With Present-Day Meaning," in Fath, *Deir Yassin, 1948, Zeita, Beit Nuba and Yalu, 1967* (n.p., [1969]), p. 5; Tom Segev, *One Palestine Complete: Jews and Arabs Under the British Mandate* (New York, 2000), p. 507 (citing the manuscript of Bernard de Bunsen's "Memoirs," entry for 11 April 1948); MEC GB165-0128/1/1: Gurney, *Palestine*, entry for 15 April 1948; Glubb, *Soldier*, p. 82; "Editorial: Deir Yassin," *Arab News Bulletin*, no. 61 (The Arab Office, London), 23 April 1948, p. 1. The Arab Office was the propaganda organ of the Arab League in London. In a propaganda booklet published twenty years later by the permanent delegation of the Arab League to Geneva, Deir Yassin was compared to both Lidice and Oradour-sur-Glane, and the affair was asserted to be genocide, a prelude to a "final solution." Délégation Permanente de la Ligue des Etas Arabes a Genève, *Il y a vingt ans – Deir Yassin: Comment oublier? Comment pardonner?* (Geneva, April 1968), pp. 1–2, 12, 14.

10. See e.g. McGowan and Hogan, *Saga*, pp. 32–34. McGowan and Hogan, ardent believers in the massacre narrative, devoted several pages to prove Pa'il's credibility, arguing, for example, that the very fact that he produced photographs of the event was "a very good corroboration of his claim that he was there" (ibid., p. 33).

11. See e.g. 'Awawda, *Dhakira*, p. 86 (testimony by Mustafa Hamida, chairman of *Jam'iyyat Dayr Yasin al-Khayriyya*); Kana'na, "Madhbahat," pp. 172–173; 'Ubaydu, "Khamsun," p. 15.

12. HA 20/253: Avraham [Meir Pilavsky] to District Commander, "Pe'ulat ha-Porshim be-Dir Yasin," 10 April 1948; YTA 16-12/52/82: interview with Shraga Peled; Pa'il, "Ra'ayonot Anshey Shay," pt. 1, 1:23 and 5:40 (interview with same); Peled, *Sipurim*, pp, 136–137; Conversation between the author and Peled, 13 February, 2011; Pail and Isseroff, "Deir Yassin"; Pa'il, *Meirke*, pp. 37–38;

MacGowan and Ellis, *Remembering*, pp. 40, 44–45 (interview with Meir Pa'il); Silver, *Begin*, p. 93 (citing same); Avrahami, "Ruhot," p. 29 (interview with same); YTA 15-46/169/6: letter, Yisrael Galili to Amotz Peleg (Hulda), 22 April 1978. For years, Pa'il refused to divulge the identity of the photographer. Peled, a long-time volunteer in the Haganah archives in Tel Aviv, approached the author of this book in one of his visits to the archives, introduced himself as the photographer, and acquainted him with his memoirs.

13. HA 20/253: The Haganah's Operations Branch – Intelligence Officer, "Ha-Nadon: Leqah Pe'ulat Dir Yasin," 12 April 1948, including Avraham to District Commander, "Pe'ulat ha-Porshim be-Dir Yasin," 10 April 1948, Intelligence Officer ... [Gicherman] to Section Commander, "Doh Kibush Dir Yasin 'al-Yedey ha-Porshim," 10 April 1948, and Company Commander, 4th Company, 4th [should be 6th] Battalion (Palmach), to Jerusalem's District Commander, "Doh Dir Yasin," 10 [should be 11] April 1948; Avrahami, "Ruhot," pp. 13, 29; Morris, *Revisited*, p. 294. On 12 April, Yitzhak Levy compiled a report, based on information derived from "Ram" (Pilavsky), which claimed that seven women and old men had been executed in the quarries after having been paraded in Jerusalem. See IDFA 372/5254/49: Yavne [Levy] to Tene (D), "Ma'asy ha-Zva'a shel ha-Porshim bi-F'ulat Dir Yasin," 12 April 1948.

14. IDFA 584/4944/49: Company Commander (4th Company, 6th Battalion) to Jerusalem's District Commander, "Doh Dir Yasin," 11 April 1948 (Weg's original report); YTA 15-34/13/5: testimony by Moshe Vachman, "Dir Yasin." Weg was killed in late May in the battle over Latrun, so he could not supply further information.

15. YTA 16-12/52/82: interview with Shraga Peled; Pa'il, "Ra'ayonot Anshey Shay," pt. 1, 5:33, 11:54 and 13:31 (interviews with same, Meir Pa'il and Yehezkel Rabi' – it should be noted that both Peled and Rabi' delivered their versions in Pa'il's presence); Peled, *Sipurim*, p, 137; Pail and Isseroff, "Deir Yassin"; Interview with Yehuda Lapidot, 24 August 2010; Lapidot, *Lahav*, p. 320; Milstein, *History*, vol. 4, p. 379, and *Myth*, pp. 93–94; Rozen, "Kol," p. 47 (interviewing Uri Milstein).

16. YTA 15-34/13/5: testimony by Meir Pa'il, "Dir Yasin"; YTA 12-3/41/14: interview with Moshe Edelstein; Milstein, *History*, vol. 4, pp. 355, 378, and *Myth*, pp. 39, 92 (interview with same); Lapidot, *Lahav*, p. 318; Interview with Yehuda Lapidot, 24 August 2010; Regev-Yarkoni and Regev, *Lohem*, p. 135.

17. Phone conversation with Mordechai Gichon, 21 May 2014; Milstein, *History*, vol. 4, pp. 368, 378, and *Myth*, pp. 66, 93 (interview with same); Gichon, *Mate*, pp. 252–253; YTA 12-3/9/3: Gichon, "Parashat Dir Yasin Tashah."

18. Avraham [Meir Pilavsky], "Dir Yasin ve-Herpoteha," *ba-Mahane*, 5–6, 16 April 1948, p. 1.

19. YTA 15-34/13/5: testimony by Meir Pa'il, "Dir Yasin," 10 May 1971, with answers to questions. The original, unavilable to the public, may be found in HA 167.15. The section on Deir Yassin in Pa'il, *Meirke*, pp. 35–37, is a modified version of this testimony.

20. Pail and Isseroff, "Deir Yassin"; Ilan Kfir, "Shalosh Girsot 'al Parashat Dir Yasin," *Yedi'ot Aharonot*, 4 April 1972, p. 2; Meir Pa'il, "Ha-Emet ha-Hatzuya be-Farashat Dir Yasin," *Yedi'ot Aharonot*, 20 April 1972, pp. 14, 23.

21. JA 'EP-19/1: testimony by MK Meir Pa'il.

22. Ron Maiberg, "Dir Yasin – Har'u lanu et ha-Tzilumim," *Monitin*, 32 (April 1981), pp. 36–40; Banks, *Country*, pp. 55–58, 65–66 (emphasis in the original); Eric Silver, "New Accounts of Deir Yassin," *The Guardian*, 9 April 1983, p. 15; Idem, *Begin*, pp. 93–94; Palumbo, *Catastrophe*, pp. 49–50, 52, 56; YTA 12-3/9/3: David Segal "Parashat Dir Yasin" (Efal Seminary, 1984), p. 6.

23. Rozen, "Kol," p. 47; Avrahami, "Ruhot," pp. 12–13, 29; Michal Kedem, "Raq Psikhiater Yakhol le-Hasbir – Dr Meir Pa'il: Hayiti Sham ve-Ra'iti et ha-Tevah," *Hadashot*, 2 September 1991, p. 13; "A Jewish Eye-Witness: An Interview with Meir Pa'il," in MacGowan and Ellis, *Remembering*, pp. 35–46; BBC, "50 Years," 13:37; Bregman and Tahri, *Fifty Years*, pp. 29, 32; Pail and Isseroff, "Deir Yassin."

24. YTA 16-12/52/81: interview with Meir Pa'il; Norman Rose, *'A Senseless Squalid War': Voices from Palestine 1945–1948* (London, 2009), pp. 193, 196; Pa'il and Yurman, *Mivhan*, p. 332; Pa'il, "Ra'ayonot Anshey Shay," pts. 1 (especially 3:50, 5:33, 11:54, 13:15, and 14:31) and 2.(1:56). In another interview, Peled explicitly said that "This village deserved 'treatment'." YTA 16-12/52/82: interview with Shraga Peled.

25. Ministry for Foreign Affairs, Information Division, *Background Notes on Current Themes: Dir Yassin* (Jerusalem, 16 March 1969), no. 6. See also Joseph B. Schechtman, "The Truth About Dir Yassin: An Official Vindication of Libeled Heroes of 1948," *The American Zionist*, 59:10 (June 1969), pp. 17–20. Schechtman's article, based on the booklet, was also published in *The Canadian Zionist*, and as a booklet in its own, *Israel Explodes Dir Yassin Blood Libel* (New York, [1969]).

26. Morris, "Historiography," pp. 80–84, 101; Tzur, *Shomer*, pp. 40–41 (testimony by Meir Pa'il); Pail and Isseroff, "Deir Yassin"; Uri Avneri, "Dir Yasin," *ha-'Olam ha-Ze*, 3 July 1972, p. 13; Menachem Begin, "Be-Regashot Me'oravim," *Ma'ariv*, 8 January 1971, p. 17, and "Hazmana le-Vaqer be-London," *Ma'ariv*, 23 April 1971, p. 13; YTA 12-3/9/3: letter, Levy to Begin, 12 April 1971 (with handwritten remarks by Meir Pa'il); YTA 15-46/48/9: letter, Gideon Rafael (Ministry for Foreign Affairs, Jerusalem) to Sh[aul] Avigur (Tel Aviv), 18 April 1971, and letter, Abba Eban to Galili, 10 May 1971. On the very same day Pa'il gave his

first testimony about Deir Yassin after 23 years of silence. One may wonder whether there was a connection between this affair and his decision to speak.

27. Yehoshua Ofir, *'Al ha-Homot* (Tel Aviv, 1961), pp. 44–67; Ezra Yakhin, *Sipuro shel Elnaqam* (Tel Aviv, 1977), pp. 250–260; Yehuda Lapidot, *'Al Homotayikh: Zikhronot Lohem Etzel* ([Tel Aviv], 1992), pp. 146–166, and *Be-Lahav ha-Mered: Ma'arkhot ha-Etzel bi-Yerushalayim* ([Tel Aviv], 1996), pp. 299–329. The affair was also described in detail in Etzel's official history, David Niv, *Ma'arkhot ha-Irgun ha-Tzva'i ha-Le'umi* (Tel Aviv, 1980), vol. 6, pp. 79–94, and Lehi's official history, Nechemia Ben-Tor, *Sefer Toldot Lohamey Herut Yisra'el (Lehi)* (Jerusalem, 2010), vol. 4, pp. 455–474.

28. Yardena Golani, *Ha-Mitos shel Dir Yasin* (Tel Aviv, 1976); Baruch Nadel, "Siluf History mul Siluf History," *Yedi'ot Aharonot, Tarbut, Sifrut, Amanut* supplement, 30 July 1976, p. 2 (it should be noted, though, that Nadel arrived in Deir Yassin only the next day, see Marton, *Death*, p. 29); Interview with Yehuda Lapidot, 24 August 2010.

29. Uri Milstein, *'Alilat Dam be-Dir Yasin* ([Tel-Aviv], 2007), pp. 9–84, *Toldot Milhemet ha-'Atzma'ut* (Tel-Aviv, 1991), vol. 4, pp. 251–281, *History of Israel's War of Independence* (Lanham MD, 1998), vol. 4, pp. 343–396, and *The Birth of a Palestinian Nation: The Myth of the Deir Yassin Massacre* (Jerusalem and New York, 2012), pp. 3–111.

30. Morton A. Klein, *Deir Yassin: History of a Lie* (The Zionist Organization of America, March 1998), and "Deir Yassin: The 1948 'Jewish Massacre of Arabs' that Never Was," 18 March 1998, radiobergen.org/history/deir-1.html.

31. Netanel Lorch, *The Edge of the Sword: Israel's War of Independence, 1947–1949* (Jerusalem, [1961] 2nd ed. 1968), p. 96; Ben-Zion Dinur and others (eds.), *Sefer Toldot ha-Haganah* (Tel Aviv, 1954-72), vol. 3, pt. 2, pp. 1546–1548; Yitzhak Levy, *Tish'a Qabin: Yerushalayim bi-Qravot Milhemet ha-'Atzma'ut* ([Tel Aviv], 1986), pp. 340–345. Uri Ram of Ben-Gurion University was to complain that Lorch did not emphasize enough that the massacre took place after the battle, that he did not clarify that brutalities took place against women and children, and that he did not mention rape and mutilation. Uri Ram, "Ways of Forgetting: Israel and the Obliterated Memory of the Palestinian Nakba," *Journal of Historical Sociology*, 22:3 (2009), p. 373. The possibility that these things never happened did not even occur to Ram.

32. 'Arif, *Nakbat*, vol. 1, p. 173 ('Arif devoted pp. 169–175 of his book to the affair); 'Arafat Hijazi, *Dayr Yasin: Judhur wa-Ab'ad al-Jarima fil-Fikr al-Sahyuni* ([Amman?], 1978); Sharif Kana'na and Nihad Zaytawi, *Dayr Yasin* (Birzeit, 2nd rep. 1987). Several years later, Kana'na published an additional article about the affair, based on a lecture he delivered concerning his findings. Sharif Kana'na, "Madhbahat Dayr Yasin: Qira'a Jadida," *Al-Shatat al-Filastini: Hijra am Tahjir?* (Bira, 2000), pp. 152–181.

33. Walid al-Khalidi, *Dayr Yasin: Al-Jum'a, 9 Nisan/Abril 1948* (Jerusalem, 1999); Fadi Salayima, *Dayr Yasin: Al-Qarya al-Shahida* (Damascus, 2008); Harold Levius, *Conflict of Lies: History of the 1948 Palestinian Catastrophe and Its Continuing Genocidal Aftermath* (n.p., 2012), pp. 78–80 (about 'Arafat's alleged participation). The survivor Muhammad Mahmud Radwan set up a private library in his home to document the history of the village. He, too, said that he had a map of all the houses and roads of the village, and he prepared a paper recounting the details of the affair. See "Abu Mahmud," p. 8, and BUPA: Muhammad Mahmud As'ad [Radwan] 'Aql, "Haqa'iq Waqi'iyya min Majzarat Dayr Yasin al-Basila (1948)."

34. Dan Kurzman, *Genesis 1948: The First Arab-Israeli War* (New York, 1970), pp. 138–149; Larry Collins and Dominique Lapierre, *O Jerusalem!* (Jerusalem, 1972), pp. 272–281. See also Levius, *Conflict*, pp. 85–86, who claims that Collins and Lapierre were influenced in this "one-sided" narrative by their research assistant Lilly Rivlin, who, according to him, disapproved of Begin. Regarding Rivlin's share in the Deir Yassin chapter of this book, see also Doron Geller, "O Writer," *Jerusalem Post*, 23 March 2001, p. 10.

35. Matthew C. Hogan and Daniel A. McGowan, "Anatomy of a Whitewash: A Critical Examination and Refutation of the Historical Revisionist 'Deir Yassin: History of a Lie,' Issued by the Zionist Organization of America (March 8, 1998)," www.deiryassin.org/op0005.html; Daniel A. McGowan and Matthew C. Hogan, *The Saga of Deir Yassin: Massacre, Revisionism and Reality* (Geneva NY, 1999), www.deiryassin.org/pdf/SAGAA4.pdf; Daniel A. McGowan and Marc H. Ellis (eds.), *Remembering Deir Yassin: The Future of Israel and Palestine* (New York, 1998); Matthew Hogan, "The 1948 Massacre at Deir Yassin Revisited," *The Historian*, 63:2 (2001), pp. 309–333. See also Morris, "Historiography," p. 97, defining *Remembering Deir Yassin* as a "propagandistic volume." For the attitude of the survivors and their descendants toward McGowan, see Hillel Cohen, "Shel Mi ha-Tevah ha-Ze, le-'Azazel," *Kol ha-'Ir*, 20 June 1997, p. 73.

36. Benny Morris, "The Historiography of Deir Yassin," *The Journal of Israeli History*, 24:1 (2005), pp. 79–107, *The Birth of the Palestinian Refugee Problem Revisited* (Cambridge, 2004), pp. 237–240 (and pp. 113–115 of the 1987 version), and *1948: A History of the First Arab-Israeli War* (New Haven and London, 2008), pp. 125–128; Yoav Gelber, "Propaganda as History: What Happened at Deir Yassin?," in idem, *Palestine 1948: War, Escape and the Emergence of the Palestinian Refugee Problem* (Brighton, 2006), pp. 307–318, which is an enlarged version of the respective section in his Hebrew *Qomemiyut ve-Nakba: Yisra'el, ha-Palestinim u-Medinot 'Arav, 1948* (Or Yehuda, 2004), pp. 153–161.

37. E-mails from Ilana Alon (IDFA director) to the author, 2 December 2014; Dan Izenberg, "Court to Decide Whether Army Must Release All Material on Deir Yassin," *Jerusalem Post*, 5 May 2010, p. 5; Ruling of the High Court of Justice, Case 10343/07, 24 May 2010, eyloni.court.gov.il/files/07/430/103/p08/07103430.

p08.htm; See also Avrahami, "Ruhot," pp. 13, 29, and Paʿil, *Meirke*, p. 38. The student from Bezalel, Neta Shoshani, later filmed a documentary about Deir Yassin, which included interviews with some of the Etzel and Lehi veterans. While the film was perceived by some as adopting the massacre narrative, a careful examination of the testimonies shows that, although expressing their shock at the results of the battle, none of them admitted to a massacre. (The only one to state in the film that a massacre had taken place, was, again, Meir Paʿil.) Neta Shoshani (dir.), "Born in Deir Yassin," 2016, f2h.io/utym1u59uqbi. Regarding the photos, see also YTA 16-12/52/82: interview with Shraga Peled, and Peled, *Sipurim*, p. 137. In addition to the documents and the photos, there existed in the IDF archives a movie of some portions of the battle, filmed by the cameraman Ben Oyserman for Movieton News. He talked about the film with a colleague, who secretly also worked for the Haganah. Following this indiscretion the film was switched in Lydda airport, and Movieton News received 400 feet of film of clouds. By the 1970s the film was already in unusable condition and by the 1980s it no longer was in the archives, probably having been destroyed. YTA 12-3/43/45: interview with Gideon Sarig; Silver, *Begin*, p. 89; phone conversations with Yaakov Gross, 23 March and 30 June 2014.

NOTES FOR CONCLUSIONS

1. Muhammad Mahmud Radwan, interviewed by Elias Zananiri, in "Interviews: 50th Anniversary of Deir Yassin Massacre," *ArabicNews.com*, 10 April 1998.

2. Yehoshua Zettler, interviewed by Ilan Kfir, in "Shalosh Girsot ʿal Parashat Dir Yasin," *Yediʿot Aharonot*, 4 April 1972, p. 3.

3. "Plan D," 10 March 1948, cited in *Sefer Toldot ha-Haganah*, vol. 3, pt. 3, p. 1957.

4. Interview with Shraga Peled, in Paʿil, "Raʾayonot Anshey Shay," pt. 2, 2:56; HA 58.49: testimony by Zalman Mart; ISA P-2878/5: interview with Shimon Moneta; LC 3/29: testimony by [Yehuda] Lapidot; Asʿad, "Dhikra," p. 3.

5. See expressions by Yunus Ahmad Asʿad Radwan, in ibid., Mustafa Hamida and ʿAbd al-Qadir Zaydan, in ʿAwawda, *Dhakira*, pp. 86, 88, ʿAyish Muhammad ʿAyish Zaydan, in PACE 240, and many other survivors.

6. The fact that the Deir Yassin villagers had a "localist" mentality, rather than sharing in a countrywide national perception, could be demonstrated by the following seemingly trivial fact. In the list of the villagers killed there were eight women from other villages, married to men from Deir Yassin. They were all called after their village of origin, Zaynab al-Malihiyya (after Maliha), Ruqya al-Subaniyya (after Suba), etc., despite the fact that some of them had been married to their husbands for years. Some came from very close villages,

like Maliha, less than four kilometers to the south, but nevertheless, all were considered foreign enough to be called after their villages of origin.

7. Muhammad Mahmud Radwan, cited in Bregman and Tahri, *Fifty Years*, p. 33. See also MEC GB165-0346/4/5: interview with Hazem Nusseibeh. Khalidi was well aware of the accusations cast against him and tried to justify himself in his memoirs.

8. 'Adil Yahya interviewing Wahid and Ibtisam Zaydan, in PACE 237.

9. Matza, *Shney Eqdahim*, p. 50, and testimonies by Naziha Radwan, in Khalidi, *Dayr Yasin*, p. 69, and Assad, *Palestine*, p. 119 (also cited by her brother, Da'ud, in "Survivor," 13:30).

10. Lehi's David Gottlieb explained that initially, they too did not refute the massacre allegation, precisely because it accelerated the Palestinian flight. Denying it could hamper the flight. At that point, according to him, there actually was a consensus of the Arabs, the Jewish Agency, and Etzel and Lehi to say that a massacre had happened. See JA 'EG-28/2: testimony by David Gottlieb. See also Amos Kenan's opinion in Barne'a, "'Amos,'" p. 30, Gertz, *Da'at*, p. 202, and Tzipi Shohat, "Shnayim Shlosha Dvarim she-Lo Yada'tem 'al 'Amos Qeynan," *ha-Aretz*, supplement, 15 March 1996, p. 52, and Gelber's opinion in his "Propaganda," pp. 307–308.

11. 'Ayish Muhammad 'Ayish Zaydan, cited in La Guardia, *War*, p. 200. Cf. Freedom Fighters of Israel Heritage Association: letter, Giora [Yehuda Feder] (Jerusalem), 12 April 1948, mentioning that he shot an armed Arab who was shooting at him, and two young girls who assisted the Arab.

12. PACE 241: interview with Muhammad 'Ayish Zaydan.

Bibliography

DOCUMENTS

Israel
Central Zionist Archives, Jerusalem.
    L4: Zionist Commission, Jaffa
    L18: Palestine Land Development Company
    MM: Printed Maps
    NSC: Fritz Schlesinger Collection
    PHG: General Photograph Collection
    PHO: Zvi Oron (Orushkes) Collection
    S25: Political Department of the Jewish Agency
    S63: Office of Levi Eshkol
    S100: Protocols of the Executive of the Jewish Agency

Freedom Fighters of Israel Heritage Association (FFI-LEHI), Tel Aviv.

Haganah Archives, Tel Aviv.
    20: Underground and Other Organizations
    105: Arab Intelligence

106: Testimonies

Israel Defense Forces Archives, Tel ha-Shomer.
446/48: Etzioni Brigade, Headquarters
500/48: Etzioni Brigade, Headquarters
481/49: Chief of the General Staff Office
2504/49: Etzioni Brigade, Headquarters
2605/49: Etzioni Brigade, Headquarters
2644/49: Etzioni Brigade, Headquarters
4944/49: Etzioni Brigade, Headquarters
5254/49: Etzioni Brigade, Headquarters
5440/49: Etzioni Brigade, Headquarters
5942/49: Karmeli Brigade, Headquarters
900/52: Foreign Ministry, Research Branch
1559/52: Chief of the General Staff Office
100001/57: Captured Arabic Materials
922/75: Historical Branch
150/86: David Shaltiel Files
70/2004: Lehi Archives
421/2004: Lehi Archives
Large Posters Collection
Photo Collection
Posters Collection

Israel State Archives, Jerusalem.
G: Prime Minister Office
M: Palestine Government – Chief Secretary and Governor of
the Jerusalem District
P: Yad Yitzhak Ben-Tzvi Collection

Jabotinsky Archives, Tel Aviv.
'E: Testimonies
H13: Max Seligman Archives
K4: Etzel Collection
K'E: Periodicals
TTZ: Photos

National Photo Collection, Jerusalem (www.gpophoto.gov.il).

Palmach Photo Gallery, Palmach House, Tel Aviv.

Survey of Israel, Tel Aviv.
Aerial Photos
Maps

Yad Tabenkin Archives, Ramat Efal.
12: Security
15: Personal Archives
16: Paper Collections

Palestinian Authority
Birzeit University Palestine Archive (www.awraq.birzeit.edu).

Palestinian Association for Cultural Exchange, Ramallah.
Mashru' al-Laji'in (Interviews Archive)

Red Cross
Archives du Comité International de la Croix-Rouge, Geneva.
B G 59/I/GC: Guerre civile en Palestine
B G 3/82: Missions-Délégations en Palestine
Photo Library

United Kingdom
Bodleian Library of Commonwealth and African Studies, Rhodes House, Oxford.
MSS. Brit. Emp. s. 527: 'End of Empire' Transcripts

Imperial War Museum, London.
06/43/1: Peter F. Towers-Clark Diary

Middle East Centre, St. Antony's College, Oxford.
GB165-0072: Alan Cunningham Papers
GB165-0128: Henry Gurney Diary

GB165-0282: Thames Television Palestine Series
GB165-0346: The Fifty Years War – Israel and the Arabs

National Archives, Kew.
AIR 23: Air Ministry – Royal Air Force Overseas Commands
CO 537: Confidential Original Correspondence
CO 733: Palestine Original Correspondence
CO 793: Palestine – Registers of Correspondence
FO 371: Political
FO 816: Legation and Embassy, Amman
WO 261: Middle East Land Forces
WO 275: Sixth Airborne Division, Palestine

United Nations
United Nations Information System on the Question of Palestine (unispal.un.org).

United States
Foreign Broadcast Information Service (infoweb.newsbank.com).
Daily Reports

Library of Congress Prints and Photographs Division, Washington DC.
G. Eric and Edith Matson Photograph Collection

National Archives and Records Administration, College Park MD.
LM163: Confidential U.S. State Department Central Files – Palestine and Israel
M1390: Records of the Department of State Relating to Internal Affairs of Palestine
RG 84: Foreign Service Posts of the Department of State – Jerusalem Consulate General Classified Records

Special Collections Research Center, Georgetown University, Washington DC.
GTM.GAMMS315: Larry Collins Papers

NEWSPAPERS

Ha-Aretz (Tel Aviv), 1948
Ha-Boqer (Tel Aviv), 1948
Daily Telegraph (London), 1948
Davar (Tel Aviv), 1927, 1948
Al-Difaʿ (Jaffa), 1948
Filastin (Jaffa), 1948
Hashqafa (Jerusalem), 1906
Herut (Tel Aviv), 1952–1953
'Iton ha-Magen (Jerusalem), 1948
Ha-Mashqif (Tel Aviv), 1948
Mishmar (Tel Aviv), 1948
New York Herald Tribune (New York), 1948
New York Times (New York), 1948
Palestine Post (Jerusalem), 1948
Ha-Tzofe (Tel Aviv), 1948

BOOKS, ARTICLES AND DISSERTATIONS

"37 ʿAman ʿala al-Majzara: Shuyukh Dayr Yasin Yatadhakkaruna," *Sawt al-Bilad*, 40 (1985), pp. 9–12.

"50 ʿAman ʿala Madhbahat Dayr Yasin – Muʾarrikh Israʾili: Madhabih Afzaʿ lam Tudhkar!," *al-Safir*, 7 April 1998, p. 12.

"60 Shaʿot be-Dir Yasin (Sipuro shel ha-Lohem Yaʿaqov)," in Oren [Nadel], Baruch, *Ba-Matzor: Emet Yerushalayim* (Tel Aviv, 1949), pp. 34–37.

ʿAbd al-Hadi, Fayhaʾ, "Majzarat Dayr Yasin: Shahadat man Shahidu al-Majzara," *Dawriyyat Dirasat al-Marʾa*, 3 (2005), pp. 8–20.

ʿAbd al-Majid, Faʾiza, "Sutur min Kifah Filastin: Shahidat Dayr Yasin Hayat Salim al-Balbisi," *al-ʿArabi*, 65 (1964), pp. 118–122.

Abdel Jawad, Saleh, "Zionist Massacres: The Creation of the Palestinian Problem in the 1948 War," in Benvenisti, Eyal, Gans, Chaim and Hanafi, Sari (eds.), *Israel and the Palestinian Refugees* (Berlin, 2007), pp. 59–127.

Abu Gharbiyya, Bahjat, *Fi Khidamm al-Nidal al-'Arabi al-Filastini: Mudhakkirat al-Munadil Bahjat Abu Gharbiyya 1916–1949* (Beirut, 1993).

"Abu Mahmud ma Zala Shahidan 'ala Majzarat Dayr Yasin," *al-Safir*, 8 April 2001, p. 8.

Abu Mu'tazz, "Shuhada' Majzarat Dayr Yasin 1948," *Shabakat al-Quds lil-Hiwar*, elqudos.com/vb/showpost. php?p=146840&postcount=1.

Abu-Sitta, Salman H., *Atlas of Palestine 1948* (London, 2004).

———, *The Palestinian Nakba 1948: The Register of Depopulated Localities in Palestine* (London, 1998).

Amikam, Eliahu, "Ha-Hagana Hiskima me-Rosh le-Kibush Kfar Dir Yasin," *Yedi'ot Aharonot*, 19 August 1960, *7 Yamim* Saturday's supplement, p. 3.

Amir, Ehud, *Gadna' Yerushalayim be-Tashah* (n.p., 2003).

'Aql, Muhammad, "'Alaqat Ahali Dayr Yasin al-Tayyiba bil-Yahud lam Tamna' al-Madhbaha," 1 April 2010, www.arabs48. com/?mod=articles&ID=69887.

'Aql, Muhammad Mahmud As'ad [Radwan], "Haqa'iq Waqi'iyya min Majzarat Dayr Yasin al-Basila (1948)," www.awraq.birzeit.edu/ sites/default/files/PDF_153.

"'Aql Yakshifu Tafasil Murawwi'a 'an Madhbahat Dayr Yasin," *Ida'a*, 15 April 2013, eda2a.com/news/3/35534.

Arbel, E[liyahu], "Hayiti Qtzin ha-Haganah she-Siyyer be-Dir Yasin le-Mohorat ha-Pe'ula," *Yedi'ot Aharonot*, 2 May 1972, p. 20.

'Arif, 'Arif al-, *Nakbat Filastin wal-Firdaws al-Mafqud 1947–1952* ([Sidon, 1956]), vols. 1, 6.

Arnold, Michael S., "The Ghosts of Deir Yassin," *The Jerusalem Post Magazine*, 3 April 1998, pp. 8–10.

As'ad [Radwan], Da'ud Ahmad, *Filastin Tashu: Ahdath wa-Masir – Kayfa Najawtu min Madhbahat Dir Yasin* ([Bloomington IN], 2012).

As'ad [Radwan], Yunus Ahmad, "Al-Dhikra al-Khamisa li-Majzarat Dayr Yasin Yaktabuha Ahad Abna'iha," *al-Urdunn*, 9 April 1953, p. 3.

Assad [Radwan], Dawud A., *Palestine Rising: How I Survived the 1948 Deir Yasin Massacre* ([Bloomington IN], [2010] 2nd rep. 2011).

Avigdori-Avidov, Hadassah, *"Ba-Derekh she-Halakhnu...": Mi-Yomana shel- Melavat Shayarot* (Tel Aviv, 1988).

Avizohar, Meir, *Moriya bi-Yerushalayim be-Tashah: Gdud ha-Hish ha-Rishon bi-Qravot Yerushalayim* (Lod, 2002).

Avner, Yehuda, "The Ghosts of Deir Yassin," *Jerusalem Post*, 8 April 2007, pp. 13–14.

Avneri, Uri, "Dir Yasin," *ha-'Olam ha-Ze*, 3 July 1972, p. 13.

Avrahami, Avner, "Ruhot ha-Refa'im shel Dir Yasin," *Ma'ariv of Sukkot*, 11 October 1992, pp. 12–13, 29.

'Awawda, Wadi', *Dhakira la Tamutu* ([Haifa], 2000).

——, "Isra'il Tarfadu Fath Milaff Dayr Yasin," *al-Jazira Net*, 8 April 2011, www.palestineremembered.com/Jerusalem/Dayr-Yasin/Story19755.html

——, "Isra'il Tuwasilu al-Takattum 'ala Majzarat Dayr Yasin," *al-Jazira Net*, 9 April 2008, www.palestineremembered.com/Jerusalem/Dayr-Yasin/Story9260.html.

——, "Majzarat Dayr Yasin Tuthiru al-Jadal bayna al-Isra'iliyyin," *al-Jazira Net*, 9 April 2008, www.palestineremembered.com/Jerusalem/Dayr-Yasin/Story9261.html.

'Awda, 'Awda Butrus, *Masra' Filastin* (Jerusalem, [1950]).

Banks, Lynne Reid, *Torn Country: An Oral History of the Israeli War of Independence* (New York, 1982).

Bar'el, Tzvi and Shay, Eli, "Be-Hazara le-Dir Yasin," *Kol ha-'Ir*, 1 May 1981, pp. 22–25.

Bar-Zohar, Michael, *Ben-Gurion* (Tel Aviv, 1977), vol. 2.

Barnea, Nahum, "'Amos Qeynan: Ha-Shanim ha-Shhorot," *Koteret Rashit*, 108, 26 December 1984, pp. 29–32.

——, "Dir Yasin Hazarnu Elayikh Shenit," *Davar*, 9 April 1982, p. 13.

Be'er, Yizhar, "Ha-Kfarim ha-Smuyim min ha-'Ayin," *Kol ha-'Ir*, 25 November 1988, pp. 35–36.

Bedein, David, "The Big Lie of a Massacre at Deir Yassin: New Facts behind Deir Yassin – The Witness Who Was Not There"

(Jerusalem), 9 April 1998, radiobergen.org/history/deir-6. html.

Begin, Menachem, *Ba-Mahteret* (Tel Aviv, 1961), vol. 4.

———, "Be-Regashot Me'oravim," *Ma'ariv*, 8 January 1971, p. 17.

———, "Hazmana le-Vaqer be-London," *Ma'ariv*, 23 April 1971, p. 13.

———, *The Revolt* (Tel Aviv, [1952]).

———, "Why the Irgun Fought the British: The Former Commander of the Irgun Zvai Leumi Gives his Personal Account of Dir Yassin," *Times*, 14 April 1971, p. 21.

Bell, J. Bowyer, *Terror Out of Zion: The Fight for Israeli Independence* (New Brunswick NJ and London, 1996).

Ben-Vered, Amos, "Dir Yasin, 'Adayin Lo 'Inyan le-Historyonim Bilvad," *ha-Aretz*, 19 April 1989, p. B4.

Ben-Ami, Shuki, "Dir Yasin – Petza' she-lo Higlid," *'al ha-Mishmar*, 8 April 1983, Saturday's supplement, pp. 4–5.

Ben-Ami, Yitshaq, *Years of Wrath, Days of Glory: Memoirs from the Irgun* (New York, 2nd ed. 1983).

Ben-Gurion, David, *Zikhronot* (Tel Aviv, 1971), vol. 1.

Ben-Tor, Nechemia, *Sefer Toldot Lohamey Herut Yisra'el (Lehi)* (Jerusalem, 2010), vol. 4.

Ben-Tor, Nechemia and others (eds.), *Lehi – Anashim: Sipur Hayeyhem shel 840 Lohamim ve-Lohamot* (Tel Aviv, 2002), vols. 1–2.

Bender, Aryeh, "Matzpunenu Naqi," *Ma'ariv*, 3 August 1986, p. 11.

Benvenisti, Meron, *Sacred Landscape: The Buried History of the Holy Land Since 1948* (Berkeley CA, 2002).

Berger, Earl, *The Covenant and the Sword* (London, 1965).

Bethell, Nicholas, *The Palestine Triangle: The Struggle between the British, the Jews and the Arabs 1935–48* (London, 1979).

Binyamin, Avraham, "Ha-Bor shel Saba," *'Olam Qatan*, 442, 28 March 2014, pp. 8–9.

Bregman, Ahron and al-Tahri, Jihan, *The Fifty Years War: Israel and the Arabs* (London, 1998).

Bronstein, Eitan, *Zokhrot et Dir Yasin* (Tel Aviv, 2006).

Budeiri, Musa, "A Chronicle of a Defeat Foretold: The Battle for Jerusalem in the Memoirs of Anwar Nusseibeh," *Jerusalem Quarterly File*, 11–12 (2001), pp. 40–51.

Bulos, Nassib and Thicknesse, S[ubylla] G[ratiana], *Arab Loss in Palestine, November 1947-December 1949* (n.p., 1 March 1950).

Childers, Erskine, "The Other Exodus," *The Spectator*, 12 May 1961, pp. 8–11.

———, "The Wordless Wish: From Citizens to Refugees," in Abu Lughod, Ibrahim (ed.), *The Transformation of Palestine: Essays on the Origin and Development of the Arab-Israeli Conflict* (Evanston IL, 1971), pp. 165–202.

Cohen, Hillel, "'Amutat Zekher Dir Yasin Tehapes et Gufot Harugey ha-Tevah be-1948 mi-tahat le-Migrash ha-Rusim," *Kol ha-'Ir*, 29 April 1998, p. 31.

———, "Shel Mi ha-Tevah ha-Ze, le-'Azazel," *Kol ha-'Ir*, 20 June 1997, pp. 70–73.

Cohen, Meir, "Yerushalayim shel HA," *Bit'on Heyl ha-Avir*, 91 (1973), pp. 74–76, 209–210.

Cohen, Yonah, *Yerushalayim ba-Matzor* (Tel Aviv, 1976).

Cohen, Zehava, Letter to the Editor, *Ma'ariv*, 19 May 1974, p. 25.

Collins, Larry and Lapierre, Dominique, *O Jerusalem!* (Jerusalem, 1972).

Cull, Brian, Aloni, Shlomo and Nicolle, David, *Spitfires over Israel* (London, [1994]).

Darwaza, Muhammad 'Izzat, *Al-Qadiyya al-Filasiniyya fi Mukhtalif Marahiliha* (Sidon and Beirut, [1960]), vol. 2.

Dayan, David, *Ken, Anahnu No'ar! Sefer Toldot ha-Gadna'* (Tel Aviv, 1977).

"Dayr Yasin (Madhbaha – 1948)," *Al-Mawsu'a al-Filastiniyya* (Damascus, 1984), al-Qism al-'Amm, vol. 2, pp. 432–435.

"Dayr Yasin (Qarya)," *Al-Mawsu'a al-Filastiniyya* (Damascus, 1984), al-Qism al-'Amm, vol. 2, p. 432.

"The Deir Yassin Massacres," *Proche-Orient: Near East Monthly Review*, 6:1 (May 1950), pp. 35–37.

de Reynier, Jacques, *A Jerusalem un drapeau flottait sur la ligne de feu* (Neuchâtel, 1950).

Delorme, Roger, *Inni Attahimu* (Montreal, 2nd ed. 1983).

Derogy, Jacques and Saab, Edouard, *Les deux Exodes* (Paris, 1968).

"Al-Dhikra 58 'ala Madhbahat Dayr Yasin wa-Dhikra Istishhad 'Abd al-Qadir al-Husayni," 8 April 2006, www.arabs48. com/?mod=articles&ID=35979.

Dinur, Ben-Zion and others (eds.), *Sefer Toldot ha-Haganah* (Tel Aviv, 1954–72), vol. 2, pt. 1, vol. 3, pts. 2–3.

"Dir Yasin – Kol ha-Emet," *Ma'oz*, 18, October 1970, pp. 14–16, 18.

"Dir Yasin – Tragedya ba-Historya shel Etzel – Ulam ha-Avedot Nigremu be-Qrav; Lo Haya Tevah!," *Yedi'ot Aharonot*, 22 June 1979, p. 8.

Douglas, William O., *Strange Lands and Friendly People* (New York, 1951).

Dror, Eliel, "Dir Yasin," *Herut*, 19 May 1950, p. 5.

"Editorial: Deir Yassin," *Arab News Bulletin*, no. 61 (The Arab Office, London), 23 April 1948, p. 1.

[Egypt], Wizarat al-Irshad al-Qawmi – Al-Hay'a al-'Amma lil-Isti'lamat, *Dayr Yasin: Ramz Falsafat al-Sahyuniyya, al-Saytara bil-Satw wal-Tahakkum bil-Irhab, 9 Abril 1948 – 9 Abril 1969* ([Cairo, 1969]).

Eldad, Israel, *Ma'aser Rishon: Pirkey Zikhronot u-Musar Haskel* (Tel Aviv, 3rd ed. 1975).

Even-Or, Shmuel, "Dir Yasin," *Qardom: Mivhar Ma'amarim bi-Yedi'at ha-Aretz*, 1–11 [1982], pp. 161–164.

Farsakh, 'Awni, "Majzarat Dayr Yasin fi Dhikraha al-Sittin," 12 April 2008, www.arabs48.com/?mod=articles&ID=53368.

Flapan, Simha, *The Birth of Israel: Myths and Realities* (London and Sydney, 1987).

Fleishmann, Ellen, "Young Women in the City: Mandate Memories," *Jerusalem Quarterly File*, 2 (1998), pp. 31–39.

Gani, Pesach, "Silufey Dir Yasin," *Ma'ariv*, 18 April 1973, p. 5.

[Gefen, Shay] Dvir, Y. (pseud.), "Dir Yasin: Ha-Sipur ha-Male," *ha-Shavu'a*, parashat Tazri'a-Metzora', April 1998, pp. 18–20.

Gelber, Yoav, *Jewish-Transjordanian Relations 1921–48* (London, 1997).

————, "Propaganda as History: What Happened at Deir Yassin?," in idem, *Palestine 1948: War, Escape and the Emergence of the Palestinian Refugee Problem* (Brighton, 2006), pp. 307–318.

————, *Qomemiyut ve-Nakba: Yisra'el, ha-Palestinim u-Medinot 'Arav, 1948* (Or Yehuda, 2004).

Geller, Doron, "O Writer," *Jerusalem Post*, 23 March 2001, p. 10.

Gertz, Nurith, *'Al Da'at 'Atzmo: Araba'a Pirqey Hayim shel 'Amos Qeynan* (Tel Aviv, 2008).

Gervasi, Frank, *The Life and Times of Menahem Begin: Rebel to Statesman* (New York, 1979).

Gichon, Mordechai, *Mate Mordechai* ([Reut], 2010).

Giniewski, Paul, *De Massada à Beyrouth: Une leçon d'Histoire* (Paris, 1983).

————, "Dir Yassine: un drame," *Memoir de l'Histoire*, no. 286, Spécial 12: *Les Combats d'Israël*, 9 April 1973, pp. 272–278.

Glubb, John Bagot, *A Soldier with the Arabs* (London, 1957).

Golan, Aviezer, *Milhemet ha-Atzma'ut* (Tel Aviv, 1968).

Golan, Aviezer and Nakdimon, Shlomo, *Begin* (Jerusalem, 1978).

Golani, Motti, *The End of the British Mandate for Palestine, 1948: The Diary of Sir Henry Gurney* (Basingstoke, 2009).

————, *Hanhagat ha-Yishuv u-Sh'elat Yerushalayim be-Milhemet ha-'Atzma'ut, Detzember 1947 – May 1948* (MA thesis, Hebrew University, 1988).

————, *Ha-Natziv ha-Aharon: Ha-General Seyr Elen Gordon Qaningham, 1945–1948* (Tel Aviv, 2011).

Golani, Yardena, *Ha-Mitos shel Dir Yasin* (Tel Aviv, 1976).

Goldfoot, Stanley, "I Was There," *The Times of Israel*, 23 April 1970, p. 11.

Goldstein [Golan], Aviezer, *Lehavot bi-Shmey Yerushalayim* (Tel Aviv, 1949).

Graves, R[ichard] M., *Experiment in Anarchy* (London, 1949).

Habib Allah, Ghanim, "Majzarat Dayr Yasin fil-Fikr wal-Mumarasa al-Sahyuniyya," *Kan'an*, 3 (1991), pp. 62–71.

Hadawi, Sami, *Bitter Harvest: A Modern History of Palestine* (New York, 4th ed., 1991).

Hanania, Ray, "Forward from the Ansar Code: The Palestinian Book of 'Exodus'," www.themediaoasis.com/ansarcodeforward. htm.

Haskin, Gilad, "Parashat Dir Yasin – Tevah, Ta'ut Metza'eret, o 'Alila?," [2006], www.gilihaskin.com/Article.Asp?ArticleNum=897.

Hasso, Frances S., "Modernity and Gender in Arab Accounts of the 1948 and 1967 Defeats," *International Journal of Middle East Studies*, 32:4 (2000), pp. 491–510.

Hassuna, Khadija, "Al-'Alaqat bayna al-'Arab wal-Yahud qabla 'Am 1948 – Dayr Yasin: Dirasat Hala," *al-Turath wal-Mujtama'*, 41 (2005), pp. 115–122.

Hijazi, 'Arafat, *15 Ayyar 'Am al-Nakba* ([Amman, 1968]).

———, *Dayr Yasin: Judhur wa-Ab'ad al-Jarima fil-Fikr al-Sahyuni* ([Amman?], 1978).

Hirbawi, Najat, "Deir Yassin: My Memories," *Palestine-Israel Journal*, 5:2 (1998), pp. 70–72.

Hogan, Matthew, "The 1948 Massacre at Deir Yassin Revisited," *The Historian*, 63:2 (2001), pp. 309–333.

Hogan, Matthew C. and McGowan, Daniel A., "Anatomy of a White-wash: A Critical Examination and Refutation of the Historical Revisionist 'Deir Yassin: History of a Lie', Issued by the Zionist Organization of America (March 8, 1998)," www.deiryassin. org/op0005.html.

Holmes, Paul, "Deir Yassin a casualty of guns and propaganda" (Jerusalem), [6 April 1998], radiobergen.eu/palestine/deir-02. html.

Hovav, Meir, *Gal – Dmuto shel Lohem: Hayav u-Ma'asav shel Lohem ha-Etzel Yehush'a Yeruham Goldshmid* (Tel Aviv, 1990).

Howeidy, Amira, "It's Difficult to Count," *Al-Ahram Weekly*, 9–15 April 1998, weekly.ahram.org.eg/1998/1948/372_yass.htm.

Humphries, Isabelle and Khalili, Laleh, "Gender of Nakba Memory," in Sa'di, Ahmad H. and Abu-Lughod, Lila (eds.), *Nakba: Palestine, 1948, and the Claims of Memory* (New York, 2007), pp. 207–227.

IDF Historical Branch, *Toldot Milhemet ha-Qomemiyut* (Tel Aviv, [1959] rep. 1978).

Igbariyyeh, Umar, "The 60th Anniversary of the Deir Yassin Massacre," 17 April 2008, www.palestineremembered.com/Jerusalem/Dayr-Yasin/Story9373.html.

International Committee of the Red Cross, *The International Committee of the Red Cross in Palestine* (Geneva, July 1948).

[Israel], Ministry for Foreign Affairs, Information Division, *Background Notes on Current Themes: Dir Yassin* (Jerusalem, 16 March 1969).

Israel, State Archives, and World Zionist Organization, Central Zionist Archives, *Te'udot Mediniyot ve-Diplomatiyot Detzember 1947-May 1948* (Jerusalem, 1979).

Isseroff, Ami, "Coming to Terms with Deir Yassin," February 2000, middle-east.yu-hu.com/peacewatch/dy/.

———, "Deir Yassin: The Conflict as Mass Psychosis," 10 April 2005, www.mideastweb.org/log/archives/00000350.htm.

———, "Deir Yassin – The Evidence," [updated February 2000], middle-east.yu-hu.com/peacewatch/dy/dycg.htm.

'Iyad, Shafiqa, "Shuhud 'Iyan min Madhbahat Dayr Yasin," www.awraq.birzeit.edu/sites/default/files/PDF_154.

Izenberg, Dan, "Court to Decide Whether Army Must Release All Material on Deir Yassin," *Jerusalem Post*, 5 May 2010, p. 5.

The Jewish Agency, *The Jewish Agency's Digest of Press and Events*, no. 219 (Jerusalem), 18 April 1948.

John, Robert and Hadawi, Sami, *The Palestine Diary* (New York, 1970), vol. 2.

Joseph, Dov, *The Faithful City* (New York, 1960).

Juburi, Salih Sa'ib al-, *Mihnat Filastin wa-Asraruha al-Siyasiyya wal-'Askariyya* (Beirut, 1970).

Junod, Dominique-D., *The Imperiled Red Cross and the Palestine–Eretz-Yisrael Conflict 1945–1952* (London and New York, 1996).

Kana'na, Sharif, "Madhbahat Dayr Yasin: Qira'a Jadida," in *Al-Shatat al-Filastini: Hijra am Tahjir?* (Bira, 2000), pp. 152–181.

———, "Reinterpreting Deir Yassin," in *Still on Vacation! The Eviction of the Palestinian in 1948* (Jerusalem, 2000), pp. 145–172.

Kana'na, Sharif and Zaytawi, Nihad, *Dayr Yasin* (Birzeit, 2nd rep. 1987).

Kanaaneh, Rhoda and Nusair, Isis (eds.), *Displaced at Home: Ethnicity and Gender among Palestinians in Israel* (Albany NY, 2010).

Kark, Ruth and Oren-Nordheim, Michal, *Jerusalem and its Environs: Quarters, Neighborhoods, Villages 1800–1948* (Jerusalem and Detroit, 2001).

Karpel, Dalia, "Zikhronot mi-Dir Yasin," *ha-Aretz*, supplement, 12 August 2011, p. 34.

Katz, Samuel, *Days of Fire* (London, 1968).

Katzman, Avi, "Ha-Mitos be-Lav Hakhi Ma'afil 'al ha-'Uvdot," *ha-Aretz*, 25 April 1993, p. B9.

Kedem, Michal, "Raq Psikhiater Yakhol le-Hasbir – Dr Meir Pa'il: Hayiti Sham ve-Ra'iti et ha-Tevah," *Hadashot*, 2 September 1991, p. 13.

Keydar, Renana, "'I Was in a War, and in a War Things Like That Happen': On Judgement and Ethical Investigation in Israeli Law and Literature," *Jewish Social Studies*, NS 18:3 (2012), pp. 212–224.

Kfir, Ilan, "Shalosh Girsot 'al Parashat Dir Yasin," *Yedi'ot Aharonot*, 4 April 1972, pp. 2–3.

Khalidi, Husayn Fakhri al-, *Wa-Mada 'Ahd al-Mujamalat: Mudhakkirat Husayn Fakhri al-Khalidi* (Amman, 2014), vols. 1–3.

Khalidi, Walid al- (ed.), *All That Remains: The Palestinian Villages Occupied and Depopulated by Israel in 1948* (Washington DC, [1992] rep. 2006).

———, *Dayr Yasin: Al-Jum'a, 9 Nisan/Abril 1948* (Jerusalem, 1999).

———, *From Haven to Conquest: Readings in Zionism and the Palestine Problem until 1948* (Beirut, 1971).

———, *Kay la Nansa: Qura Filastin Allati Dammaratha Isra'il Sanat 1948 wa-Asma' Shuhada'iha* (Beirut, [1997]).

Kimche, John, *Seven Fallen Pillars: The Middle East, 1915–1950* (London, 1950).

Kimhi, Yoel, "Sin'a 'Iveret le-Irguney ha-Mahteret," *Yedi'ot Aharonot*, 2 May 1972, p. 21.

Klein, Morton A., *Deir Yassin: History of a Lie* (The Zionist Organization of America, 9 March 1998).

————, "Deir Yassin: The 1948 'Jewish Massacre of Arabs' that Never Was," 18 March 1998, radiobergen.org/history/deir-1.html.

Koestler, Arthur, *Promise and Fulfilment: Palestine 1917–1949* (New York, 1949).

Krystall, Nathan, "The De-Arabization of West Jerusalem 1947–50," *Journal of Palestine Studies*, 27:2 (1998), pp. 5–22.

Kurtzman, Daniel, "Israelis, Palestinians still dispute tragic 1948 battle," 10 April 1998, www.jweekly.com/article/full/8039.

Kurzman, Dan, *Ben-Gurion: Prophet of Fire* (New York, 1984).

————, *Genesis 1948: The First Arab-Israeli War* (New York, 1970).

La Guardia, Anton, *War Without End: Israelis, Palestinians, and the Struggle for a Promised Land* (New York, [2001] updated ed. 2003).

Langer, Felicia, *Be-Darki sheli* (Tel Aviv, 1991).

Lapidot, Yehuda, *'Al Homotayikh: Zikhronot Lohem Etzel* ([Tel Aviv], 1992).

————, *Be-Lahav ha-Mered: Ma'arkhot ha-Etzel bi-Yerushalayim* ([Tel Aviv], 1996).

————, "Ha-'Uvdot Kvar Yedu'ot," *ha-Aretz*, 18 May 1993, p. 16.

————, Letter to the Editor, *ha-Aretz*, 2 February 1998, p. B6.

League of Arab States, Permanent Delegation to Geneva, *Il y a vingt ans – Deir Yassin: Comment oublier? Comment pardonner?* (Geneva, April 1968).

League of Arab States, Secretariat General, Palestine Department, Political Section, *Israel's Aggression prior to the Israeli Attack of October 29, 1956, on Egypt* (Cairo, 1957).

Lev-'Ami, Shlomo, *Ba-Ma'avaq u-va-Mered* (Tel Aviv, 1979).

Lever, Walter, *Jerusalem Is Called Liberty* (Jerusalem, 1951).

Levin, Harry, *Jerusalem Embattled: A Diary of the City under Siege, March 25th, 1948 to July 18th, 1948* (London, 1950).

Levius, Harold, *Conflict of Lies: History of the 1948 Palestinian Catastrophe and Its Continuing Genocidal Aftermath* (n.p., 2012).

Levy, Yitzhak, *Tish'a Qabin: Yerushalayim bi-Qravot Milhemet ha-'Atzma'ut* ([Tel Aviv], 1986).

Lohamey Herut Yisra'el – Ktavim (Tel Aviv, 1959), vol. 2.

London, Yaron, "Al Tivki America," *Yedi'ot Aharonot*, 14 February 1992, 7 *Yamim* Saturday's supplement, pp. 27–31.

Lorch, Netanel, *The Edge of the Sword: Israel's War of Independence, 1947–1949* (Jerusalem, [1961] 2nd ed. 1968).

Lynd, Staughton, Bahour, Sam and Lynd, Alice (eds.), *Homeland: Oral History of Palestine and Palestinians* (New York, 1994).

Madsen, Ann N., *Making Their Own Peace: Twelve Women of Jerusalem* (New York, 2003).

Maiberg, Ron, "Dir Yasin – Har'u lanu et ha-Tzilumim," *Monitin*, 32 (April 1981), pp. 36–40.

Martin, Ralph G., *Golda – Golda Meir: The Romantic Years* (New York, 1988).

Marton, Kati, *A Death in Jerusalem* (New York, 1996).

Matza, Yehoshua, *Shney Eqdahim: Praqim me-Havayot Politiyot* (Tel Aviv, 2014).

McGowan, Daniel A. and Ellis, Marc H. (eds.), *Remembering Deir Yassin: The Future of Israel and Palestine* (New York, 1998).

McGowan, Daniel A. and Hogan, Matthew C., *The Saga of Deir Yassin: Massacre, Revisionism and Reality* (Geneva NY, 1999), www.deiryassin.org/pdf/SAGAA4.pdf.

Milstein, Uri, *'Alilat Dam be-Dir Yasin* ([Tel-Aviv], 2007).

———, *Be-Dam va-Esh Yehuda* (Tel Aviv, 1973).

———, *The Birth of a Palestinian Nation: The Myth of the Deir Yassin Massacre* (Jerusalem and New York, 2012).

———, "Dir Yasin," *ha-Aretz*, 30 August 1968, pp. 16–19.

———, "Ha-Hartza'a she-Lo Nitna," *ha-Aretz*, 10 March 1989, p. 15.

———, *History of Israel's War of Independence* (Lanham MD, 1998), vol. 4.

———, *Toldot Milhemet ha-'Atzma'ut* (Tel-Aviv, 1991), vol. 4.

"Min Mudhakkirat Khalil Sammur bi-Khatt Yadihi Ya'uddu fiha Ba'd Asma' al-Shuhada' fil-Madhbaha," www.palestineremembered. com/OralHistoryMP3/Jerusalem/Dayr-Yasin/Muhammad-Sammur/docs/Picture002.jpg.

Moneta, Shimon, *Gam Ele Toldot: Asufat Dapim* (Jerusalem, 2011).

————, "Kavana Re'uya, Aval Shiqul Mut'e," *ha-Aretz, Tarbut ve-Sifrut* supplement, 1 May 2009, p. 4.

Morris, Benny, *1948: A History of the First Arab-Israeli War* (New Haven and London, 2008).

————, *The Birth of the Palestinian Refugee Problem, 1947–1949* (Cambridge, [1987] rep. 1994).

————, *The Birth of the Palestinian Refugee Problem Revisited* (Cambridge, 2004).

————, "The Causes and Character of the Arab Exodus from Palestine: The Israel Defence Forces Intelligence Service Analysis of June 1948," in idem, *1948 and After: Israel and the Palestinians* (Oxford, 1994), pp. 83–102 (previously published in *Middle Eastern Studies*, 22:1, 1986, pp. 5–19).

————, "The Historiography of Deir Yassin," *The Journal of Israeli History*, 24:1 (2005), pp. 79–107.

Al-Munazzama al-Filastiniyya li-Hquq al-Insan, *Al-Kitab al-Aswad: Al-Majazir al-Isra'iliyya fil-Qarn al-'Ishrin* (Beirut, 2001).

Nadel, Baruch, *Retzah Bernadot* (Tel Aviv, 1968).

————, "Siluf History mul Siluf History," *Yedi'ot Aharonot, Tarbut, Sifrut, Amanut* supplement, 30 July 1976, p. 2.

[Nadel] Oren, Baruch, *Ba-Matzor: Emet Yerushalayim* (Tel Aviv, 1949).

Nevo, Yosef, *'Abdallah ve-'Arviyey Eretz Yisra'el* (Tel Aviv, 1975).

Netach, Israel, *Yisra'el Netah – Patriyot Yisra'eli* (Ramat Gan, [2003]).

Nijim, Basheer K. and Muammar, Bishara, *Toward the De-Arabization of Palestine/Israel 1945–1977* (Dubuque IA, 1984).

Nimr, 'Abbas, *Dayr Yasin fi Atun al-Ma'raka* ([Ramallah?], n.d.).

Nimrod, Yoram, *Breyrat ha-Shalom ve-Derekh ha-Milhama: Hithavut Dfusim shel Yahasey Yisra'el-'Arav, 1947–1950* (Givat Haviva, 2000).

————, "Dir Yasin o Mishmar ha-'Emeq? Shtey Astrategyot Menugadot be-Milhemet ha-Shihrur," in idem, *Mifgash be-Tzomet: Yehudim ve-'Aravim be-Eretz Yisra'el – Dorot Aharonim, Pirqey Mehqar ve-Hora'a* (Haifa University-Oranim, 1985), pp. 121–126.

————, "Golda Meir beyn Ben-Gurion ve-'Abdallah: Shtey Pgishot Shney Dgeshim Halifiyim," in Nevo, Yosef and Nimrod, Yoram (eds.), *Ha-'Aravim el mul ha-Tnu'a ha-Tziyonit veha-Yishuv ha-Yehudi 1946–1950* (Oranim, 1987), pp. 59–98.

"Nipeah et Parasat Dir Yasin; Hashash mi-Begin," *Hadashot*, 2 July 1987, p. 3.

Niv, David, *Ma'arkhot ha-Irgun ha-Tzva'i ha-Le'umi* (Tel Aviv, 1980), vol. 6.

Nusseibeh, Hazem Zaki, *Jerusalemites: A Living Memory* (Nicosia, 2009).

O'Ballance, Edgar, *The Arab-Israeli War 1948* (London, 1956).

Oded, Haim, "Oto Mifne," *Herut*, 2 March 1951, p. 6.

Ofir, Yehoshua, *'Al ha-Homot* (Tel Aviv, 1961).

————, "Dir Yasin – Az ve-ha-Yom," *Herut*, 5 April 1957, p. 5.

————, "Kovshey Dir Yasin Motetu et ha-Hazit ha-'Aravit," *Herut*, 7 February 1964, p. 5.

————, "Sha'alti'el Biqesh me-Etzel le-Hahaziq be-Dir Yasin Kekhol she-Yukhal," *Herut*, 5 April 1949, p. 3.

————, *Tirat al-'Amawi* (Givatayim, 1987).

Orenstein, Yaakov, "Aluf David Sha'alti'el: Ha-Kni'a Hayta be-Nigud le-Hora'otay," *Hed ha-Hagana*, 11 (October 1960), pp. 87–89.

Ottewell, Guy, "Deir Yassin: A Forgotten Tragedy With Present-Day Meaning," in Fath, *Deir Yassin, 1948, Zeita, Beit Nuba and Yalu, 1967* (n.p., [1969]), pp. 3–13.

Pa'il, Meir, "Ha-Emet ha-Hatzuya be-Farashat Dir Yasin," *Yedi'ot Aharonot*, 20 April 1972, pp. 14, 23.

[Pa'il-Pilavsky, Meir] Avraham, "Dir Yasin ve-Herpoteha," *ba-Mahane*, 5–6, 16 April 1948, p. 1.

Pail, Meir and Isseroff, Ami, "Deir Yassin: Meir Pail's Eyewitness Account," 1 October 1998, www.ariga.com/peacewatch/dy/dypail.htm.

Pa'il, Meir and Yurman, Pinchas, *Mivhan ha-Tnu'a ha-Tziyonit 1931–1948: Marut ha-Hanhaga ha-Medinit mul ha-Porshim* (Tel Aviv, [2003]).

Pa'il, Opher (ed.), *Meirke – Meir Pa'il: Mefaqed, Mehanekh, Historyon u-Politiqay – Pirqey Hayim u-Ma'amarim* ([Kiryat Ono], 2014).

Palumbo, Michael, *The Palestinian Catastrophe: The 1948 Expulsion of a People from Their Homeland* (London, [1987] 1989).

"Parashat Dir Yasin," *Esh*, no. 8, 15 April 1948, p. 5.

Peled (Stahl), Shraga, *Sipurim min ha-Arkhiyon* (Tel Aviv, 2006).

Perlmutter, Amos, *The Life and Times of Menachem Begin* (Garden City NY, 1987).

"Qaryat wa-Madhbahat Dayr Yasin – Film Wtha'iqi bi-Shahadat Najin," *al-Quds al-'Arabi*, 10 April 2013, www.alquds.co.uk/index.asp?fname=online\data\2013-04-10-18-15-06.htm.

Qasim, Samih al-, *Min Famika Udinuka: Qira'at fi Watha'iq Isra'iliyya Khatira* (Acre, 1974).

Qusari, Muhammad Fa'iz al-, *Harb Filastin 'Am 1948* (Damascus, 1962), vol. 2.

Raday, Itamar, *Beyn Shtey 'Arim: Ha-'Aravim ha-Palestinim bi-Yerushalayim uve-Yafo 1947–1948* (Tel Aviv, 2015).

———, *Ha-Kohot ha-Bilti Sdirim ve-ha-Hit'argenut ha-'Arvit be-Ezor Yerushalayim me-Reshit Detzember 1947 'ad ha-19 be-May 1948* (MA thesis, Hebrew University, 2002).

Ram, Uri, "Ways of Forgetting: Israel and the Obliterated Memory of the Palestinian Nakba," *Journal of Historical Sociology*, 22:3 (2009), pp. 366–395.

Rees, Matt, "Village of Blood and Lies," *Newsweek* (International ed.), 4 May 1998, p. 29.

Regev-Yarkoni, Hadas and Regev, Ofer, *Lohem Herut Yerushalayim: Zikhronotav shel Yehoshu'a Zetler* (Tzur Yigal, 2007).

Ronel, Eti, "Kikar ha-Mantziha Ketem," *'al ha-Mishmar*, 12 August 1986, p. 2.

Rose, Norman, *'A Senseless Squalid War': Voices from Palestine 1945–1948* (London, 2009).

Rozen, Rami, "Kol Ehad ve-ha-Tashah shelo," *ha-Aretz*, supplement, 19 April 1991, pp. 4–7, 47.

Rubinstein, Dani, "Ha-She'ela eyna Kama, Ela Lama," *ha-Aretz*, 28 January 1998, p. B2.

Sa'd, Khalid al-(ed.), *Khutab al-Shaykh al-Qaradawi* (Cairo, 2003), vol. 5.

Safieh, Hanna, *A Man and His Camera: Photographs of Palestine 1927–1967* (Jerusalem, 1999).

Sakakini, Hala, *Jerusalem and I: A Personal Record* (Jerusalem, 1987).

Salayima, Fadi, *Dayr Yasin: Al-Qarya al-Shahida* (Damascus, 2008).

Salihiyya, Muhammad 'Isa, "Al-Nuzuh al-Kabir," *Al-Qadiyya al-Filastiniyya fi Arba'in 'Aman – Bayna Darawat al-Waqi' wa-Tumuhat al-Mustaqbal: Buhuth wa-Munaqashat al-Nadwa al-Fikriyya Allati Nazzamatha Jam'iyyat al-Khirrijin fil-Kuwayt* (Beirut and Kuwait, 1989), pp. 109–144.

Schechtman, Joseph B., *Israel Explodes Dir Yassin Blood Libel* (New York, [1969]).

———, "The Truth About Dir Yassin: An Official Vindication of Libeled Heroes of 1948," *The American Zionist*, 59:10 (June 1969), pp. 17–20.

Schmidt, Dana Adams, *Armageddon in the Middle East* (New York, 1974).

Schossberger, J[anos A.], "Therapeutic Atmosphere in a Work Village for Mental Patients in Israel," in Masserman, Jules H. and Moreno, J. L. (eds.), *Progress in Psychotherapy* (New York and London, 1959), vol. 4, pp. 279–288.

Segal, Yisrael, "Tiq Dir Yasin," *Koteret Rashit*, 19 January 1983, pp. 6–8.

Segev, Tom, *1949: The First Israelis* (New York, 1986).

———, *One Palestine Complete: Jews and Arabs Under the British Mandate* (New York, 2000).

Shafrir, Yaakov, Letter to the Editor, *ha-Aretz*, 9 February 1998, p. B6.

Shapira, Yosef (ed.), *David Sha'alti'el: Yerushalayim Tashah* (Tel Aviv, 1981).

Sharvit, Soli, *Akiva Azulay Ish Yerushalayim* ([Jerusalem, 1987]).

Shipler, David, *Arab and Jew: Wounded Spirits in a Promised Land* (London, 1988).

Shlaim, Avi, *Collusion Across the Jordan: King Abdullah, the Zionist Movement, and the Partition of Palestine* (Oxford, 1988).

Shohat, Tzipi, "Shnayim Shlosha Dvarim she-Lo Yada'tem 'al 'Amos Qeynan," *ha-Aretz*, supplement, 15 March 1996, pp. 50–54.

Shweki, Yitzhak, "Shkhunat Giv'at Sha'ul," www.shimur.org.

Silver, Eric, "Arab Witnesses Admit Exaggerating Deir Yassin Massacre," *The Jerusalem Report*, 2 April 1998, p. 6.

————, *Begin: A Biography* (London, 1984).

————, "New Accounts of Deir Yassin," *The Guardian*, 9 April 1983, p. 15.

Spicehandler, David, *Let My Right Hand Wither* (New York, 1950).

Steigman, Yitzhak, *Shelah David: Ha-Yishuv ha-Yehudi el mul ha-Hitnagdut ha-'Aravit la-Mif'al ha-Tziyoni be-Eretz Yisra'el 1918–1948* (Tel Aviv, 1997).

Stern, Gabriel, "Ani mi-Dir Yasin," *'al ha-Mishmar*, 4 August 1982, p. 8.

Stewart, Catrina, "A massacre of arabs masked by state of national amnesia," *The Independent*, 10 May 2010, www.independent.co.uk/news/world/middle-east.

Sultan, Cathy, *Israeli and Palestinian Voices: A Dialogue with Both Sides* (Minneapolis MN, 2nd ed. 2006).

Sykes, Christopher, *Cross Roads to Palestine* (London, 1965).

Tabenkin, Yosef, *Ha-Mifne be-Milhemet ha-'Atzma'ut: Mitqefet Gdud Palmah "ha-Portzim" be-Mivtze'ey Nahshon ve-Har'el* (Ramat Efal, 1989).

Tall, 'Abdallah al-, *Karithat Filastin: Mudhakkirat 'Abdallah al-Tall Qa'id Ma'rakat al-Quds* ([Cairo, 1959], 2nd ed. 1990).

Tamari, Salim (ed.), *Jerusalem 1948: The Arab Neighbourhoods and Their Fate in the War* (Jerusalem and Bethlehem, 1999).

Tannous, Izzat, *The Palestinians: A Detailed Documented Eyewitness History of Palestine under British Mandate* (New York, 1988).

Tauber, Eliezer, *Military Resistance in Late Mandatory Palestine: The Activities of the Jewish and Arab Military Organizations as Reflected in the Reports of High Commissioner General Sir Alan Cunningham* (Ramat Gan, 2012).

Temko, Ned, *To Win or to Die: A Personal Portrait of Menachem Begin* (New York, 1987).

Tidhar, David, *Entziqlopedya le-Halutzey ha-Yishuv u-Bonav: Dmuyot u-Tmunot* (Tel Aviv, 1947–1971).

Tilbert, George William, "Parashat Dir Yasin," *Yediʿot Aharonot,* 7 October 1949, p. 6.

Tzabar, Shimon, "What Really Happened in Deir-Yassin 54 Years Ago?," *Israel Imperial News,* 2003-pt. 1, www.israelimperial-news.org/summo3A.htm#yassin.

Tzur, Eli, *Shomer le-Yisraʾel: Pirqey Hayav shel David Shaʾaltiʾel* (n.p., 2001).

'Ubaydu, Rim, "Khamsun ʿAman ʿala al-Nakba – Qaryat Dayr Yasin Sarat Mustashfa lil-Majanin al-Yahud," *al-Nahar,* 16 May 1998, p. 15.

United States Department of State, *Foreign Relations of the United States, 1948* (Washington DC, 1976), vol. 5, pt. 2.

UNRWA, "The Legacy of Hind al-Husseini," 8 March 2008, unis-pal.un.org.

Vered, Avraham, *Ariʾela: Leʾa Prizant, Lohemet Herut Yisraʾel* (Tel Aviv, 2001).

———, *Yerushalayim Zo Hazit ha-Merkaz* (Tel Aviv. 1998).

Vester, Bertha Spafford, *Our Jerusalem: An American Family in the Holy City 1881–1949* (New York, 1950).

Waxman, Yosef, "Mefaqdey ha-Etzel le-she-'Avar Hitkansu be-Lish-kato shel Rosh ha-Memshala," *Maʾariv,* 18 June 1979, p. 4.

"Welcome to Dayr Yasin," www.palestineremembered.com/Jerusalem/Dayr-Yasin/index.html.

Yahav, Dan, *Tohar ha-Nesheq: Etos, Mitos u-Metziʾut 1936–1956* (Tel Aviv, 2002).

Yahya, Adel H., "The Birth of the Palestinian Refugee Problem in 1947–1948," in Scham, Paul, Salem, Walid and Pogrund, Benjamin (eds.), *Shared Histories: A Palestinian-Israeli Dialogue* (Jerusalem, 2005), pp. 220–227.

———, *The Palestinian Refugees 1948–1998 (An Oral History)* (Ramallah, 1999).

Yakhin, Ezra, *Sipuro shel Elnaqam* (Tel Aviv, 1977).

Yanait, Rachel, Avrahami, Yitzhak and Etzion, Yerah (eds.), *Ha-Hagana bi-Yerushalayim: 'Eduyot ve-Zikhronot mi-Pi Haverim* (Jerusalem, 1975), vol. 2.

Yasin, Walid, *Dayr Yasin Abadan Tatamarradu 'ala al-Nisyan* (Jerusalem, 1984).

Yavin, H. Y[ehoshua], "Li-Mlot Shana le-Mivtza Dir Yasin," *Herut*, 25 March 1949, p. 3.

Yechiel, Ben, "Jerusalem Letter (January 1948)," *The New Judaea* (January–February 1948), pp. 64–65.

Yehudayof, Avichai, "Dir Yasin," *ba-Sa'ar*, 11 March 1949, p. 11.

Yellin-Mor, Nathan, *Lohamey Herut Yisra'el* (Jerusalem, 1974).

———, "Refuting a Libel," *New Outlook*, 12:4 (1969), pp. 63–64.

Yerushalmi, Y., "Dir Yasin: Me-'Az Yatza Matoq," *Herut*, 5 May 1965, p. 5.

Yitzhaki, Aryeh, "Dir Yasin – Lo bi-R'i 'Aqum," *Yedi'ot Aharonot*, 14 April 1972, p. 17.

———, *Latrun: Ha-Ma'arakha 'al ha-Derekh li-Yerushalayim* (Jerusalem, 1982), vol. 1.

[Zananiri, Elias], "Interviews: 50th Anniversary of Deir Yassin Massacre," *ArabicNews.com*, 10 April 1998, www.arabicnews.com/ansub/Daily/Day/980410/1998041030.html.

Zaru, Nawaf al-, *Min Dayr Yasin ila Mukhayyam Jinin* (Amman, 2002).

Zimmerman, John, "Radio Propaganda in the Arab-Israeli War 1948," *The Wiener Library Bulletin*, 27, NS nos. 30/31 (1973/4), pp. 2–8.

Zoghby, James, "Remembering Deir Yassin," *Al-Ahram Weekly*, 16–22 April 1998, weekly.ahram.org.eg/1998/1948/373_zgby.htm.

Zu'aytar, Akram, *Al-Qadiyya al-Filastiniyya* (Cairo, 1955).

VIDEOS

BBC, "The 50 Years War: Israel and the Arabs" (London), 15 March 1998, www.youtube.com.

Daoud, Eyad al- (prod.), "Deir Yassin: The Agony" (Jerusalem), 1999, www.youtube.com.

Dirbas, Sahera (prod.), "Deir Yassin Village and Massacre" [Jerusalem], 15 December 2012, www.youtube.com.

"Jacob Shafrir – Deir Yassin Massacre," 2 June 2010, pts. 1–2, www.youtube.com.

Middle East Crisis Committee, "The Struggle: Survivor of Deir Yassin," [Woodbridge CT], 5 October 2013, www.youtube.com.

Pa'il, Hassida (prod.), "Parashat Dir Yasin, Yom Shishi 9/4/48, Ra'ayonot 'im Anshey Shay 60 Shana Aharey," [2008], pts. 1–2, www.meirpail.co.il.

———, "Parashat Dir Yasin, Yom Shishi 9/4/48, Ra'ayonot 'im Gadna'im 60 Shana Aharey," 2008, pts. 1–2, www.meirpail.co.il.

Pa'il, Orrin, "Teqes li-Khvod Me'ir Pa'il, Hashaqat ha-Sefer 'Me'irke', Beyt ha-Palmah, Oqtober 2014," 13 November 2014, www.youtube.com.

Qanat al-Hiwar, "Qadiyya wa-Hiwar: Dayr Yasin .. al-Dhakira al-Hayya" (London), 1 May 2012, www.youtube.com.

Shoshani, Neta (dir.), "Born in Deir Yassin," 2016, f2h.io.

INTERNET SITES

info.palmach.org.il
infoweb.newsbank.com
jpress.org.il
radiobergen.org
unispal.un.org
weekly.ahram.org.eg
www.arabs48.com
www.awraq.birzeit.edu
www.deiryassin.org
www.gpophoto.gov.il
www.meirpail.co.il
www.palestineremembered.com
www.youtube.com

MISCELLANEOUS

Conversation with Shraga Peled, 13 February 2011.

E-mails from Ezra Yakhin to the author, 30 March and 1 April 2014.

E-mails from Ilana Alon (IDFA director) to the author, 2 December 2014.

E-mail from Lilly Rivlin to the author, 22 November 2013.

Hansard (London), 12 April 1948, cols. 626–630.

High Court of Justice, ruling on case 10343/07, 24 May 2010, eyloni. court.gov.il/files/07/430/103/p08/07103430.p08.htm.

Interview with Yehuda Lapidot (Jerusalem), 24 August 2010, and e-mails to the author, 26 August 2010, 20 April 2012, 6, 7 and 9 March, 24 August and 27 October 2014.

Phone conversation with Ben-Zion Cohen, 15 February 2015.

Phone conversation with Mordechai Gichon, 21 May 2014.

Phone conversations with Shimon Moneta, 1 April and 7 August 2014.

Phone conversations with Yaakov Gross, 23 March and 30 June 2014.

Sources of Photographs

Fig. 1: Survey of Israel, map 5075.

Fig. 2: CZA NSC/100591 (photographer: Fritz Schlesinger).

Fig. 3: CZA L18M/5194.

Fig. 4: Library of Congress Prints and Photographs Division, G. Eric and Edith Matson Photograph Collection, LC-DIG-matpc-05994.

Fig. 5: Palmach Photo Gallery 9818 (photographer: Israel Netach).

Fig. 6: JA TTZ-1359_002.

Fig. 7: JA TTZ-1903_002.

Fig. 8: IDFA AZ 209 (photographer: Yehuda Eisenstark).

Fig. 9: Wikipedia, "Yehoshua Zettler."

Fig. 10: Palmach Photo Gallery 11628.

Fig. 11: Courtesy of Rama Schiff (daughter of Yeshurun Schiff).

Fig. 12: JA TTZ-9195 (photographer: Alexander Archer).

Fig. 13: CZA MM/34/1.

Fig. 14: Courtesy of Aviva Friedman (niece of Yehoshua Goldschmidt).

Fig. 15: IDFA RAG 74280.

Fig. 16: Hebrew Wikipedia, "Sten" (photographer: Ilan Rosenman).

Fig. 17: CZA L18M/5194.

Fig. 18: Survey of Israel, photo 5114, sortie DEV7, 25 January 1946.

Fig. 19: Tidhar, *Entziqlopedya*, vol. 12, p. 4083.

Fig. 20: JA TTZ-4473 (photographer: Photo Kovetch).

Fig. 21: JA TTZ-517.
Fig. 22: Courtesy of Anat Liberman (daughter of Petahya Selivansky).
Fig. 23: Survey of Israel, photo 5114, sortie DEV7, 25 January 1946.
Fig. 24: Ben-Tor and others, *Lehi – Anashim*, vol. 1, p. 179.
Fig. 25: Courtesy of Aviva Friedman.
Fig. 26: JA TTZ-807.
Fig. 27: JA TTZ-1359_001.
Fig. 28: CZA NSC/100590 (photographer: Fritz Schlesinger).
Fig. 29: JA TTZ-98.
Fig. 30: National Photo Collection D850-065.
Fig. 31: Tidhar, *Entziqlopedya*, vol. 19, p. 5633.
Fig. 32: Ben-Tor and others, *Lehi – Anashim*, vol. 1, p. 76.
Fig. 33: Palmach Photo Gallery 5443.
Fig. 34: Courtesy of Yehuda Lapidot.
Fig. 35: Courtesy of Yehuda Lapidot.
Fig. 36: Palmach Photo Gallery 5442.
Fig. 37: Palmach Photo Gallery (courtesy of Nadav Man, son of Yaakov Weg).
Fig. 38: Survey of Israel, photo 5114, sortie DEV7, 25 January 1946.
Fig. 39: Courtesy of Yehuda Lapidot.
Fig. 40: Courtesy of Aviva Friedman.
Fig. 41: Courtesy of Aviva Friedman.
Fig. 42: Courtesy of Ofer Regev.
Fig. 43: CZA MM/34/1.
Fig. 44: ACICR V-P-PS-N-00043-08.
Fig. 45: Ben-Tor and others, *Lehi – Anashim*, vol. 1, p. 213.
Fig. 46: IDFA LH 3013.
Fig. 47: IDFA AZ 202 (photographer: Yehuda Eisenstark).
Fig. 48: JA TTZ-546.
Fig. 49: JA TTZ-1358.
Fig. 50: Ben-Tor and others, *Lehi – Anashim*, vol. 2, p. 539.
Fig. 51: JA K4-10/4.
Fig. 52: CZA PHG/1006618.
Fig. 53: CZA PHO/1390627 (photographer: Zvi Oron Orushkes).
Fig. 54: National Photo Collection D711-074 (photographer: Yaacov Saar).

Index